Texts in Philosophy
Volume 13

Beyond Description:
Naturalism and Normativity

Volume 3
Monsters and Philosophy
Charles T. Wolfe, ed.

Volume 4
Computing, Philosophy and Cognition
Lorenzo Magnani and Riccardo Dossena, eds.

Volume 5
Causality and Probability in the Sciences
Federica Russo and Jon Williamson, eds.

Volume 6
A Realist Philosophy of Mathematics
Gianluigi Oliveri

Volume 7
Hugh MacColl: An Overview of his Logical Work with Anthology
Shahid Rahman and Juan Redmond

Volume 8
Bruno di Finetti: Radical Probabilist
Maria Carla Galavotti, ed.

Volume 9
Language, Knowledge, and Metaphysics. Proceedings of the First SIFA Graduate Conference
Massimiliano Carrara and Vittorio Morato eds.

Volume 10
The Socratic Tradition. Questioning as Philosophy and as Method
Matti Sintonen, ed.

Volume 11
PhiMSAMP. Philosophy of Mathematics: Sociological Aspects and Mathematical Practice
Benedikt Löwe and Thomas Müller, eds.

Volume 12
Philosophical Perspectives on Mathematical Practice
Bart Van Kerkhove, Jonas De Vuyst and Jean Paul Van Bendegem, eds.

Volume 13
Beyond Description: Naturalism and Normativity
Marcin Miłkowski and Konrad Talmont-Kaminski, eds.

Texts in Philosophy Series Editors
Vincent F. Hendriks   vincent@hum.ku.dk
John Symons   jsymons@utep.edu
Dov Gabbay   dov.gabbay@kcl.ac.uk

Beyond Description:
Naturalism and Normativity

edited by
Marcin Miłkowski
and
Konrad Talmont-Kaminski

© Individual author and College Publications 2010. All rights reserved.

ISBN 978-1-904987-91-8

College Publications
Scientific Director: Dov Gabbay
Managing Director: Jane Spurr
Department of Computer Science
King's College London, Strand, London WC2R 2LS, UK

http://www.collegepublications.co.uk

Original cover design by orchid creative   www.orchidcreative.co.uk
Printed by Lightning Source, Milton Keynes, UK

All rights reserved. No part of this publication may be reproduced, stored in a retrieval system or transmitted in any form, or by any means, electronic, mechanical, photocopying, recording or otherwise without prior permission, in writing, from the publisher.

Contents

1. *Naturalism Beyond Description* — 1
   Konrad Talmont-Kaminski
2. *Is Normativity Natural?* — 14
   Mark H. Bickhard
3. *Why We Don't Need Naturalistic Epistemic Norms* — 31
   Jonathan Knowles
4. *Status of Naturalistic Epistemology – Problem of Autonomy* — 60
   Barbara Trybulec
5. *Making Naturalised Epistemology (Slightly) Normative* — 72
   Marcin Miłkowski
6. *Naturalistic Epistemologies and A Priori Justification* — 85
   Lisa Warenski
7. *The Proper Role of Intuitions in Epistemology* — 101
   Adam Feltz & Michael Bishop
8. *Naturalism: Progress in Epistemology?* — 123
   Timo Vuorio
9. *Naturalism without Representationalism* — 136
   Huw Price
10. *Two kinds of Nonscientific Naturalism* — 157
    Jonathan Knowles
11. *Postscript: Reply to Knowles* — 176
    Huw Price

12. *A Dilemma for Naturalism?*   180
    Shane Oakley
13. *Understanding Quine in Terms of the Aufbau:*
    Another Look at Naturalized Epistemology   195
    Stefanie Rocknak
14. *Descriptive Epistemology and Normativity:*
    A Humean Approach   211
    Treasa Campbell
15. *Naturalising Logic. The inference-marker view*   226
    María J. Frápolli
16. *Naturalising Illocutionary Rules*   243
    Maciej Witek
17. *Naturalising the Design Process:*
    Autonomy and Interaction as Core Features   265
    Argyris Arnellos, Thomas Spyrou, John Darzentas
18. *Causality Naturalised?*   289
    Piotr Leśniak
19. *Can Mental Illness Be Naturalised?*   300
    Andrzej Kapusta
20. *Technologised Epistemology*   313
    Marek Hetmański

1

Naturalism Beyond Description

KONRAD TALMONT-KAMINSKI

1 Introduction

That 'naturalism' is not a univocal term is a philosopher's commonplace. At the same time, it seems fair to say that normativity is one issue naturalist philosophers of all stripes keep returning to. That this is the case might appear surprising given that all too often naturalism is mischaracterised as the straightforward rejection of normativity. Such exclusive focus on description might have been true of a moment in Quine's philosophical development but, even there, the interpretation is contentious. A closer-to-the-truth characterisation of at least some ontological versions of naturalism would hinge on the rejection of normativity as ontologically independent of the sphere of facts – physical facts, in particular. For some naturalists this means the elimination of the normative. For most it only means some kind of reduction. However, ontology is hardly the only area in which naturalist approaches have been applied, with methodological naturalism being the normally cited alternative. And issues of normativity also impact methodological naturalism, though quite differently.

The search for the reasons why issues of normativity have continued to play such a significant role in naturalist discussions could lead to an historical examination of the philosophical doctrines collected under that rubric. Apart from the already named Quine, such a recapitulation would

Beyond Description: Naturalism and Normativity.
Marcin Miłkowski and Konrad Talmont-Kaminski (eds.).
Copyright © 2010 The Author.

have to touch on Hume's discussion of the is/ought distinction, Moore's formulation of the issues in terms of a naturalist fallacy, Dewey's instrumentalism, the rejection of 'metaphysics' by the Vienna Circle, and any of a number of current positions that are the intellectual inheritors of those earlier approaches. Such an approach would have the advantage of helping to show the historical roots to which most of today's versions of naturalism can be traced back; showing that, even though naturalism isn't necessarily a species, it is perhaps a clade – at least within analytical philosophy. However, such an historical approach to the question of why issues of normativity have continued to play a central role for naturalists would have two serious short-comings. The first is that it seeks numerous proximate explanations – the intellectual influence of one writer upon another, the development of a particular tradition at a certain university – where a single, ultimate explanation may turn out to be sufficient. One doesn't need to know how individual animals died to understand a species was driven to extinction by loss of habitat. Similarly, it may be that a more fundamental explanation would be sufficient in the case of the rise of naturalism. While appreciation for the historical details is valuable in and of itself, it would be a shame if it were to serve to hide the big picture. Particularly, if no attempt to look for that picture is made in the first place. The second short-coming with a historical review of naturalist philosophers is that, by discussing naturalism in what are – in truth – anti-naturalist terms, such philosophical history does not do justice to it. Naturalists, in so far as generalisations can be made about this disparate group, have tended to place great store upon the continuity of philosophy with the sciences. This was already the case with such philosophers as Peirce, who may have not used the term 'naturalist' but who would clearly fall within naturalism's ambit. As such, the influence of science upon philosophical thought is a naturalist's staple. To the degree that a hermetically philosophical history of naturalism were adequate it would, therefore, show the naturalists failing to be true to their word.

The solution may seem simple enough: The intellectual history that is to explain why naturalists have continued to concern themselves with issues of normativity needs to consider the significance of scientific developments and practices for this issue. It is clear, for example, that shifts in philosophical outlooks over the span of the twentieth century are connected to developments first in logic, then in physics and computer science, and most recently in biology. More fundamentally, even when philosophers became most suspicious of talk of norms, scientific practice remained very much full of references to normativity. This is clear whenever one reads a scientific paper or watches a scientific experiment being undertaken. To remain true to this scientific practice, naturalist philosophers have to consider normativity, even if it is with the aim of ultimately eliminating it from the picture – even a merely descriptive account of science must talk at length about how scientists frame and make use of claims that are, at face value, normative. Such focus upon actual scientific practices is, of course, no more than what Kuhn argued for. And, just like his arguments, it opens the way to the charge of scientistic tribalism. The charge is misplaced yet it does serve to clarify naturalists' commitments. Naturalists do not focus on scientific practices because of a fondness for lab coats but, ultimately, because science offers the very best epistemic methods that are currently available to us. This focus does not free naturalists from consideration of the limitations of the social institutions of science – the research institutes, the funding bodies or the informal culture of the scientific community. Indeed, it has forced naturalist philosophers in many cases to also become sociologists of science. However, this focus does underscore that the naturalist's commitment is conditional upon science holding up its end of the bargain. It also means that naturalists must, ultimately, be willing to look at effective epistemic methods regardless of whether they are scientific or not. As a result, naturalists have found themselves considering the evolutionary antecedents of human epistemic abilities, including of science, as well as the physiological – and especially neurological – mechanisms underlying these abilities. Very often, these investigations, also, have proved to call for consideration of the apparently normative aspects of the phenomena under investigation.

It is here, therefore, that we find the ultimate reason why naturalists continue to discuss normativity – epistemic practices, be they scientific or otherwise, are shot through with normativity. A non-naturalist account might perhaps hope to get away from all talk of normativity by positing the existence of a perfect form of reason that does not call upon norms. A naturalist, however, is not so free to range over the field of the imaginable but must hook their deliberations to the actual. By no means does this entail that the picture of norms the naturalists will end up putting together will be one familiar to philosophers of more traditional tenor. It is a rare naturalist that would not make fundamental changes in how we should understand normativity. Yet, the naturalist's contention must be that, no matter how surprising the ultimate product ends up being, it will be the 'best deserver' for the term due to the lack of anything to refer to that is less challenging to previous conceptions.

2 Articles

It is possible to identify three aspects of discussions of normativity within the context of naturalised philosophy: the ontological, the epistemic and the methodological. This tripartite grouping of issues is also to be met in this volume, although to a different degree in the various papers.

The ontological aspect of naturalist debates concerning normativity focuses upon finding the right balance between the need to do justice to the apparent ubiquity of calls to normativity while avoiding ontological claims that cannot be justified within a naturalist world-view. Not surprisingly, that balance is thought to lie in very different places depending upon just which naturalist is asked. The positions range from a minimalist position that denies that anything like norms needs to be considered as part of a naturalist ontology, all the way to full-blown dualism. A different sort of debate among naturalists that concerns normativity may be characterised as epistemic in nature. Accepting normativity in general, it focuses on the content of particular epistemic norms and how those norms are to be justified. Typically, the background for such discussions is constituted by the views presented by more traditional approaches to philosophy, with naturalists aiming to explain how it is that their views differ from those positions. Finally, methodological debates come to deal with concrete examples of how norms are applied within particular epistemic endeavours – the various sciences, foremost – and often concern issues that arise out of the nature of those disciplines. As such, these debates may be thought to fall within the scope of the philosophies of the individual sciences rather than within a general naturalised epistemology. Such a flow from philosophical to scientific discussions is only to be applauded from a naturalist point of view. Of course, the various levels of debate inform each other. This means that it would be impossible to divide the papers in this volume neatly into those that deal with only ontological or only methodological questions. None-the-less, an effort has been made to try to order the papers in such a way that the collection moves from the most general to the most specific of discussions.

The picture of normativity put forward by Mark Bickhard in chapter 2 is very much a realist one. Bickhard argues that entities such as norms only appear problematic due to a substance metaphysics being implicitly accepted. A substance metaphysics is forced to deny the essential reality of anything other than the most fundamental building blocks of the universe, while at the same time assuming that these are unchanging and that all change is due to their rearrangement. The problem with normativity is therefore just one example of the problems this metaphysics has with emergent phenomena in general. While that result might be disappointing, disappointment is not necessarily a sufficient reason to abandon such metaphysics. However, substance metaphysics has a much more serious difficulty according to Bickhard – it runs counter to what modern physics tell us about the structure of the world. Taken together with the argument that incorrect assumptions regarding the introduction of new terms with the use of definitions led Hume to reject the possibility of obtaining norms from facts, this problem leads Bickhard to conclude that there are no good grounds for rejecting the possibility of the emergence of norms from facts. He bases his own positive account upon a process metaphysics according to which organisation, at all scales, becomes the locus of causality. According to Bickhard, normativity emerges through the operation of recursively self-maintenant far-from-equilibrium stable systems. The essential notion is that of the function different parts of such autonomous systems play in maintaining their stability. The normativity that emerges is relative to the systems and consists in how well their parts fulfil their functions.

If anyone should need further evidence of the differences between naturalist positions, the contrast with Jonathan Knowles' position presented in chapter 3 provides it in spades. Where Bickhard's account aimed to show how normativity can be included in a naturalist account, Knowles argues that norms are wholly superfluous: not just logically unnecessary but, more importantly, that people do not require them to effectively investigate the world. Also, where Bickhard's focus was ontological, Knowles sees epistemic issues as front and centre for evaluating norms. Interestingly, however, the two approaches are not necessarily incompatible as Knowles explicitly does not equate denying the significance of norms with expunging normativity from naturalism. In the process of arguing for his conclusion, Knowles carefully distinguishes several different versions of naturalism. The main distinction he uses is that between anti-apriorist and anti-foundationalist positions – the second being opposed to all foundations whereas the first allows for the possibility that some norms come to play a foundational role through a posteriori means. The first a posteriori option he considers is psychologistic, with our natural, evolved cognitive inclinations serving the foundational role – a naturalist interpretation of intuitions (unlike the other positions he does not discuss this version of naturalism at length within the article). The second a posteriori option is anti-psychologistic and depends upon reaching a reflective equilibrium between, at minimum, the norms and assessments of individual cases. The point Knowles makes in relation to this approach for deriving norms is that it presumes people's ability to make judgements without recourse to such norms and, indeed, relies upon its reliability, thus undermining any significance of the role played by the norms. Knowles also discusses two varieties of anti-foundationalist naturalism that he considers particularly significant: instrumentalism, which sees norms as hypothetical imperatives, and inductivism, which holds that epistemic norms come to be justified and refined inductively. In the case of inductivism, Knowles argues that norms do not add anything to the shaping of hypotheses beyond what is achieved by observation and, possibly, general claims about the nature of the world. In the case of instrumentalism, Knowles reaches much the same conclusion on the grounds that, since hypothetical imperatives rely upon factual claims regarding connections between the desired aims and the means to reach them, the aims plus factual claims are sufficient to direct action.

Partly in response to Knowles, a different view is presented by Barbara Trybulec who attempts to deal with a question that has bothered many naturalised epistemologists since Quine, i.e. whether there is anything for the epistemologist to do over and above what the sciences of cognition achieve. She puts her question in terms of whether epistemology, once naturalised, can retain autonomy. Her conclusion is that while, of course, any attempt to carry on without the aid of the sciences is mistaken, this does not entail that epistemology as a separate discipline must disappear. Trybulec appears to agree with Knowles in so far as she claims that what had been thought to be independent norms are merely descriptions of reliable processes. Nonetheless, she sees the source of epistemology's autonomy in epistemology's concern with the meta-methodological task of picking the optimal set of processes. In effect, while no longer capable of being carried out independently of science, epistemology on this view retains its status of being a metascience and, in a very altered form, its focus remains on normative issues.

Marcin Miłkowski also tries to reconcile Knowles' critique with retaining some notion of epistemic norms while drawing upon Quine to do so. However, unlike Trybulec, Miłkowski expands upon Quine's talk of normativity as engineering. The resulting instrumentalist view of norms is meant to be humble enough to avoid Knowles' objections to this kind of approach. The problem identified by Miłkowski is that while rejecting claims to providing a priori justified methodology, naturalised epistemology has given up on methodology in general by handing it over wholesale to scientists. Miłkowski examines what epistemology can do concerning methodology at three different roughly distinguished levels, that of cognitive system interactions as well as those of the personal and the subpersonal. In focussing upon the subpersonal, he draws out the similarities between the structures and processes studied by cognitive science and the categories and other mechanisms that Kant tried to show as structuring experience. While rejecting an apriorist attitude to efforts of this kind, he argues for their significance to a methodological naturalised epistemology. The essential point for Miłkowski's argument is that naturalised epistemology relies upon the notion of function, a normative notion that he, following Dennett, sees as vital to the design stance that epistemology shares with cognitive science and evolutionary theory. As such, his account is close to that developed by Bickhard, even though the concept of function he uses is somewhat different. The methodological epistemology Miłkowski sees this engineering approach leading to is focussed primarily on artificial cognitive systems – the investigation of their abilities being akin to an a posteriori version of what Kant had aimed at. Significantly, the norms that such interdisciplinary work leads to are not the typically general and vague philosophical norms that Knowles can be seen as railing against but will be limited heuristics.

The next paper in this volume is by Lisa Warenski and pursues an altogether different and prima facie unlikely path to naturalised normativity, that is by developing a naturalised account of the a priori. While surprising, the resultant divorce between naturalism and empiricism is not easy to ignore. The essential strategy pursued by Warenski is to strip the a priori of nonessential elements, leaving a core notion that most naturalists can swallow. The only ones who cannot, according to Warenski, are just those that reject all normativity. Warenski's first choice of what needs to be abandoned for the a priori to be acceptable is the idea that a priori justification is infallible – the difficulty being to reconcile empirical indefeasibility with fallibility. The point Warenski makes is that, given fallibilism, we can be justified to think a proposition a priori justified even if we merely fallibly but justifiably judge it to be empirical indefeasible. Thus, one can be a fallibilist about the truth of some a priori claim as well as about its warrant being a priori in nature. While infallibility is the most troubling aspect of the traditionally understood a priori to Warenski, she is also careful to reject its connections to notions of metaphysical necessity, abstract objects and rational intuition. This leaves her open to the objection that her notion of the a priori is compatible with naturalism only because it lacks a positive account of a priori justification. In response, she sketches out not one but several accounts that might be fitted into different versions of naturalism. With nonnormative naturalist approaches, an account of a priori justification cannot be given but not because of the a priori aspect of it – the problem is simply that justification of any kind is rejected by such accounts. Even so, Warenski argues, a priori of a kind survives in belief-forming processes indifferent to what the sensory inputs are. Normative versions of naturalism allow for a more full-blooded a priori, however. Thus, for example, in the case of reliabilism, the conditions are the same as above except the belief-forming processes have to be reliable. Most significantly, Warenski believes that her approach may open the way to naturalist a priori accounts of logic and mathematics. Even though this can at best be described as a possibility at this point the value of such as achievement is such as to be the major reason for making this approach worth investigating.

After a naturalist defence of the a priori, it may be less of a surprise to find a naturalist defence of some uses of epistemic intuitions – which is precisely what Adam Feltz and Michael Bishop provide in their chapter. Careful to start by abstracting away from the details of a theory of epistemic intuitions, they ask what precisely it is that we might hope to get from intuitions, whatever they are. This, they argue, will depend upon the precise epistemological project we are engaged in. They distinguish between five possibilities: capturing our intuitions, expounding the theory that underlies the intuitions, analysing the underlying concepts, characterising the true nature of knowledge or guiding our reasoning. Being most interested in the last two of these options, Feltz and Bishop argue for a moderate position that allows intuitions play a vital role in everyday cognition but, nonetheless, shows that they are not solid enough to base philosophical projects upon. Given the general fallibilism of naturalism, this does not mean that naturalist philosophers should eschew intuitions but that they ought to think of them as a relatively fallible input.

The chapter written by Timo Vuorio develops a discussion between what are often presented as different takes upon Sellars' work. Rather than opting for the more typical naturalist take such as is pursued by Ruth Millikan, among others, Vuorio prefers the general approach taken by Robert Brandom, Richard Rorty and Huw Price, among others. His paper focuses upon the central question differentiating these two camps, that of what to say about normativity given a shared disbelief in the possibility of providing it with an a priori foundation. On this issue, Vuorio sides with Rorty in claiming that philosophers should give up on trying to provide a theory of normativity. Whether the result is one that should be called 'naturalism' is not an issue Vuorio takes a strong stance on. It is interesting, however, to consider this issue in the light of Knowles' argument that naturalism does not require normativity as well as his arguments against the position Huw Price puts forward in the paper that follows Vuorio's.

The proposals put forward by Feltz and Bishop as well as by Warenski, if accepted, would perhaps leave naturalism largely unchanged, simply adding to it the ability to draw upon concepts that are not usually seen as belonging within its scope. This is not the case, however, with Huw Price's stated proposal. Price's basic claim is that naturalists tend to begin their philosophising from the wrong starting place and, once the error is corrected, a very different naturalism results. In particular, Price argues that the currently popular object naturalism – as he calls it – should be replaced by subject naturalism. The vital difference between them is that object naturalism starts from the view that science sets the standard for what exists and what is knowledge while subject naturalism starts from the scientific view of ourselves. What is more, according to Price, subject naturalism is prior to object naturalism as it could be used to show object naturalism to be incorrect. Indeed, that is precisely what Price aims to do. The tool he uses is what he, after Frank Jackson, calls placement problems – the problems caused by phenomena such as meaning or qualia that are difficult for philosophers to put into the naturalist picture – a problem that Bickhard might be seen to be trying to deal with. In a further move that is typical of many Australian philosophers, he then argues these problems must be seen as ultimately linguistic in nature. The result is a rejection of standard object naturalism on the basis of several arguments against representationalist interpretations of linguistic behaviour.

Price's position is one of the main foci of the Knowles paper that follows it – Knowles' second contribution to this volume. In that paper, Knowles aims to defend what he sees as the standard scientific naturalism against two versions of naturalism that Knowles thinks would give science a lesser role and which were earlier defended by Vuorio and Price. The first of these – called 'expansionist naturalism' by Knowles – is tied to the figure of John McDowell, the second is the pragmatic naturalism (Knowles' term again) developed by Price, among others. Knowles' argument against Price is to draw out what seem to be two different aspects of Price's position that appear to be very much in tension with each other. The first is an a priori scepticism regarding naturalistic representational semantics, the second is a commitment to a posteriori investigation of human linguistic behaviour. The problem with the first is that it is hard to see what is naturalist about it, while the problem with the second is that it seems to be reliant for the requisite explanations on the very scientific naturalism that Price would seem to have us reject. While this does not, of course, show that Price's position is incorrect, it does show – according to Knowles – that Price does not provide a naturalist alternative to Knowles' own scientific naturalism. This leaves McDowell's expansionist nonscientific naturalism. Knowles sees expansionists as running two mutually inconsistent lines of argument to show that science has no special status for naturalists. The first of these is that apart from natural phenomena that are dealt with adequately by science, there are also other phenomena that science can not deal with but which, none-the-less, are natural. The second is that there is no way to identify an unambiguously scientific methodology or metaphysics, making a scientific naturalism, likewise, unclear. The two lines of argument are in tension since, if it is impossible to identify scientific metaphysics, it must be impossible to unambiguously identify naturalist phenomena whose explanations fall outside of that metaphysics. While generally siding with the view that any identification of science must be at best provisional, Knowles points out that even so the determination of what is natural and what is not is reliant upon the work science has done in rejecting supernatural explanations. In effect, Knowles argues for the recognition that the choice of scientific naturalism is predicated upon the context of the scientific worldview being a central element of our culture. He, thinks, however, this is in-line with the way in which naturalism does not seek to give ultimate answers to general sceptical worries.

In his short response to Knowles, Price opts for the second of the two options Knowles outlines for pragmatic naturalism – the recognition that any empirical investigation of human linguistic behaviour must assume the bulk of scientific metaphysics. None-the-less, he feels that his position differs from Knowles' scientific naturalism for a couple of reasons, including him not favouring the explanatory project whose centrality he feels Knowles' argument assumes.

Shane Oakley's contribution is aimed at a particular kind of argument that has been put forward against naturalism. The argument is that naturalised epistemology can either be defended independently of its naturalist basis, in which case it is actually false, or that it cannot and any defence relies upon naturalist assumptions, in which case it is circular. Oakley's response is to point out that the same form of argument can be used for all other epistemological positions. In effect, the argument cannot be seen to particularly disadvantage naturalism. Indeed, Oakley suggests that naturalism may be in a particularly advantageous position in so far as some naturalists are able to make concessions to the sceptical argument.

Unlike the previous chapters in this volume, which focus almost solely upon modern discussions in naturalism, Stephanie Rocknak's reaches back to the beginning of naturalism by looking at the way in which Quine's work was a reaction to that of Carnap. In particular, Rocknak looks at the way Quine's philosophy responded to the project of the Aufbau. She argues that Quine saw what she calls 'circles' within Carnap's work: to acquire knowledge one already had to possess knowledge, to acquire logic one had to already possess logic and, finally, to define analyticity one had to already have a definition of analyticity – each tied to the appearance of basic normative considerations within epistemology. In her chapter, Rocknak focusses on the first of the circles and argues that Quine's naturalism allowed him to avoid the problem of needing to presume that knowledge was possessed to show how it could be obtained.

Treasa Campbell seeks to understand naturalism by casting her eyes even further back – at Humean naturalism. She sees it as based on the 'causal instinct' that is an 'unavoidable, indispensable and universal' feature of human cognition. As such, it restricts any considerations of epistemic 'oughts', since 'ought' implies 'can' and humans cannot but see events as causally connected. In effect, Campbell argues for a close interconnection between epistemic norms and the cognitive capabilities actually possessed by humans. The argument would seem to be quite challenging to the position presented earlier by Feltz and Bishop in that, if correct, Campbell would seem to have identified a way in which human instincts can play a central role within philosophy.

A similar close connection between human capabilities and normative issues is central to María Frápolli's chapter. In it, she argues that logic can be given an adequate naturalist account so long as meaning and content can be naturalised, where Frápolli points out that naturalisation of those linguistic phenomena is central to the naturalist project and the point of Bickhard's contribution to this volume. Frápolli achieves her goal by showing that terms of standard logic get their meaning from linguistic practice. The vital step is Frápolli's assertion that formal inferences depend upon material ones, rather than the other way around. This allows her to retain a close connection between human reasoning and logic, unlike Gilbert Harman, for example. While Frápolli requires logic to be a priori she argues that the sense in which logic is a priori is the unproblematic one for naturalists that is identified by Lisa Warenski in her chapter of this volume. At the same time, it appears that Frápolli's position must run counter to that proposed by Knowles, in so far as it identifies logic as containing a set of rules that even a naturalist must accept in order to be rational.

Frápolli places philosophy of logic within the philosophy of language and Maciej Witek's contribution, which follows hers in the volume, is concerned with naturalising another aspect of the philosophy of language – speech acts. Indeed, the two papers share more than the general topic and approach in that both follow the strategy of explaining the rules of language use in terms of the practice of language use, thereby inverting the more usual antinaturalist direction of explanation. Witek presents his argument as a way of making it possible to talk about Searle's illocutionary rules in the context of Millikan's picture of convention. The reason for the appearance of the illocutionary rules, according to Witek, is that in a given physical context the locally recurrent natural signs make it possible to conventionalise the illocutionary acts that serve to supplement those natural signs.

Argyris Arnellos, Thomas Spyrou and John Darzentas also seek to present a naturalist account of a human activity. However, their topic is one that has to a large degree escaped mainstream philosophical attention – the process of design. One virtue of focussing on it, therefore, is showing the relevance of naturalism to such topics. However, the insights feed back into Quine's use of the idea of engineering and Miłkowski's discussion of the design stance. The main theoretical tools that Arnellos et al. use are those developed by Bickhard and others in the context of autonomous dynamical systems theory. They argue for a cognitivist view of design as an open-ended, future-anticipatory and interactive process that involves two or more autonomous agents. This allows for the on-going modification of both the aims and the means used, the progressive nature of the process being spelled out in terms of the autonomy of the agents.

As Piotr Leśniak observes, the concept of causality is one that has been problematic for naturalists since Hume. This motivates him to pursue a modification of naturalism that in some ways is similar to the suggestion made by Price. However, Leśniak's proposal is based upon Kant's distinction between conceptual structure and the non-conceptual aspect of sensations, the second of which he feels had been underappreciated by naturalists even though it offers a way to argue that causation is directly perceived. Using recent work on the perception of causation, Leśniak develops a view of it which he argues is connected to Gibson's affordances.

Andrzej Kapusta considers the naturalist approach to a normative category that is central to clinical psychology, i.e. mental illness. As Kapusta explains, current folk-psychological and clinical conceptions of mental illness do not provide us with a category that fits well into a naturalist view of the world, both in terms of mental illnesses as a whole and in terms of what are conceived of as individual illnesses. The key concept that allows him to naturalise mental illness is that of biological function. Looking as mental illness at this level requires that a design stance rather than an intentional stance be taken, however. Kapusta recognises the connected tension between an evolutionary and a mechanistic concept of function – an issue that Bickhard and Arnellos et al. try to deal with.

Finally, Marek Hetmański considers the significance of technology for a naturalist epistemology. On the one hand this involves an externalist view of knowledge which is able to explicitly take into the various technologies used to obtain, store, modify and communicate knowledge. On the other, it involves the need to consider what effects particular technologies have upon how humans deal with knowledge and the kinds of knowledge accessible to them. Hetmański argues that in the context of the technologies of knowledge the traditional epistemic problems re-arise, though in a substantially altered form. In particular, technology raises anew traditional issues of the normativity of the process of dealing with knowledge.

3 Acknowledgements

The papers in this volume began as presentations at the Kazimierz Naturalised Epistemology Workshops held in 2006 and 2007, the idea for a volume being born from the connections among those presentations.

The editors would like to thank the referees who provided the authors with valuable feed-back, including Tadeusz Ciecierski and John Collier. Also, they would like to thank Vincent Hendricks who accepted the volume for his book series, Jane Spurr at College Publications who helped to guide this volume from idea to physical book, and Patrick Trompiz who helped to edit some of the contributions. Finally, they would like to thank the contributors to this volume for their patience in waiting for its much-delayed publication, and to Centre for Time in the Department of Philosophy at the University of Sydney for financial support.

"Naturalism Without Representationalism," by Huw Price reprinted by permission of the publisher from NATURALISM IN QUESTION, edited by Mario De Caro and David Macarthur, pp. 71–88, Cambridge, Mass.: Harvard University Press, Copyright © 2004 by the President and Fellows of Harvard College.

2

Is Normativity Natural?

MARK H. BICKHARD

Why do naturalism and normativity pose a problem? What makes normativity so difficult to account for within a naturalism? I will argue that normativity is in fact a natural class of phenomena, but that to outline how that is so requires three steps: 1) A diagnosis of a conceptual barrier to the possibility of a metaphysical integration of naturalism and normativity, 2) Arguing for an alternative metaphysical orientation that removes that in-principle barrier, and 3) Sketching how an account of normativity can be grounded in a naturalistic framework. The central shift is from a metaphysical framework in which the possibility of the natural *emergence* of normativity is blocked to one in which it can be accounted for.

1 A Diagnosis

The Pre-Socratics — particularly the Parmenidean argument against change and Empedocles' and Democritus' developments of and reactions to the Parmenidean arguments — established an assumption of *substance* as the foundational metaphysical form of the world. Parmenides had argued that change among substances could not occur, and, therefore, post-Parmenidean metaphysics of substance assumed that the basic substances did not change, and, in fact, that they remained unchanging as a matter of metaphysical necessity. Apparent change, then, could be accounted for in terms of superficial changes in the mixtures or locations of substances (or

Beyond Description: Naturalism and Normativity.
Marcin Miłkowski and Konrad Talmont-Kaminski (eds.).
Copyright © 2010 The Author.

equally unchanging atoms), even though they did not themselves change (Graham, 2006).

But a world of such substances or atoms is a world of basic metaphysical realities, plus the causal interactions, and the factual relations among them. In particular, this world, or at least this realm of the world, does not include intentionality or normativity. This Pre-Socratic legacy, therefore, has three basic presumptive consequences:

1) The explanatory default is stasis. Substances do not change unless made to change: change requires special explanation.
2) Emergence is precluded. For example, it is not possible to derive a fifth substance from Empedoclean earth, air, fire, and water.[1]
3) The natural world of substances or atoms, cause, and fact, is split from the realm of normativity and intentionality. This is a necessary presupposition of the metaphysics of the substance framework.

Various forms of substance metaphysical frameworks and their consequences have dominated Western thought since the Pre-Socratics. In particular, given the split between the realm of substance and that of intentionality and normativity, there are only three possible kinds of positions to adopt:

1) Accept two metaphysical realms as basic. These could be, for example, the matter and form of Aristotle, the two substances of Descartes, the noumenal world and that of the transcendental subject of Kant, or the realm of science and the realm of conventional and tautological normativity of the logical positivists.
2) Attempt to account for the world in terms of just the intentional, normative realm. Idealists, such as Green or Bradley, exemplify this position.
3) Attempt to account for the world in terms of just the material world of substances or atoms. Hobbes, Hume, and Quine exemplify this possibility.

---

[1] This point is made more complex by the Aristotelian assumption that earth, air, fire, and water could change into one another, but these were not the metaphysical foundation for Aristotle. That foundation, usually called prime matter, still honored the Parmenidean necessity for an unchanging metaphysical ground (Gill, 1989; Graham, 1984, 1987).

The contemporary world, post-Quine, is dominated by this third possibility, with some form of materialistic or physicalistic "naturalism" generally assumed or argued for. This assumptive framework has permeated far beyond philosophy into even far corners of the sciences. One anecdotal illustration is the response of a major psychologist to a question about the normativity of representation: "I'm not interested in that mystical stuff". If the world is assumed to be constituted in some strictly materialistic or physicalistic way, then issues such as normativity can seem merely "mystical".

2 Why Not Emergence?

Some form of *emergence* of normative phenomena within the natural world can seem to be an intuitively attractive possibility, but such fundamental emergence is precisely one of the kinds of phenomena that substance was supposed to preclude — and it does. Two illuminating ways in which this preclusion of emergence has visited itself on modern thought can be found in arguments of Hume and of Kim.

Hume

Hume famously argued against the possibility of deriving norms from facts (Hume, 1978). Actually, he didn't fill in that argument much, but the manner in which it is usually understood is as follows: In a valid argument that begins with strictly factual premises, only factual conclusions are possible. If there are any terms in the conclusion that are not present in the premises, then they must have been introduced by definitions. These definitions might have involved still other terms not in the premises, but those too would have to have been introduced via definition, with any such hierarchy of definitions grounding out in the terms available in the premises. All of the terms in the conclusion, then, can be replaced by their defining phrases or clauses, and this back-translation through the definitions can proceed until the conclusion is stated solely using terms that were in the original premises. But these were, by assumption, strictly factual, so any valid conclusion will likewise be strictly factual. Therefore, beginning with strictly factual premises, a valid argument can arrive only at strictly factual conclusions.

In its general form, this argument precludes any possibilities other than various logical re-arrangements of the original premise terms. In restricting to "nothing but re-arrangements" the argument precludes not only the derivation of norms from facts, but it precludes any form of emergence: emergence is supposed to be a phenomenon of something more than just such re-arrangements.

But Hume's argument is unsound: Not all valid forms of definition permit the requisite back-translations upon which the argument depends. In particular, implicit definition does not permit back-translation because there is no defining phrase or clause that can substitute for the defined term — there is no phrase or clause for which the defined term is an abbreviation.

Hume didn't know about implicit definition, but it was introduced in a major way by Hilbert (and others) around the beginning of the twentieth century (Hilbert, 1971; Otero, 1970). Implicit definitions define via a pattern of interrelationships among the terms, which are initially *not* defined. The pattern then implicitly defines the class of all the ways in which the terms can be interpreted that will successfully honour the interrelationships. In Hilbert's case, for example, the patterns were given by uninterpreted axioms, and the axioms implicitly defined geometry. The terms, then, can be interpreted in ways that conform with our notions of point, line, etc. except that these have never been explicitly defined on any foundational base.[2]

The very possibility of implicit definition, then, renders Hume's argument unsound — back-translation is not necessarily possible[3] — and thereby removes this block against the possibility of emergence. Hume's argument is effectively a logical rendition of the substance metaphysical prohibition of anything other than mixtures and re-arrangements, and this logical aspect of a substance framework must be rejected.

Kim

Jaegwon Kim (1991) has elaborated a powerful argument against the possibility of emergence, at least of any form of emergence that could claim to be causally efficacious. The central intuition of the argument is that various organisations or configurations of particles do not yield any new causal power: all genuine causality is carried by the particles, and, although they will interact differently depending on their organisation, it is only the causality of the particles per se that is being manifest.

The argument is set up as a dichotomous pair of possibilities: 1) physics (i.e., whatever the basic particles turn out to be) is causally closed in

---

[2] In general, implicit definitions can permit multiple satisfying interpretations, and the entire class of such interpretations is what is implicitly defined.
[3] For more on some technical issues concerning implicit definition, including the related notion of the implicit definition of single terms, see Chang & Keisler (1990), Doyle (1985), Hale & Wright (2000), Kolaitis (1990).

the sense that anything that has any cause at all has its cause in terms of such particles, or 2) new organisation will generate new causality, in which case the physical world is *not* causally closed. In the first case, any purported causality at the level of configurations or organisations of particles is pre-empted by — rendered superfluous to — the causality of the particles acting within that organisation. Configurations, then, are nothing more than the stage setting in which the genuine causality of the particles is engaged. In the second case, in which new causality does emerge, the causal closure of the (particle) physical world fails, and, therefore, naturalism fails. Therefore, either emergence is at best causally epiphenomenal, or naturalism is false.

Kim's argument, however, turns on its assumption of a particle metaphysics in a crucial way. Particles have causal power and do not have organisation, though they can participate in organisation. Thus, that which has genuine causality does not have organisation, and organisation is nothing more than initial and boundary conditions for the causal interactions of those particles. Emergence is supposed to be manifest, if at all, in new organisations, but organisation is precluded as a potential locus of causal power by the assumed metaphysical framework. Organisation is neither stuff nor thing: it is not the right metaphysical kind to have any causal power. So emergence is precluded by that assumed metaphysical framework.

But, like Hume's argument, Kim's argument is unsound, and for similar reasons. Hume's argument fails because it fails to recognise the possibility of relational organisation itself constituting a definition — relational organisation cannot, in Hume's assumptions, have definitional power. In Kim's argument, it is presupposed that that which has causal power does not have organisation, and, therefore, organisation cannot have causal power without violating physical closure, thus violating naturalism. In both cases, organisation is excluded from consideration by underlying presuppositions, and in both cases those presuppositions are false.

In the case of Kim's argument, the assumption of a particle metaphysics is both false and ultimately incoherent. In a world of point particles, nothing would ever happen because they would have a zero probability of ever hitting each other. In a world of point particles interacting via fields (the standard contemporary naïve view), Kim's argument no longer holds: fields have causal power, and have their causal power in part in virtue of their organisation. Thus organisation cannot be excluded as a potential locus of causal power without eliminating all causality from the world.

Even worse for Kim's assumption, according to our best current physics, *there are no particles*. Everything is quantum fields, and the only remaining particle-like properties are that various properties of those fields are quantised and conserved in field interactions, and those field interactions are sometimes relatively localized (Bickhard, 2003; Cao, 1999; Clifton, 1996; Halvorson & Clifton, 2002; Huggett, 2000; Kuhlman et al, 2002; Weinberg, 1977, 1995; Zee, 2003). The quantisation of quantum field processes is akin to the quantisation of the vibrations of a guitar string, and, just as there are no guitar sound particles, there are no physical particles. There are instead quantised and conserved excitations of the processes of quantum fields.

Quantum fields, in turn, have causal power, and do so in part in virtue of their organisation. Again, organisation cannot be excluded as a potential locus of causal power without eliminating causality entirely.

But, if organisation is a potential locus of genuine causal power, and everything is (just) organisations of quantum field processes, then there is no longer any metaphysical block against the possibility of new organisation manifesting new causal power. This includes, for example, the quantum field organisations constituting Kim himself, as well as you and me.

The removal of this metaphysical block against causally efficacious emergence, of course, is just brush clearing. It eliminates a barrier to the possibility of the construction of models of emergence, and therefore, potentially, models of the emergence of normative and intentional phenomena. But it does not in itself provide any such models. That construction remains to be outlined.

3 Process

The basic metaphysical shift that is required in order to address issues of emergence has already been indicated: unlike particle and substance frameworks, a process metaphysics manifests causality, insofar as it does at all, in virtue of its organisation. Therefore, organisation becomes a potential locus of causal power, including at the macro-scales of biological organisms and central nervous systems — and, therefore, potentially for normative and intentional phenomena.[4] A process metaphysics, there-

---

[4] For consideration of a superficially apparent rejoinder that, even with quantum fields, all causality obtains at micro-scales, and everything above some quantum scale will be epiphenomenal, see Bickhard (2000, in preparation).

fore — a return to Heraclitus, if you wish — is required for both logical and physical reasons, and it legitimates the possibility of emergence.

In fact, a process metaphysics reverses all three of the consequences of a substance or particle metaphysics — a metaphysics of some unchanging substratum for all change:

1) Change becomes the explanatory default, and stability requires explanation,
2) Emergence in organisation becomes a metaphysical possibility, and
3) Therefore, it becomes metaphysically legitimate to explore the possibility of the emergence of normative (and intentional) phenomena *within the natural world*.

4 Normative Emergence

Viewed from the perspective of the non-normative world, the fundamental novelty manifested by normativity is an asymmetric differentiation between the positive and negative sides of normative properties: functional and dysfunctional with regard to biological function, for example, or truth and falsity for representation. Physics provides multitudinous differentiations among directions, energy levels, charges, and so on. But none of these provide anything like the asymmetry of normativity. The single major exception to this is in thermodynamics, and I will argue that that thermodynamic asymmetry provides the ground for the natural emergence of normativity.

To begin, however, we must return to the base out of which this entire metaphysical issue evolved: change. Unlike for substances and atoms, in a process metaphysics, change is the default — it's what happens if nothing prevents or modifies it. Stability requires special explanation.

Stability clearly occurs, and the first step toward normativity is to explore kinds of stability. I begin with a differentiation between two basic kinds of stable organisations of process, and these kinds are distinguished in terms of their thermodynamic character.

The first is a process organisation that is stable so long as no energy from the environment impinges on it that is sufficient to disrupt that organisation. The organisation is in a kind of energy well, and will stay there, in that organisation, unless sufficient energy to knock it out of the well hits it. This form of process organisational stability is exemplified by atoms and molecules — it constitutes much of the basic furniture of our world.

Energy well stabilities remain stable should they go to thermodynamic equilibrium. Therefore, they remain stable if they are isolated from their environments — they simply go to equilibrium and stay there.

The second kind of stability differs in these two respects. These stabilities are far from thermodynamic equilibrium. They cannot go to equilibrium without ceasing to exist, and they cannot be isolated without going to equilibrium. Far from equilibrium organisations of process will not be stable unless they are *maintained* in their far from equilibrium conditions.

Often, such maintenance is from outside of the far from equilibrium process itself: a fire maintains a temperature differential between the bottom of a pan of water and the top, or the sun maintains a flow of energy through the biosphere of the earth. As evidenced by the emergence of Bénard cells in the boiling water (and by the evolutionary processes in the earth's biosphere — Bickhard & Campbell, 2003; Bickhard, in preparation), process held in far from equilibrium conditions tend to self organise into systematic patterns.

Some such self-organised organisations of far from equilibrium processes manifest a special emergent property: they contribute to their own maintenance. They help maintain the far from equilibrium conditions upon which their existence depends. A canonical example here is a candle flame: it maintains above combustion threshold temperature, vaporizes wax in the wick so that it can burn, melts wax in the candle so that it can percolate up the wick, and induces convection that brings in fresh oxygen and gets rid of waste. Candle flames exhibit *self-maintenance* in several ways (Bickhard, 1993, 2004, 2009, in preparation).

Candle flames can only burn — they have no alternative ways of contributing to their own maintenance. But some systems do have more than one way in which they can contribute to self-maintenance, and they can switch among those ways in a manner that is appropriate to relevant changes in their environments. A canonical example here is Don Campbell's bacterium that can swim and continue swimming if it finds itself headed up a sugar gradient, but can tumble instead if it finds itself headed down a sugar gradient (Campbell, 1974, 1990). With such switches among alternatives, such a system maintains its condition of being self-maintenant in the face of changes with respect to its environment that can render what might be contributions to self-maintenance instead as being detrimental to self-maintenance if they were to continue. Thus, swimming contributes to the self-maintenance of the bacterium under some conditions — e.g., it's pointed up a sugar gradient — but would be detrimental to self maintenance if it were to continue to swim when pointed down the gradient. Instead, however, the bacterium switches to tumbling. In this manner, the bacterium maintains its condition of being self-maintenant in differing orientations. It is in that sense *recursively self-maintenant*.

Normative Function

With these notions of self-maintenant systems — or, more generally, *autonomous* systems (Bickhard, 2004, 2009, in preparation; Christensen & Bickhard, 2002) — we already have, I claim, the framework for a model of the emergence of normativity: If what constitutes normative phenomena is given in implicit definition, then we can have a model that satisfies such (an) implicit definition(s), and thus constitutes (some kind of) normative phenomena.[5] The task, then, is to show how self-maintenant systems satisfy what is arguably an implicit definition of a kind of normative phenomena. The kind that I will be focusing on is that of normative function.

The central point is that far from equilibrium systems require maintenance in order to be stable, and such contributions are functional for that stability — they *serve the function* of helping to maintain the persistence of that organisation of process. In the simplest of cases, these functions may be served entirely from outside of the system itself. Such cases serve as a kind of primitive starting point for the evolution of more complex function-relevant systems — with self-maintenant systems the first step in which an organisation of processes is functional for itself. As such systems become more and more complex, they become increasingly

---

[5] Note that a model could satisfy an implicit definition of some normative phenomena whether or not the model used normative terms, and whether or not there were any recognition or understanding of the relevant implicit definition(s). This point has particular force against, for example, dynamic system or autonomous agent approaches that reject or eschew normative notions such as representation — e.g., Brooks (1991) or van Gelder (1995). If the relevant organizations of process exist in a system, then accurate models of those systems will satisfy the implicit definitions of normative phenomena, whether or not the modelers recognize or wish to accept that: if normativity is a natural aspect of the natural world, then complete models of the (natural) world will have to model normativity.

autonomous[6] in the sense that they are increasingly more competent at making use of their environments to functionally contribute to their stability.

The normativity in this model of function is strictly relative to the system, the process organisation, that is the focus of consideration. And that relativity can completely alter functionalities or lack thereof across differing systems: For example, the heart beat of a parasite may be functional for the parasite, but dysfunctional for the host, and have no functionality at all for some unrelated distant organism. There is no non-relative sense of normativity here; no God's eye view.

Furthermore, there is no assumption that the persistence of a process organisation is itself good or normatively positive. If it is normatively positive, that will in its turn be relative to some other system. Functionality is normative relative to the stability of a system, but that stability need not be normative in itself at all. The crucial point is that far from equilibrium systems are the only case for which *stability requires maintenance* — thus constituting a natural property with respect to which functional maintenance is relative.

Contrast: The Etiological Approach to Function

The dominant approach to normative function today is the evolutionary etiological approach — modelling function in terms of the evolutionary origins of functional relations and systems (Millikan, 1984, 1993). For Millikan's model, an organ having a function is constituted in its ancestral organs having had the right kind of evolutionary selection history (or various ingenious ways in which function can be derivative from these selection-history functions). This model provides an illuminating contrast for the autonomy-based model of function introduced above, and helps to indicate some of the strengths of the autonomy model as well as some of the specific differences from the etiological approach. I begin with a critique of the etiological approach, and then use the contrast to develop a few additional properties of the autonomy model of function.

Etiological approaches to function make use of a design metaphor: some subsystems have been "designed" to have certain functions by evolutionary processes, and that both explains why those subsystems exist

---

[6] Autonomy, therefore, is a graded concept (Christensen & Bickhard, 2002; Bickhard, 2004).

and constitutes their having a function. I certainly have no objection to evolutionary processes being explanatory for the existence of biological (sub)systems (Bickhard & Campbell, 2003), and the design metaphor can enrich such accounts: evolutionary selection histories can impose important constraints on what exists, what comes into existence, and how they function.

A serious problem with such historical accounts as addressing what constitutes function, however, is that they yield a causally epiphenomenal model of function. Evolutionary history is in the past, and, if that is what constitutes having a function, then it can have causal efficacy for the present only via present states or conditions. But the etiological account is not just an account of the (evolutionary) *origins* of functional systems, it claims to provide an analysis of what *constitutes* having a function, and because that history is in the past, it can make a current causal difference only if it is somehow constituted in the current dynamics of the system, regardless of its history — causality is inherently local.[7] But it cannot be constituted in the current dynamics, as is illustrated by examples that Millikan discusses.

In particular, Millikan's thought experiment of the lion that pops into existence that is molecule by molecule identical to a lion in the zoo provides a clear example. The thought-experiment lion is dynamically, causally, identical to the zoo lion, but the zoo lion has organs that have the right evolutionary history to have functions, while the thought-experiment lion has organs that have no evolutionary history, and, therefore, cannot have functions. So here are two lions that are causally identical, yet one has functions and the other doesn't. Etiological function is causally epiphenomenal. Etiological history can explain the etiology of systems, including systems that have the right history to have functions (according to this account), but those systems having functions or not having functions is not determined by anything concerning the current dynamics of the systems: identical current dynamics can be the outcome of quite different histories, some of which may, according to the etiological account, yield function and some of which may not.

This thought experiment example (along with others such as the swampman: Millikan, 1984, 1993) might be dismissed as having no real implications for modelling function, since it is not something that could

---

[7] Setting aside as irrelevant for these purposes potential quantum nonlocalities.

ever actually happen. But there are quite real versions of the point as well.

Consider the first time in the evolutionary history of a species that some part of an organism belonging to that species makes a contribution to the survival of the organism. This contribution, according to the etiological account, has no evolutionary history, and, therefore, cannot constitute a functional contribution. With a sufficient number of generations of the species being subject to selection pressures regarding such a contribution, that part will come to have making that sort of contribution as (one of) its functions (Godfrey-Smith, 1994). This is a scenario that *must* occur for *every* function, according to this account. Yet that part making that contribution may well be dynamically identical between the first time and some later time sufficient for "function" to have come into existence. Again, we find dynamically, causally, identical systems that differ in terms of having or not having functions. Etiological function is causally epiphenomenal.

Furthermore, the original contribution that is selected for, as well as subsequent contributions, are precisely the kinds of contributions that the autonomy based model takes as constituting function — as serving a contributory function for the continued existence of the system.[8] The evolutionary etiological approach, then, presupposes the autonomy approach (even if it is not *called* function in the etiological model), and, therefore, presupposes a normative kind of phenomenon in its model of the emergence of normative function. It provides a causally epiphenomenal model of function, and is circular as an account of emergent normativity.

Serving a Function; Having a Function

One important contrast between etiological approaches and the autonomy approach to function is that etiological approaches focus on "*having* a function" as the primary property to model, while the autonomy approach takes "*serving* a function" as the focal property. An etiological approach, then, can model serving a function in terms of something that has a function successfully serving the function that it has. Conversely, it is at best

---

[8] Contributions to the reproductive continuation of a species are functional for the species, in this model (though not necessarily for the individual organism), and considerations of species as autonomous systems in themselves yield some interesting complexities (Bickhard, & Campbell, 2003; Bickhard, in preparation).

difficult in this approach to model serving a function when nothing has that function.

Certainly there seem to be cases in which functions are served by phenomena and (sub)systems that do not have those functions. One example would be the sense in which leg muscles can serve the function of contributing to blood flow on long airplane flights even though they do not have that function. The autonomy model has no difficulties with such examples, nor with examples in which functional contributions are distributed across many organs or organ systems, and in which one organ may have multiple functions — but these are again at best difficult to model in terms of evolutionary selection histories for specific organs (Christensen & Bickhard, 2002).

On the other hand, in taking "serving a function" as primary, the autonomy model also undertakes an obligation to account for "having a function" within the framework of the model of serving a function. Having a function must (when it exists) in some sense be derivative from serving a function.

The central property for this purpose is a relation between some activity that might be functional and the conditions under which it would in fact serve a function. Engaging in such an activity, then, involves a presupposition — a functional presupposition — that the necessary supporting conditions hold. Continued swimming in the case of the bacterium, for example, functionally presupposes that supporting conditions hold for that swimming to be making a functional contribution, such as that the bacterium is heading into higher concentrations of sugar.

Some functionally presupposed conditions will be in the environment, such as the sugar gradient, but others may be internal to the organism. In particular, some activities of some parts of a system may be functional or not depending on contributions from other parts of the system being present. Kidneys can filter blood only if the blood is being circulated, for example, and the circulatory system can circulate blood only if something in a particular location is pumping that blood. The functional activities of some parts of a system, in other words, may presuppose functional contributions from other parts. They functionally presuppose that those other parts are serving their own particular functions, making their own functional contributions upon which other contributions depend. In that sense, the other parts *have the functions* of serving the functions that are presupposed. The overall system, then, will, in its activities, presuppose various contributions from its parts[9], which can, in turn, involve still further presuppositions. To *have a function*, then, is to be presupposed as serving that function by the other or overall organisation and functioning of the system. In this manner, having a function can be accounted for in a way that is constituted in the current dynamic organisation of the system, and, therefore, it too (along with serving a function) is causally efficacious.

A Word about Representation

The relational property of functional presupposition is central to the account of having a function. It is also central to the account of the emergence of another form of normativity: representation. Roughly, when interactive activities of the system involve functional presuppositions about the environment, those presuppositions may in some cases be correct, and in other cases not correct. That is, the presuppositions about the environment may be true or false: they constitute (implicit) contents predicated about the environment by the activities of the overall system. This, I claim, captures the emergence of the most primitive version of representational truth value. More complex kinds of representation are constructable out of this base, and these models have important consequences for higher level cognitive and representational phenomena, such as perception, rational thought, and language (Bickhard, 1993, 2004, 2009, in preparation).

5 Conclusion

The natural emergence of such normative phenomena as normative function and representation forms the foundation for multiple further normative emergences, such as memory, learning, social realities, language, and so on, up to and including ethics and morality. These further developments require their own extensive discussions and arguments (Bickhard, 2004b, 2005, 2006, 2007, 2009, in preparation). In itself, however, the model of the emergence of foundational normativity, in the form of normative function, constitutes a claim that normativity in general is emergently natural. To model normative emergence, however, requires first the possibility of metaphysical emergence, which, in turn, requires a

---

[9] Assuming it has parts (Bickhard, 2004, in preparation).

foundational shift from a substance or particle based metaphysics to a process metaphysics.

References

Bickhard, Mark H. (1993). "Representational Content in Humans and Machines". *Journal of Experimental and Theoretical Artificial Intelligence* 5, pp. 285–333.
Bickhard, Mark H. (2000). "Emergence". In *Downward Causation*, ed. by P. B. Andersen, C. Emmeche, N. O. Finnemann, P. V. Christiansen. Aarhus, Denmark: University of Aarhus Press, pp. 322–48.
Bickhard, Mark H. (2003). "Variations in Variation and Selection: The Ubiquity of the Variation-and-Selective Retention Ratchet in Emergent Organizational Complexity, Part II: Quantum Field Theory". *Foundations of Science* 8(3), pp. 283–93.
Bickhard, Mark H. (2004a). "Process and Emergence: Normative Function and Representation". *Axiomathes — An International Journal in Ontology and Cognitive Systems* 14, pp. 135-69. Reprinted from: Bickhard, Mark H. (2003). "Process and Emergence: Normative Function and Representation". In *Process Theories: Crossdisciplinary Studies in Dynamic Categories*, ed. by Johanna Seibt. Dordrecht: Kluwer Academic. pp. 121–55.
Bickhard, Mark H. (2004b). "The Social Ontology of Persons". In *Social Interaction and the Development of Knowledge*, ed. by J. I. M. Carpendale, U. Muller. Mahwah, NJ: Erlbaum. pp. 111–32.
Bickhard, Mark H. (2005). "Consciousness and Reflective Consciousness". *Philosophical Psychology* 18(2), pp. 205–18.
Bickhard, Mark H. (2006). "Developmental Normativity and Normative Development". In *Norms in Human Development*, ed. by L. Smith and J. Voneche. Cambridge: Cambridge University Press. pp. 57–76.
Bickhard, Mark H. (2007). "Language as an Interaction System". *New Ideas in Psychology* 25(2), pp. 171–87.
Bickhard, Mark H. (2009). "The Interactivist Model". *Synthese* 166(3), pp. 547–591.
Bickhard, Mark H. (in preparation). *The Whole Person: Toward a Naturalism of Persons — Contributions to an Ontological Psychology*.
Bickhard, Mark H., Campbell, Donald T. (2003). "Variations in Variation and Selection: The Ubiquity of the Variation-and-Selective Retention Ratchet in Emergent Organisational Complexity". *Foundations of Science* 8(3), pp. 215–82.
Brooks, Rodney A. (1991). "Intelligence without Representation". *Artificial Intelligence* 47(1-3), pp. 139–159.

Campbell, Donald T. (1974). "Evolutionary Epistemology". In *The Philosophy of Karl Popper*, ed. by Paul A. Schilpp. La Salle, IL: Open Court. pp. 413–63.

Campbell, Donald T. (1990). "Epistemological Roles for Selection Theory". In *Evolution, Cognition, and Realism*, ed. by Nicholas Rescher. Lanham, MD: University Press. pp. 1–19.

Cao, Tian Yu (1999). *Conceptual Foundations of Quantum Field Theory*. Cambridge: University of Cambridge Press.

Chang, C. C., Keisler, Howard J. (1990). *Model Theory*. North Holland.

Christensen, Wayne D., Bickhard, Mark H. (2002). "The Process Dynamics of Normative Function". *Monist* 85(1), pp. 3–28.

Clifton, Rob (1996). *Perspectives on Quantum Reality*. Kluwer Academic.

Doyle, Jon (1985). "Circumscription and Implicit Definability". *Journal of Automated Reasoning* 1, pp. 391–405.

Gill, Mary-Louise (1989). *Aristotle on Substance*. Princeton, NJ: Princeton University Press.

Godfrey-Smith, Peter (1994). "A Modern History Theory of Functions". *Nous* 28(3), pp. 344–62.

Graham, Daniel W. (1984). "Aristotle's Discovery of Matter". *Archiv für Geschichte der Philosophie* 66, pp. 37–51.

Graham, Daniel W. (1987). "The Paradox of Prime Matter". *Journal of the History of Philosophy* 25, pp. 475–90.

Graham, Daniel W. (2006). *Explaining the Cosmos*. Princeton, NJ: Princeton University Press.

Hale, Bob, Wright, Crispin (2000). "Implicit Definition and the A Priori". In *New Essays on the A Priori*, ed. by Paul Boghossian, Christopher Peacocke. Oxford: Oxford University Press. pp. 286–319.

Halvorson, Hans, Clifton, Rob (2002). "No Place for Particles in Relativistic Quantum Theories?" *Philosophy of Science* 69(1), pp. 1–28.

Hilbert, David (1971). *The Foundations of Geometry*. La Salle: Open Court.

Huggett, Nick (2000). "Philosophical Foundations of Quantum Field Theory". *The British Journal for the Philosophy of Science* 51(supplement), pp. 617–37.

Hume, David (1978). *A Treatise of Human Nature*. Index by L. A. Selby-Bigge; Notes by P. H. Nidditch. Oxford: Oxford University Press.

Kim, Jaegwon (1991). "Epiphenomenal and Supervenient Causation". In *The Nature of Mind*, ed. by David M. Rosenthal. Oxford University Press. pp. 257–65.

Kolaitis, Phokion G. (1990). "Implicit Definability on Finite Structures and Unambiguous Computations". In *Proc. 5th IEEE LICS*, pp. 168–80.

Kuhlmann, Meinard, Lyre, Holger, Wayne, Andrew (2002). *Ontological Aspects of Quantum Field Theory*. River Edge, NJ: World Scientific.

Millikan, Ruth G. (1984). *Language, Thought, and Other Biological Categories*. Cambridge, MA: MIT Press.

Millikan, Ruth G. (1993). *White Queen Psychology and Other Essays for Alice*. Cambridge, MA: MIT Press.

Otero, Mario H. (1970). "Gergonne on Implicit Definition". *Philosophy and Phenomenological Research* 30(4), pp. 596–99.

van Gelder, Tim J. (1995). "What Might Cognition Be, If Not Computation?". *The Journal of Philosophy XCII*(7), pp. 345–381.

Weinberg, Steven (1977). "The Search for Unity, Notes for a History of Quantum Field Theory". *Daedalus* 106(4), pp. 17–35.

Weinberg, Steven (1995). *The Quantum Theory of Fields. Vol. 1. Foundations*. Cambridge: Cambridge University Press.

Zee, Anthony (2003). *Quantum Field Theory in a Nutshell*. Princeton: Princeton University Press.

3

Why We Don't Need Naturalistic Epistemic Norms

JONATHAN KNOWLES

Naturalised epistemology is more a movement than a philosophical position; it is inspired by the idea of making epistemology more continuous with natural science than it traditionally has been, but in detail the expression means different things to different people. In the sense with which I am concerned here, 'naturalised epistemology' denotes various different theories about what epistemic norms we should follow in order to form our beliefs rationally, and, in particular, about how these norms should be justified. Each kind of naturalised (or naturalistic) epistemology provides its own – naturalistic – account of justification. In my view, when we look at how these different accounts of justification work, we come to see that none of them is such that the norms justified can be seen both as probative and necessary for fully rational belief-formation. In a word, all naturalised epistemology is either defunct or superfluous – or (as I more frequently tend to argue) to the extent it is not defunct, it is superfluous. In my book *Norms, Naturalism and Epistemology: The Case for Science without Norms* (Knowles 2003), I attempted to provide a thoroughgoing demonstration of this 'overarching thesis' for all possible varieties of naturalised epistemology[1]. In this paper-length treatment of

---

[1] The book is henceforth referred to as 'NNE'.

Beyond Description: Naturalism and Normativity.
Marcin Miłkowski and Konrad Talmont-Kaminski (eds.).
Copyright © 2010 The Author.

essentially the same topic, I will confine myself to what I see as the three most important argumentative strategies of the book. I will also provide some clarification of both the content and import of the thesis, and respond to a published criticism of my book that has appeared in a review.

In section 1 I provide a brief overview of naturalism as a perspective within epistemology (something I endorse), and spell out its relationship to naturalised epistemology, understood as above (henceforth 'NE'). In section 2 I outline the main different varieties of NE that I will consider in this paper. In section 3 I discuss the variety I dub 'antipsychologism' and show why the norms it delivers cannot be both probative and necessary for rational belief-formation. In section 4 I do the same though more briefly for what I call 'inductivism' and 'instrumentalism', both subvarieties of what I call 'antifoundationalism'. By way of conclusion, I respond briefly to a published objection to my overarching thesis.

Before all of this, I would like to make a couple of clarificatory comments. Firstly, what I am arguing for is specifically this: that to the extent any epistemic norms may appear to be justifiable in a naturalistically kosher way, they are not necessary for (fully) rational belief formation. By this I mean not just that the norms are not logically necessary, but that we humans have no rational need for them in order to function in an epistemically optimal manner. (The thesis is thus not refuted if some particular individual has to have things put in the imperative if she is to do anything she isn't naturally inclined to! See further § 4.2 below.) The idea is that to the extent naturalism thought it could perform the same kind of service for science or knowledge as traditional a priori epistemology (allegedly) did, or at least something similar, it is mistaken. I am thus not making any claims about the metaphysical status of epistemic norms or normative statements: whether they exist, whether they can be reduced to non-normative states of affairs or statements, whether they express truths that can be known, and so on. Moreover, though I am sceptical about the need for naturalistic epistemic norms, I do not in any way seek to undermine the idea of epistemic normativity; indeed, I presuppose that there are worse and better ways of forming our beliefs and that what these ways are is in a broad sense accessible to us. Thus, though my project is no doubt reasonable to describe as 'meta-epistemological', this should not be understood in the sense that carries over its meaning from the customary concerns of metaethics.

Secondly, in talking of epistemic norms, I mean to speak broadly, and thus do not restrict myself to rules or principles that might be seen as special in applying to belief-formation directly - and hence as things which we may not, assuming an involuntarist conception of belief-formation, be in a position to take heed of anyway[2]. In other words, my notion of epistemic norm covers, at least in addition to these latter things, principles and rules concerning what we should do - how to act - in order to alter and/or steer the course and/or nature of our belief-forming processes. Whether this is an important distinction is not something I take a stand on here, but it is important that I am in any case concerned with what we can in principle take heed of in forming our beliefs.

1 Naturalism in Epistemology

I take my lead from Quine (and especially Quine 1969). For Quine, naturalising epistemology involves, in the first place, renouncing the foundationalist project of traditional epistemology, associated with the modern tradition initiated by Descartes, which sees our scientific knowledge world as warranted in virtue of its provenance from a logically prior set of normative rules for how to form beliefs. In the second place, naturalising epistemology means shifting our investigation from principles for how we should form our beliefs to how in fact we do so - tentatively assuming a modern scientific world-view as the basis for such an account. However, as this latter project is just as reasonable to see as psychology rather than epistemology, and as this is in any case something science will want to provide, it is reasonable to see Quine – at least in 'Epistemology naturalised' – as simply sounding the death-knell of traditional epistemology.

Naturalism as I understand the expression – epistemological naturalism, one might say[3] – is the result of accepting Quine's arguments in this

---

[2] I allude her to a debate about the so-called deontological conception of epistemic justification (cf. Alston 1988).

[3] Though I will not; indeed I regard the term as less appropriate insofar as it suggests that there are other, coeval forms of naturalism, in particular metaphysical naturalism, such that one might be committed to one but not the other. In my view by contrast any view that could with justification claim to be metaphysically naturalistic would ipso facto be epistemologically naturalistic (see Knowles 2008).

area: it is what you are left just insofar as you reject traditional epistemology. By way of positive characterisation naturalism can be seen as committed to the following:

> a) a broadly coherentist, pragmatist and fallibilist conception of belief and justification, in which no belief is fundamental or absolutely a priori, but only gains its acceptability by reference to its place in relation to other beliefs, all of which are in principle open to revision (viz. Quine's 'web of belief', cf. Quine and Ullian 1970);
> b) a broadly natural scientific construal of the content of this 'web of belief', rather than anything non-scientific, such as a religious or magical content.

These aspects of naturalism are to an extent mutually reinforcing insofar as the modern scientific world-view is precisely of a world that is causally interconnected, without sustenance from exterior forces or entities; coherence in our beliefs could therefore be expected to be a reasonable guide to the truth about it. Conversely, our most coherent theories seem to coincide with those of science. However, it would be stretching things to think that coherence, pragmatism, fallibilism and/or some combination of these features - whatever exactly they amount to - uniquely demand the world view of science, or *vice versa*. Moreover, our two features of naturalism would need in this case to cohere with one another, and there are limits to the extent to which we can make sense of such coherence (cf. Knowles 2008). What this means is that being a naturalist must also involve a kind of quietism (or perhaps scepticism in the ancient, classical sense): at some level, we must simply accept the scientific world-view predominant in the Western world today, together with the cogency of our most basic cognitive practices, as the framework within which to work. Naturalism is thus essentially a negative position that rejects the aspirations of *prima philosophia*[4].

---

[4] Talk of 'basic cognitive practices' need not be understood as any more committing than the general assumption noted in the introduction that there are epistemic wrongs and rights and that our epistemic activity is fundamentally on course (though a more full-blooded interpretation is also possible – see section 2). Apart from this, the content of the last four sentences, though very much part of what naturalism is on my view, are essentially optional when it comes to the theses defended in this paper.

That then is naturalism. It is clearly neutral about the prospects for naturalised epistemology (i.e. NE), understood, as above, as some or other theory of epistemic norms and how these might be justified. At the same time, it does not rule out such a theory, and indeed many who subscribe to naturalism in epistemology are attracted to the idea that something more than the mere negative project of rejecting the *a priori* norms of traditional epistemology might be in the offing. Can we not make sense of naturalistic norms, based, not on *a priori* intuition, but somehow or other on what we have available within the scientific world view and/or the idea of belief-justification as essentially 'situated' (cf. points a) and b) above)? These norms would not play exactly the same fundamentalistic role as those of traditional epistemology, but might have a point nevertheless. As we shall see, Quine himself later came to suggest a way of understanding normativity and norms in scientific inquiry on the basis of his underlying epistemological naturalism. But his is only one amongst many. It is time to turn to the varieties of NE.

2 Naturalised Epistemology

The idea of a 'web' of belief is one famous metaphor employed by Quine; that of Neurath's raft is another. The latter idea is often used to underline the non-foundationalist conception of knowledge he prefers, and to rebut charges of vicious circularity. A mariner can stand on some part of his raft while repairing other parts, and can continue to do this without ever docking at port and standing on dry land. Similarly we scientists can assume some part of our knowledge to assess another and then later assess that which we before used as a benchmark for assessment on the assumption of the correctness of some other bit of knowledge.

However, it seems there are two distinct ways of understanding what might be happening in such a situation. On what seems fair to call the standard reading, the idea of repairing the raft while afloat suggests that there is no one plank or set of planks that is somehow privileged as a place to stand on in repairing others: each may take its turn at some point as both evaluator and evaluated. Call this the *antifoundationalist* reading. However, we can also imagine that the sailor, having investigated and repaired many planks, comes to regard certain planks as particularly suited to standing on in repairing others. This wasn't something she could know without having tried out various planks first, but it turns out that some are indeed sturdier than the others - indeed, sturdy enough to function as a kind of 'foundation'. Call this the *antiaprioristic* reading of the raft metaphor.

I have introduced this distinction as a way of classifying kinds NE, as we shall see shortly. As things stand, however, it is important to note that neither reading yields anything like a theory of norms directly. What we have in both cases is a picture on which our beliefs are evaluated against other beliefs, where what the latter are varies indefinitely or after some time emerges as a particular, privileged set. But in neither case need the beliefs be anything more than factual beliefs. One could of course always formulate the normative impact of such beliefs by way of prescriptive statements, such as 'take heed of p in evaluating q, r, s etc.'. The manifest futility of so doing serves as a first, simple illustration of my overarching thesis concerning the superfluity of naturalistic epistemic norms.

However, this is not the only way in which one might seek to motivate a theory of epistemic norms (that is, a naturalistic one, a qualification I shall drop henceforth). Taking the antiaprioristic reading first, we might see the 'planks' the sailor stands on to repair his ship as corresponding to what I called in section 1 our *basic cognitive practices*. On a traditional epistemological picture, such practices would be conceived as our intuitive grasp and application of *a priori* norms, but naturalism does not rule that some other conception of such practices might be viable. Perhaps the most straightforward understanding of what 'basic cognitive practices' might amount to for a naturalist would be something like a psychological capacity for reasoning, perhaps bequeathed to us through evolution in somewhat the same manner as language (at least according to Noam Chomsky). And indeed such a view of epistemic norms has been defended (cf. e.g. Antony 1987, Pollock 1987; cp. Cohen 1981). For reasons in broad outline familiar I think this view fails, but the dialectic involves complexities which space precludes relating here (cf. NNE: ch. 5 for a full presentation).

But *psychologism* (as I dub the above view) is not the only way of understanding 'basic cognitive practices' naturalistically. Firstly, Quine's 'raft' and 'web of belief' metaphors are not obviously meant to refer to the cognitive processes of individual thinkers. Further, though our cognitive practices as a whole may turn out to be something we may view as an agglomerate of those of individual minds in interaction with one another, we cannot just assume that such a reduction will be in the offing. Secondly, it is arguably legitimate to think of cognitive practices in a non-psychologistic way even without entering the debate on socially distributed cognition, insofar as naturalism presupposes the idea that there are better and worse ways of manipulating our beliefs in relation to one another. Such manipulation must, arguably, involve the idea of a cognitive practice, and if psychologism about norms fails - as there is independent reason to think - then a naturalist may be justified in taking the notion as a primitive. This will be the case even if cognitive practices are in some way supervenient on natural psychological capacities, a view that need not imply reduction to them. (For more detailed discussion of the relationship between psychological capacities and non-psychologistic norms, see NNE: ch. 2.2, 3.1).

It is essentially this idea that forms the basis for the first type of NE I will discuss in this paper, which I dub 'antipsychologism'[5]. The basic idea is that naturalistic epistemic norms can be seen as yielded through the explication of our basic cognitive practices. Moreover, I contend that it is natural to see this explication (i.e. justification) along the lines of a process of *reflective equilibrium*, as first advocated by Nelson Goodman in his discussion of the justification of rules of deductive and inductive inference (Goodman 1965: 63-4)[6]. Indeed, Goodman's idea here, though not usually linked directly to discussions about naturalism in epistemology, seems to me to articulate precisely one potentially viable naturalistic conception of epistemic norms and how they are derived[7]. According to the process he advocates, epistemic norms should be arrived at and justified by reference to judgements and intuitions about what is a valid inference in concrete cases. If a proposed norm comports well with our judgements about concrete cases, then it has *prima facie* justification. However, it is not the case that a norm must be immediately rejected

---

[5] 'Antipriorism' is thus a superordinate category embracing both psychologism and antipsychologism.

[6] The expression 'reflective equilibrium' is first used by Rawls (1974), who also develops the notion into something more like an explicit method, but the essentials of the idea are essentially to be found in Goodman – who, moreover, applies it to the derivation of epistemic rather than moral norms. See also below on *wide* reflective equilibrium.

[7] In Goodman's discussion the concern is first and foremost with inductive and deductive rules of inferences, but I see no reason not see his proposal as applying to epistemic norms more generally (or, to the same effect, to understand 'induction' very broadly), and I will frame my discussion accordingly.

simply because it conflicts with one or more judgements about particular cases: such judgements do not form an incorrigible bedrock for epistemological reflection. We may need to revise one or more of them, especially if a proposed principle accords well with many other such judgements – in somewhat the same way the existence of anomalies for an otherwise highly explanatory and well-confirmed theory in science may reasonably lead to rejecting or reconceptualising these in ways conducive to the theory. The aim of the enterprise is to arrive, by gradual mutual adjustment of norms to concrete judgements, at a coherent set of epistemic norms which accord with the judgements we are disposed to make about particular cases – indeed, at precisely something like a *theory* of these judgements, where the hypotheses constituting this theory yield our set of norms, justified insofar as they are arrived at in the manner just described.

As noted, Goodman himself did not connect his suggestion to naturalised epistemology, at least as such (his original discussion predates Quine's 'Epistemology naturalised' by over a decade). Nevertheless, that something like a process of reflective equilibrium (henceforth 'RE') should function as at least a central component in justifying epistemic norms is a quite widely-held view amongst many naturalists today (cf. e.g. Stein 1996, Henderson 1994) – with the proviso that the process be one of so-called *wide* reflective equilibrium, as opposed to the 'narrow' variety initially proposed by Goodman. Like 'reflective equilibrium', the expression 'wide reflective equilibrium' stems from Rawls (1971), and was used by him to denote a process whereby one seeks to bring intuitions about concrete cases and rules into accord with wider philosophical theories, for example from ethics or metaphysics. In co-opting the idea of wide reflective equilibrium, naturalists stress the need to take account of *empirical* evidence concerning the structure of our reasoning capacities and other psychological data in the reflective process of deriving valid epistemic norms.

Notwithstanding, I wish to maintain that RE, even in a relatively narrow, unmodified form, already enunciates a naturalistic perspective on epistemology – or at least does so when interpreted in a manner that makes it plausible as a way of justifying norms. This interpretation of RE tends to be obscured because the intuitions about rules or principles are themselves often seen as having the role of *data*, along with the judgements about concrete cases, both of which are then fed into and steer the process toward reflective equilibrium. On this understanding, it becomes natural to regard the intuitions about rules as corresponding to philosophical or a priori elements, and the whole process as differing from traditional accounts of justification insofar as these are fallible and susceptible to correction by taking into account judgements about concrete cases as well (also viewed as fallible). Not only is this account inherently problematic (cf. NNE: ch. 2.2), moreover, it is non-compulsory: we can take the whole process as a *theoretical* enterprise in which one must proceed *in situ*, seeking to improve upon the *theory* – about the norms – that one has at any given time by taking account of further *data* – i.e. judgements about concrete cases – and modifying the theory on the basis of these, though in a manner, no less scientific, that also permits rejection of the concrete judgements. There is thus no *a priori* starting point for the justification of epistemic norms, fallible or otherwise, and the picture is consonant with Quine's idea of science as an ever-evolving web of belief (or a raft afloat at sea). RE is thus inherently naturalistic. At the same time, the basic procedure is also open to modifications in order to take account of 'wider' considerations, e.g. empirical data from psychology or other sciences. (The impact of adopting a narrow or wide conception of RE will be discussed in the following section.)

It is also worth pointing out that essentially this same method, RE, seems to be employed in at least one dominant research strategy in philosophy of science: the appeal to the practice of actual, prominent scientists as the basis for providing a set of normative methodological rules for science (cf. Lakatos 1974, 1978; Chalmers 1990: ch. 2.3;; Kosso, 1991: 351 ff; Laudan 1996: 128). On this line the data for the construction of a theory of scientific rationality are the judgements and actions of scientists whose science we today judge to have been most successful and thus to constitute the canon of scientific knowledge (Galileo, Newton, Lavoisier et al.). At the same time, the norms we arrive at can (or at least should)[8] function as a corrective and guide to subsequent scientists, and, insofar as the methodological theory is generally well-confirmed, they can to an extent resist certain seeming counterexamples. Clearly this

---

[8] There is much debate about concrete proposals. For discussion of Lakatos, cf. Feyerabend (1981: 202-30), Couvalis (1996: 74 ff.).

method has much in common with RE, the main difference appearing to lie in the database: in philosophy of science we use scientists' judgements, with RE, those of ordinary people. (We shall consider the relationship between everyday and scientific rationality further in the following section.)

Let us now turn to varieties of naturalised epistemology that fall under the rubric of *antifoundationalism*. According to antifoundationalist theories of epistemic norms, contra antipriorism – *a fortiori* antipsychologism – there is no stable set of standards for evaluating our beliefs that endures over time. This does not have to mean any standards are relative; rather, an antifoundationalist can say that *what it is* to be a correct standard for reasoning and belief-formation has to take its lead from the state of our knowledge at any given time. There is of course no guarantee that this will converge on some unchanging conception of 'the truth', though it also seems clear that the process as a whole being in some way rational and/or goal-directed must be assumed if our enquiries are to be other than a kind of game. On the other hand, since this would seem to be entailed by the presuppositions of our naturalism – that there are better and worse ways of forming our beliefs that are in some broad sense accessible to us – this need not be a problem for antifoundationalism. The question thus arises: what prospects exist by way of a theory of norms for this view of science and knowledge?

There are in fact rather many subvarieties of it. Indeed, RE itself might be put in the service of one such view – after all, the process might continually 'destabilize'. This particular kind of antifoundationalism will not be discussed here: it fails for reasons somewhat similar to those to be marshalled against AP in the following section, but again complexities in the dialectic preclude details. (For what aims to be an exhaustive catalogue of the varieties of antifoundationalism and their weaknesses, see NNE: ch. 4).

In this paper I will focus on what I see as the two most important varieties of antifoundationalism. One of these I call *instrumentalism*, an idea we find in Quine, Laudan and many other naturalised epistemologists of recent years. On this line, empirical evidence can ground norms for belief-formation insofar as the latter are conceived not categorically but hypothetically, as telling you what to do *given* you have a certain epistemic goal. Such an account is antifoundationalist at least insofar as it stays silent about which fundamental goals we should be pursuing. Nevertheless, it does, assuming an overall rational direction to our cognitive activity, seem to allow us to motivate cogent norms for empirical work.

The other important sub-variety (which I will critique first) is essentially an idea of John Stuart Mill's in *A System of Logic* (Mill 1895), to the effect that norms for science can be motivated by reference to what we learn through successful and non-successful inductive practice. A clearly naturalistic suggestion, the cogency of such norms assumes that induction in a broad sense is a rational mode of inquiry into the natural world. More details will be given below of this position, which I dub 'inductivism'.

It is time to turn to critique[9].

3 Antipsychologism

My basic argument against antipsychologism (henceforth AP) as a viable naturalised epistemology is very simple. It aims to establish the superfluity any norms that are sanctioned in the manner prescribed – the problem that, according to me, infects all varieties of NE. I will first present it in relation to the simplest form of AP, i.e. that based on a narrow form of RE, and then show it remains in force in the face of several different replies and however one might seek to 'widen' this process.

According to the simplest form of AP, norms are derived through RE, that is, on the basis of inferences made by ordinary people and/or scientists that, in the first instance, are not governed by norms or rules (at least, by explicit rules) but merely, so to speak, 'flow' from their ability.

---

[9] I should perhaps underline that an important aim of NNE was to offer an exhaustive taxonomy of naturalised epistemology, one which also took into account the possibility of 'mixed' varieties, that is, epistemologies which are, say, partly antifoundationalist and partly antipsychologist – as well as, possibly, partly non-naturalistic (what I call *weak* versions of NE). It all gets rather complicated. Exactly what labels get attached to which views is in the end of subordinate importance; what I try to do here is focus on what are arguably three of the most central conceptions of naturalistic epistemic norms today in a way that also relates them to what still strikes me as an most important divide in the terrain, namely, between epistemologies that seek something like an unchanging set of standards as a way of understanding rational belief formation (antiapriorism), and those that demur at giving a direct answer to that problem but nevertheless insist that norms can be made sense of and have a role to play in science (antifoundationalism).

These abilities collectively constitute what we have been calling our basic cognitive practices. Now, though these abilities may supervene on some psychological competence or competencies, insofar as AP opposes itself to psychologism, there is no question of the norms gleaned being identified with the principles contained in any such competence. Nevertheless, one can surely still legitimately wonder what the point of deriving explicit rules might be. After all, if the process presupposes certain abilities in people, why shouldn't we simply let these people *get on with it* – using the abilities, natural or acquired, which constitute what we are calling 'basic cognitive practices'? We might indeed be able to uncover certain rules that they (in some sense) might be said to be following: implicitly guiding principles, perhaps mirrored in their actual psychological make-up. But why should we go to this trouble when it seems doing so is not necessary for their rational belief-formation? I see this as *the fundamental objection* to AP, and will refer to it as such in what follows.

An initial first reply might be that insofar as the abilities in question are not considered individualistically (or as a mere sum thereof), there will still be a point in deriving norms for the regulation of individuals' inferences and reasoning. But the fundamental objection does not rest on such an individualistic conception of ability or cognitive practices, but only on the idea that what is in question is *an ability*. If the ability is individualistic then the norms in question will be aimed at regulating the individual's belief-formation; if it is not, they will be aimed at regulating this supra-individualistic ability. If the fundamental objection applies in the first case, then presumably it does so in the second as well.

A better reply from a supporter of AP would be that the rules would not be redundant insofar as they could play a role in *streamlining* and/or *expediting* the *application* of the ability we possess. But even if we accepted this, it is another matter whether explicitly setting up the principles underlying this ability would be the only let alone the most effective way of doing this. Consider an analogy with our linguistic ability. One could no doubt imagine that speaking grammatically correctly could, to an extent, be improved by making people aware of the rules of grammar.[10] However, it seems clear that this same goal would probably be

---

[10] I am not here assuming a cognitivist construal of grammar as something actually known or internally represented.

more effectively ensured by advising people to concentrate properly on what they are saying, on whether their utterances really mean what they want them to mean, and so on – in short, to apply their ability more *competently* or *assiduously*. Someone might retort there are relevant disanalogies (beyond those alluded to in footnote 10) between the linguistic case and that of epistemic norms conceived as derived through RE. However, it is unclear what these should be insofar as RE operates on a cognitive ability, for it would seem unexceptionable to speak of more or less competent use of any such ability. In any case, the present defence hardly shows that setting up epistemic norms explicitly is *necessary* for optimal belief-formation. Moreover, I think it is fair to say that the burden of proof rests on my opponent to show that doing this would expedite this process to a greater extent than simply applying our ability more assiduously.

Does the possibility of using a wide form of RE affect these points in any way? A wide process of RE is often seen as encompassing one or more of the following elements in addition to straightforward intuitions (cf. Stich 1991: ch. 4; Stein 1996: 149-55, 256-63; Knowles 2002a):

  i) considered intuitions;
  ii) empirical data concerning our ability to reason;
  iii) other empirical data;
  iv) philosophical theories and ideas.

As far as the present discussion is concerned, iii) and iv) can be set aside. 'Philosophical theories and ideas' smack of *a priori* elements, which would yield at best what I call a weak version of NE, which I am not considering here (see footnote 9). Empirical data beyond our ability to reason would not seem relevant given that AP is a quasi-foundational version of NE, based precisely on our reasoning ability.

Let us consider the other two sources. Basing the norms on considered intuitions rather than ordinary – let us call them 'rash' – intuitions might indeed yield norms that would be useful for the rash individual. However, insofar as the individual is not rash, but considers her belief-formation in any particular case, it seems the fundamental objection against AP must continue to apply.

Consider now empirical data concerning our ability to reason. Those who have stressed these factors have been concerned first and foremost with contingent facts about our computational and cognitive limitations. Presumably, the idea for the supporter of AP would be that knowledge of certain limitations could rule out certain intuitively attractive norms that would have emerged through a narrow process of RE,[11] for example, exhaustive consistency-checking (I will focus on this example).[12] Thus, it might seem that there would be a point to deriving and explicitly setting up the norms delivered through a wide process of RE – in the present case, to get people to abjure exhaustive consistency-checking (for the reasons spelled out in footnote 12). However, if consistency-checking really were countenanced by a process of narrow RE, it surely must have *something* going for it. Some degree of consistency-checking would seem therefore to be apposite, or at least legitimate. Concerning the question of to what extent we should check for consistency, we can imagine two possibilities: that there should be a norm, or several norms – for different, specified situations – regulating the degree of consistency-checking one should go in for; or that it should be irreducibly a matter of context-dependent, individual judgement. In the latter case, a norm proscribing exhaustive consistency-checking would not be required, because we could instead just inform people about their computational limitations, and let them limit their natural disposition to seek consistency as they see fit, according to the circumstances. In the former case, the relevant norm or norms would have to be derived and justified – which, for a supporter of AP, would go *via* a process of RE seeking to derive a theory of norms by simultaneously taking into account concrete judgements together with knowledge of human computational limitations. But then it seems my argument for the non-necessity of these norms would go through in much the same way as before: instead of using the thus-derived norms, one could simply apply one's cognitive ability assiduously, taking into account as one did so knowledge of human computational limitations.

---

[11] To simplify the following discussion, 'narrow RE' will be understood as involving considered intuitions.

[12] As is now well known, such checking for even a relatively modest number of beliefs is far beyond the cognitive resources we have at our disposal (cf. Cherniak 1986). Details of our perceptual and memory systems also seem to have relevance to normative matters (cf. ibid.; Goldman 1986).

A further, distinct answer to the fundamental objection might build on the fact that we can distinguish *different kinds* of ability, existing in different groups of people, as the basis upon which to derive norms of reasoning. In the recent literature on the use of RE in gleaning epistemic norms, the idea of *reasoning experts* has been discussed, viewed as people whose reasoning ability is somehow 'enhanced' relative to the rest of the population (they are standardly assumed, amongst other things, to understand logic and probability theory; cf. Stich ibid.; Stein 1996: §§ 3.3, 3.5). Thus it is often suggested the correct epistemic norms are those that are in *expert reflective equilibrium* (which might also take into account some or more of the wide factors listed above), rather than the reflective equilibrium ordinary people would reach. In relation to AP, the important point is that whilst experts would perhaps not need to have their principles made explicit for themselves – for the reasons already outlined – nevertheless, doing this would be beneficial for ordinary people, for it would enable them to form their beliefs in a more rational fashion than they could by employing their own ability.

I have no particular quarrel with the idea of reasoning experts, but I do not think it can aid the plight of AP. We must ask exactly how we are to conceive of such experts. One alternative might to view of them as traditional philosophers, engaged in developing theories of reasoning based on detailed knowledge of logic and statistics. However, this suggests that expert RE will build in *a priori* elements, in which case the norms they delivered could not be classed as fully naturalistic.

Another alternative would be to view the experts as offering empirically-based advice about what kinds of reasoning methods are most conducive to rational belief-formation, given certain goals one might have (e.g. securing a greater proportion of true beliefs). However, if this is the view in question, we are no longer really considering AP at all, where norms are derived through RE, but rather a version of NE based on knowledge of empirical connections (on which, see section 4.2 below.)

The only other remaining feasible alternative would seem to be that the experts in question must simply be scientists. Thus one could again concede that scientists do not themselves need the norms that might be gleaned from a reflective analysis of their own activity, but also insist that those of us who are not scientists may do so to reason optimally – given that science represents the most advanced means of finding out about the world, and goes beyond the competence enshrined in everyday reasoning ability.

I think this last suggestion is really very far-fetched. Is there really a monolithic set of rules for science? Moreover, are these such that one could use them to function as or become a scientist? Much recent philosophy of science has emphasised the historical variation in concrete scientific methods (cf. Chalmers 1999: ch. 11; Laudan 1984, 1996), whereas any general prescriptions appear either inherently vague or merely common-sensical (i.e. part of everyday ability) (cf. Chalmers 1999: 171; Kuhn 1970; NNE: ch. 4.5). As Kuhn has also argued, the idea that scientists function by following rules at all, even implicitly, is undermined by the amount of situation-specific practical know-how involved in science (cf. Kuhn 1970, 1977; NNE: ch. 3.4). But even if there were such implicit rules, supporters of AP would still have to establish that these could be used by ordinary people to function as or become a scientist, which would seem highly unlikely, or at least unsubstantiated. I admit that these considerations are not one 100% watertight. Nevertheless, this last ditch attempt to save AP does seem to be a very long shot (see NNE: Conclusion for further reflection on this 'caveat' to my overarching thesis).

That ends my discussion and critique of AP.

4 Antifoundationalism

In this section, I consider two sub-varieties of AF, *inductivism* and *instrumentalism*. The presentation will, for reasons of space, be somewhat more compact than that of AP, but will I hope manage to convey the essentials of my arguments.

4.1 Inductivism

According to this line, first espoused by Mill (1895),[13] science is fundamentally an inductive cognitive practice, but we can also learn how to

---

[13] My presentation is largely inspired by Couvalis (1997: ch. 3), which in turn is indebted to Skorupski's (1990) study of Mill. For a similar kind of account, cf. Papineau (1993: ch. 5). Although Mill considers only induction in a narrow sense, there would seem to be scope for developing the kind of justification Mill proposes to inductive canons in a wide

improve upon what at any time these concrete practices are. Here is George Couvalis' rendering:

> [...] Mill thinks that we start our investigations of nature by assuming all enumerative inductions with true premises prove their conclusions. [...] However, Mill holds that our starting assumption needs to be substantially modified. We quickly realise that enumerative inductions over some sorts of cases produce many cases which are falsified [...] For example, we quickly realise that when we infer from the colour of a few instances of a species that all members of that species have that colour, our premise provides little support for its conclusion. However, in other sorts of cases, enumerative induction seems to produce statements that are not falsified, so we come to understand that enumerative inductions over such cases provide stronger support for their conclusions. [.... E.g. ...] generalisations about broad structural anatomy of all the members of species [...] are rarely wide of the mark. [...W]e can and do decide on the basis of large numbers of trials that enumerative inductive arguments about some sorts of cases are at least much less probative than arguments about other cases. (Couvalis 1997: 77-8)

Thus, the inductive canons of science – our epistemic norms (or at least some of them) – can be justified in pretty much the same way that we justify 'first-order' scientific hypotheses, that is, by proposing general hypotheses on the basis of observation, and refining them in the light of subsequent observation. What Mill advocates is a *system* of inductively based generalisations, with higher level norms being used to steer the creation of lower level hypotheses, and the higher level norms in their turn being modified in relation to the observational success of the lower level hypotheses they generate. There need be no end to this process, even though one might hope for greater stability to emerge in our inductive canons after a while, and even though it seems reasonable to suppose we will thus be making progress towards ever more adequate canons. Pictorially, the idea can be represented as follows:

---

sense, i.e. including those that are sometimes called *abductive* (*viz.* inferences to the best explanation), as well as to higher level inductive norms.

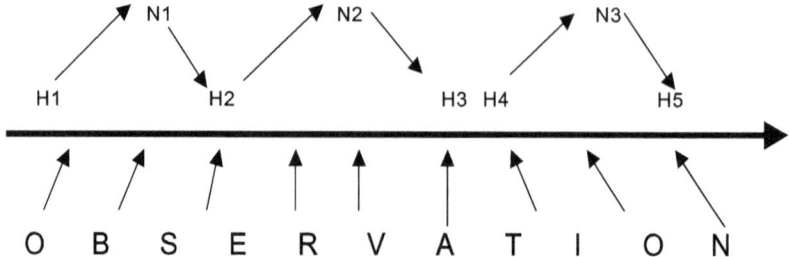

Is this view of scientific norms and their justification tenable? Let us suppose that the process of refining hypotheses iteratively in relation to observation is fundamentally apt as a way of gaining ever more adequate hypotheses (in accord with the presuppositions of our naturalism). With the assumption in place, it would seem unexceptionable that using information about which kinds of hypotheses have turned out most reliable in relation to past observations in order to derive norms about which hypotheses to form in the face of future observations can be assumed to be a reliable method for deriving norms too (bearing in mind any such will always be fallible). The question I want to raise, however, is this: why, given that we must assume that shaping one's hypotheses in relation to observation is a reliable process in the first place, will it be necessary also to postulate norms in order to steer these hypotheses – from 'above' as well as from 'below', so to speak? In other words, why will such norms be *necessary* to form optimally rational beliefs?

This might seem like an obtuse question. It might just seem obvious – under the general assumption that induction is basically reliable – that there will be a potential for greater steering of hypotheses by generating more refined norms. But what grounds this feeling of obviousness, and what kind of steering is this really meant to be? Note first that it is not a steering whose epistemic authority differs in *kind* from the steering hypotheses gain from observation. If there is anything fundamentally lacking in the latter with regard to the *kind* of steering it gives, steering by norms as Mill conceives of them will clearly not compensate for it.

The idea must then presumably be that the norms will somehow *assist* observation in the creation of good hypotheses – that they will lead to better hypotheses than observation alone could sanction. However, on reflection, it is in fact highly unclear how they can be in a position to do this. Remember that the norms are derived merely on the basis of hypotheses so far chosen, just as the latter are derived on the basis of available observational data. If our norm is 'Draw inductions based on structural anatomy, but not colour' (call this 'N'), we need to know in what way this will genuinely aid further enquiry. The hypotheses we have used to ground N might after all turn out to be faulty, to a greater or lesser extent. All we can say, given our background assumptions, is that, through trial and error, gradual convergence on truth (or rational progress of some kind) will obtain through inductive reasoning. In other words: to what extent our hypotheses stand the test of time is only something time will tell (to put it in what I hope is an illuminatingly tautological manner!). But the same thus goes for the norms: they are in no worse, but also no better position than the hypotheses. Since there is, *ex hypothesi*, no *a priori* way of delimiting the correct set of inductions, but only further observation, it seems the norms cannot – in the absence of further assumptions – play any substantive role in this delimitation. They are a mere summary presentation of where we have got to so far – an inessential overlay to the (assumed) underlying rationality of the practice.

To see this more clearly, we can note that 'grue-like'[14] norms such as the following are also consistent with our data about which hypotheses have been confirmed and which not:

N': Draw inductions based on structural anatomy up to 31st December 2020, but on colour thereafter.

N'': Draw inductions based on structural anatomy for birds, mammals and fish, but on colour for reptiles and insects.

It cannot on Mill's account count against a norm that it is intuitively invalid, as I take it N' and N'' are: we have to find this out empirically. Until we make the relevant observations or else some other assumptions, N' and N'' must, for Mill, be as good guides to hypothesis-formation as N. But that just shows that none are of any real use.

Of course, first-order hypotheses might in principle take a branching, 'grue' form too (e.g. 'All pigs will have four legs before 2020 and three thereafter'). However, indeterminacy in the norms will always go beyond

---

[14] Cf. Goodman's new riddle of induction, in which the predicate 'grue' means *green before [a certain date in the future], blue thereafter* (Goodman 1965: 80 ff.).

any that exists at the level of the hypotheses. In other words, though we might legitimately balk at grue-like hypotheses – for whatever reason, perhaps that 'having four legs' is some sort of natural kind or predicate – we cannot use precisely *that* reason to balk at grue-like norms. Having said this, however, I think we are now in a position to understand why we are strongly inclined to think that steering by higher level norms of the kind Mill proposes *must* have some kind of useful role to play in scientific progress. Though N' or N'' might be just as 'rational' as the original norm in the absence of further assumptions, there are, in the usual case, precisely further assumptions in play: that N, and other 'valid' norms, correspond to what we take to be deeper, underlying laws or principles of nature. If one assumes that nature is governed by general and simple underlying principles, and that such principles are the *basis* of more specific laws of nature (e.g. pigs having four legs), then one can see how hypotheses about the former would be helpful in constraining hypotheses about the latter. If the world really does partake of deeper levels of organization, then knowledge, albeit partial and fallible, of what these are will clearly expedite our understanding of more superficial levels. To be a little more specific, one might justifiably assume that the world is carved up into natural kinds at various levels of generality. If this were the case, then hypotheses about which categories of thing are natural kinds would, if correct, clearly expedite research. If antifoundational inductive norms correspond to or are backed up by correct assumptions about what the relevant natural kinds are, or about other fundamental principles of nature, they will therefore also be in a position to expedite the progress of science. However – and this is the rub as far as we are concerned – they will still not be necessary to do this, since the substantive, factual assumptions about the nature of the world will themselves be sufficient to do it insofar as scientists perforce will take heed of these in their reasoning.

There are some further rounds of possible riposte and replies to this argumentative line, for which the interested reader is referred to NNE: ch. 4.1. For now our conclusion is that AF in its inductivist form does not avoid the dilemma of NE: the superfluity or inadequacy of its proposed norms.

4.2 Instrumentalism

According to instrumentalism, epistemic norms are fundamentally hypothetical imperatives or 'instrumentalities'. They say not 'Do X!', but 'If you want Y (i.e. if Y is one of our cognitive aims or goals), do X!' (cf. Laudan 1984, 1996). What status goals or aims have is a further issue, but, at least for an antifoundationalist, there need be nothing inherently or intrinsically valuable about them. Aims may vary across individuals or across times; the idea is that nevertheless, given a certain aim is held, and given that there are worse and better ways of attaining it, statements of the above form will have normative force. Moreover, there need only be a reliable connection between X and Y to ground such norms, something that is presumably empirically ascertainable, hence rendering the norms naturalistically kosher.

The instrumentalist conception of epistemic norms is quite widespread amongst naturalists today (cf. e.g. Laudan 1984, 1996, Giere 1989, Kornblith 1993, Kitcher 1992, Goldman 1986, Maffie 1990, Stich 1990, Henderson 1994, Bishop & Trout 2005)[15]. Quine's later writings also promote an instrumental notion of rationality as part of naturalised epistemology. Here is an oft-cited passage:

> Naturalisation of epistemology does not jettison the normative and settle for indiscriminate description of ongoing practices. For me normative epistemology is a branch of engineering. It is the technology of truth-seeking or, in a more cautiously epistemological term, prediction. Like any technology, it makes free use of whatever scientific findings may suit its purpose. There is no question here of ultimate value, as in morals; it is a matter of efficacy for an ulterior end. (Quine 1986. 664)

There is a great deal that might be said about instrumentalism (and indeed of different varieties thereof), and I cannot go into all sides of the controversy here. Suffice it to say that in my opinion, the view is not decisively refuted by the considerations that have been adduced against it (cf. Freedman 1999; Knowles 2002b). The complaint here will rather, yet

---

[15] Indeed, it is also espoused by some non-naturalists, e.g. Foley (1987).

again, be one of superfluity of the proposed norms. To begin to see this, I will consider first an objection made by Alexander Rosenberg against Laudan's account of norms (Rosenberg 1990). According to Laudan, on an instrumentalist conception of epistemic norms there is mutual 'reticulation' between norms and facts, whereby the facts decide which norms we should adopt and the norms in turn steer our understanding of what is fact. Rosenberg claims that factual theories must in fact be more fundamental, since they explain why the former work or fail to work, but not *vice versa* (ibid.: 36). Laudan replies to this that, intuitively, norms can, if justified, explain why theories work; and that otherwise the question of which comes first, norms or theories, is like the proverbial 'chicken-and-egg' (Laudan 1996: 164-5).

Now I think Laudan is right that norms, as he conceives of them, can explain why theories are chosen. However, this does not mean there is no meaningful issue as to which is prior. Indeed, a simpler point than Rosenberg's is just this: since hypothetical norms are justified on the basis of empirical connections between means and ends, why not just stick with claims about these empirical connections and jettison the norms? Knowledge of such connections will be at least as useful as knowledge of the norms in guiding action towards the attainment of one's goals. Indeed, rational action in the instrumental sense in question here is not generally conceived of as involving explicit norms or rules – at least beyond the background rules of decision theory (if such exist – and which in any case are not *epistemic* norms). I desire certain things, have beliefs about what will most likely lead to these things, and I act accordingly; I don't need to formulate a rule (additional to those of decision theory) to the effect *If you want such and such, do so and so in order to achieve this*. So the question is, given hypothetical norms of an epistemic variety will also be justified by reference to ordinary, fact-stating empirical beliefs, why bother with the former?

How might instrumentalists react to this criticism? Perhaps by saying that a hypothetical imperative could be in force in a given scientific community without all the members having access to the empirical reasons for it being in force – just as ordinary citizens are required to obey society's laws even though they are partially ignorant as to why they should obey them. But what precisely does it mean to say scientists would not have 'access to the empirical reasons for it being in force'?

This could mean either (i) they are not acquainted with the empirical claim or claims on which the rule is based; or (ii) they are not acquainted with the detailed empirical evidence used to justify the empirical claim or claims on which the norm is based. The second possibility here seems reasonable, given the cooperative and communal nature of science. However, it seems far less clear that possibility (i) would be acceptable in a scientific community. Practitioners are told *If you want such and such an aim (A), use such and such a method (M)*. Surely, in a *scientific* community it would only be acceptable to conform to such a rule if one also were given reasons for it, such as: *M leads to A in the large majority of cases and nothing other than M has been found, so far, to lead to A in as many cases*. At the very least, it seems these purely factual statements would be *assumed*, possibly tacitly, by those who embraced the hypothetical imperative and used it, in a rational manner, to steer their belief-formation. In either case, the norm itself would be redundant.

But what, someone might say, about non-scientific communities? Presumably an instrumental norm could be accepted by ordinary people without them having to be acquainted, even tacitly, not just with the *grounds* for the empirical claim underlying it, but with the empirical claim itself. Moreover, it might seem that science could precisely play a role here in supplying lay people with epistemic norms for the achievement of their goals – so that we get a situation analogous to the kind envisaged in the previous section where, though perhaps reasoning experts will not need the norms themselves, these will be essential for the optimal epistemic practice of ordinary people.

However, this line of argument is also easy to rebut. The bottom line is again very simple: why not just inform people of the relevant empirical connections, rather than provide the norm? Given what I argued above about the structure of instrumental reasoning, information to the effect that a certain desired consequence is reliably brought about by a certain kind of action and (let us say) only by this action would be just as effective in expediting optimal epistemic practice as a conditional norm. Perhaps one might say that the normative formulation is more streamlined, and better gets across the essential point. However, there is surely nothing in the way of introducing some standard non-normative formulation that is equally streamlined and succinct, for example of the form 'X is the most reliable known way of securing Y'. Moreover, it is not even clear that avoiding the complications of the precise nature of the empirical connection, at least in the total way a hypothetical norm does, is actually conducive to maximally rational behaviour. If the only viable, known way of attaining a given goal is in fact far from being a *very* reliable means to that end, this presumably ought to be taken account of by those concerned to achieve it. But even if one disagreed about this, the idea that norms should be necessary, or have some kind of advantage relative to non-normative formulations in steering optimal belief-formation, seems implausible.

A further objection to my line might be that the best means to attaining a given aim could stand alone as a norm for belief-formation. There may be people who do not know that Y is a relevant goal of their cognitive activity, or perhaps do know but do not care. Nevertheless, if it is, it may be true that these people should still do X given X leads reliably to Y; moreover, they will then need specifically to be told to do X. To be somewhat more concrete, it seems there will always be people within, say, a scientific community who need to be told explicitly what to do – technicians who follow procedures and instructions, or even 'higher-level' scientists mostly concerned about money and prestige – who lack concern for what scientific ends following these methods leads to.

In response to this, I should first concede that science, indeed, knowledge-gaining activity generally, probably does need *some* kind of rules or norms if it is to function optimally. If cognitive inquiry requires, as a matter of practical fact, the cooperation of people who are just not interested in truth or rational belief (or whatever general characterisation we give of specifically epistemic activity) then, just as there will be a need for societal rules in general, so there will also be a need for rules governing the belief-forming practices of this kind of people. However, the question is whether such norms should qualify as epistemic in nature. Note first that the present point would seem to be quite a general one in relation to NE, not having anything particularly to do with an instrumentalistic conception of norms. For example, if certain people are needed to reason well when they are not interested in using their reasoning ability – of the kind AP assumes we possess – well, we might need to set up explicit norms dictating the way they should reason, norms which, for those willing to use their ability properly, would not be required. This in turn suggests that the people for whom norms (of whatever kind) would be essential are best described as *performing a job in the service of* scientific or cognitive enquiry, not actually *conducting* that enquiry. For the latter group, who value the relevant aims, it would remain the case that norms would not be required for optimal epistemic activity. Further, for the former group, though perhaps the norms will *coincide* with those genuine scientists or enquirers would countenance, they could not really be said to be playing an *epistemic* role for them. They would, after all, be upheld through incentives for abidance (i.e. salaries), and possibly sanctions for violations. In view of this, the norms, insofar as they play the role they do, could reasonably be said not to be epistemic but merely practical in nature. Instrumentalism thus still fails to yield a variety of NE whose norms are required for optimal belief-formation, insofar as NE is concerned with specifying *epistemic* norms for the *conducting* of scientific enquiry.

At this juncture, a supporter of instrumentalistic NE might say that she can, at least for the sake of argument, go along with my conclusion here, but say that it really has no impact on what practitioners of NE aim to achieve. Whether or not we need normative formulations of the empirical connections between means and cognitive ends, it remains a fact that this knowledge is required for optimal epistemic progress. Hence we need instrumentalistic NE, even if we do not need norms, because we need to be told what the best means are for achieving our cognitive goals[16].

However, this description of what cognitive agents need to know is tendentious. Talk of what is 'best' only makes an essential entrance in relation to *individuals'* consideration of how to achieve their cognitive aims in particular circumstances. Practitioners of the present version of NE do not offer information about what is best or optimal or anything of that kind, or at least doing so is unnecessary (and, possibly, as I indicated above, misleading); their contribution can and should be restricted to empirical information which individuals may then make use of in their own decision-making. These practitioners might still retort that they are needed for optimal epistemic activity – for optimal cognitive progress. However, that empirical information is needed for such progress is not really very surprising – indeed, it is a cornerstone of naturalism. In say-

---

[16] This objection was put to me by David Henderson.

ing this, I am in a way admitting that what some people who call themselves naturalistic epistemologists do might be necessary for optimal epistemic progress; and thus, if NE is by definition what these people do, then NE is not superfluous. However, it strikes me as highly significant to point out that this discipline and those who practice it are *nothing more* than scientists investigating certain empirical connections in the natural world. That this will be of significance in the progress of knowledge is beyond doubt; but then the same can be said of all other scientific activity. I take it that naturalistically-inclined epistemologists have seen their role as something beyond that of ordinary scientists, and at least that those who read them have taken it that they see their role as something beyond this. It strikes me, therefore, as highly significant to point out that it does not do so[17].

5 Conclusion

This paper is almost at its end. There is nothing really to add by way of conclusion to the details of the foregoing (apart from the embellishments to be found in NNE, to which the interested reader is again referred). Instead I will therefore consider an objection to my overarching thesis that has been made by Harvey Siegel (Siegel 2005), and try to show why I think my view survives it.

According to Siegel, it is one thing to show that explicit norms may not be necessary for forming optimally rational beliefs; it is another, however, to think that they are therefore superfluous. The reason is simply that we may need to *know* that the beliefs we have formed are rational, and that we can only do this by considering whether our beliefs are formed in conformity to the relevant epistemic norms:

> Even if Knowles is correct that explicit consideration of explicit norms is not necessary for rational belief-formation, it nevertheless remains that establishing that beliefs are indeed rational depends on such norms. And if so, even Knowles' quietist naturalist will not be able to do without norms, if part of her task in-

---

[17] I think these considerations serve to question the epistemological significance of much recent work carried out in the name of 'naturalised epistemology', *inter alia* that presented in the much celebrated book by Bishop & Trout (2005).

volves establishing particular (especially controversial) beliefs and theories as rational. (Siegel 2005: 429).

But what does the expression 'depends on […] norms' really amount to here? What Siegel is concerned with is the justification of our beliefs, and I agree that this is something we might want to know obtains or not. More specifically, what we want to know is whether our beliefs have been formed in a certain way, plus whether these ways are suitably reliable and/or rational. However, as far I can see, this knowledge need involve no normative statements (at least, those of a naturalistically kosher origin). Though the knowledge might indeed be expressed as 'our beliefs satisfy/fail to satisfy the relevant norms', it could also be expressed in terms that comprise no normative vocabulary, but merely record what the relevant belief-forming practices are, and what the relevant facts are (at least this will be possible if what I have argued about NE is right). Normative statements will thus be required neither for forming optimally rational beliefs, of either first- or second-order, nor for the expression of second-order belief about the justifiability (or otherwise) of our first-order beliefs. Naturalised epistemology (in our sense) is still – to the extent it is not defunct – superfluous.

References

Alston, William (1988). "The deontological conception of epistemic justification". *Philosophical Perspectives* 2, pp. 257–299.

Antony, Louise M. (1987). "Naturalised epistemology and the study of language". In *Naturalistic Epistemology*, ed. by Abner Shimony & Debra Nails, Dordrecht: Reidel.

Bishop, Michael and Trout, J. D. (2005). *Epistemology and the Psychology of Human Judgement*. Oxford: Oxford University Press.

Chalmers, Alan (1990). *Science and its Fabrication*. Milton Keynes: Open University Press.

Chalmers, Alan (1999). *What is this thing called science?* 3rd edition. Milton Keynes: Open University Press.

Cherniak, Christopher (1986). *Minimal Rationality*. Cambridge, Mass.: MIT Press.

Cohen, Jonathan (1981). "Can human irrationality be experimentally demonstrated?". *Behavioural and Brain Sciences* 4, pp. 317–31.

Couvalis, George (1997). *Philosophy of Science: Science and Objectivity*. Sage.

Feyerabend, Paul (1981). *Problems of empiricism: Philosophical Papers Volume II*. Cambridge: Cambridge University Press.

Freedman, Karyn (1999). "Laudan's naturalistic axiology". *Philosophy of Science*, 66 (Proceedings), pp. S526–S537.

Giere, Ronald (1989). "Scientific rationality as instrumental rationality". *Studies in the History and Philosophy of Science* 20, pp. 377–84.

Goldman, Alvin (1996). *Epistemology and Cognition*. Cambridge, Mass.: Harvard University Press.

Goodman, Nelson (1965). *Fact, Fiction and Forecast*, 2nd edition. Indianapolis: Bobbs-Merrill.

Henderson, David K. (1994). "Epistemic competence". *Philosophical Papers*, 23, pp. 139–167.

Kitcher, Philip (1992). "The naturalists return". *Philosophical Review* 101, pp. 53–114.

Knowles, Jonathan (2002a). "Do we need norms in a naturalised epistemology?". *Croatian Journal of Philosophy* 2, pp. 283–97.

Knowles, Jonathan (2002b). "What's really wrong with Laudan's normative naturalism". *International Studies in Philosophy of Science,* 16, pp. 171–86.

Knowles, Jonathan (2003). *Norms, Naturalism and Epistemology: The Case for Science without Norms.* Palgrave Macmillan.

Knowles, Jonathan (2008). "Is naturalism a threat to metaphysics?". *Norsk filosofisk tidsskrift* 43, pp. 23–32.

Kornblith, Hilary (1993). "Epistemic normativity". *Synthese* 94, pp. 357–76.

Kosso, Peter (1991). "Empirical epistemology and philosophy of science". *Metaphilosophy* 22, pp. 349–63.

Kuhn, Thomas (1970). *The Structure of Scientific Revolutions*, 2nd edition. Chicago: Chicago University Press.

Kuhn, Thomas (1977). "Objectivity, value-judgement, and theory-choice". In Thomas Kuhn, *The Essential Tension: Selected Studies in Scientific Tradition and Change*. Chicago: Chicago University Press.

Lakatos, Imre (1974). "Falsificationism and the methodology of scientific research programmes". In *Criticism and the Growth of Knowledge*, ed. by Imre Lakatos & Alan Musgrave, Cambridge: Cambridge University Press.

Lakatos, Imre (1978). "History of science and its rational reconstruction". In *Imre Lakatos. Philosophical Papers, Volume 2: Mathematics, Science and Epistemology*, ed. by John Worral and Gregory Currie. Cambridge: Cambridge University Press.

Laudan, Larry (1984). *Science and Values*. University of California Press.

Laudan, Larry (1996). *Beyond Positivisim and Relativism*. Westview.

Maffie, James (1990). "Recent work on naturalized epistemology". *American Philosophical Quarterly* 27, pp. 281–93.
Mill, John Stuart (1895). *A System of Logic*, 8th edition. Longman.
Papineau, David (1993). *Philosophical Naturalism*. Blackwell.
Pollock, John (1987). "Epistemic norms". *Synthese* 71, pp. 61–95.
Quine, W.V.O. (1969). "Epistemology naturalized" in his *Ontological Relativity and Other Essays*. Cambridge, Mass.: Harvard University Press.
Quine, W.V.O. (1986). "Reply to Morton White". In *The Philosophy of W.V. Quine*, ed. by Lewis E. Hahn & Paul A. Schilpp. Open Court.
Quine, W.V.O. & Ullian, J. (1970). *The Web of Belief*. Random House.
Rawls, John (1971). *A Theory of Justice*. Cambridge, Mass.: Harvard University Press.
Rosenberg, Alex (1990). "Normative naturalism and the role of philosophy". *Philosophy of Science*, 57, pp. 34–43.
Siegel, Harvey (2005). Review of Knowles (2003). *Mind* 114, pp. 424–9.
Skorupski, John (1990). *John Stuart Mill*. Routledge.
Stein, Edward (1996). *Without Good Reason: The Rationality Debate in Philosophy and Cognitive Science*. Oxford: Oxford University Press.
Stich, Steven (1990). *The Fragmentation of Reason*. Cambridge, Mass.: MIT Press.

4

Status of Naturalistic Epistemology – Problem of Autonomy

BARBARA TRYBULEC

1 Introduction

The main problem with naturalising epistemology concerns its normative character. Epistemologists' main task is to formulate epistemic norms which guide cognisers during the process of knowledge acquisition. In traditional epistemology norms are derived from an infallible source by an aprioristic method and are meant to constitute the foundation for all knowledge about the world. Many philosophers who continue within the Cartesian paradigm understand epistemology as an autonomous discipline, with its own subject matter and method of epistemic enquiry. Naturalism, however, rejects the aprioristic method of deriving epistemic norms and places their source in empirical phenomena. For this reason many critics accuse naturalised epistemology of falling into chapter of natural sciences which leads straightforwardly to loosing by this discipline the status of autonomous philosophical enterprise. In this article I plan to show that cognitive sciences are not able to solve all epistemological problems and therefore naturalised epistemology as a separate discipline is indispensable. However, I do not want to argue that epistemology should be completely independent of scientific achievements, namely that it does not need help from the sciences. What I will argue for is that although the sciences could have significant impact on philosophical analyses, the most important epistemological questions are not reducible to problems solved by different sciences alone. And this is what I understand by the autonomy of epistemology.

In order to justify my thesis, I analyse the consequences of naturalising normativity, as this is the source of the most difficult problems within naturalism. If naturalistic epistemic norms are derived from statements about facts, as many naturalists claim, it seems to be enough to refer to the natural sciences that analyse these facts in order to form norms. If this is right, there is little left to do for naturalised epistemology. I will argue, however, that although naturalism has to refer to natural sciences in order to fulfil its normative tasks it does not lose the status of a separate autonomous discipline. Moreover, I plan to show that naturalised epistemology is a strong alternative to the traditional foundational project, for it is able to solve old epistemological problems more effectively and truthfully. I will justify this thesis with reference to two representatives of naturalised epistemology – Willard Quine and Alvin Goldman. Firstly, however, I will analyse the main problems concerning the autonomous status of epistemology that remain once the Cartesian tradition is abandoned.

2 Epistemology's status post the Cartesian tradition

Traditional epistemologists avoid the "naturalistic fallacy", namely they do not derive norms from factual knowledge[1]. They argue that epistemic norms should be justified on an a priori basis that is claimed to be obvious and completely reliable. According to them, the existence of such a basis is an inevitable presupposition that must be taken as true in order to avoid viciously circular reasoning. Descartes wanted to identify the criteria for acceptance and rejection of beliefs and, on their basis, to show which judgments could be called knowledge. Therefore, he divided beliefs into two groups: basic beliefs justified directly and others justified

---

[1] The category of "naturalistic fallacy" was introduced by G. E. Moore in *Principia Ethica*, however its history starts with Hume's *Treatise of Human Nature* where he noticed the problem with deriving conclusions containing "ought" from descriptive premises (Moore 2002: 57–72, Hume 1978: 469–470).

by being in appropriate relations to the basic beliefs (Kim 1988: 35–36). Basic beliefs are "clear and distinct", obvious and true; these are, for example, beliefs about the subject's actual mental states. A subject recognizes the certainty of such beliefs by introspecting or reflecting on their content. Hence, within the Cartesian tradition justification is understood as a logical relation between two groups of propositions: reasons and conclusions. To justify a belief one has to refer to another belief already justified. This is the Cartesian structure of knowledge as based on an infallible fundament. Epistemological analyses conducted in this tradition are independent of empirical research, as they solve normative problems by an a priori method.

Naturalists are united in putting forward two central objections against traditional epistemology. Firstly, they reject the existence of a necessary and infallible foundation for knowledge, consisting of epistemic norms derived from an a priori source. Secondly, they do not agree with the argument that justification should be understood exclusively as a logical relation between the contents of a subject's beliefs (Knowles 2003: 14–18). This fundamental disagreement with traditional accounts of normativity is caused by a very different attitude to the "naturalistic fallacy". According to traditional epistemologists genuine epistemic norms are derived from an infallible, a priori source which ensures that they are obvious and have normative, universal power[2]. Naturalists argue however that one cannot specify criteria of evidence and indubitability acceptable to most epistemologists and that, therefore, reaching an agreement about the sources and criteria of epistemic norms is almost impossible (Knowles 2003: 14–18). According to them, epistemic norms are derived from empirical information about both the circumstances in which the beliefs are formed and the subject's cognitive processes. Consequently, naturalism is inclined to commit the "naturalistic fallacy". However, these naturalists hold that it is not a fallacy at all or, else, that it is a "fallacy" that cannot be avoided.

---

[2] It is possible to find naturalistic positions which are partially constructivist about epistemic norms and, therefore, are not committed to the naturalist fallacy. I would like to thank Marcin Miłkowski for this suggestion. In this article, however, I am dealing with the most common types of epistemic naturalism and most contemporary naturalists do commit the "naturalistic fallacy".

It seems that epistemology loses its elevated status after the naturalistic turn. It is no longer able to solve normative epistemic problems on its own but is forced to use scientific methods to analyse how a subject should achieve fallible knowledge about the world. Nevertheless, according to naturalists this is not the reason to abandon epistemological enterprise. They argue, that one can provide normative analyses on the basis of possessed knowledge and without assuming the existence of some mysterious source of epistemic norms. It is hard to disagree with the fact that naturalistic normativity is much "weaker" than traditional normativity, for it does not deliver an infallible, stable foundation. From a traditional point of view, naturalism reduces epistemic norms to descriptions of unstable empirical phenomena and for this reason cannot be an epistemology but is merely another descriptive discipline analysing human cognitive systems. One cannot, however, expect naturalism to satisfy traditional standards of normativity and to provide a traditional theory of epistemic norms. Naturalists should continue the normative project according to naturalistic standards which allow reference to scientific achievements. Consequently, they formulate conditions of rational belief in cooperation with scientists, particularly in reference to research concerning cognitive processes. Hence, empirical studies are the source of epistemic normativity and this is the reason for the doubts about the autonomous status of naturalised normativity.

3 Consequences of naturalising traditional epistemological problems

It is a common view among traditional philosophers that naturalising classical epistemological problems must lead to them being taken over by natural sciences. There is no doubt that naturalised epistemology refers to the achievements of science in order to analyse problems concerning epistemic norms or justification. Does this mean, however, that epistemology as a separate discipline is no longer needed? I will show next the consequences of naturalising normativity within Quine's and Goldman's naturalism and discuss whether, accordingly, epistemology is able to sustain its autonomous status.

3.1 Status of epistemology within Quine's naturalism

Quine's famous article "Epistemology Naturalized" is one of the most influential papers in contemporary epistemology (Quine 1969: 15–30). Theses stated there give the impression that Quine rejects the normative project focused on the task of justifying our knowledge about the world from some "external" point of view. According to Quine, epistemology, in order to evaluate whether a belief is rational, must refer to science, for it does not possess its own means to formulate the criteria of justified beliefs. Science, however, examines only causal relations between phenomena, cognitive processes and beliefs. Hence, the normative function of epistemology is reduced by Quine to the task of evaluating the reliability of cognitive processes. This problem is undertaken by cognitive sciences, however, thus one could say that epistemology loses its subject and, what follows, its autonomous status. Quine argues that the main epistemological task, namely justifying beliefs about the world, cannot be performed for it is impossible to solve Humean problem of induction and to translate the laws of nature into sensory terms. Consequently, he suggests abandoning this problem and replacing epistemological analyses with psychological research into the causal relation between empirical data and beliefs. Quine says that epistemology "falls into place as a chapter of psychology and hence natural science" (Quine 1969: 25). This thesis, called "psychologism" or "the replacement thesis" has had a crucial influence on the discussion of the status of naturalised epistemology. Epistemology is no longer considered to be the First Philosophy that builds the foundation for science. It is continuous with science in the sense that it assumes the validity and warrant of the scientific project and cooperates with the sciences in order to form the criteria of justified belief. It is worth noticing that although Quine argues in favour of replacing traditional epistemology with science he does not abandon normativity altogether. He understands epistemic normativity as "the technology of truth-seeking": epistemic norms are, according to him, recommendations based on empirical studies, indications of how to reach a particular cognitive goal in the most effective manner[3].

I do not wish to argue that Quine rejects epistemology as a discipline without content or subject. In his article, he indicates a few times that "epistemology still goes on, though in a new setting and a clarified status (...) as a chapter of psychology. (...) There is thus reciprocal containment, though containment in different senses: epistemology in natural science and natural science in epistemology" (Quine 1969: 25). Taking however his position as stated both in "Epistemology Naturalized" and "Reply to Morton White" it is really hard to find a task for epistemologists which cannot be performed by cognitive scientists. This is the reason why epistemology naturalised seems to be redundant as, if the goal is given, "technology of truth-seeking" is a purely descriptive and not a normative enterprise. Hence, to sum, Quine changes the traditional meaning of "epistemic norm" rather radically, transforming it into empirical information about appropriate processes of reasoning (Quine 1969). In order to formulate an epistemic norm one has to examine how humans actually form beliefs, which processes they use when they succeed and which when they err. Epistemic norms, therefore, point to human cognitive processes that are reliable. As far as the condition of reliability is concerned it is worth focussing on Goldman's position on the relationship between epistemology and the sciences.

3.2 Consequences of naturalising justification within Goldman's naturalism

Alvin Goldman's reliabilism – the theory of justification representative for naturalism – is very well known. This theory, however, has one feature which is controversial to more radical naturalists. Goldman builds a naturalistic, causal theory of justification using means which are commonly identified with traditional epistemology, namely the conceptual analysis of our commonsensical intuitions and assumptions. More precisely, Goldman defines "justified belief" as a belief that is a product of a reliable process, that is a process that leads in the majority of cases to the

---

[3] Quine writes the following: "For me normative epistemology is a branch of engineering. It is the technology of truth-seeking. The normative here, as elsewhere in engineering, becomes descriptive" (Quine 1986: 663–5).

truth (Goldman 1979: 115). Despite the somewhat aprioristic method of constructing this definition, Goldman's theory belongs to the naturalistic camp because of its content. The epistemic status of a belief depends on the reliability of belief-causing processes, namely on the causal relation between a fact and the belief concerning this fact. If one accepts the naturalistic assumption that humans in the majority of cases execute cognitive processes which are reliable then it seems to be enough to refer to the cognitive sciences that study these processes in order to form epistemic norms that say how to reason correctly. In other words, within Goldman's epistemology epistemic norms are derived from empirical information about the processes executed by thinkers in order to gain knowledge. Humans do not need to make a special effort and consciously obey some epistemic norms in order to form rational beliefs, they just do so by nature as this is the way their cognitive systems work (Knowles 2003: 55–60). Hence, naturalistic norms are actually descriptions of facts about human cognitive abilities examined by science and have rather little in common with traditionally understood epistemic norms. To sum, naturalising justification could be understood as the process of changing the focus from the logical analysis of relations between propositions to the examination of the cognitive processes that form beliefs. In effect, traditional "reasons" have changed within naturalism into "causes" and the aprioristic epistemic norms which were to be the foundation of knowledge have changed into statements describing reliable cognitive processes performed by humans. It is clear that epistemology within Goldman's naturalism is dependent on scientific studies, for it should be based on appropriate descriptions of mental states and this could be delivered only by cognitive psychology. Goldman, however, is not as radical as Quine, and he recognises specifically philosophical problems that cannot be answered by the sciences. Specifically, Goldman argues that psychology cannot determine the correct set of epistemic norms on its own. It needs help from logic and philosophy to decide which of available cognitive processes best achieve such ends as truth as well as to design the optimal set of operations that would lead to truth and to the avoidance of error (Goldman 1985: 55–56). Hence, epistemology has a fairly stable and safe position within Goldman's naturalism, although it has to cooperate with cognitive sciences, especially with psychology, in order to solve any problem. Therefore, one could say that it is not autonomous for it is dependent on scientific studies but on the other hand it is indispensable in the sense that scientists cannot solve epistemological problems without its help.

As was already said, naturalists changed the main problem of epistemology from aprioristic analyses performed from the subject's point of view to scientific studies focused on the causes of beliefs regarded as justified. Doing this, however, they do not abandon the problem of justification, they just change the factors that determine the epistemic status of beliefs. Naturalists form objective criteria of justification as well as other epistemologists, but they derive them from knowledge about human reasoning processes. Therefore, they have to work along with scientists. Below, I will present the final considerations concerning the functions of naturalised epistemology within the interdisciplinary project of dealing with problems of cognition and knowledge. This will help to show why epistemological investigations are necessary and why they cannot be replaced by purely scientific studies.

4 Is naturalistic epistemology an 'autonomous' enterprise?

What does it mean to claim that that some philosophical discipline is autonomous? Does it need to answer its problems by itself and without help from other disciplines or rather it is sufficient that it should raise specific questions which, however, this discipline is not able to answer on its own? Does epistemology need to be independent of science to receive the status of a separate discipline? – this sounds rather implausible. In that case, what factors make naturalised epistemology "autonomous"? Namely, what are the specific tasks handled by it that scientists do not perform?

For most naturalists epistemology is a continuation of the cognitive sciences, yet they do not equate these two disciplines. Epistemology once naturalised is not as independent as traditional epistemology, nevertheless, this does not mean that it should be replaced by the sciences. Epistemology can be deemed, according to naturalists, autonomous for it asks different questions from the sciences, namely it analyses different aspects of cognition[4]. Epistemological problems do not arise within the cognitive sciences; questions about justification, normativity or evidence are "external" and stable no matter how the content of particular sciences changes. However, they cannot be answered without the support of cognitive sciences. As a result, the status of naturalised epistemology is not clear and this is the reason for confusion over its autonomy (Kornblith 2002: 170–3). Analysing the relation between cognitive sciences and epistemology one can notice that the prior are more specific and detailed. Consequently, scientific solutions cannot function as epistemological, for these two kinds of disciplines study problems which have a different level of generality (Kornblith 1994: 7–10). Nevertheless, both epistemologists and scientists should take into account their achievements and restrain each other. More precisely, psychologists should analyse properties epistemologists indicate as the most important for processes causing justified beliefs. Epistemologists, on the other hand, should not ignore scientific research on human cognitive systems. This mutual adjustment allows both disciplines to develop more effectively then they could do alone (Kornblith 1994: 10).

From what was stated above it follows that in order to make their efforts fruitful epistemologists should cooperate with scientists. Whether scientists need to employ epistemologists is less obvious. However, naturalists are keen to affirm that this support is two-sided. Those who are engaged in empirical activity are rarely interested in strictly philosophical problems, for they often do not have the sufficient theoretical background. Therefore, only philosophers who are trained in a particular scientific discipline are ready to answer epistemological problems. From this claim it does not follow that epistemology that is empirically informed must become a chapter of the cognitive sciences. This only establishes continuity between science and epistemology. This continuity is multi-dimensional, for it could be seen in many different aspects – contextual, epistemological, methodological and axiological[5]. Taking into

---

[4] Among naturalists who defend the autonomous status of epistemology are Hilary Kornblith H. (Kornblith, 2002: 25–27), Jaegwon Kim (Kim 1988: 33–55), and Alvin Goldman (Goldman 1985: 29–68).

[5] Firstly, epistemology naturalised rejects the idea of a first philosophy and conducts its research within broadly understood science. Secondly, naturalists stress that epistemological problems are empirical and therefore should be answered by a posteriori methods. Thirdly, only scientific methods are permitted as there are no strictly epistemological

account this tight relationship between naturalised epistemology and cognitive sciences the most worrisome problem becomes how to differentiate between them. It is claimed that normative investigation is specifically an epistemological kind of activity. However, it is essential to remember that naturalism cannot deliver traditionally understood epistemic norms which are derived from an aprioristic, infallible source. According to naturalists, the normative character of epistemology could be sustained in spite of the fact that epistemic norms are derived from empirical knowledge already possessed by humans. Hence, epistemologists, by reference to scientific achievements, formulate advice concerning the most effective way to reach some epistemic goal. Consequently, only through cooperation with scientists are epistemologists able to succeed in their normative investigations concerning the conditions for possessing knowledge (Kornblith 1994: 51–52).

To sum, the cognitive sciences, psychology and neurosciences in particular, provide information concerning the processes that cause particular beliefs, moreover they are able to formulate the norms these beliefs should satisfy to be justified[6]. Nevertheless, these disciplines do not conduct important meta-epistemological research, namely they do not evaluate and justify different methods for solving epistemological problems. Scientists, moreover, very rarely provide meta-scientific analyses about the epistemic status of their activity. Beyond meta-epistemological considerations the main task of epistemology is to clarify what it means to possess knowledge and what properties a belief should have to be justified. Scientists on the other hand, analyse when exactly beliefs have those properties, namely what cognitive processes should be performed by a subject. In spite of these differences one can notice a remarkable phenomenon appearing among the specialists working together on cognition and knowledge. More and more frequently they refuse to divide themselves between scientists and epistemologists, as the epistemologists must possess a strong scientific background to be reliable partners for the

---

methods of enquiry. Hence, naturalists use scientific methodology in order to solve more general epistemological problems. And, finally, as far as the axiological dimension is concerned, in order to specify epistemic norms naturalists conduct actual empirical studies.

[6] By norms I understand here for example the psychological norms indicating how an agent should act to form a set of rational beliefs and what actions lead to errors.

scientists. Hence, for a contemporary naturalised epistemologist deep philosophical knowledge though necessary is not sufficient as it must be combined with a high level of scientific competence. In conclusion, the autonomous status of naturalised epistemology is not endangered, but it is necessary to remember that "autonomous" does not mean in this case independent of scientific achievements but indispensable and not reducible to sciences. Epistemologists are still necessary, as in addition to scientific research that they often conduct they are able to analyse scientific achievements from an epistemological point of view. Specialists with this ability are always welcomed within interdisciplinary projects on cognition, since scientists who lack philosophical knowledge cannot give appropriate and complete answers to several crucial questions, such as what to it means to reason?

References

Goldman, Alvin (1985). "The Relation between Epistemology and Psychology". *Synthese* 64, pp. 29–68.

Goldman, Alvin (1979). "What is justified belief". In *Naturalising epistemology*, ed. by Hilary Kornblith. (1994), 2nd edition. Cambridge, Mass.: MIT Press, pp. 105–130.

Hume, David (1978). *The Treatise of Human Nature,* ed. L. A. Selby-Bigge, P. H. Nidditch. Oxford: Oxford University Press.

Kim, Jaegwon (1988). "What is 'naturalised epistemology'?". In *Naturalising epistemology,* ed. by Hilary Kornblith. (1994), 2nd edition. Cambridge, Mass.: MIT Press, pp. 33–55.

Knowles, Jonathan (2003). *Norms, Naturalism and Epistemology.* Palgrave, Macmillan.

Kornblith, Hilary (1994a). "Naturalism: Both Metaphysical and Epistemological". *Midwest Studies in Philosophy* XIX, pp. 39–52.

Kornblith, Hilary (1994b). "Introduction: What is naturalistic epistemology?". In *Naturalising epistemology,* ed. by Hilary Kornblith, 2nd edition. Cambridge, Mass.: MIT Press, pp. 3–14.

Kornblith, Hilary (2002). *Knowledge and its Place in Nature.* Oxford: Clarendon Press.

Moore, George Edward (2002). *Principia Ethica,* Cambridge: Cambridge University Press.

Quine, W.V.O (1969). "Epistemology Naturalized". In *Naturalizing epistemology*, ed. by Hilary Kornblith (1994), 2nd edition. Cambridge, Mass.: MIT Press, pp. 15–31.

Quine, W.V.O. (1986). "Reply to Morton White". In *The philosophy of W. V. Quine*, ed. by Lewis Hahn, Paul Schilpp. La Salle: Open Court, pp. 663–665.

5

Making Naturalised Epistemology (Slightly) Normative

MARCIN MIŁKOWSKI

1 Engineering Epistemological Normativity

The standard objection against naturalised epistemology is that it cannot account for normativity in epistemology (Putnam 1982; Kim 1988). There are different ways to deal with it. One of the obvious ways is to say that the objection misses the point: It is not a bug; it is a feature, as there is nothing interesting in normative principles in epistemology. Normative epistemology deals with norms but they are of no use in practice. They are far too general to be guiding principles of research, up to the point that they even seem vacuous (see Knowles 2003).

In this chapter, my strategy will be different and more in spirit of the founding father of naturalised epistemology, Quine, though not faithful to the letter. I focus on methodological prescriptions supplied by cognitive science in re-engineering cognitive architectures. Engineering norms based on mechanism design were not treated as seriously as they should in epistemology, and that is why I will develop a sketch of a framework for researching them, starting from analysing cognitive science as engineering in section 3, then showing functional normativity in section 4, to eventually present functional engineering models of cognitive mechanisms as normative in section 5. Yet before showing the kind of engineering normativity specific for these prescriptions, it is worthwhile to review briefly the role of normative methodology and the levels of norm complexity in it, and show how it follows Quine's steps.

Quine insisted on reducing normativity to engineering as taught at technical universities, even ethical normativity (Quine 1994). He seemed to accept (Q1) or (Q2):

(Q1) Engineering helps to explain what normativity is.

(Q2) Engineering helps to reduce normative propositions to practical/technical knowledge.

(Q2) seems to be more coherent with Quine's position, as he is not in general interested in explaining previous theories or frameworks in terms of his reductive proposals. The idea is to reduce meaning to behaviour, and replace mentalism with behaviourism, and not to explain why mentalist talk is justified. The explanatory task hinted in (Q1) does not exclude (Q2) but seems less entrenched in his project.

It is still an open question how far one can go with substituting normativity with engineering principles. I doubt that ethical theories are just like engineering and should be developed at technical universities by engineers, as Quine bluntly claimed. For most moral philosophers today, naturalised ethics is supposed to save the phenomenon of normativity and explain it rather than to replace it with engineered principles and explain it away. A Nietzschean kind of moral philosophy that is committed to naturalism and sceptical about the validity of any received moral principles is rare, as naturalism is hardly committed to overarching scepticism. Partial scepticism about the validity of the received view is, however, one of the reasons why naturalism remains attractive for many philosophers. In epistemology, naturalists can be sceptical about norms in epistemology or justification as the most important theme in theory of knowledge. Yet Quine's suggestion is antisceptical in this regard: "Insofar as theoretical epistemology gets naturalised into a chapter of theoretical science, so normative epistemology gets naturalised into a chapter of engineering: the technology of anticipating sensory stimulation" (Quine 1992: 19).

Pace Quine, anticipating sensory stimulation is not the essential aspect of normative epistemology, as cognition is not only about sensory stimulation and external behaviour, as behaviourists thought. Moreover, the goal of science should not be conflated with prediction (described as anticipation of sensory stimuli) while science is also interested in explanation, understanding and description. Quine could be right about engineering but knowledge engineering is not only about anticipating sensory stimuli; it is about generating knowledge, but not necessarily predictive knowledge. So the claim inspired by Quine becomes (Q*):

(Q*) By using engineering knowledge, it is possible to define normative criteria for naturalised epistemology.

The term "normative criteria" is deliberately kept abstract enough to cover various kinds of norms. These are not only the principles of cognitive action that are endorsed by agents but also the guidelines for developing cognitive agents, either by natural selection, or artificially. Another kind of normative criteria is connected to those conditions of interaction among groups of cognitive agents and with environment that prove to be fruitful for development of knowledge. So there are at least three categories of norms: (1) endorsed by individuals, (2) embodied by individuals and (3) embodied by interaction of individuals with each other and with their environment. They are all methodological.

Methodology does not help us develop norms that are valid categorically. As instrumental, they are valid conditionally. In other words, methodology does not supply us with the norms that are justified the way the moral obligations were supposed to be justified with the help of Kant's categorical imperative. It is rather on a par with the hypothetical imperative that supplies conditional norms such as: If you want to achieve X, you should do Y. As Quine would say, if you want to anticipate sensory stimulation X, you should do Y (see also Hookway 2002: 39). However, the antecedent of such conditionals does not have to be universally valid or true. In this regard, I agree with Knowles 2003 that obligatory universal normative principles are rare in epistemology, if they exist at all. This does not mean that there are no prescriptions in epistemology. Sometimes they are even more restricted than simple conditionals: A methodological prescription can suggest a method that fails in some cases, for example a heuristic method, or a method that is sometimes advisable but not strictly required.

2 Methodological Naturalised Epistemology

In naturalised epistemology, methodology seems to have been largely ignored. For example, neither reliabilism nor evidentialism seems to have any bearing for methodology. They just piggy-back on methodology but give nothing in return, being motivated solely by philosophical interest in reducing epistemic concepts to nonepistemic or by an attempt to define knowledge in a Gettier-proof way. This is not, however, based on any principled argument against normative methodology in sciences. In non-armchair epistemology, methodological questions are to be settled by scientists rather than with conceptual analysis alone but nothing prevents from integrating those questions into the research program of naturalised epistemology.

I suggest that nonfoundational epistemology can be methodological and as such normative. A nonmethodological normative epistemology (foundational or not) does not seem to make much sense for non-armchair naturalism, or otherwise it could not be of any use for science. Methodology cares about proper methods of acquiring and justifying knowledge by cognitive agents.

Naturalised epistemology can be analysed as operating at least on three levels of complexity:

- *cognitive system interaction* (fashions, traditions, groups, niches…)
- *personal* (beliefs, webs of beliefs, theories, desires…)
- *subpersonal* (perceptual subsystems, faculties, cognitive modules…)

The distinction between the personal and subpersonal level of description (Dennett 1969) is sometimes difficult to spell out precisely, yet I need it only for showing that naturalised epistemology can operate on many levels of complexity (the notion of level used in this chapter is the same as in Craver 2001). The additional cognitive system interaction level hints at developments connected with notions of embodiment and embeddedness in cognitive science.

Cognitive system interaction is a dimension of epistemology that is explored by science studies, sociology of knowledge, evolutionary epistemology and other disciplines that are not committed to methodological solipsism and/or methodological individualism. In my terminology, it covers also interpersonal processes. Interaction between individuals generates a new level of complexity that is different not only quantitatively but also qualitatively from individual cognitive achievements[1].

---

[1] Traditionally, sociology of knowledge has been treated as a forerunner of relativism or even irrationalism by philosophers of science, but it is just an empirical assumption that individual researchers always act like strictly rational and good-willing angels that care only about truth and the growth of knowledge, and not about their own careers and eco-

On the personal level, one can describe the capabilities of a cognitive agent to acquire knowledge, the ways she justifies her beliefs, etc. These descriptions require using intentional predicates, especially in the realm of individual webs of beliefs. The personal level is preferred by antipsychologist, nonnaturalist epistemology, as it is possible to analyse beliefs in a pure logical fashion, for example to criticise the logical structure of reasoning. Yet, logical hermeneutics deals with just one kind of idealisations of personal-level beliefs, and not always the most important kind: psychotic beliefs can be logically coherent but completely out of sync with reality.

On the subpersonal level, epistemology specifies the mechanisms within the cognitive agent that contribute to her personal-level cognitive abilities. In traditional epistemology, subpersonal properties were construed of as psychological (in terms of a philosophical, rational psychology). Nowadays, cognitive science deals with this level of explanation. As cognitive science is a multidisciplinary research program rather than a unified science, the predicates that describe subpersonal properties do not have to be psychological only but to span multiple levels and disciplines (for multiple-level explanations in neuroscience, see Craver 2007).

Antinaturalist and nonnaturalist philosophy denies the importance of the subpersonal level in epistemology, which is sometimes motivated by antipsychologism. At the same time, all epistemological theories, including antinaturalist epistemology, use the intentional idiom to speak about cognitive capabilities. So what antipsychologism denies is not the usage of intentional predicates such as "believe", "think" or "perceive" but citing nonintentional psychological facts in justifying knowledge. In epistemology, rationality, logical structures and justification count, and these concepts can be analysed without knowing any underlying psychological mechanisms in cognitive agents.

Interestingly, many modern philosophers, including especially Immanuel Kant, were analysing the underlying mental structures, by assuming that they are inaccessible to introspection, in order to vindicate the concepts of rationality and justification. Kantian categories and other theoretical mechanisms or entities such as transcendental apperception are on the subpersonal level. The way the category of causality operates is not the way the cognitive agent acts. According to antipsychologism,

---

nomic interests. At least in some cases, this assumption is evidently false. Not to mention that science is only possible not as an individual but a collective achievement.

this must be viewed as a commitment to psychologism, and implies a serious methodological error, or Kant's theory is to be reconstructed in terms of logical structures. I suggest otherwise.

In Kantian epistemology, the hypothesised subpersonal structures are *a priori*: Their use is justified independently of experience[2]. In cognitive science, empirical hypotheses about analogous structures and processes are being developed, and naturalised epistemology cheerfully endorses those hypotheses (if confirmed by empirical data).

The subpersonal level is necessary for any cognitive system to be cognitive. While it is possible to abstract from the way the cognitive personal level capabilities are realised on the lower level, and describe the logical structure of beliefs or theories, those capabilities are instantiated always and only if underlying lower level properties are also instantiated; higher level properties depend on the lower level properties of the system. Note that because there could be external factors on higher levels, such as other cognitive systems, time pressure, or tiredness, that may affect cognitive performance, higher level properties in most cases will never be fully reducible to lower level properties[3].

At the subpersonal level, the cognitive architecture that generates knowledge in a system is the most important factor. Note that on any analysis of the notion of knowledge (traditional, reliabilist, disjunctivist...), you cannot ascribe true knowledge to a dysfunctional cognitive system. In next sections, I will focus on the subpersonal level and its functional characteristics to show one of the kinds of normativity in naturalised epistemology.

The body of knowledge in scientific methodologies concerns mostly personal level achievements of cognitive agents, and as far as it is empirically valid, naturalised epistemology cannot question it. Environmental and other interaction-dependent factors, which are now being taken into account (if sometimes exaggerated) in embodied and embedded cognition theories, also play a role in cognitive processes. The norms on the personal level are most likely to be methodological prescriptions

---

[2] If you understand Kant's project nonfoundationally, you can see that a priori does not mean conceptual; for a nonfoundational reading of Kantian project, see Kitcher 1995 and Miłkowski 2007.

[3] This is because systems on all three abovementioned levels of organization are never fully isolated or completely autonomous, and they can be influenced from the outside.

to be followed consciously, and their normative character is just of the kind displayed by the hypothetical imperative.

In order to be a successful cognitive agent, you should behave the way other successful cognitive agents behave according to scientific methodology prescriptions. For example, a nonpractical norm of scientific methodology would be, as Knowles 2003 shows, "avoid contradiction", as you cannot effectively rule out contradiction in most real-world cases due to the immense computational complexity of the task (in decidable logical systems; it is not feasible in incomplete systems). However, more detailed norms, like "change beliefs if you find a deep contradiction" or "treat contradiction as a nondirect proof" are more viable in some cognitive niches, like mathematics. Another viable norm at the personal level for a modern scientist would be "submit your papers to peer-reviewed journals".

On the interaction level, the norms are also instrumental. There are functional systems that interact and their interactions may become dysfunctional, so there could be functional normativity. Cognitive agents can communicate and share hypothetical imperatives. It is an open question whether conscious sharing and debating norms among cognitive agents should be accounted for as generating simply personal-level norms, or as involving larger systems (i.e., organizations such as research agencies) with their level of hypothetical imperatives. I leave the personal and interaction level questions mostly aside as they are outside of the scope of the current paper. However, norms on all levels stay instrumental and are not normative *sui generis*: they are reducible to hypothetical imperative conditionals that do not express obligations.

3 Cognitive Science and Evolutionary Theory as Engineering

As Dennett (1995) argues, cognitive science and evolutionary biology are engineering sciences, construed of along the lines of the "sciences of the artificial" in Herbert Simon's sense (Simon 1996). These sciences use the "design stance" to describe and predict phenomena. The difference between the standard engineering practice and these sciences is that the latter are focused mainly on reverse engineering, while nonreverse engineering is used to confirm the hypotheses about the reliability of the design being reverse-engineered. At the same time, there is a growing research community on artificial life and artificial intelligence, which are clearly closely linked with engineering, evolutionary theory and cognitive science.

I suggest that naturalised epistemology uses exactly the same stance as cognitive science to describe cognitive processes on the subpersonal level. The notion of "function" is not a physical notion, and it is not ascribed from the physical stance but from the design stance (Dennett 1971). Subpersonal structures are functional: the human mind is conceived of as a complex system of interacting faculties (or modules) that contribute to personal-level cognitive capabilities (for a vindication of massive modularity, see Carruthers 2006).

The task of cognitive science is to discover the functional structures and processes of mind on the subpersonal level, and these structures are of interest for normative naturalised epistemology. Most (if not all) naturalised theories of cognition should be translatable into engineering projects: if you know how cognition proceeds, you should be able to replicate the process in an artefact or explain why it cannot be replicated.

In other words, in order to build successful cognitive agents, you need to engineer and/or reverse-engineer their cognitive architecture. By investigating the individual components of the architecture and their interaction, you can see which solutions are functional and which are not. If you know why a system fails to function normally, and know the way to fix it, you can repair it. After finding a viable way to extend its cognitive abilities, you can supply the system with new cognitive components that will enhance its cognitive performance. All three cases: discovery of the architecture, maintaining the performance of the architecture, and extending the architecture, imply a specific kind of normativity. This normativity is embedded in the engineering of the cognitive architecture.

4 Cognitive Architecture Functions in Normative Epistemology

Subpersonal level cognitive architecture is described from the design stance. Design stance specifications provide descriptions of functions or functional complexes. The notion of function has been discussed in philosophy of science for several decades, and at least three kinds of function concepts have been proposed: causal role based, etiological, and structural. The causal role account ascribes function to a system component that contributes causally to the system level capability (Cummins

1975). The etiological account ascribes function to a system component that has been selected in the system because it contributed causally to the system capability in the past (Wright 1973; Millikan 1984). The structural account ascribes function to a system component when it serves a function in the system design (Krohs 2004, Krohs 2009) or contributes to the system autonomy (Bickhard 2000, Bickhard 2004). The design-based notion requires that a component of the system be ascribed function not just because it has a causal role or was inherited but because it is selected by the design for this function. The selection process can be natural or artificial.

It is often noted that functional attributions are normative in a very specific sense: something may fail to function properly, and this failure is used for evaluative purposes. The causal account of function fails to make the distinction between function and dysfunction: if a TV set breaks, the causal chains still occur and they contribute to the system capability of keeping the screen black, for example. The etiological account fails for first tokens of the system, as they have no selection history that would specify the components. For this reason, the prototypes of AI systems will always be dysfunctional. Autonomy account would also make partial AI systems dysfunctional: as long as you do not have the model of the whole iguana, no part of the iguana can be functional. But because the research starts with relatively isolated subsystems that are not fully autonomous, it would be useful to be able to distinguish the properly functioning systems from the broken ones. This is what the design-based account enables (Krohs 2009). It is a happy coincidence that the design account uses the notion of design also used in the notion of the design stance. In what follows, I will assume that design stance functions be analysed in a design-based account.

A design-stance description refers to a functional structure (design) of the system. Cognitive architecture description provides criteria for evaluation of the functioning of a cognitive system and its subsystems. If something essential in the architecture is missing, system becomes dysfunctional, and fails to fulfil cognitive functions. The notion of architecture, i.e., the abstract specification of the system component interactions, is equivalent to the notion of the system design.

Functional normativity is instrumental. If a TV set stops functioning, it is not a failure to fulfil a moral prescription. It is just useless as a TV set. This kind of normativity can be analysed either in terms of means and ends (the end is to watch television on the device, the means is the architecture that works in home environment), or in terms of instrumental values. In both cases, it is a derived kind of normativity, subsumable under the hypothetical imperative. But we do not need any more normativity on the subpersonal level in naturalised epistemology.

5 Artificial Cognitive Systems As Models for Epistemology

In research on cognition, one can take a biologically inspired approach (reverse engineering) or artefact-inspired approach (engineering). These approaches can intermingle, as artefacts are often also biologically inspired, like wings of a plane. But there are artefacts that have no counterparts in the evolutionary world, such as wheels, that cannot be evolved for morphological reasons but remain–in their niche–a very good technical solution. It remains an open question whether artificial systems that are able, for example, to prove theorems in a way that is too difficult for a human being (like the four colours theorem), are minimally cognitive. We may expect, however, that future cognitive systems will have capacities that are more like wheels than like wings.

These wheel-like cognitive capacities are at least as important in naturalised epistemology as research on biological cognition. Building cognitive systems that are not modelled on animal or human cognition has always been the goal of epistemological theories. Specifically, one can set out to sketch the overall design specifications for a cognitive robot–these would serve roughly the same role as the traditional notion of the transcendental subject. For that purpose, conceptual arguments will not suffice. Naturalised epistemology must consult engineering sciences such as AI and cognitive science.

So joining the forces between philosophical analysis of cognition per se and engineering of cognitive systems can lead to android epistemology, as Clark Glymour dubbed it–to epistemology that can analyse non-biological cognitive systems (see Ford, Glymour & Hayes 1995; Ford, Glymour & Hayes 2006). They could be arbitrarily stronger or weaker than natural cognitive systems. Just by juxtaposing those artificial models with natural agents, one could try to see the really cognitive aspect of their actions.

The research on artificial cognitive architectures has several benefits. First of all, it is ethical to test which dysfunctions are caused by switching off some modules in a simple artificial cognitive system. This is impossible with research on human beings, and it can be argued that such experiments on animals are also too cruel. A second benefit is that translation of abstract models into engineering specifications requires that the conceptual vagueness be replaced with specific solutions. Thirdly, unexpected consequences of idealised models are discovered: the frame problem can be thought of as an unexpected implication of the propositional model of cognition that reduces cognition to reasoning in classical logic. Even approaches that were mildly hostile to engineering in investigating cognition, like Heidegger's, can be turned into requirements for making cognitive systems as embedded in their environments. In the process, the hermeneutical model of interpreting Heidegger's *Sein und Zeit* is replaced with actually improving upon his ideas (see for example Wheeler 2005).

Another benefit is that it becomes testable whether a given model of cognition works or not. Though initially it can be unclear why a given system is dysfunctional, after comparing different implementations of the similar architecture, one can see if it can really work. This is of course impossible for armchair conceptual analysis.

The cognitive science on the subpersonal level can supply normative principles for cognitive architectures, and these normative principles, which would generally determine what is minimally required for certain cognitive capacities, are available for use in naturalised epistemology. Similarly, personal-level intentional requirements of rationality as studied by methodology and psychology supply normative principles. They are instrumental as well–if they do not involve any moral obligation. The interaction level is the same in this regard, as it uses both kinds of principles. To wit, naturalised epistemology can be normative if it uses detailed results of cognitive science, science methodology, psychology and other sciences. The normative principles in epistemology are not however vague and general norms like "avoid contradiction", but specific and constrained heuristic principles of design.

There is no general and effective algorithm for discovering the laws of nature or deducting all possible true propositions, as Tarski and Gödel proved. Hume's problem of induction will remain unsolved for limited beings. So there is no hope that a single methodological prescription would say what to do to get all true knowledge as it would presuppose that there is an effective algorithm to get them. At the same time, there are effective algorithms that deal only with discovering some laws in a limited domain or deducting some true propositions (if the system is incomplete). So there might be constrained algorithms with a limited scope of application in normative epistemology, but there is no hope for a groundbreaking normative philosopher's stone.

References

Bickhard, Mark H. (2000). "Autonomy, Function, and Representation". *Communication and Cognition - Artificial Intelligence* 17(3–4), pp. 111–131.

Bickhard, Mark H. (2004). "Process and Emergence: Normative Function and Representation", *Axiomathes - An International Journal in Ontology and Cognitive Systems* 14, pp. 135–169.

Carruthers, Peter (2006). *The Architecture of the Mind. Massive Modularity and the Flexibility of Thought*. Oxford: Clarendon Press.

Craver, Carl F. (2001). "Role Functions, Mechanisms, and Hierarchy". *Philosophy of Science* 68, pp. 53–74.

Craver, Carl F. (2007). *Explaining the Brain*, Oxford: Oxford University Press.

Cummins, Robert (1975). "Functional Analysis". *Journal of Philosophy*, 72 (20), pp. 741–765.

Dennett, Daniel C. (1971). "Intentional systems". *Journal of Philosophy* 68 (February), pp. 87–106.

Dennett, Daniel C. (1995). *Darwin's Dangerous Idea: Evolution and the Meanings of Life*. New York: Simon & Schuster.

Ford, Kenneth M., Glymour, Clark, Hayes, Patrick, eds. (1995). *Android Epistemology*, Cambridge, Mass.: MIT Press.

Ford, Kenneth M., Glymour, Clark, Hayes, Patrick, eds. (2006). *Thinking about Android Epistemology*. Cambridge, Mass.: MIT Press.

Hookway, Christopher (2002). "Naturalism and Rationality". In *Quine. Naturalised Epistemology, Perceptual Knowledge and Ontology*, ed. by Lieven Decock and Leon Horsten, Poznań Studies in the Philosophy of the Sciences and the Humanities. Amsterdam: Rodopi.

Kim, Jaegwon (1988). "What is 'Naturalised Epistemology'?". *Philosophical Perspectives* 2, pp. 381–405.

Kitcher, Patricia (1995). "Revisiting Kant's Epistemology: Skepticism, Apriority, and Psychologism". *Nous* 25 (3), pp. 285–315.

Knowles, Jonathan (2003). *Norms, Naturalism and Epistemology: The Case for Science without Norms*. Palgrave Macmillan.

Krohs, Ulrich (2004). *Eine Theorie biologischer Theorien*, Berlin: Springer Verlag.

Krohs, Ulrich (2009). "Functions as Based on a Concept of General Design", *Synthese* 166 (1), pp. 69–89.

Millikan, Ruth G. (1984). *Language, Thought, and Other Biological Categories. New Foundations for Realism*. Cambridge, Mass.: MIT Press.

Miłkowski, Marcin (2007). "Siemek, dialektyka, rzeczywistość. O transcendentalnej filozofii społecznej". *Przegląd Filozoficzno-Literacki* 16 (1), pp. 99–113.

Putnam, Hilary (1982). "Why Reason Can't Be Naturalised". *Synthese* 52 (1), pp. 3–23.
Quine, Willard Van Orman (1992). *The Pursuit of Truth*. Revised edition. Cambridge, MA: Harvard University.
Quine, Willard Van Orman (1994). *In Conversation – W. V. Quine. The Dennett panel* (VHS cassette). London: Philosophy international.
Simon, Herbert (1996). *The Sciences of the Artificial*. Cambridge, Mass.: MIT Press.
Wheeler, Michael (2005). *Reconstructing the Cognitive World. The Next Step*. Cambridge, Mass.: MIT Press.
Wright, Larry (1973). "Functions". *The Philosophical Review* 82 (2), pp. 139–168.

6

Naturalistic Epistemologies and A Priori Justification*

LISA WARENSKI

1 Introduction

Broadly speaking, a naturalistic approach to epistemology seeks to explain human knowledge – and justification in particular – as a phenomenon in the natural world, in keeping with the tenets of naturalism. Naturalism is typically defined, in part, by a commitment to scientific method as the only legitimate means of attaining knowledge of the natural world. Naturalism is often thought to entail empiricism by virtue of this methodological commitment. For example, Michael Devitt (1996: 2) writes "there is only one way of knowing, the empirical way that is the basis of science… So I reject a priori knowledge." However, scientific methods themselves may incorporate a priori elements, so empiricism does not follow from the methodological commitments of naturalism alone. And given a suitably-naturalistic conception of the a priori, a priori forms of justification may be compatible with naturalism generally.

---

* I would like to thank the editors and the participants in the 2006 Kazimierz Naturalised Epistemology Workshop, especially Michael Bishop, for helpful discussion. I am indebted to Konrad Talmont-Kaminski for many constructive comments on an earlier draft of the paper. My participation in the 2006 workshop was funded by a faculty development grant from Union College.

Beyond Description: Naturalism and Normativity.
Marcin Miłkowski and Konrad Talmont-Kaminski (eds.).
Copyright © 2010 The Author.

In the discussion to follow, I will argue that that a priori justification is, in principle, compatible with naturalism – and hence naturalistic epistemologies – if the a priori is understood in a way that is free of some of the inessential properties that have been associated with the concept. I argue that some of the more prominent strategies for accommodating normative notions within a naturalistic framework allow for the possibility of a priori justification. These include reliabilism, instrumental rationality, and (partial) nonfactualism about justification. A priori justification thus need not be seen as standing in opposition to all naturalistic epistemologies. It is only with nonnormative naturalistic epistemologies that a priori justification *per se* is incompatible, and this only because the notion of justification itself has no role to play within a nonnormative approach to epistemology.

2 A Naturalistic Conception of A Priori Justification

2.1 The A Priori/A Posteriori Distinction

The a priori/a posteriori distinction is at root an epistemological distinction that contrasts two different types of justification.[1] The a priori is often defined in the negative in the following way:

    apj: A priori justification is justification that does not rely upon the particulars of sensory experience for its justificational force.

The locution 'justificational force' is due to Tyler Burge (Burge 1993; 1998), and it makes explicit Kant's original understanding of a priori justification as justification that is independent of the particulars of experience, but allowing that experience may be needed to acquire the relevant concepts involved in an a priori claim. Although the a priori/a posteriori distinction is typically understood to contrast two types of justification, the distinction could be extended to contrast weaker forms of positive epistemic appraisal such as entitlement or epistemically-blameless acceptance.

---

[1] The naturalistic conception of a priori justification that I present here is the same as the conception that I defend in "Naturalism, Fallibilism, and the A Priori" (Warenski 2009). My concern in that paper is to articulate the fallibilist thesis, with fallibilist apriorism as a particular case, for claims of a general and theoretical nature. In the discussion below, I characterize fallibilism more broadly in order to encompass individual-relative claims of the form 'S believes that P'.

One objection that might be raised by the naturalist at this juncture is that the a priori/a posteriori distinction as stated above is unclear. However, the problem of characterising justification based on sensory experience is a problem for the empiricist and apriorist alike. Although it is generally agreed that a more illuminating account of the a priori is needed, the prospects for providing such an account may depend upon our acquiring a more perspicuous understanding of the cognitive and physiological processes involved in experience. And to the extent that we have a clear understanding of what a justification based on sensory experience is, we can contrast it with a justification that is not so based. While I acknowledge that the a priori/a posteriori distinction is in need of further refinement, I take the distinction to be clear enough to merit serious philosophical consideration.

What makes a given subject matter empirical or a priori? We classify a claim as a priori or empirical based on what we take its ideal justification conditions to be (ideal in the sense of ignoring individual limitations of computational capacity). It is important to keep in mind that, in the words of Susan Haack, a naturalistic epistemology rejects "knowledge without a knowing subject" (Haack 1979). Hence, justification must not be construed as a property that some propositions possess independently of the beliefs or judgments of cognitive agents. In what follows, I will speak of an "a priori proposition", but this expression is elliptical for "a proposition with a priori justification conditions", where justification is understood to be, at root, doxastic[2].

Insofar as it might be used to classify a particular subject matter then, the notion of the a priori that I will be defending is as follows:

app: A proposition is a priori iff (1) it can be justifiably believed without empirical evidence, and (2) it is empirically indefeasible, if so justified.

The notion of an a priori subject matter can be extended to incorporate rules:

---

[2] There are some delicate issues here. A proposition's being justified requires neither that it be justified for all agents nor that it be justified for any particular agent. A proposition is ratified (or not) within an epistemic community if it meets the prevailing evidential standards of a contextually-relevant subset of the community. However, standards may vary within the relevant subset of the community, and so in a given case, there may be disagreement with respect to judgments of justification.

apr: A rule or system of rules is a priori iff (1) it can be justifiably employed without empirical evidence, and (2) it is empirically indefeasible, if so justified.

The extension of the a priori/a posteriori distinction to a system of rules is important to the question of whether scientific methods presuppose a priori elements.

If the basic notion of the a priori that I have outlined above is to be suitably naturalistic, the empirical indefeasibility claim will need to be understood in such a way that we can be fallibilist about a priori justification. An infallibilist interpretation of empirical indefeasibility would be in direct conflict with naturalism: Scientific method is characterized *inter alia* by its ongoing responsiveness to new evidence and the revisability of theory in light of new evidence, so recognising some class of claims as in principle immune to empirical evidence – should such evidence ever arise – would be in conflict with the naturalist's commitment to scientific method.

2.2 A Fallibilist Conception of A Priori Justification

A fallibilist apriorist thinks that an apriori-justified belief or claim is empirically indefeasible, but she allows that we are imperfect cognitive agents, and so it may be simply a failure of our imagination to see how experience should come to defeat it. In general, if one is fallibilist about knowledge claims, one allows that (under contextually-relevant conditions) knowledge claims are defeasible by the expansion of evidence or further conceptual developments. An apriori-justified claim is just a particular instance of the more general case.

Fallibilism, as I understand it, is not equivalent to the denial that we have knowledge with absolute certainty. P is known with absolute certainty just in case it is impossible for our belief or claim that P to be mistaken. For example, beliefs about one's own immediate sensory experience and *cogito*-type statements have been thought to belong to a special class of beliefs or claims that are immune to error. By contrast, fallibilism is a thesis about evidence or grounds. If P is thought to be known infallibly, we think we know that P will never come to be legitimately undermined, but we aren't thereby taking the belief or claim that P to belong to a special class of beliefs or claims for which, antecedent to evidence, mistake is impossible.

On a fallibilist understanding of a priori justification, one can be fallibilist about both *claims* that are said to be a priori warranted and *a priori warrants* for claims. If a proposition held to be a priori true were to come to be defeated on empirical grounds, both the proposition and our a priori warrant for it would be simultaneously overturned. However, a proposition might also come to be revised on *a priori* grounds. The revision of naïve set theory would be a case in point. If an a priori claim were to be revised on purely conceptual grounds, the revision would not undermine its a priori status. Likewise, we might come to discover that a proposition held to be true a priori is, in fact, empirically supported. In this imagined case, only our a priori justification, not the proposition itself, would be defeated. In the 19th Century, Carl Frederich Gauss doubted the a priori status of Euclid's parallel postulate, understood as a claim about physical space; however, he thought it to be empirically corroborated[3]. Had the parallel postulate been upheld on empirical grounds, only the warrant for the postulate, not the postulate itself, would have been undermined.

Fallibilism, and hence fallibilist apriorism, need not be construed solely as a thesis about knowledge claims or internally-accessible beliefs. An externalist may want to adopt a fallibilist account of justification and belief formation. For example, if a belief formed by a reliable process is justified, but reliability doesn't have to be perfect, the reliable process may generate some false beliefs. The reliable process would be fallible because the reliability of the process doesn't guarantee the truth of the target belief. (I discuss externalist versions of apriori-justified belief in Section 3.2.1.1.)

2.3 The Compatibility of A Priori Justification with Naturalism

Some of the naturalist's objections to the a priori have to do with associated claims that are not part of the core epistemological notion. These include the association of the a priori with metaphysical necessity, a commitment to a realm of Platonic objects as the truth-makers of a priori

---

[3] Gauss' skepticism regarding the a priori status of the parallel postulate and his conception of the possibility of alternative geometries is documented in his correspondence with Friedrich Wilhem Bessel and H.C. Schumacher. The relevant portions of the correspondence are reprinted in Ewald (1996).

propositions[4], and the assumption that rational intuition is the means by which we have access to the Platonic truth-makers. The modest notion of the a priori that I have given above is unencumbered by these attendant claims. A key worry is that countenancing a priori justification would conflict with the naturalist's commitment to scientific method by taking a class of claims to be immune to new evidence. But a fallibilist interpretation of the empirical indefeasibility requirement removes this conflict.

The naturalist might object that without a positive account of a priori justification, it is not clear just how a priori justification is compatible with naturalism, and hence, naturalistic epistemologies. First, it should be noted that there may be multiple forms of a priori justification. Alleged apriori-justified claims include not only the traditional subject matters of logic and mathematics, but also basic belief-forming methodologies, conceptual truths, Descartes' *cogito*, and second-order beliefs about the contents of occurrent first-order thoughts. It is not clear that any single positive characterisation of a priori justification would encompass these diverse claims. But more importantly for present purposes, a positive account of a priori justification will depend on how justification itself is understood within a particular naturalistic epistemology. In what follows, I give a sketch of how a positive account of a priori justification might be developed within several naturalistic epistemologies.

3 Naturalistic Epistemologies and A Priori Justification

By way of providing a framework for the discussion to follow, I first divide naturalistic epistemologies into the categories of nonnormative and normative. I then I consider some different approaches within each category. I argue that the normative epistemologies can, in principle, accommodate forms of a priori justification, if a priori justification is understood in the minimal and fallibilist way outlined above. By definition, normative notions like a priori justification have no place in a nonnormative epistemology, but an analogue of a priori justification may survive within naturalistic epistemologies of this type.

---

[4] Naturalists who take the indispensability of mathematics to science to commit us to the existence of numbers will not object to the admission of abstracta *per se* but only in the absence of a theoretical mandate.

3.1 Nonnormative Naturalistic Epistemologies

A nonnormative epistemology aims to reconcile normative epistemological notions with a naturalistic orientation either by reconceiving them in nonnormative terms or by treating them as superfluous to optimal belief formation. These positions may be characterized, respectively, as *eliminative* and *noneliminative nonnormativism*[5]. Nonnormative epistemologies are not epistemologies in the sense that they attempt to give a naturalistic account of norms from within an epistemological theory; rather they are attempts to reconcile epistemology within a naturalistic orientation by reinterpreting the role of normative discourse.

An example of an eliminative strategy is Quine's proposal, famously expressed in "Epistemology Naturalized" (Quine 1969), to reclassify epistemology as descriptive psychology. On this view, what the epistemologist studies is just the relation between a subject's sensory inputs and his output of beliefs about the external world. In *Theories and Things*, Quine extends the assimilation of epistemology to science more broadly:

> ... Science itself tells us that our information about the world is limited to irritations of our surfaces, and then the epistemological question is in turn a question within science, the question how we human animals can have managed to arrive at science from such limited information. Our scientific epistemologist pursues this inquiry and comes out with an account which has a good deal to do with the learning of language and the neurology of perception.... Evolution and natural selection will doubtless figure in his account, and he will be free to apply physics if he sees a way (Quine 1969: 72).

On Quine's proposal, justification and related normative notions do not survive because they are to be reconstructed as part of descriptive science.

A noneliminative nonnormativism proposes to ignore, rather than eliminate, normative notions. This strategy is employed by Jonathan Knowles who takes the position that naturalistic norms are not needed for optimally-rational belief-formation; hence *naturalised epistemology is either defunct or superfluous* (Knowles 2003: 4). Knowles argues that naturalism requires us to accept some beliefs and basic cognitive prac-

---

[5] This classification is due to Harvey Siegel (Seigel 1996).

tices as fundamentally valid (although not infallible) because for anything we might call a justification—or justified formation—of a belief about the world, we cannot *dig deeper* than to other beliefs about the world and to basic cognitive practices. But whatever is needed for optimal belief formation is reflected in the basic cognitive practices (Knowles 2003: 24–26).

If normative notions such as justification are not integral to a naturalistic understanding of optimal belief formation – either because they are to be replaced or because they may safely be ignored, then a priori justification is likewise inessential. But we would find an analogue of a priori justification within a nonnormative reconstruction of the epistemological enterprise if we were to discover processes of belief formation that are indifferent to the particulars of sensory input. We might classify the outputs of such processes, in total or in part, as a priori in a modified sense. The a priori would no longer be a normative notion; instead, it would be a classification of a type of process, or output of a process, in which the particulars of sensory input played no role. Default computational processes would be "a priori" in this derivative, nonnormative sense, and their default status might be of interest within the disciplines of cognitive science and artificial intelligence.

3.2 Normative Naturalistic Epistemologies

A normative naturalistic epistemology aims to reconcile normativity with naturalism within an epistemological theory. The reconciliation may take the form of a reduction, whereby normative notions are explained in terms of nonnormative processes, or an analysis of epistemic norms as partially nonfactual. I consider these two strategies in turn.

3.2.1 Reductive Accounts of Normativity

Many epistemologists attempt to accommodate normative notions within a naturalistic framework by identifying them with nonnormative processes and methods. Normative notions are naturalised but not eliminated on this strategy. I will discuss two noneliminative reductive strategies: reliabilism and instrumental rationality. Reliabilism specifies the conditions for which a particular agent S either knows or is justified in believing that P, where S may not be aware of the mechanisms by which she forms a belief. Instrumental rationality attempts to explain the normativity of rationality and methods of belief formation that involve deliberative choice. Instrumental rationality is arguably a leading strategy for naturalising epistemology within the philosophy of science, and its advocates aim to show that the normativity of methodologies employed in the evaluation of scientific theories can be understood in terms of instrumental value. I will argue that forms of a priori justification can, in principle, be accommodated within these reductive strategies.

3.2.1.1 Reliabilism

Reliabilism identifies justification with nonepistemic notions such as causal connections between a thinker and the world, psychological processes, and actual reliability. Here is a simple formulation of the reliabilist thesis:

> S's belief that p is justified iff it is caused (or causally sustained) by a reliable cognitive process (or history of reliable processes) (Goldman 1994: 309).

A distinction is usually made between native psychological *processes* and acquired *methods*, with native processes being the more basic. A key feature of reliablism is its rejection of the "KK" thesis, which says that in order for a believer to know something, she must know that she knows it. According to reliabilism, a believer need not know that her belief that P was generated by a reliable process in order to know P.

A priori justification is readily accommodated within the reliabilist framework. Georges Rey (1993; 1998; 2005), Alvin Goldman (1999), and Louise Antony (2004) have each argued that there might be a priori beliefs that result from processes or methods that meet the conditions for being a priori warranters. (The authors differ with respect to the details.) Both Rey and Antony explicitly develop their view within a Quinean empiricist framework, whereby we might come to discover that certain cognitive processes are a priori warranting, with the result that individuals may form either fully apriori-justified beliefs or beliefs with an a priori component. Empiricism could thus be preserved for propositional claims of a general and theoretical nature, while allowing that there is apriori-justified belief for individuals at particular times and in particular circumstances. (Of course Quine identifies the a priori with analyticity and rational irrevisability, both of which he denies. But neither of these features is a required component of the notion of a priori justification that I have articulated here.)

A belief is a priori justified on the reliabilist picture just in case it is exclusively produced by a reliable cognitive process that is indifferent to the particulars of sensory input (an "a priori warranter"). A belief formed exclusively by such a process would be a priori justified. A belief formed partially, but not exclusively, by an a priori warranter would be partially a priori justified. More fully, beliefs that are the output of operations of a priori warranters on reliably-formed input beliefs that originate in perception would have apriori-justified elements, but they would not be entirely a priori justified.

The following example, due to Georges Rey (Rey 1998: 33–34) illustrates how an apriori-warranting process might operate to produce a fully apriori-justified belief:

> Suppose we have a Gentzen-style natural deduction system built into our heads. Suppose further that the system generates
>
> (R) Nothing bites all and only those things that do not bite themselves.
>
> (R) would be an apriori-justified belief because (by hypothesis) it is produced by a reliable process, and it would be a priori because the process involves no (undischarged) premises, *ergo* it involves no empirical premises.

An apriori-warranting process might yield a belief that is partially a priori justified as the following example illustrates:

> Suppose modus ponens is a part of a natural deduction system built into our heads and it causes S to make the following inference:
>
> 1. According to the odometer in my car, I have driven 123 kilometers in the southeast direction from Warsaw.
> 2. If I have driven 123 kilometers in the southeast direction from Warsaw, then I have arrived at Kazimierz Dolny.
> _____
> ∴ 3. I have arrived at Kazimierz Dolny.

The belief that I arrived at Kazimierz Dolny, if the odometer in my car is reliable, is the result of an inferential process applied to beliefs that originate, in part, in experience.

Candidate a priori-warranting processes include processes that subserve deductive reasoning, numerical cognition, and perhaps basic inductive methodologies. A learned method might also be a candidate for an a priori warranter, but only if it can be determined to be reliable by a priori means. The a priori elements of knowledge would be those elements that reflect or derive solely from the operations of a priori warranters.

3.2.1.2 Instrumental Rationality

Instrumental rationality analyzes the normativity of rationality in terms of the efficacy of a set of chosen means with respect to achieving our epistemic goals. If rationality can be given a means-end analysis, the normative element reduces to description when optimal or effective methods that bring about desired ends are identified. The instrumental relation of a particular method to a targeted end is understood to be subject to empirical scrutiny and evaluation. Proponents of the view thus take the normative element of epistemology to be adequately accounted for and preserved within a naturalistic framework.

Many philosophers operating in the naturalist tradition advocate some form of instrumental rationality[6]. The view can be traced back to Quine, and it is articulated in a number of his writings, such as this passage from his "Reply to White":

> Naturalization of epistemology does not jettison the normative and settle for indiscriminate description of the on-going process. For me, normative epistemology is a branch of engineering. It is the technology of truth-seeking, or, in more cautiously epistemic terms, prediction .... There is no question here of ultimate value, as in morals; it is a matter of efficacy for an ulterior end, truth or prediction. The normative here, as elsewhere in engineering, becomes descriptive when the terminal parameter has been expressed (pp. 664–65).

Whether Quine should be interpreted as an eliminativist about justification or as noneliminative reductionist is a matter of some dispute. A number of interpreters of Quine, including Richard Foley (1994), Roger Gibson (1988), and Susan Haack (1993), have suggested that, contrary to what he says in "Epistemology Naturalized," Quine's best-considered view may be that epistemology is instrumentally normative.

Although it may not be immediately apparent, some forms of a priori justification are consistent with instrumental rationality. We may discover that basic belief-forming methodologies are presupposed by the method whose instrumentality is being evaluated, and moreover, that

---

[6] This strategy is developed in different ways by Ronald Giere (1985; 1988), Larry Laudan (1984; 1990), Stephen Stich (1990), and Hilary Kornblith (1993), to name just a few.

they are presupposed in the evaluation itself. Candidates for methods that would need to be presupposed would be basic deductive and inductive belief-forming methodologies. These methods are instrumental to science and to knowledge claims generally, but they are not themselves empirical if they are presupposed, rather than tested by, scientific methods.

A number of philosophers, for example Thomas Nagel (1997) and Crispin Wright (2004), have recognized our need to presuppose certain principles in reasoning as an important component of our a priori grounds for accepting them and Ernest Nagel (1956) develops an explicitly a priori instrumentalist account of logic. Although facts about presupposition could not plausibly be extended to cover the full range of alleged cases of a priori justification, it is one way that there could be a priori justification within an instrumentalist account of normativity.

3.2.2 Nonreductive strategies

An alternative to the reductive strategies discussed above is a meta-epistemological view known as *nonfactualism* or *evaluativism*. On this view, justification and other terms of positive epistemic appraisal are understood as evaluative – as opposed to fully-factual – judgments. An attribution of justification is a judgment that a cognitive agent(s) makes according to a set of epistemic norms. Epistemic evaluations have a factual component in that they depend on the relevant facts, but they are ineliminably evaluative and thus partially nonfactual.

Evaluativism is a naturalistic view in that it does not take justification to be a primitive and irreducible property of rules or propositions. However, evaluativism shares with nonnaturalism the view that epistemological properties are irreducibly normative; their normativity is to be explained naturalistically in terms of judgments that we might make in accordance with our epistemic goals or norms. To say that S justifiably believes P is to say that S's belief is licensed by an accepted epistemic norm or system of norms. An epistemic norm is a set of standards, principles, or rules by which beliefs and belief-forming practices are guided and appraised. To accept a norm is to be in a complex psychological state of a certain kind that would be described computationally (or otherwise naturalistically) by a psychology of normative governance. Evaluativism differs from the reductive naturalistic strategies, not only by taking normativity to be irreducible, but in rejecting realism about justification.

Evaluativists differ on the question whether there could be disagreement with respect to epistemic norms. John Pollock, an early proponent of the view, argues that we could not disagree about our basic norms without employing different concepts (Pollock 1986). Hartry Field, who advocates a norm-expressivist version of evaluativism, argues that evaluative judgments are relative to the norms of the evaluator, and that we could, at least in theory, differ with respect to our goals and evaluative standards for belief formation (Field 2000). (See also Chrisman 2007.) On Field's view, evaluativism in epistemology is analogous to norm-expressivism in ethics[7].

An important question for a norm-expressivist epistemology is whether there could be differences with respect to the value of truth, i.e., whether the value of truth could be "up for grabs." Recent work by Mark Bickhard (Bickhard 2006 and 2010) and Michael Lynch (Lynch 2009) aims to show that truth must be accepted as a primary epistemic value. Bickhard argues that normativity is an emergent, causally-efficacious property of physically-realized processes, and the value of truth is a fundamental normative aspect of representation for biological organisms. Lynch argues that truth is a constitutive norm of correctness for belief and inquiry and that expressivism about truth is self-undermining. (These papers take up the question of the value of truth independently of the debate between factual and nonfactual accounts of justification. The recognition of truth as an epistemic value is compatible with either.)

Attributions of a priori justification are compatible with evaluativism: We may judge the justification conditions for knowledge of a proposition or our grounds for employing a rule of inference to be a priori. In assessing the target claim, we employ norms of evaluation. The a priori justification for any given claim will depend on what reasons or considerations can be given in its favour and on what standards must be met for the claim to count as justified.

4 Concluding Remarks

Naturalistic epistemologies reject epistemology as "first philosophy", the project of providing internally-accessible, a priori grounds for beliefs and knowledge claims that are indubitable, incorrigible, and infallible. To the

---

[7] See Alan Gibbard (1993) for the classical articulation and defense of norm expressivism in ethics.

extent that a conception of a priori justification incorporates these attributes, a priori justification must be rejected along with first philosophy. However, a philosophically interesting notion of a priori justification can, in principle, be accommodated within some naturalistic epistemologies – if empirical indefeasibility is interpreted in such a way that we can be fallibilist about a priori justification.

The advantage to reconceiving a priori justification along naturalistic lines is that it opens up new possibilities for explaining traditionally a priori subject matters – such as mathematics and logic – within naturalistic epistemologies. Given an appropriately naturalistic conception of the a priori, this avenue of explanation is not foreclosed merely by virtue of a commitment to naturalism.

References

Antony, Louise (2004). "A Naturalized Approach to the A Priori". *Philosophical Issues* 14. *Epistemology*, pp. 1–17.

Bickhard, Mark (2010). "Is Normativity Natural". In this volume.

Bickhard, Mark (2006) "Developmental Normativity and Normative Development". In *Norms in Human Development*, ed. by Leslie Smith and Jacques Vonèche. Cambridge: Cambridge University Press.

Burge, Tyler (1993). "Content Preservation". *Philosophical Review* 102, pp. 457–488.

Burge, Tyler (1998). "Computer Proof, A Priori Knowledge, and Other Minds". In *Philosophical Perspectives* 12, ed. by James Tomberlin. Malden, MA: Blackwell, pp. 1–17.

Chrisman, Matthew (2007). "From Epistemic Contextualism to Epistemic Expressivism". *Philosophical Studies* 135 (2), pp. 225–254.

Devitt, Michael (1996). *Coming to Our Senses: A Naturalistic Program for Semantic Localism.* Cambridge: Cambridge University Press.

Ewald, William, ed. (1996). *From Kant to Hilbert*, Vol. I. (Oxford: Oxford University Press).

Field, Hartry (2000). "Apriority as an Evaluative Notion". In Field (2001), pp. 361–90.

Field, Hartry (2001). *Truth and the Absence of Fact.* New York: Oxford University Press.

Foley, Richard (1994). *Midwest Studies in Philosophy*, 19, *Philosophical Naturalism*, ed. Peter French et al., pp. 243–60. Notre Dame, IN: Univ. of Notre Dame Press.

Gibbard, Alan (1993) *Wise Choices, Apt Feelings.* Cambridge, MA: Harvard University Press.

Gibson, Roger (1988). *Enlightened Empiricism: An Examination of W. V. Quine's Theory of Knowledge*. Tampa: Univ. Presses of Florida.
Giere, Ronald (1985). "Philosophy of Science Naturalized". *Philosophy of Science* 52, pp. 331–356.
Giere, Ronald (1988). *Explaining Science*. Chicago: University of Chicago Press.
Goldman, Alvin (1999). "A Priori Warrant and Naturalistic Epistemology". In *Philosophical Perspectives* 13, *Epistemology*, ed. by James Tomberlin. Cambridge, MA; Oxford: Blackwell, pp. 1–28.
Haack, Susan (1979). "Epistemology *with* a Knowing Subject", *Synthese* 41, pp. 37–63.
Haack, Susan (1983). "Two Faces of Quinean Naturalism." *Synthese* 94, pp. 335–356.
Kornblith, Hilary (1993). "Epistemic Normativity". *Synthese* 94, pp. 357–376.
Knowles, Jonathan (2003.) *Norms, Naturalism, and Epistemology: The Case for Science without Norms*. Houndmills: Palgrave Macmillan.
Laudan, Larry (1984). *Science and Values*. Berkeley: University of California Press.
Laudan, Larry (1990). "Normative Naturalism". Philosophy of Science 57, pp. 44–59.
Lynch, Michael (2009). "Truth, Value and Epistemic Expressivism". *Philosophy and Phenomenological Research* LXXIX (1), pp. 76–97.
Nagel, Ernest (1956). *Logic Without Metaphysics*. Glencoe, IL: Free Press.
Nagel, Thomas (1997). *The Last Word*. New York: Oxford University Press.
Pollock, John (1986). *Contemporary Theories of Knowledge*. Totowa, NJ: Rowman & Littlefield.
Rey, G. (1993). The Unavailability of What We Mean: A Reply to Quine, Fodor, and Lepore. *Grazer Philosophical Studien* 96, pp. 61–101.
Rey, Georges (1998). "A Naturalistic A Priori". *Philosophical Studies* 92, pp. 25–43.
Rey, Georges (2005). "The Rashness of Traditional Rationalism and Empiricism". In *New Essays in the Philosophy of Language and Mind*, *Canadian Journal of Philosophy*, Supplementary Volume 30, ed. by M. Ezcurdia, R. Stainton, and C. Viger, pp. 227–58.
Quine, Willard V. O. (1969). *Ontological Relativity and Other Essays*. New York: Columbia University Press.
Quine, Willard V. O. (1981). *Theories and Things*. Cambridge, MA: MIT Press.
Quine, Willard V.O. (1986). "Reply to White". In *The Philosophy of W.V. Quine*, ed. by Hahn and Schilpp. La Salle, IL: Open Court, pp. 663–65.
Siegel, Harvey (1996). "Naturalism and the Abandonment of Normativity". In *The Philosophy of Psychology*, ed. by William O'Donohue and Richard Kitchener. London: Sage Publications.
Stich, Stephen (1990). *The Fragmentation of Reason*. Cambridge, MA: MIT Press.

Warenski, Lisa (2009). "Naturalism, Fallibilism, and the A Priori". *Philosophical Studies* 142 (3), pp. 403–426.
Wright, Crispin (2004). "Warrant for Nothing: Notes on Epistemic Entitlement". *Proceedings of the Aristotelian Society*, Supplementary Volume 78, pp. 167–212.

7

The Proper Role of Intuitions in Epistemology

ADAM FELTZ & MICHAEL BISHOP

Intuitions play an important role in contemporary philosophy. It is common for theories in epistemology, morality, semantics and metaphysics to be rejected because they are inconsistent with a widely and firmly held intuition. Our goal in this paper is to explore the role of epistemic intuitions in epistemology from a naturalistic perspective. Here is the question we take to be central:

(Q) Ought we to trust our epistemic intuitions as evidence in support of our epistemological theories?

We will understand this question as employing an epistemic 'ought' – insofar as we aim at developing a correct epistemological theory, ought we to trust our epistemic intuitions as evidence for or against our epistemological theories? As it stands, (Q) needs further clarification. *Whether something is trustworthy is relative to (a) what it is and (b) what we're asking it to do.* Sam might trust Marie but not George to care for his children, while he might trust both to care for his pet fish. So in order to address (Q), we first need to explore two questions: What are epistemic intuitions? And what sort of epistemological theories do we want? We will take up each of these questions in the following sections.

Beyond Description: Naturalism and Normativity.
Marcin Miłkowski and Konrad Talmont-Kaminski (eds.).
Copyright © 2010 The Authors.

1 What Are Epistemic Intuitions?

We can distinguish various views about the nature of intuitions by focusing on the following four questions.

Are intuitions beliefs / inclinations to believe? According to David Lewis, "'intuitions' are simply opinions" where "some are commonsensical, some are sophisticated; some are particular, some are general, some are firmly held, some less. But they are all opinions" (1983: x). An objection to this view holds that it is possible to have an intuition that p without believing that p. For example, one might have the intuition but not the belief that parallel lines never intersect. In reply, one might argue that intuitions can include a feeling or inclination to accept a belief. According to Peter van Inwagen, for example, "'intuitions' are simply beliefs—or perhaps, in some cases, the tendencies that make certain beliefs attractive to us, that 'move' us in the direction of accepting certain propositions without taking us all the way to acceptance" (1997: 309). So one can have an intuition without a belief insofar as one can have an inclination to believe without a belief. A worry about this view is: Do are all our beliefs count as intuitions? It would be strange to say that S's belief that (say) she is an employee of IBM is an intuition. If this is right, the belief view of intuitions is incomplete: What is it about some beliefs that makes them intuitions?

Many philosophers insist that intuitions and beliefs are distinct kinds of propositional attitude. According to Ernest Sosa, an intuition is "a representationally contentful conscious state that can serve as a justifying basis for belief while distinct from belief, not derived from certain sources, and possibly false" (2007: 57). George Bealer argues that intuition is a "sui generis, irreducible, natural (i.e., non-Cambridge-like) propositional attitude that occurs episodically..." They are distinct from "physical intuitions, thought experiments, beliefs, guesses, hunches, judgments, common sense, and memory... not reducible to inclinations, raisings-to-consciousness of non-conscious background beliefs, linguistic mastery, reports of consistency; and so forth" (1998: 213).

Are intuitions non-inferential? Most philosophers who write about intuitions claim that they are non-inferential. For example, Lisa Osbeck claims that "the salient feature common to various accounts of intuition is its non-inferential status" (2001: 119). Alvin Goldman and Joel Pust "assume, at a minimum, that intuitions are some sort of spontaneous mental judgments. Each intuition, then, is a judgment 'that p', for some suitable class of propositions p" (1998: 179). But some naturalistically inclined philosophers take intuitions to be the result of some inferential process. Michael Devitt claims that "intuitive judgments are empirical theory-laden central-processor responses to phenomena, differing from many other such responses only in being fairly immediate and unreflective, based on little if any conscious reasoning" (2006: 491). Hilary Kornblith argues that intuitions "are corrigible and theory-mediated. The extent of agreement among subjects on intuitive judgments is to be explained by common knowledge, or at least common belief, and the ways in which such background belief will inevitably influence intuitive judgment, although unavailable to introspection, are none the less quite real" (2002: 13).

Are intuitions untutored judgments? Philosophers disagree about whether intuitions are commonsense, untutored judgments or whether they can arise (non-inferentially) after considerable learning and reflection. So L.J. Cohen contends that "an intuition that p is... just an immediate and untutored inclination, without evidence or inference, to judge that p" (1981: 318). On the other hand, Laurence BonJour takes intuitions to be "judgments and convictions that, though considered and reflective, are not arrived at via an explicit discursive process" (1998: 102).

Do intuitions come with special seemings? Some philosophers believe that intuitions come with a characteristic feeling or conviction that what is intuited is true. Guy Claxton thinks that intuition "comes to mind with a certain aura (or even conviction) of 'rightness'" (1998: 217). Stephen Hales thinks that "to have an intuition that A is for it to seem necessarily true that A" (2000: 137). But as we have already seen, those philosophers who take intuitions to be beliefs do not suppose that intuitions *must* come with these sorts of seemings, although they can include an inclination to accept a belief.

There is a cacophony of views about intuitions. When we ask whether our epistemic intuitions should count as evidence for or against our epistemological theories, there are a number of different sorts of things we might mean by this question, depending on what we mean by 'intuitions'.

We can capture some of the variation in views about intuitions in terms of the following menu:

> Menu I: Choose one each from the As, the Bs and the Cs.
> A1. Epistemic intuitions are beliefs or inclinations to believe.
> A2. Epistemic intuitions are sui generis propositional attitudes.
>
> B1. Epistemic intuitions are inferential judgments.
> B2. Epistemic intuitions are non-inferential judgments.
>
> C1. Epistemic intuitions include only untutored judgments.
> C2. Epistemic intuitions include tutored and untutored judgments.

This menu defines eight different views about intuitions (in terms of the various possible combinations of As, Bs and Cs). So recall our central question:

> (Q) Ought we to trust our epistemic intuitions as evidence in support of our epistemological theories?

We can distinguish eight different interpretations of (Q) depending on what we take intuitions to be. For the purposes of this paper, we are going to adopt a neutral characterization of intuitions: they are quickly formed epistemic judgments of the sort that have played vital roles in the development of epistemological theories over the past half-century or so. We take no stand on whether these judgments are beliefs, whether they are non-inferential or whether they can be the result of specialized training.

2 What Sort Of Epistemological Theory Do We Want?

Different philosophers have different conceptions of what an epistemological theory is supposed to deliver. Unlike disagreements about intuitions, however, we cannot make these disagreements disappear by adopting a neutral position. Let's restrict our focus to theories of epistemic knowledge. Following Stephen Stich (2009), let's distinguish five possible projects we might embark upon in developing a theory of knowledge:

1. Intuition capturing: A theory of knowledge must entail our intuitions about epistemic knowledge (perhaps with some light revisions in the service of clarity or theoretical power).
2. Implicit theory: There is an implicit theory that underlies our abilities to produce epistemic intuitions. A theory of knowledge must give an account of that implicit theory.
3. Conceptual analysis: There is a concept that underlies our abilities to produce epistemic intuitions. A theory of knowledge must give an account of that concept. (Note: On some views of concepts, this project will be identical to the second project.)
4. True nature: A theory of knowledge aims to characterize the nature and conditions of knowledge. This assumes that knowledge is something that is distinct from our concept of knowledge or our implicit theories about knowledge, in the same sense that characterizing the nature of water or whales is different from providing an account of our concept of water or whales.
5. Reason-guidance: A theory of knowledge (or justification) aims to tell us what we epistemically ought to believe, ceteris paribus. The ceteris paribus hedge is important: a reason-guiding epistemological theory gives advice that can be overridden by other, non-epistemic considerations. For example, a reason-guiding theory might tell us that we ought (epistemically) to believe p, even though there are competing moral or pragmatic considerations that, all things considered, advise against believing that p.

We don't mean to suggest that this list exhausts the projects epistemologists might be embarked upon in their theorizing about knowledge. But they are sufficiently different that the right answer to (Q) might depend on which project we have in mind. For example, one might reasonably argue that the appropriate role of epistemic intuitions in epistemological theorizing are quite different for project 1 (intuition capturing) and project 5 (reason-guidance). Now let's turn to the various possible answers we might give to some interpretation of (Q).

3 The Optimism-Pessimism Divide

Our central question is (Q): Ought we to trust our epistemic intuitions as evidence in support of our epistemological theories? The following schema sets out 16 different ways we might answer this question.

Schema I: Choose one from A and one from B.
> Our epistemic intuitions ought __A__ to count as __B__ substantive evidence for our epistemological theories.
>> A: always, usually, sometimes, seldom
>> B: the only, the primary, some, no

By *substantive* evidence, we mean evidence that does not simply involve theoretical considerations of power, simplicity, etc. We do not mean to suggest that the answers we might give to (Q) are restricted to these 16 possibilities and their various possible consistent conjunctions and disjunctions. Many plausible answers are ignored by the above schema; for example, a philosopher might argue that our intuitions are always "default reasonable" evidence for our epistemological theories. But it is a useful exercise to note that we can give at least 16 different answers to (Q) and we are assuming that there are five different interpretations of (Q) – one for each epistemological project.

Perhaps the most noteworthy feature of contemporary analytic epistemology is that regardless of what project is being pursued, analytic philosophers put a lot of evidential weight on epistemic intuitions. Our reading of the contemporary philosophical landscape leads us to hypothesize that the practice of most contemporary epistemologists embraces an answer to (Q) that is extremely optimistic:

> (O) Our epistemic intuitions ought always to count as the only substantive evidence for our epistemological theories.

Are we guilty of foisting on the optimist an overly polarized view of intuitions? We don't think so. Optimists believe that epistemic intuitions ought to play roughly the role they're actually playing in (nonsceptical) epistemological theorizing; pessimists believe that epistemic intuitions ought to count for less than they do in contemporary epistemology. For those who think we have made life too tough for optimists by setting the standard so high, we challenge them to find examples of theories of knowledge that have been defended by appealing to substantive, nonintuitional evidence after their counterintuitive results have been recognized. Except for the occasional sceptic, such examples are exceptionally hard to find. Despite having canvassed a dozen or so experienced epistemologists, we have been hard pressed to come up with any examples in which a philosopher defends an epistemological theory that he or she recognizes is counterintuitive. In fact, the only exception we have found is Weatherson (2003). But Weatherson argues that theoretical considerations of power and simplicity can outweigh a theory having some counterintuitive consequences. So even Weatherson seems to be an optimist insofar as he seems unwilling to appeal to substantive non-intuitional evidence in support of a theory of knowledge.

For some epistemological projects, optimism is perfectly warranted. Epistemic intuitions are clearly extremely important evidence for project 1, intuition capturing. Epistemic intuitions are also very important evidence for projects 2 and 3 (implicit theory and conceptual analysis). But other substantive evidence, particularly psychological evidence about what underlies our abilities to produce epistemic intuitions, is likely to be important to projects 2 and 3 as well. So it is a mistake for the naturalist, or for anyone, to embrace a general pessimism about the proper role of epistemic intuitions in epistemology. There are plenty of legitimate philosophical projects, projects that distinguished philosophers have pursued, where pessimism would be absurd. On our view, however, a moderate pessimism about projects 4 and 5 is warranted. That's because these theories explicitly aim to tell us about something beyond our intuitions – either about the nature of knowledge (project 4) or about what we epistemically ought to believe (project 5).

4 The Coherence of a Moderate Pessimism about Epistemic Intuitions

A moderate pessimism about epistemic intuitions consists of an optimistic component and a pessimistic component. The optimistic component holds that epistemic intuitions are practically indispensable. A person totally bereft of these sorts of intuitions would make Hamlet seem reckless. Indeed, given the many beliefs we must come to in order to navigate our environment, we would not long survive without quickly formed judgments about what we epistemically ought to believe in particular evidential situations. Not only have epistemic intuitions played an essential role in our everyday cognitive accomplishments, they have played a vital role in the quite impressive intellectual achievements of our species. The pessimistic component of a moderate pessimism about epistemic intuitions holds that despite their considerable practical utility, contemporary philosophical practice gives way too much credence to epistemic intuitions as evidence for or against epistemological theories that aim to tell us something about matters that go beyond our intuitions (e.g., theories that aim to characterize the nature and conditions of knowledge [project 4] or that aim at a reason-guiding theory of knowledge [project 5].)

Moderate pessimism, with its optimism about the practical utility of our intuitions and its pessimism about the evidential potential of intuitions on epistemological projects 4 and 5, is perfectly consistent. An analogy might be useful. Different people have different physical intuitions. Most people (including some who have learned Newtonian physics) have largely Aristotelian physical intuitions; while some people tutored in Newton's theory have Newtonian physical intuitions. From a practical perspective, having either type of physical intuition helps one get along effectively in the world. In the normal course of events, there is enough overlap in the Aristotelian and Newtonian intuitions that in everyday matters, the theoretical differences are invisible. Those with Newtonian intuitions and those with Aristotelian intuitions come to spontaneous physical judgments that allow them to catch fly balls and navigate traffic. But from a theoretical perspective, these differences are deep and important. The Newtonian intuitions give a much more accurate representation of the physical world. The moderate pessimist about intuitions wants to make a perfectly parallel point: Everyone's epistemic intuitions are practically very useful, even if there is diversity in people's epistemic intuitions; but it doesn't follow that our intuitions accurately represent the nature and conditions of knowledge (project 4) or that they issue effective reasoning guidance (project 5).

Let's consider two related arguments optimists have proposed for thinking that pessimism about epistemic intuitions is a non-starter. On our view, both arguments attack a straw man. The first argument is that intuitions are so vital to our intellectual lives that we cannot give them up without engendering intellectual catastrophe. For example, against "those who reject philosophical intuitions as useless", Ernest Sosa thinks that we merely need to reflect on how widespread and accurate appeal to intuition actually is.

[W]e surely do and must allow a role for intuition in simple arithmetic and geometry, but not only there. Indeed, I ask you to consider how extensively we rely on intuition. I myself believe that intuition is ubiquitous across the vast body of anyone's knowledge (Sosa 2009).

We rely on intuition in a wide variety of areas; "by parity of reasoning, therefore, it would be an overreaction to dismiss intuition just because it misleads us systematically in certain known circumstances" (1998: 65). As BonJour pointedly argues, to offer a blanket condemnation of our intuitions is to commit "intellectual suicide" (BonJour 1998: 5). (See also Bealer 1992, 1996, 1998.)

Another version of this basic argument contends that pessimists about our intuitions must use their intuitions in coming to their epistemological views; and as a result, pessimism about our intuitions is ultimately self-defeating. For example, Harvey Siegel argues that "in one respect the naturalized epistemologist's position is self-defeating. For it seeks to justify naturalized epistemology in precisely the way in which, according to it, justification cannot be had" (1984: 675). And Mark Kaplan thinks that "the naturalist's attempt to show the errors of aprioristic methodology depends for its success on consulting, and finding naturalist arguments in accord with the very sorts of armchair intuitions whose advice the naturalists would have us ignore" (1994: 360). (See also DePaul 1998.)

From our perspective, these arguments attack straw men because they commit the naturalist to an implausibly extreme pessimism. As we have argued, a reasonable pessimism can hold both of the following theses:

1. Restricted optimism: Our epistemic intuitions are reasonably reliable at identifying beliefs that have the property of being knowledge (project 4) or identifying what subjects epistemically ought to believe (project 5).
2. Restricted pessimism: Our epistemic intuitions are not reliable enough to serve as the only (or even the primary) substantive evidence for our theories that aim to characterize the nature and conditions of knowledge (project 4) or that aim at a reason-guiding theory of knowledge or justification (project 5).

The moderate pessimist is not arguing that we should abandon all our epistemic intuitions about everything (which would lead to "intellectual suicide"). Nor is she arguing that we can construct an epistemological theory without ever relying on any epistemic intuitions. Instead, the moderate pessimist merely holds that certain sorts of epistemological theories (e.g., those aimed at projects 4 and 5) cannot be supported entirely (or perhaps even primarily) by epistemic intuitions. These arguments against a moderate pessimism don't work.

5 The Vicissitudes of Epistemic Intuitions

Why might anyone be pessimistic about whether our epistemic intuitions ought to be trusted as the primary (or only substantive) evidence for a theory of knowledge that aims to characterize the nature and conditions of knowledge (project 4) or guide reasoning (project 5)? From our perspective, a fundamental reason for pessimism is driven by evidence for what we will call the *epistemic diversity thesis*. This thesis holds that different people have different, incompatible epistemic intuitions. This diversity, we will argue, calls into question whether our epistemic intuitions serve *by themselves* as the only substantive evidence for an epistemological theory that aims to tell us about something other than our epistemic concepts and intuitions.

5.1 Epistemic Intuitions Are Culturally Variable

Jonathan Weinberg, Shaun Nichols, and Stephen Stich (henceforth, WNS) present a series of empirical studies that suggest that there are systematic cultural and socio-economic differences in people's epistemic intuitions (2001). Consider that for over 40 years, every philosopher who was published on the Gettier Problem has had the intuition that subjects in Gettier conditions do not have knowledge. Here is a typical Gettier case.

> Bob has a friend, Jill, who has driven a Buick for many years. Bob therefore thinks that Jill drives an American car. He is not aware, however, that her Buick has recently been stolen, and he is also not aware that Jill has replaced it with a Pontiac, which is a different kind of American car. Does Bob really know that Jill drives an American car, or does he only believe it?
> REALLY KNOWS   ONLY BELIEVES

The majority of Westerners (75%) agree with philosophers that Bob only believes that Jill drives an American car and does not really know it. But a majority of subjects from East Asia and India disagreed with philosophers (and most Western subjects). 55% of East Asians and about 60% of Indians judged that Bob has knowledge (WNS 2001: 443–4). WNS also found cases in which there were significant differences between the epistemic judgments of people of high socioeconomic status (SES) and of low SES (2001: 447–448).

The cross-cultural diversity in epistemic intuitions is important but it is not the whole story. WNS emphasize that they did not merely find random variation in people's epistemic judgments across cultures. Instead, these differences reflected deeper cross-cultural differences in how people reason. The psychologist Richard Nisbett and his colleagues have identified some significant differences in the thought patterns of East Asians (Chinese, Japanese and Koreans) and non-Asian Westerners (from the U.S. and Europe) (Nisbett, Peng, Choi and Norenzayan 2001; Nisbett 2003). The reasoning of Westerners tends to be more analytic, "involving detachment of the object from its context, a tendency to focus on attributes of the object to assign it to categories, and a preference for using rules about the categories to explain and predict the object's behaviour. Inferences rest in part on the practice of decontextualizing structure from content, the use of formal logic, and avoidance of contradiction." The reasoning of East Asians tends to be more holistic, "involving an orientation to the context or field as a whole, including attention to relationships between a focal object and the field, and a preference for explaining and predicting events on the basis of such relationships. Holistic approaches rely on experience-based knowledge rather than on abstract logic and are dialectical, meaning that there is an emphasis on change, a recognition of contradiction and of the need for multiple perspectives, and a search for the 'Middle Way' between opposing propositions" (Nisbett, et al. 2001: 293). An example will help make this distinction concrete.

In the "Michigan Fish" study, Japanese and American subjects viewed animated underwater scenes and then reported what they had seen (Masuda & Nisbett 2001). The first statement by Americans usually referred to the fish, while the first statement by Japanese usually referred to background elements, e.g., "There was a lake or a pond." The Japanese made about 70 percent more statements than Americans about background aspects of the environment, and 100 percent more statements about relationships with inanimate aspects of the environment, e.g., "A big fish swam past some grey seaweed" (Nisbett, et al. 2001: 297). In this study, the Westerner subjects focused on objects detached from their background, while the Japanese subjects focused on the context and the relationships between objects in the field. Referring to this study, Nisbett has joked that for Westerners, if it doesn't move, it doesn't exist.

The cognitive differences that Nisbett and his colleagues found between East Asians and Westerners are reflected in WNS's epistemic diversity findings. For example, WNS gave participants three variations of a Truetemp case (in which a person unwittingly is able to reliably form beliefs about the ambient temperature). In the individualistic version, Charles alone gets the Truetemp ability as a result of getting hit in the head by a rock. In the elders version, John alone gets the Truetemp ability as a result of the elders in his community deciding to have John's brain rewired for this ability. And in the community version, radiation causes the rewiring of the entire community of people of which Kai is a member. In all three versions, Westerners' intuitions about stayed about the same (32%, 35%, and 20% respectively thought the person knows). But East Asians' tend to ascribe knowledge more often as more of the community was involved (12%, 25%, and 32% respectively thought the person knows). So in the individualistic version, more Westerners ascribed knowledge; in the elders version, there was no significant difference; and in the community version, more East Asians ascribed knowledge (WNS 2001: 439–441). These results are consistent with the findings of Nisbett and his colleagues. Because Westerners focused on the properties of the individual and those properties remained the same in the Truetemp cases, their intuitions remained basically stable. However, because East Asians focused on relational properties that changed in 1–3, their intuitions about the cases changed accordingly. WNS argue that

> [t]he differences between Ws [Westerners] and EAs [East Asians] look to be both systematic and explainable. EAs and Ws appear to be sensitive to different features of the situation, different *epistemic vectors*, as we call them. EAs are much more sensitive to communitarian factors, while Ws respond to more individualistic ones. Moreover, Nisbett and his colleagues have given us good reason to think that these kinds of differences can be traced to deep and important differences in EA and W cognition… What our studies point to, then, is more than just divergent epistemic intuitions across groups; the studies point to divergent epistemic concerns – concerns which appear to differ along a variety of dimensions (2001: 451).

This consilience suggests some pretty deep differences in how people in different cultures evaluate reasoning.

5.2 Epistemic Intuitions Are Influenced By Irrelevant Considerations

Stacy Swain, Joshua Alexander, and Jonathan Weinberg (henceforth SAW, 2008) have found that people's intuitions are influenced by the order in which examples are presented. SAW presented participants with a Truetemp case: Charlie is hit in the head which causes his brain to be rewired so that he can accurately judge the ambient temperature. The Truetemp case is presented either before or after one of the following two cases.

Non-Knowledge: Dave sometimes gets a special feeling about which side of a coin is going to come up. When he feels which side will come up, he forms a belief to that effect.

Knowledge: Karen is a chemist who has recently read that mixing two chemicals together will create a toxic gas, and she forms the belief that mixing those two chemicals will create a toxic gas.

Two experimental results are particularly interesting. In the first, experimental subjects are presented with Non-Knowledge first, then Truetemp; the control subjects are presented with Truetemp first, then Non-Knowledge. Those who get Non-Knowledge first are more likely to judge that Charlie knew the ambient temperature. In the second experiment, experimental subjects are presented with Knowledge first, then Truetemp; the control subjects are presented with Truetemp first, then Knowledge. Those who got Knowledge first are less likely to judge that Charlie knew the ambient temperature. SAW conclude that these "results build on an existing body of empirical research demonstrating that intuitions vary according to factors irrelevant to the issues thought-experiments are designed to address" which indicates that epistemic intuitions "may in fact be built on an unacceptably shifting foundation" (2008: 154).

5.3 Philosophers Are Mistaken about "Our" Epistemic Intuitions

Philosophers who build theories on the basis of epistemic intuitions rely on their own intuitions. Why do they believe that their intuitions are shared by most people? Frank Jackson claims that "we [philosophers] know that our own case is typical and so can generalize from it to others" (1998: 37). But sometimes this is not true. For example, in *Knowledge and Practical Interests*, Jason Stanley argues that the practical facts of a situation play a role in ordinary knowledge ascriptions. In particular, keeping a person's evidence fixed, when the costs of having a false belief are high, people are less likely to ascribe knowledge to a person, and when the costs of having a false belief are low, people are more likely to ascribe knowledge to a person. "Ordinary assertions of knowledge are made on such a basis that we can envisage someone [who possesses knowledge] in a higher-stakes situation (often a much higher-stakes situation), whom we would not think of as possessing that knowledge, given similar evidence" (2005: 8).

Adam Feltz and Chris Zarpentine (manuscript) have tested Stanley's claim. They began with the examples Stanley takes to show that practical facts influence ordinary knowledge ascriptions (although the examples are slightly modified so as to eliminate potential confounding factors[1]).

Low Stakes: Hannah and her wife Sarah are driving home on a Friday afternoon. They plan to stop at the bank on the way home to deposit their paychecks. It is not important that they do so, as they have no impending bills. But as they drive past the bank, they notice that the lines inside are very long, as they often are on Friday afternoons. Realizing that it isn't very important that their paychecks are deposited right away, Hannah says, 'I know the bank will be open tomorrow, since I was there just two weeks ago on Saturday morning. So we can deposit our paychecks tomorrow morning.'

High Stakes: Hannah and her wife Sarah are driving home on a Friday afternoon. They plan to stop at the bank on the way home to deposit their paychecks. Since they have an impending bill coming due, and very little in their account, it is very important that they deposit their paychecks by Saturday. Hannah notes that she was at the bank two weeks before on a Saturday morning, and it was open. But, as Sarah points out, banks do change their hours. Hannah says, 'I guess you're right. I don't know that the bank will be open tomorrow.' (Stanley 2005: 5)

---

[1] The sentence, "But, as Sara points out, banks do change their hours," is present in High Stakes but not in Low Stakes. In their study, Feltz and Zarpentine removed this sentence because it made a possible justification defeater salient that may have confounded the results.

When Feltz and Zarpentine gave these examples to subjects, their pattern of responses did not conform to Stanley's predictions. 41% disagreed that Hannah knows in Low Stakes whereas 43.5% disagreed that Hannah knows in High Stakes. The costs of being wrong or right did not significantly influence people's knowledge ascriptions. Feltz and Zarpentine tested Stanley's hypothesis against several different scenarios, and none of the results conformed to Stanley's predictions. It would appear that most people do not share Stanley's intuitions about knowledge.

6 From Epistemic Diversity to Moderate Pessimism

The case for a moderate pessimism begins with three assumptions. First, a theory of knowledge aims to give us an account of a target beyond our concepts and intuitions. Perhaps the aim is to give us an account of the nature and conditions of knowledge (project 4) or an account of what we ought epistemically to believe (project 5). (It will be useful to focus on just one of these projects in our discussion below, so we'll focus on project 4. The following arguments apply mutatis mutandis to project 5.) The second assumption is that crude relativism about these projects is false. So the nature and conditions of knowledge are not determined by the content of our concept of knowledge or by our knowledge intuitions. And the third assumption is that the diversity thesis is correct: different people have different knowledge intuitions. Given these three assumptions, we are faced with what we might call the adjudication problem: We need a principled way to adjudicate between competing inconsistent knowledge intuitions – to decide which knowledge intuition is correct and which is incorrect. Since the target of our inquiry is not our knowledge intuitions, a solution to the adjudication problem must appeal to evidence beyond the knowledge intuitions at issue. But there's the rub: Optimists don't think they need to appeal to substantive evidence beyond our knowledge intuitions in constructing a theory of knowledge. So they can't solve the adjudication problem.

Some optimists try to avoid the adjudication problem by denying the existence of genuine diversity in people's epistemic intuitions. Let's start with two related avoidance strategies.

A. Thin slicing knowledge: Diversity does not imply any disagreement about what beliefs count as knowledge because those who apparently disagree are really talking past one another. The diversity findings show only that 'knowledge' has different meanings in different people's idiolects. So there can be no large-scale, systematic disagreements about knowledge. And so there is no need to adjudicate any disagreements.

B. Thin slicing epistemology: The diversity findings show that some people don't have epistemic concepts at all. So, for example, WNS have not shown that East Asians have different *epistemic* intuitions concerning Gettier cases. Rather, WNS have shown that East Asians have *non-epistemic* intuitions concerning Gettier cases. And the diversity findings show no large-scale, systematic disagreements about epistemological matters.

The main worry about the thin slicing strategies is that it is not clear that a plausible semantic theory can support them. After all, while WNS found systematic diversity in people's epistemic intuitions, they also found plenty of widespread cross-cultural agreement. For example, the vast majority of all cultural groups agreed that beliefs based on "special feelings" were not knowledge (WNS 2001: 430). More importantly, the epistemological project we're considering does not concern itself with our concept of knowledge or what we mean by 'knowledge'. It concerns itself with the nature and conditions of knowledge – with the referent of 'knowledge'. It is overwhelmingly plausible that individuals can have quite different opinions about something while still referring to it (Kripke 1972, Putnam 1975). If people with very different ideas about what atoms are can all refer to atoms, then it seems plausible to suppose that people with somewhat different ideas about the nature and conditions of knowledge can all refer to knowledge. There's much more to say about this, of course, but it is plausible to conclude that as an attempt to explain why epistemology never tackles the adjudication problem and relies entirely on philosophers's agreed upon intuitions, the thin slicing strategies are fraught with difficulties.

A third avoidance strategy is convergence. The basic idea is that all epistemic diversity is merely apparent diversity; it always arises because someone is making some kind of mistake. Once the errors are eliminated, the diversity in people's epistemic intuitions will disappear. It is important to distinguish two sorts of convergence strategies. The first holds that diversity will disappear (or at least ought to disappear) when people are introduced to evidence about knowledge (not about our concept of knowledge or our knowledge intuitions). This is not an avoidance strategy, since it essentially refers to evidence beyond our intuitions about knowledge in order to resolve the adjudication problem. It adjudicates between different, competing intuitions by introducing non-intuitional evidence. Here is a convergence strategy that does involve denying the existence of real epistemic diversity:

> C. Convergence: All diversity about intuitions concerning epistemic knowledge is merely apparent diversity. It will always disappear after people engage in a process of reflection *solely on their epistemic knowledge intuitions*.

The problem with the convergence strategy is that it must avoid stacking the deck in favour of some particular set of epistemic intuitions. We suspect that at least some philosophers who favour the convergence strategy do so because they are confident that they can convince people who have (from their perspective) "mistaken" intuitions to change their minds and adopt "correct" intuitions. But that way of eliminating diversity does not show that the original diversity was merely apparent. Even if those with T1 intuitions can implement some argumentative or pedagogical regime and convince those with T2 intuitions to adopt T1 intuitions, it doesn't follow that those original T2 intuitions were the result of some kind of mistake. After all, those with T2 intuitions might be able to implement a different argumentative or pedagogical regime and convince those with T1 intuitions to adopt T2 intuitions. The convergence strategy must show that an unbiased process of reflection *solely on knowledge intuitions* will lead people to a single set of knowledge intuitions. This is a brute empirical claim. We do not know how to test it. But we see no reason to take convergence seriously in absence of at least some evidence that it is true.

The final avoidance strategy we will consider simply involves the claim that certain people are experts in matters epistemological and their intuitions are correct – or at least more likely to be correct than other people's intuitions.

> D. Claiming expertise: Some privileged class of people, perhaps those with a certain sort of expertise, have the correct intuitions – or at least they have the intuitions we ought to accept.

We have no objections to well-founded claims of expertise and the practice of deferring to experts. But if two people have different intuitions about nature and conditions of knowledge, what makes one of them an expert? It can't just be that she has *these* intuitions rather than *those*. It must be that her intuitions are correct – or at least that we have good evidence for thinking that her intuitions more accurately reflect the nature and conditions of knowledge. If this is right, then this isn't really an avoidance strategy, since it must provide evidence beyond the knowledge intuitions under consideration for why some of these intuitions are correct and others are not.

So given epistemic diversity, why do contemporary analytic epistemologists construct theories of knowledge relying solely on their agreed upon knowledge-intuitions? Perhaps there is an explanation we have missed, or perhaps one of the avoidance strategies we've considered can overcome its prima facie difficulties. But we have an alternative hypothesis which we will frame in terms of the following argument:

1. Analytic epistemology is committed to relying solely upon the agreed upon knowledge intuitions of philosophers as the substantive evidence for theories of knowledge.
2. A well-supported theory of knowledge that aims at projects 4 or 5 (characterizing the nature and conditions of knowledge or developing a reason-guiding account of knowledge) must appeal to more substantive evidence than simply the agreed upon knowledge intuitions of philosophers.
3. Therefore, analytic epistemology cannot deliver a well-supported theory of knowledge that aims at projects 4 or 5.

7 Naturalized Epistemology: Intuitions and Beyond

If we want a theory to tell us about the nature and conditions of knowledge (project 4), our knowledge intuitions are likely to be reasonable guides. If we want a theory that delivers a reason-guiding conception of knowledge (project 5), our knowledge intuitions (or our justification-intuitions) are likely to be reasonable guides. But there is some plausible evidence that people's epistemic intuitions about knowledge vary in systematic ways. Not all these various, inconsistent intuitions can be accurate representations of the true nature and conditions of knowledge (project 4). And it is unlikely these inconsistent intuitions will always provide high quality guidance about what we epistemically ought to believe (project 5). How might we determine whose knowledge intuitions are right? We submit that philosophy must face the adjudication problem squarely:

We must find some evidence that would show us that *these* intuitions are correct while *those* intuitions are not. One might reasonably wonder what such evidence might be. This is one of the challenges facing naturalized epistemology: What, besides our epistemic intuitions, might reasonably count as substantive evidence for or against our epistemological theories? We want to briefly sketch an answer to this question.

A naturalistic approach to philosophy will begin by considering humans in our natural settings. We find ourselves interacting with various parts of the natural and social world, and we try to navigate and arrange our natural and social environments in ways that (if all is going well) make our lives go better. Normative concepts and practices – moral, epistemic, pragmatic – play important roles in guiding certain aspects of our thought and behaviour in ways that are (if all is going well) generally effective at helping us to navigate and arrange our environments in ways that make our lives – and the lives of others – go better. Where do our epistemological theories fit into this picture? To some degree, this is an empirical question and subject to various lines of evidence. Our epistemic intuitions are certainly an important line of evidence – from them we can perhaps learn about the role of our epistemic concepts, norms and practices in guiding our reasoning and our beliefs (Ahlstrom 2008). What's more, sociological and anthropological evidence are relevant to limning the (perhaps variable) role of epistemic norms and practices in the lives of people in different cultures.

On the view we are pressing, the contents of our epistemic concepts are not handed down from above as Iron Laws of Reason. Rather, they are cultural artefacts that betray how reasoning and belief are guided in an environment that is to some degree successful in promoting people's well being. And this brings out another line of evidence we take to be relevant to epistemological theorizing: evidence concerning human well-being. On our view, epistemological excellence in reasoning and belief tends to promote human well-being. It does not necessarily, or even always, do this. (Pragmatists might insist that epistemic excellence always promotes well-being. But we think it is a mistake to suppose that all epistemic considerations are grounded directly in considerations of well-being [Bishop 2009; Bishop & Trout 2008].) If we suppose there is some sort of loose connection between epistemic excellence and well-being, this provides another line of evidence to consider in adjudicating between competing intuitions. Other things being equal, epistemic intuitions are more likely to reflect genuine epistemic factors insofar as they recommend ways of reasoning or believing that consistently foster greater well-being.

So what role do epistemological considerations play in our cognitive lives? Here is a plausible speculation, based on the philosophical study of our epistemic concepts and on evidence (some of it anecdotal) concerning the role of epistemic practices in various cultural settings (including science, the law, medicine, etc.): Our epistemological concepts and practices are largely aimed at directing us to reason reliably about significant matters and believe significant truths. We hope this speculation seems obvious and trivial. That's because accepting it opens up many new lines of evidence that are relevant to epistemological theorizing. In particular, our epistemological theories must answer to psychological evidence concerning how people can become better, more reliable reasoners (e.g., Bishop & Trout 2005). Indeed, given the aim of epistemological concepts, norms and practices, we might find lots of ways to revise and improve our concepts, norms and practices so that they more effectively fulfil their appropriate roles.

Given the naturalistic perspective we're pressing, theories of epistemology must fit coherently with a wide range of interesting theories and evidence about how we get along in the world and how we might get along better in the world. These theories and evidence come from psychology, sociology, anthropology as well as philosophy. Many of these theories are in their infancy. Viewed in this light, the philosophical debate over the role of intuitions in supporting epistemological theories appears stilted and cramped. The real issue is not whether to trust our epistemic intuitions in building our epistemological theories. Of course we should. The real issue is: In building our epistemological theories, why stop with our intuitions?

References

Ahlstrom, Kristoffer (2008). *Constructive Analysis: A Study in Epistemological Methodology*. Acta Universitatis Gothoburgensis: Goteborg, Sweden.
Bealer, George (1992). "The incoherence of empiricism". *The Aristotelian Society* Supplementary Volume 66, pp. 99–138.
Bealer, George (1996). "A priori knowledge and the scope of philosophy". *Philosophical Studies* 81, pp. 121–142.

Bealer, George (1998). "Intuition and the autonomy of philosophy". In *Rethinking Intuition: The Psychology of Intuition and Its Role in Philosophical Inquiry*, ed. by M. D. a. W. Ramsey. Lanham: Rowman and Littlefield, pp. 201–239.

Bishop, Michael, and Trout, J. D. (2005). *Epistemology and the Psychology of Human Judgment*. New York: Oxford University Press.

Bishop, Michael & Trout, J.D. (2008) "Strategic Reliabilism: A Naturalistic Approach to Epistemology". *Philosophy Compass* 3/5, pp. 1049–1065. Blackwell Publishing (Web Services).

Bishop, Michael (2009). "Reflections on Cognitive and Epistemic Diversity: Does a Stich in Time Save Quine?" In *Stephen Stich and His Critics*, ed. by Dominic Murphy and Michael Bishop, Blackwell Press, pp. 113–136.

BonJour, Laurence (1998). *In Defense of Pure Reason: A Rationalist Account of A Priori Justification*. Cambridge: Cambridge University Press.

Claxton, Guy (1998). "Investigating human intuition: Knowing without knowing why". *The Psychologist* 11, pp. 217–220.

Cohen, L. Jonathan (1981). "Can human irrationality be experimentally demonstrated". *The Behavioral and Brain Sciences* 4, pp. 317–331.

DePaul, Michael (1998). "Why bother with reflective equilibrium". In *Rethinking Intuition: The Psychology of Intuition and Its Role in Philosophical Inquiry*, ed. by W. R. M. DePaul. Lanham: Rowman and Littlefield, pp. 293–309.

Devitt, Michael (2006). "Intuitions in linguistics". *British Journal for the Philosophy of Science* 57, pp. 481–513.

Feltz, Adam & Zarpentine, Chris (manuscript). "Do you know more when it matters less?"

Goldman, Alvin, and Pust, Joel (1998). "Philosophical theory and intuitional Evidence". In *Rethinking Intuition: The Psychology of Intuition and Its Role in Philosophical Inquiry*, ed. by W. R. M. DePaul. Lanham: Rowman and Littlefield, pp. 179–197.

Hales, Steven (2000). "The problem of intuition". *American Philosophical Quarterly* 37, 125–147.

Jackson, Frank (1998). *From Metaphysics to Ethics: A Defense of Conceptual Analysis*. New York: Oxford University Press.

Kaplan, Mark (1994). "Epistemology denatured". *Midwest Studies in Philosophy* 19, pp. 350–365.

Kornblith, Hilary (2002). *Knowledge and Its Place in Nature*. Oxford: Oxford University Press.

Kripke, Saul (1972). *Naming and Necessity*. Cambridge: Harvard University Press.

Lewis, David (1983). *Philosophical Papers*. Oxford: Oxford University Press.

Masuda, Takahiko, and Nisbett, Richard E. (2001). "Attending holistically versus analytically: Comparing the context sensitivity of Japanese and Americans". *Journal of Personality and Social Psychology* 81, pp. 992–934.

Nisbett, Richard E. (2003). *The Geography of Thought*. New York: Free Press.

Nisbett, Richard E., Peng, Kaiping, Choi, Incheol, and Norenzayan, Ara (2001). "Culture and systems of thought: Holistic vs. analytic cognition". *Psychological Review* 108, pp. 291–310.

Osbeck, Lisa (2001). "Direct apprehension and social construction: Revisiting the concept of intuition". *Journal of Theoretical and Philosophical Psychology* 21, pp. 118–131.

Putnam, Hilary (1975). "The meaning of 'meaning'". In *Mind, Language, and Reality: Philosophical Papers*, ed. by H. Putnam, Cambridge: Cambridge University Press, pp. 215–271.

Siegel, Harvey (1984). "Empirical psychology, naturalized epistemology, and first philosophy". *Philosophy of Science* 51, pp. 667–676.

Sosa, Ernest (2007). "Intuitions: Their nature and epistemic efficacy". *Grazer Philosophische Studien* 74, pp. 51–67.

Sosa, Ernest (2009). "A defense of the use of intuition in philosophy". In *Stephen Stich and His Critics*, ed. by Dominic Murphy and Michael Bishop, Blackwell Press, pp. 101–112.

Stanley, Jason (2005). *Knowledge and Practical Interests*. New York: Oxford University Press.

Stich, Steven (2009). "Reply to Bishop". In *Stephen Stich and His Critics*, ed. by Dominic Murphy and Michael Bishop, Blackwell Press.

Swain, Stacey, Alexander, Joshua, and Weinberg, Jonathan (2008). "The instability of philosophical intuitions: Running hot and cold on Truetemp". *Philosophy and Phenomenological Research* 76, pp. 138–155.

van Inwagen, Peter (1997). "Materialism and the psychological continuity account of personal identity". *Nous* 31, pp. 305–319.

Weatherson, Brian (2003). "What good are counterexamples?". *Philosophical Studies* 115, pp. 1–31.

Weinberg, Jonathan, Nichols, Shaun, and Stich, Steven (2001). "Normativity and epistemic intuitions". *Philosophical Topics* 29 (1&2), pp. 429–460.

8

Naturalism: Progress in Epistemology?

TIMO VUORIO

Introduction

The last decades of the 20th century witnessed such a triumph for the doctrine of philosophical naturalism that today the idea of philosophy as a pure, 'armchair' discipline, independent of the results of empirical science, is almost quaint. A mark of this change is the fact that the burden of proof has shifted to defenders of pure philosophy. However, despite the unquestionable merits and successes of the naturalist approach in philosophy, we seem to lack a clear conception of the nature of the achievement, at least in comparison with the definitions of the goals of the so-called 'pure' methods (those being, among other things, 'logical analysis', 'phenomenological reduction', 'the transcendental method'). For example, the problem arises: Does the naturalist solve the *same* problems as traditional 'philosophy', or is the subject matter of philosophical naturalism simply different?

In this paper I will try to clarify the nature of the naturalist approach – how it stands with respect to traditional epistemology. However, my approach will be to take a closer look at the nature of the foundationalist program, since I am convinced that a better understanding of the reasons for its failure should provide lessons for naturalist programs as well. My

Beyond Description: Naturalism and Normativity.
Marcin Miłkowski and Konrad Talmont-Kaminski (eds.).
Copyright © 2010 The Author.

leading point of reference is Richard Rorty. He is famous for declaring the death of traditional, 'pure' epistemology in his book *Philosophy and The Mirror of Nature* (1979). From one point of view, this seemed to be good news for the epistemological naturalist. Yet however tempting a conclusion this may be, it is not the correct one. Inspired by figures like Wilfrid Sellars and W.V.O. Quine, the collapse of classical foundationalism as understood by logical positivism, left a cultural void that, according to Rorty, should not be filled by *anything* at all. This idea is based on the insight that the philosophically interesting and pivotal feature of the 'theory of knowledge' is the issue of justification. And this concept in turn, in particular as expressed in Sellars' metaphor of the "space of reasons" – and very much utilized recently by Robert B. Brandom and John McDowell - is immune to the process of naturalization.

1 Rorty and Naturalism

Rorty is a difficult case. First of all, he is willing to label himself a naturalist – in his own sense of the term. Roughly speaking, for him 'naturalism' can be defined in negative terms: it stands in contrast to the desire to construct a pure philosophical program. In this sense Rorty is an extreme naturalist: there is no place for any 'a priori philosophy' that would go beyond the explanatory matrix of time and place. The naturalist believes that "all explanation is causal explanation of the actual, and that there is no such a thing as a non-causal condition of possibility" (Rorty 1991: 55). So everything can be described in causal terms, within vocabularies suited for different purposes, be it neurology or evolutionary biology or the story of Neanderthal Man through to the likes of Shakespeare and Dostoyevsky (see Rorty 1989: 15–6). This form of naturalism is consistent with the label 'historicism' (and according to Rorty, the latter is a special case of the former (Rorty 1991: 55n)), that is to say, a means of explaining events with reference to certain earlier events. More recently, Rorty described his pragmatism as a philosophical attempt to "...come to terms with Darwin..." (Rorty 1999: 66). In Rorty's view, the Darwinian lesson for us is that the history of human intelligence, culture and its accomplishments – such as science, including evolutionary biology – is basically a struggle for *life* in the sense of being a process of creating contingent vocabularies for coping with the environment. I think this sense of naturalism is quite close to what Huw Price (2004) calls 'subject naturalism' (in contrast to that of 'object naturalism'): we humans are natural creatures, and human knowledge is itself a natural phenomenon[1]. One of Rorty's provocative theses has been that of all cultural forces, philosophy has most of all tried to avoid learning the lessons of Darwin, in particular the Darwinian lessons pertinent to the philosophical enterprise. What Rorty implies is that 'reading Darwin' would have radical effects on the intellectual landscape and the basic questions posed by Plato, Descartes and Kant.[2]

But despite all this self-acclaimed naturalism[3], Rorty can be also viewed as anti-naturalist. Indeed there are thinkers among the naturalist circles who are not willing to call him a 'naturalist' at all[4]. For example, Brian Leiter (2004: 2) has recently divided English-speaking philosophers into two camps: the 'Wittgensteinian quietists' and the 'Quinean naturalists'. The difference is that, unlike the Wittgensteinians, the naturalists "...believe that the problems that have worried philosophers (about the nature of the mind, knowledge, action, reality, morality, and so on) are indeed real..," but the key for naturalist philosophers is "...either to adopt and emulate the methods of the successful sciences, or for philosophers to operate in tandem with the sciences, as their abstract and reflective branch" (ibid: 3).

However, I will not debate here the legitimate use of the term 'naturalism', and I happily stick to the definition given by Leiter (the non-Wittgensteinian definition mentioned in the previous paragraph) – the definition that Rorty surely does *not* identify himself with[5]. And, in fact, I have my own criteria by which to formulate the distinction between these two camps[6]. I will take the central claim of naturalism to be as fol-

---

[1] See Notes 5 and 6.
[2] In discussing the effect of Darwin's theory of evolution on the development of American pragmatism, Brandom (2001) talks of a 'Second Enlightenment', according to which Darwin's theory has replaced Newton's particle mechanics as a model of human knowledge.
[3] The most systematic presentation of Rorty as a consistent naturalist is Ramberg (2004).
[4] This usually happens when Rorty's historicism, antipositivism, and antiscientism – associated with such continental philosophical traditions as hermeneutics and postmodernism – are understood as forms of antinaturalism.
[5] Rorty discusses Leiter's – and also Price's – way of defining naturalism in his "Naturalism and Quietism", in Rorty (2007).
[6] The distinction between different kinds of naturalism can be drawn as Price (2004) does, for example: as that between 'subject naturalism' and 'object naturalism'. The first

lows: with the help of empirical sciences – by adopting and emulating their methods or using their results – we now have or shall have progress that was not possible before when 'pure methods' were used to address the traditional problems of epistemology. So, in this sense, the 'naturalist turn' means actual philosophical progress. I call antinaturalists those who do not share this optimism. I'll take Robert Brandom, John McDowell, and especially Rorty, as antinaturalists saying that there is a dilemma, even a fallacy, in the very heart of the naturalist program. Their conviction is based on the idea that *epistemic discourse is in principle irreducible to any sort of factual explanation*. Differently put: normative contexts are irreducible to descriptive ones. This idea can be found in a contemporary setting in a classic essay by Wilfrid Sellars, "Empiricism and Philosophy of Mind" (1956), but of course, its history can be traced back to Hume's law or to Kant's distinction between theoretical and practical uses of reason. According to those who call themselves 'left-wing Sellarsians' – in contrast to 'right-wing' Sellarsians (who take the doctrine of scientific realism as their point of departure) – the fatal error of all empiricism, including the external version of empiricism which flourishes in naturalism, is to confuse *justification* with *explanation*.

2 What is epistemology?

To make this charge sound at least plausible, it should be noted that it requires at least three further presuppositions, that are, of course, debatable. The first assumption is that the core of epistemology is the issue of justification; epistemology is a study that investigates 'claims to knowledge' in the sense of trying to establish criteria by which we may judge strong candidates from the unqualified, roughly speaking, to distinguish

---

makes use of the idea of a subject that uses tools (language, science, culture, etc.) that undergo evolutionary progress, the struggle for life and coping with the environment (the biologist's model). Object naturalism, on the other hand, is basically an ontological thesis, one taking nature as the object of research, as natural science – paradigmatically physics – does. The former approach is very close to the one Bjørn Ramberg (2004: 43) calls 'pragmatic naturalism'. Jonathan Knowles (2010) distinguishes what he calls 'non-scientific naturalism' from that of scientific naturalism, which he takes to be the only consistent naturalist position. I agree with him, and for that reason in this paper 'subject naturalists', 'pragmatic naturalists' and 'non-scientific naturalists' are treated as variants of antinaturalism, but unlike Knowles, I find this position plausible, even though I am not sure if 'naturalism' is the right word to describe it.

proper knowledge from 'mere opinion'. We wouldn't have any need of a theory of knowledge without the prior recognition of rival and contradicting beliefs. The second assumption made by the left-wing Sellarsians is that when we are talking about knowledge, we are talking about it in terms of beliefs – knowledge is only propositional. And the third presupposition is that justification is a normative notion. The aim of epistemology is to establish a theory of norms to guide the search for proper knowledge. Thereby, epistemology has a cultural task, for example, to support our respect for the results of science.

According to the story told by Rorty in *Philosophy and The Mirror of Nature*, the whole project of epistemology came about because of setting up the issue (that of justification) in terms of representational relations between mind and the world – this scenario being established in early modern philosophy by Descartes and Locke. The representational theory of mind that locates the knowing subject, the Cartesian Eye, behind the veil of ideas, inside an ontological realm of its own, was a response to the threat of epistemological scepticism. According to the premises of Descartes this threat was a serious challenge to the foundations of our culture. However, it was Kant who did the lion's share of the work, transforming the Cartesian problematic into a self-standing, academic discipline of its own. With his transcendental philosophy, Kant provided the methodological model for philosophy to stand as an independent discipline, and thereby justify its place among the other academic disciplines which were making such rapid progress. This task thereby amounted to the question of providing foundations for science – and two great movements of 20th Century philosophy, analytic philosophy and Husserl's phenomenology, can be seen as two different attempts to meet the Kantian demands for a scientific, independent discipline which could ground the other sciences. The result of this history was the rise of the program of 'pure philosophy' where the rigorous conditions of scientific philosophy were met: like any of the natural sciences or mathematics, philosophy had a research field of its own, a problematic of its own. And secure in the use of its own, autonomous methods, it was about to achieve results.

Perhaps this story of the rise and nature of pure philosophy is too sketchy, but most people calling themselves naturalists broadly accept it. That is to say, it provides a background against which to depict the rise of a naturalist challenge: the enemy is the 'purity' with its idea of the a priori, the quest for certainty, Cartesianism – all those traits that were heavily criticized in the latter part of the 20th century (and had been criticized earlier by pragmatists).

So, the demise of pure philosophy is taken to be the rise of the new naturalism. Now, let us ask if this 'naturalist turn' in epistemology represents progress thanks to new methodology, the methodology in question being borrowed from the natural sciences? The shift in methodology – using empirical rather than pure methods – marked *such* a radical break with the traditional approach that the effects of this change, I claim, are not clearly visible. The continuity of subject matter is not, at any rate, obvious. And there are a range of kinds of naturalism: that inspired by Quine and his idea of 'external empiricism' (Quine 1970) – that we should use the same 'empirical spirit' that informs the empirical sciences (Quine 1969: 26) – or what Price (2004) calls 'object naturalism', Rorty's (2007: 158) 'particle naturalism', Mark Bickhard's (2010) 'quantum naturalism' and Jonathan Knowles' (2010) 'scientific naturalism'. All these approaches carry the same message: to reject the methodological agenda prompted by the Cartesian epistemological sceptic, one that starts with the immediate and incorrigible knowledge of the contents of own mind, and methodologically doubts anything else. This is not to say that the problem of representation, and even the refutation of scepticism, cannot be taken up by naturalists. Yet the approach is different: instead of these sceptical and foundational issues being the starting point of the whole philosophical enterprise and their setting what is to be permissible methodology, these issues are now research objects to be scrutinized in the context of empirical science, constrained by its third-person observation.

But now we might ask, as I take it Rorty does indeed ask: "Is the shift in methodology not so large that we have reached the point where we have changed the very game we are playing – are we using hockey sticks to score in a game of football?" For example, what was once a starting point for philosophical theory, the most secure place to begin, now appears to be the fuzziest and most difficult issues of all: one's privileged access to one's own mental states. If there are no 'privileged representations' to start with, and to distinguish them from less accurate or more fallible representations, it is very hard to build up the whole story of representations and construct an epistemological program around that. One consequence of this is to doubt in the very idea of knowledge as a *representation* of the outer world at all. The latter conclusion is, of course, a famous thesis drawn and defended by Rorty in *Philosophy and the Mirror of Nature*. Obviously this is not something that many naturalists are willing to do – to skip the whole idea of representation. However, the fact that there has been a radical change in methodology is not a reason to doubt in the success of naturalism in epistemology. For me, the real problem lies elsewhere.

To illustrate this issue, I would now to like take up Quine's well-known proposal that epistemology should be taken as a "...chapter of psychology and hence of natural science." (Quine 1969: 82). I will try to clarify this thesis, both in a historical context, and thereby explain the radical difference between the approach of pure philosophy and naturalism.

3 Historical Case: Hume

Let us consider a great work from the past, David Hume's *A Treatise of Human Nature*. Let us tentatively ask: is it more a work of epistemology or of psychology? The first answer is the familiar and standard one that I don't think needs any clarification here – that the book is a classic of epistemological empiricism, famously addressing the problem of scepticism and so on. This reading has placed the work firmly in the canon of our philosophical tradition, and greatly influenced Kant and his epistemological followers.

But the latter, alternative reading is to see Hume's *Treatise* as a pioneering work in the field of the empirical science of psychology. Of course, this provocative reading is not much defended by scholars and may be vulnerable to a charge of anachronism. According to this reading (used for the sake of argument here), what Hume was doing, roughly speaking, was mimicking and applying to the human mind the same sort of principles and universal laws that Newton had already successfully applied to the physical world.[7] That Hume, like his forerunner Locke, troubled himself with the vocabulary of folk psychology might have ob-

---

[7] This suggestion can be seen as taking the 'naturalist interpretation' of Hume (made influential by Norman Kemp Smith, e.g. 2005) further, and thereby treating him not as a philosopher at all, but as a psychologist. Rorty occasionally suggests the possibility of this reading (see e.g. Rorty 1982: 144).

scured his point, but with hindsight we can see he had the right approach – he was a pioneer in a field that one day, with better tools and conceptual schemes at its disposal, would provide more results.

If we take this reading at face value, it has some metaphilosophical difficulties. It might be the case that Hume was not in fact very 'philosophical', or if he was, we might respond with something to the effect that, "Well, this great scientific soul, Hume, had his bad philosophical moments, but we forgive him, as we forgive Newton his moments of alchemy. They were also products of the times they lived in." Perhaps this would have been the standard reading were it not for Kant and his epistemological reading of Hume – that reading placing Hume alongside the biggest figures in the canon of philosophy. It is one of those ironies of history that Hume is the archetype of the empiricist, an epistemologist, foundationalist, the sceptic or naturalist of text books for scholars to argue about. But he wouldn't be there without the Kantian or epistemological reading – a reading that takes the philosophical problematic at face value, and abstracts from other irreducible aspects of his discourse. Simply put, Hume wouldn't be there in that canon, were it not for the program of pure philosophy.

Keeping this (admittedly unscholarly) discussion of Hume in mind, let us now compare what two consistent naturalists of today, Quine and Rorty, say about our historical thought-experiment. What Quine says in his 'Naturalized Epistemology' is that Hume was on the right track – the whole Kantian movement was a wrong turn, by taking the path of the pure philosophy as its leading theme. The actual place of epistemology, if there is indeed such a thing as epistemology, is the department of psychology, as Hume, despite his own atomism and foundationalism, was already indicating. But what makes Quine's own thesis unsound in regard to our historical example is its conceptual ambiguity: why imply that epistemology exists at all by continuing to use the word – Hume was not aware of epistemology, because the (alleged) discipline had yet to appear? Why not just say that *all there is* an empirical science called psychology.

In this sense Rorty is more consistent: he doesn't believe that there is any disciplinary space left for epistemology to occupy; the whole business and motivation for 'epistemology' disappeared with the collapse of pure philosophy – no cultural form will fill the gap left by it. According to this reading, Hume got the problem of scepticism, the existence of outer world, *right* – he didn't even try to answer the sceptic in a fair fight, but understood his challenge as being irrefutable by its own premises. Awareness of certain sentiments and impressions was good enough for him, and gave no real reason to further doubt the existence of their source. To a certain degree, this view is shared by both Quine and Rorty, who share Hume's perspective here without accepting any foundationalist implications. But Quine still thinks that the gap between impressions and our ideas about the external objects, that is, between sensory prompting and surface irradiations on the one hand and the description of the three-dimensional external world and its history on the other, as a model to make sense of how "...evidence relates to theory...," is still epistemologically fruitful. The positing of entities remains of interest when the research is relocated to the department of psychology, not just conducted by foundationalist philosophers (Quine 1969: 82–3). However, Rorty and Sellars do not think that any theoretical concept-entity that an empirical theorist would like to posit, nor the idea of 'pre-linguistic or 'pre-theoretical' awareness' are significant at all when it comes to the justification of beliefs.

4 Systematic point: Sellars

I shall try to clarify the issues surrounding theoretical concepts and (alleged) pre-linguistic awareness just touched on. It is these issues that seem to mark the difference between 'Wittgensteinian quietists' like Rorty and the constructive naturalist programs of today. The crucial point here is Sellars' insight concerning the nature of knowledge – the fact the knowledge ascriptions cannot be reduced to empirical descriptions. This thesis – encapsulated in the phrase 'the Myth of Given' – is usually taken to apply to only certain mentalist concepts, used in foundationalist programs, and that is surely the intended goal of the original critique. But if we look at the basis Sellars has for coining and using this phrase, we see that it expresses an insight into the very nature of epistemic discourse. Sellars famously writes:

> The essential point is that in characterizing an episode or a state as that of *knowing*, we are not giving an empirical description of that episode or state; we are placing it in the logical space of reasons,

of justifying, and being able to justify what one says (Sellars 1963: 169).

This passage has been quoted countless times by Rorty and other 'left-wing Sellarsians', and given the relative triviality of its content, no wonder its message has travelled further afield than was intended. But, anyway, this should not hide the fundamental moral. The point of Sellars's famous essay – as its very title implicitly says – is to show how the issues of epistemology are confused with psychological considerations of the human mind. To make this confusion is what Sellars calls "...an analogy to the naturalist fallacy in ethics..." (Sellars 1963: 131). Rorty (1979: 180n) takes this straightforwardly to mean the distinction between norms and descriptions. Lately the moral of Rorty's reading has been expressed by drawing a metaphorical distinction between 'the space of reasons' and 'the space of causes' (see McDowell 1994; Brandom 1994). I shall address the issue of whether the difference between naturalists and antinaturalists can be expressed precisely in terms of this distinction. What some think of as 'just another distinction' which needs to be surpassed, for others is a fundamental insight[8].

If we hold that that the distinction between norms and descriptions, the space of reasons and the space of causes, is the final word on the issue of justification, constructive epistemological programs have been dealt a fatal blow. For then it would be the case that the error of both foundationalist and naturalist programs is basically the same: both of them try to settle (what are in fact normative) issues by means of description, by reducing the normative into descriptive – regardless of the diversity of empirical descriptions given. If we take perception – as is usually the case – to be the right candidate for explaining the justification of one's beliefs concerning the outer world, one position will produce a story about one's introspective immediate perceptions, while another will look at the story of a third-person view of the surroundings or the causal link between the perceiver and the perceived. In any case, the founda-

---

[8] For example, one attempt to go beyond the distinction is to view it in terms of 'supervenience' (see e.g. Van Cleve 1999; cf. Lehrer 1999). However, according to the view presented here, the 'epistemological lesson' provided by Sellars takes precedence over any metaphysical issue as to how the epistemic and non-epistemic (natural) properties or terms are related to each other. This is to say that as far as the issue of justification goes, the metaphysics does not have a role there.

tionalist program is trying to show how justified beliefs derive their justification from more secure beliefs – ones which cannot be doubted. Now, what *naturalist programs* argue is that a relevant (reliable) causal origin is the basis for explaining the occurrence of a certain belief, and thereby could act as a ground for its justification. However, from the perspective of the distinction between norms and descriptions, the way a belief is acquired does not have to count as a sufficient reason to justify it in the course of a conversation – regardless of whether the story of its origin concerns immediate experience or the evolutionary history of that belief.

What Sellars argues is that a perception might be a fruitful source, and in some cases, a causal antecedent for judgements about the perceptive world. However, if these judgements are to be taken as justificatory moves made within epistemic discourse, this introduces us to a different game than that of describing the mere nature or origin of a perception. They are being taken to be moves made in a discussion, and this social practice is the place where justification occurs and, thereby, where knowledge is constituted. Even the ability to recognize and discriminate the content of one's own perceptions – whether introduced by way of first or a third person perspective – requires the use of concepts, and mastering those concepts means taking a part in a social practise, that is, acquiring language. So to claim that people have justified beliefs – or knowledge – is to say that they are able to justify their beliefs in the course of discussion, in a metaphorical 'space of reasons'. The error of the epistemological tradition was that it suggested that justification could be something else, to go *beyond* epistemic discourse – go beyond the "...game of giving and asking for reasons...", as Brandom (1994) says. Rorty interprets the idea with his thesis of 'epistemological behaviourism', according to which epistemic authority is to be explained by "what society lets us say" - so for Rorty it follows that all justification is thoroughly a social matter (Rorty 1979: 174). This thesis is a negative thesis in the sense that it aims to give up on attempts to discover any intrinsic features in justification. We might interpret this as saying that there is nothing peculiarly philosophical to say about justification. To say that justification is social, constituted by the very practices people are engaged in, is to say that only philosophy professors – being afraid of the epistemological sceptic – would ever have thought it could be anything else – a philosophical issue to be set out in terms of problems of representation.

However, in giving an account of these social habits and practices, could social epistemology help, as a variant of the naturalist approach? Instead of trying to rewrite the story of subject and object in (physical) naturalist terms, what about trying to describe how epistemic authority works in a social world? Apparently Rorty was not interested in giving *any* philosophical theory of justification – he was an 'epistemological nihilist' with respect to traditional epistemological problems – as Susan Haack (1990: 200) prefers to call his position. Rorty is consistent on this point – the idea of determining the rules or norms for any given discourse, and thereby explaining epistemic authority, would just violate the Sellarsian lesson once again, of trying to reduce the normative into the descriptive.

I have tried to argue, in the spirit of left-wing Sellarsians, that the normative character of epistemic discourse is irreducible to any naturalist explanation, and it is a fallacy to think otherwise. The fallacy of foundationalist epistemology was to think that there is such a framework, or a vocabulary, where the 'norms' could be grounded in a fundamental way. This sort of attempt, a search for certainty, was ill-guided. The mistake is easily repeated, but with a different agenda, in recent naturalism, for example, as an attempt to capture the 'nature' of normativity by providing a framework (of any kind) in terms of which to describe it.

The true merits of naturalism in its taking a lead in epistemology – if there is any progress to be gained – are similar to the benefits of the transition from a religious culture to a secular one. People simply stopped asking certain types of questions and started to ask new ones - perhaps more interesting ones. In this way, I hope I have indicated the real significance of 'the naturalist turn' in negative terms: naturalism is about what kind of questions we *should not* be associated with anymore.

References

Bickhard, Mark (2010). "Is Normativity Natural?". This volume.
Brandom, Robert (1994). *Making It Explicit*. London & Cambridge: Harvard University Press.
Brandom, Robert (2001). "When Philosophy Paints Its Blue on Grey: Irony and The Pragmatist Enlightenment", *Boundary* 2, pp. 1–28.

Haack, Susan (1990). "Recent Obituaries of Epistemology", *American Philosophical Quarterly* 27 (3), pp. 199–212.
Kemp Smith, Norman (2005). *The Philosophy of David Hume*. Palgrave Macmillan.
Knowles, Jonathan (2010). "Two Kinds of Non-scientific Naturalism". This volume.
Lehrer, Keith (1999). "Reply to Van Cleve". *Philosophy and Phenomenological Research*, LIX (4), pp. 1068–71.
Leiter, Brian (2004). "Introduction". In *Future For Philosophy,* ed. Brian Leiter. Oxford: Clarendon Press, pp. 1–24.
McDowell, John (1994). *Mind and World*. Cambridge: Harvard University Press.
Price, Huw (2004). "Naturalism without Representationalism". In *Naturalism in Question*, ed. by David Macarthur and Mario de Caro. Harvard University Press, pp. 71–88.
Quine, W.V.O. (1969). *Ontological Relativity and Other Essays*. New York and London: Columbia University Press.
Quine, W.V.O. (1970). "Philosophical Progress in Language Theory". *Metaphilosophy* 1 (1), pp. 2–19.
Ramberg, Bjørn (2004). "Naturalizing Idealizations: Pragmatism and the Interpretative Strategy". *Contemporary Pragmatism* I (2), pp. 1–63.
Rorty, Richard (1979). *Philosophy and The Mirror of Nature*. New York: Princeton University Press.
Rorty, Richard (1982). *Consequences of Pragmatism*. New York: Harvester Wheatsheaf.
Rorty, Richard (1989). *Contingency, Irony, and Solidarity*. Cambridge: Cambridge University Press.
Rorty, Richard (1991). *Essays on Heidegger and Others*. Cambridge: Cambridge University Press.
Rorty, Richard (1999). *Philosophy and the Social Hope*. Suffolk: Penguin Books.
Rorty, Richard (2007). *Philosophy as Cultural Politics*, Cambridge: Cambridge University Press.
Sellars, Wilfrid (1956). "Empiricism and Philosophy of Mind", in Sellars (1963), pp. 127–96.
Sellars, Wilfrid (1963). *Science, Perception, and Reality*. London: Routledge & Kegan Paul.
Van Cleve, James (1999). "Epistemic Supervenience Revisited". *Philosophy and Phenomenological Research* LIX (4), pp. 1049–1055.

9

Naturalism without Representationalism

HUW PRICE

1 The Relevance of Science to Philosophy

What is philosophical naturalism? Most fundamentally, presumably, it is the view that natural science constrains philosophy, in the following sense. The concerns of the two disciplines are not simply disjoint, and science takes the lead where the two overlap. At the very least, then, to be a philosophical naturalist is to believe that philosophy is not simply a different enterprise from science, and that philosophy properly defers to science, where the concerns of the two disciplines coincide.

Naturalism as spare as this is by no means platitudinous. However, most opposition to naturalism in contemporary philosophy is not opposition to naturalism in this basic sense, but to a more specific view of the relevance of science to philosophy. Similarly on the pronaturalistic side. What most self-styled naturalists have in mind is the more specific view. As a result, I think, both sides of the contemporary debate pay insufficient attention to a different kind of philosophical naturalism – a different view of the impact of science on philosophy. This different view is certainly not new – it has been with us at least since Hume – but nor is it prominent in many contemporary debates.

Beyond Description: Naturalism and Normativity.
Marcin Miłkowski and Konrad Talmont-Kaminski (eds.).
Reprinted by permission of the publisher from NATURALISM IN QUESTION, edited by Mario De Caro and David Macarthur, pp. 71–88, Cambridge, Mass.: Harvard University Press, Copyright © 2004 by the President and Fellows of Harvard College.

In this paper, I try to do something to remedy this deficit. I begin by making good the claim that the position commonly called naturalism is not a necessary corollary of naturalism in the basic sense outlined above. There are two very different ways of taking science to be relevant to philosophy. And contrary, perhaps, to first appearances, the major implications of these two views for philosophy arise from a common starting point. There is a single kind of core problem, to which the two kinds of naturalism recommend very different sorts of answer.

I'll argue that the less well-known view is more fundamental than its rival, in a sense to be explained; and that in calling attention to the difference between the two, we call attention to a deep structural difficulty for the latter. I'll thus be defending philosophical naturalism in what I take to be its more fundamental form, while criticising its popular contemporary manifestation.

Both the difficulty for the popular view and the conceptual priority of its unpopular rival turn on the foundational role of certain "semantic" or "representationalist" presuppositions in naturalism of the popular sort. This role is not well understood, in my view, but of considerable interest in its own right. (It deserves a more detailed examination than I can give it in this paper.) For present purposes, its importance lies in four facts. First, the presuppositions concerned are non-compulsory, and represent a crucial choice point for naturalism – reject them, and one thereby rejects naturalism of the popular variety. Second, the standpoint from which the choice is properly made is that of naturalism of the unpopular variety – this is the sense in which this kind of naturalism is conceptually prior to its more popular cousin. Third, the possibility of rejection of these suppositions is no mere idle threat; it is a corollary of some mainstream views in contemporary philosophy. And fourth, and potentially worst of all, the presuppositions concerned turn out to be doubtfully acceptable, by the standards of the kind of naturalism they themselves are supposed to underpin.

Concerning naturalism itself, then, my argument is something like this. To assess the prospects for philosophical naturalism, we need a clear sense of the task of philosophy, in the areas in which science might conceivably be relevant. Clarity about this matter reveals not only that the approach commonly called naturalism is not the only science-sensitive option for philosophy in these areas, but also that a different approach is the pre-eminent approach, in the various senses just outlined. As bad news for contemporary naturalists of the orthodox sort, this may sound like good news for contemporary non-naturalists. But I hope it will be clear that my intentions are much more even-handed. Many non-naturalists share the representationalist presuppositions of their naturalist opponents, and in questioning those presuppositions, we question both sides of the debate they underpin. So I oppose both naturalism and non-naturalism as popularly understood, and favour a different kind of naturalism – a naturalism without representationalism.

2 Two Kinds of Naturalism

The popular kind of naturalism – the view often called simply "naturalism" – exists in both ontological and epistemological keys. As an ontological doctrine, it is the view that in some important sense, all there is is the world studied by science. As an epistemological doctrine, it is the view that all genuine knowledge is scientific knowledge[1].

I'll call this view *object naturalism*. Though it is widely endorsed in contemporary philosophy, many of its supporters agree with some of its critics, in thinking that it leads to some profound difficulties. The view implies that in so far as philosophy is concerned with the nature of objects and properties of various kinds, its concern is with something in the natural world, or with nothing at all. For there simply is nothing else. Perhaps there are very different ways of talking about the world-as-studied-by-science – different "modes of presentation" of aspects the same natural reality. But the object of each kind of talk is an aspect of the world-as-studied-by-science, or else nothing at all. The difficulties stem from the fact that in many interesting cases it is hard to see what natural facts we could be talking about. Different people will offer different lists of these "hard problems" – common candidates include meaning, value, mathematical truth, causation and physical modality, and various aspects of mentality, for example – but it is almost an orthodoxy of contemporary philosophy, on both sides of the issue between naturalists and their opponents, that the list is non-empty.

More in a moment on these issues – *placement problems,* as I'll call them. Before we turn to such issues, I want to distinguish object natural-

---

[1] It is a nice issue whether there is any deep difference between these two versions of the view, but an issue I'll ignore for present purposes.

ism from a second view of the relevance of science to philosophy. According to this second view, philosophy needs to begin with what science tells us *about ourselves*. Science tells us that we humans are natural creatures, and if the claims and ambitions of philosophy conflict with this view, then philosophy needs to give way. This is naturalism in the sense of Hume, then, and arguably Nietzsche[2]. I'll call it *subject naturalism*.

What is the relationship between object naturalism and subject naturalism? At first sight, the latter may seem no more than an obvious corollary of the former. Contemporary "naturalists" – object naturalists, in my terms – would surely insist that they are also subject naturalists. After all, if all real entities are natural entities, we humans are surely natural entities. But in my view, the relationship between the two approaches is much more interesting than this. Subject naturalism comes first, in a very important sense.

I want to defend the following claim:

Priority Thesis: Subject naturalism is theoretically prior to object naturalism, because the latter depends on validation from a subject naturalist perspective.

What do "priority" and "validation" mean in this context? As I noted earlier, subject naturalism directs our attention to the issue of the scientific "respectability" of the claims and presuppositions of philosophy – in particular, their compatibility with the recognition that we humans are natural creatures. If the presuppositions of object naturalism turn out to be suspect, from this self-reflective scientific standpoint, then subject naturalism gives us reason to reject object naturalism. Subject naturalism thus comes first, and could conceivably "invalidate" object naturalism.

In my view, this threat to object naturalism is very real. I'll also defend this claim:

Invalidity Thesis: There are strong reasons for doubting whether object naturalism deserves to be "validated" – whether its presuppositions do survive subject naturalist scrutiny.

---

[2] Both attributions call for some qualification. As a parent of empiricism, for one thing, Hume certainly bears some responsibility for the object naturalist's conception of the nature of knowledge.

As advertised, my case for this claim will depend on the role of certain "semantic" or "representationalist" presuppositions in the foundations of object naturalism. The crucial role of such presuppositions is far from obvious, however. To make it visible, we need to examine the structure of the well-recognised hard cases for object naturalism, the cases I've termed placement problems.

3 The Placement Issue

If all reality is ultimately natural reality, how are we to "place" moral facts, mathematical facts, meaning facts, and so on? How are we to locate topics of these kinds within a naturalistic framework, thus conceived? In cases of this kind, we seemed to be faced with a choice between forcing the topic concerned into a category which for one reason or another seems ill-shaped to contain it, or regarding it as at best second-rate – not a genuine area of fact or knowledge.

One way to escape this dilemma is to reject the naturalism that produces it. If genuine knowledge need not be scientific knowledge, genuine facts not scientific facts, there is no need to try squeeze the problem cases into naturalistic clothing. Thus placement problems provide the motivation for much contemporary opposition to naturalism in philosophy. However, there are two very different ways to reject the kind of naturalism that gives rise to these problems. One way is to be non-naturalistic in the same ontological or epistemic keys – to be an object non-naturalist, so to speak. The other way is to be naturalistic in a different key – to reject *object* naturalism, in favour of a subject naturalist approach to the same theoretical problems.

At first sight, there seems to be no conceptual space for the latter view, at least in general, and at least if we want to avoid a universal subjectivism about all the hard cases. For subject naturalism rests on the fact that we humans are natural creatures, whereas the placement problems arise for topics which are at least not obviously human in nature. This is too quick, however. The possibility of a distinctive subject naturalist approach to the placement issues turns on the fact that, at least arguably, these problems *originate* as problems about human linguistic usage.

In fact, it turns out that there are two possible conceptions of the origins of placement problems – two conceptions of the "raw data" with which philosophy begins in such cases. On one conception, the problem begins with linguistic (or perhaps psychological) data; on the other, it begins with the objects themselves. These two conceptions are not often clearly distinguished, but the distinction turns out to be very important. As I'll explain, the priority of subject naturalism, and hence the vulnerability of object naturalism, rest on the thesis that the linguistic conception is the right one.

4 Where Do Placement Problems Begin?

On the face of it, a typical placement problem seeks to understand how some object, property or fact can be a *natural* object, property or fact. Ignoring for present purposes the distinction between objects, properties and facts, the issue is thus how some thing, X, can be a *natural* thing – the sort of thing revealed by science (at least in principle).

How do such issues arise in philosophy? On one possible view, the starting point is the object itself. We are simply acquainted with X, and hence – in the light of a commitment to object naturalism – come to wonder how this thing-with-which-we-are-acquainted could be the kind of thing studied by science. On the other possible view, the starting point lies in human linguistic practices, broadly construed. Roughly, we note that humans (ourselves or others) employ the term "X" in language, or the concept *X,* in thought. In the light of a commitment to object naturalism, again, we come to wonder how what these speakers are thereby talking or thinking *about* could be the kind of thing studied by science.

Let us call these two views of the origin of the placement problem the *material conception* and the *linguistic conception,* respectively. In favour of the material conception, it might be argued that the placement problem for X is a problem about the *thing* X, not a problem about the *term* "X". In other words, it is the problem as to how to locate X itself in the natural world, not the problem about how to locate the term "X".

In favour of the linguistic conception, on the other hand, note that some familiar moves in the philosophical debates to which placement problems give rise simply don't make sense, if we assume a material construal of the problem. Consider noncognitivism, which tries to avoid the placement problem by arguing that *talk* of Xs – i.e., standard *use* of the term "X" – does not have a referential or descriptive function. Here, the claim is that in the light of a correct understanding of the *language* concerned, there is no *material* problem. Of course, noncognitivism might be mistaken in any particular case, but if the material view of the placement problem is right, it is not so much wrong as completely wrong-headed – a view which simply starts in the wrong place. Perhaps noncognitivism is wrong-headed in this way. But the fact that this is not a common view reveals widespread implicit acceptance of a linguistic conception of the placement issue.

This appeal to philosophical practice isn't meant to be conclusive, of course. Instead, I'm going to proceed as follows. For the moment, I'll simply assume that the linguistic conception is correct, and explore its consequences for object naturalism. (I'll remind readers at several points that my conclusions depend on this assumption.) At the end of the paper I'll come back to the question whether the assumption is compulsory – whether object naturalism can evade my critical conclusions by adopting the material conception. I'll argue, albeit somewhat tentatively, that this is not a live option, and hence that my earlier conclusions cannot be sidestepped in this way.

5   The Semantic Ladder

If the linguistic conception is correct, then placement problems are initially problems about human linguistic behaviour (or perhaps about human thought). What turns such a concern into an issue about something else – about value, mathematical reality, causation, or whatever? The answer to this question was implicit above, when our attention shifted from the *term* to what it is *about*. The shift relies on what we may call the *representationalist* assumption. Roughly, this is the assumption that the *linguistic* items in question "stand for" or "represent" something *non-linguistic* (at least in general – let's leave aside for present purposes the special case in which the subject matter is also linguistic). This assumption grounds our shift in focus from the *term* "X" or *concept X*, to its assumed *object*, X.

At first sight, however, the required assumption may seem trivial. Isn't it a truism that "X" refers to X? Isn't this merely the referential analogue of the fact that "Snow is white" is true if and only if snow is white?

The familiarity of these principles masks a serious confusion, in my view. True, the move in question is in one sense a familiar semantic descent. A semantic relation – reference, if we are dealing with terms, or truth, if we are dealing with sentences – is providing the "ladder" that leads us from an issue about language to an issue about non-linguistic reality. But it is vital to see that in the present case, the move involves a real shift of theoretical focus, a real change of subject-matter. So this is a *genuine* logical descent, then, and not a mere reversal of Quine's deflationary "semantic ascent". Quine's semantic ascent never really leaves the ground. Quine himself puts it like this: "By calling the sentence ["Snow is white"] true, we call snow white. The truth predicate is a device of disquotation" (Quine 1970: 12). So Quine's deflationary semantic ladder never really takes us "up", whereas the present semantic ladder does need to take us "down".

If we begin with Quine's deflationary semantic notions, in other words, then talking about the *referent* of the term "X", or the *truth* of the sentence "X is F", is just another way of talking about the *object,* X. So if our original question was really about language, and we rephrase the issue in these semantic terms, we've simply changed the subject. We haven't traversed the semantic ladder, but simply taken up *a different issue,* talking in what Carnap called the formal mode about objects, rather than talking about language. On this deflationary view, then, object naturalism commits a fallacy of equivocation – a kind of mention–use fallacy, in fact[3] – on the way to its formulation of what it takes to be the central issue.

This point is easy to overlook, because we run up and down these semantic ladders so easily. But if Quine is right, the reason the climbs are so effortless is that the ladders lead us nowhere. In the present case, we do need to get somewhere. If we begin with a linguistic conception of the origins of the placement issues – if we see these issues as initially questions about linguistic usage – then it takes a genuine shift of theoretical focus to get us to an issue about the nature of non-linguistic objects. If the shift is to be mediated by semantic properties or relations of some kind, they must be substantial properties, in the following sense. They must be such that in ascribing such properties to a term or sentence we

---

[3] The fallacy turns on the fact that on the disquotational view, an expression of the form '"Snow is white" is true' contains a use masquerading as a mention. If it were a genuine mention, to call "Snow is white" true would not be "to call snow white", as Quine puts it. If we term this disquotational mention a *formal* mention, then formal mention is effective use, and the fallacy here involves a confusion between genuine and formal mention, or true mention and effective use.

are making some theoretical claim about the linguistic items concerned, rather than simply using those items to make a claim about something else.

True, these properties must also be such as to allow us to make the transition to an issue about objects. Our theoretical focus must be led from the issue about the terms and sentences to an issue about their assumed semantic objects or values. For the object naturalist's conception of the resulting program, moreover, it is vital that this transition track the disquotational schema. (How else could a concern with the use of the term "X" lead us to an interest in X itself?) My point is that unless there is more to the semantic notions than simply disquotation, the starting point is not genuinely linguistic, and so there is no transition at all. (One might argue that this is good news, because placement issue begins at the material level in any case. But for the moment we are assuming the linguistic conception of the origin of the problem, and this response is therefore excluded.)

Given a linguistic view of the placement issue, then, substantial, non-deflationary semantic notions turn out to play a critical theoretical role in the foundations of object naturalism. Without such notions, there can be no subsequent issue about the natural "place" of entities such as meanings, causes, values, and the like. Object naturalism thus rests on substantial theoretical assumptions about what we humans do with language – roughly, the assumption that substantial "word–world" semantic relations are a part of the best scientific account of our use of the relevant terms.

However, these assumptions lie in the domain of subject naturalism. Moreover, as the conceptual possibility of deflationism already illustrates, they are non-compulsory; more on this in a moment. Hence my Priority Thesis: given a linguistic conception of the origin of placement problems, subject naturalism is theoretically prior to object naturalism, and object naturalism depends on validation from a subject naturalist perspective.

6   Should Object Naturalism Be Validated? Three Reasons for Pessimism

It is one thing to establish a need, another to show that there are serious grounds for doubting whether that need can be met. However, it seems to me that there are actually strong grounds for doubting whether object naturalism can be satisfactorily validated, in the above sense. These grounds are of three kinds.

A. The Threat of Semantic Deflationism

I have already noted that deflationism about truth and reference blocks an object naturalist's access to the kind of semantic ladder needed to transform a theoretical question about terms into a question about their assumed objects. Given the attractions of deflationism, this is clearly grounds for concern, from an object naturalist's point of view.

It is worth emphasizing two further points. First, deflationism itself is clearly of a subject naturalist character. It offers a broadly scientific hypothesis about what linguistic creatures like us "do" with terms such as "true" and "refers" – what role these terms play in our linguistic lives. Of course, the use of these terms itself comprises the basis of one particularly interesting placement problem. So semantic deflationism *exemplifies* a subject naturalist approach to a particular placement problem – an approach that seeks to explain the *use* of the semantic terms in question – as well as providing a general obstacle to an object naturalist construal of placement problems at large.

Second, it is worth noting in passing how the distinctions in play at this point enable semantic deflationism to avoid Paul Boghossian's charge that any such view is inconsistent (Boghossian 1989, 1990). Boghossian argues that irrealism about semantic notions is incoherent, because irrealism involves, precisely, a *denial* that the term or sentence in question has semantic properties (a referent, or truth-conditions). If this characterisation of irrealism is indeed mandatory, then Boghossian seems right. Irrealism *presupposes* semantic notions, and hence the denial in question is incoherent in the case of the semantic terms themselves.

However, the point turns on the fact that so construed, irrealism relies on the kind of theoretical framework provided by the representational view of language. So long as a semantic deflationist simply *rejects* this theoretical framework, her position is not incoherent. Of course, one might insist that the resulting position no longer deserves to be called irrealism, but this is merely a terminological issue. The important point is that it is indisputably deflationary. A deflationist can consistently offer a use-explanatory account of semantic terms, while saying nothing of theoretical weight about whether these terms "refer", or "have truth-conditions".

The answer to Boghossian's challenge to deflationism thus depends on a distinction between *denying in one's theoretical voice* that these terms refer or have truth-conditions (which Boghossian is right to point out that a deflationist cannot do); and *being silent in one's theoretical voice* about whether these terms refer or have truth-conditions. A deflationist can, indeed must, do the latter, having couched her theoretical claims about the terms concerned in other terms entirely – and having insisted, *qua* deflationist, that the semantic notions do no interesting causal-explanatory work.

I'll return to Boghossian's argument in a moment, for in my view it does comprise a problem for my object naturalist opponents. For the moment, what matters is that it does not provide an obstacle to a well-formulated deflationism.

B. Stich's Problem

We have seen that in the light of a linguistic conception of the origins of the placement problem, semantic deflationism is incompatible with object naturalism. In so far as deflationism is an attractive view, in other words, the "validation" of object naturalism must remain in doubt.

But rejecting deflationism does not necessarily solve the object naturalist's problems. One way to appreciate this is to adapt the considerations discussed by Stephen Stich in Chapter 1 of *Deconstructing the Mind* (Stich 1996). In effect, Stich argues that even a non-deflationary scientific account of reference is unlikely to be determinate enough to do the work that object naturalism requires. Stich's own immediate concern is with eliminativism, and thus (in linguistic mode) with issues as to whether terms such as "belief" refer at all. He argues that so long as we retain a linguistic conception of our starting point in metaphysics, these questions inevitably become hostage to indeterminacies in our theory of reference. Evidently, if Stich is right then the problem is not confined to eliminativism. It affects the issue "What is belief?", for example, as much as it affects the issue "Are there any beliefs?" So realist as well as antirealist responses to the placement problem are equally afflicted.

Stich himself responds by disavowing the linguistic conception of the *explanandum*. We'll return below to the question as to whether this is really an option. For the moment, I simply help myself to Stich's useful discussion of these issues, in support of the following tentative conclusion. Even setting aside the threat of deflationism, it is very far from clear that a "scientific" account of semantic relations is going to provide what we need, in order to turn an interesting theoretical issue about *terms* ("causation", "belief", "good", and so on) into an interesting issue about *objects*.

C. Is Object Naturalism Coherent?

We have seen that if placement problems originate at the linguistic level, substantial semantic notions are needed to transform a question about linguistic usage into a question about non-linguistic objects. Object naturalism thus presupposes substantial semantic properties or relations of some kind. The two previous reasons for doubting whether object naturalism is entitled to this presupposition turned first, on the possibility of deflationism, which denies that semantic properties are load-bearing in the appropriate sense; and second, on the possibility that even a non-deflationary scientific account of reference might be too loosely constrained to be useful as the required semantic ladder.

Now to an even more serious difficulty. In view of the fact that object naturalism presupposes the semantic notions in this way, it is doubtful whether these notions themselves can consistently be investigated in an object naturalist spirit. Naturalism of this kind seems committed to the empirical contingency of semantic relations. For any given term or sentence, it must be to some extent an empirical matter whether, and if so to what, that term refers; whether, and if so where, it has a truthmaker. However, it seems impossible to make sense of this empirical attitude with respect to the semantic terms themselves.

Part of the difficulty turns on Boghossian's objection to semantic irrealism. In that context, the problem was that if semantic notions are presupposed in the issue between realists and irrealists – for example, if the realist/irrealist issue is taken to *be* that as to whether the terms and sentences of some domain refer, or have truth-conditions – then irrealism about these notions themselves is incoherent. Here, the problem is as follows. The object naturalist's project requires in general that irrealism be treated as live empirical possibility; but Boghossian's point shows that the object naturalist cannot adopt this attitude to the semantic terms themselves.

Boghossian takes the point to amount to a transcendental argument for a non-naturalist realism about semantic content. In my view, however, it is better seen as a pro-naturalist – pro-*subject* naturalist – point, in that it exposes what is inevitably a non-naturalistic presupposition in the leading contemporary conception of what is involved in taking science seriously in philosophy. Of course, the possibility of this interpretation depends on the fact that there is a consistent alternative naturalism, which walks away from the usual semantically-grounded conception of issue. (In a different way, it also depends on a linguistic conception of the starting point, a conception we are assuming at this point, and a conception to which Boghossian himself is obviously committed.)

It might seem implausible that there could be a problem here which is specific to object naturalism. After all, I have suggested that it is an empirical possibility that the subject naturalist standpoint might not yield the kind of substantial semantic relations required for object naturalism. Isn't this same possibility all that object naturalism needs to make sense of the possibility of irrealism about semantics, in its sense?

No. The empirical possibility we have discussed is not that subject naturalism will discover that there are no semantic properties of the right sort, but simply that it will find no reason to say that there are. This is the distinction I appealed to above, in explaining how deflationism escapes Boghossian's trap. The subject naturalist's basic task is to account for the use of various terms – among them, the semantic terms themselves – in the lives of natural creatures in a natural environment. The distinction just mentioned turns on the possibility that in completing this task, the subject naturalist might simply find no need for an explanatory category of semantic properties and relations. (At no point would she need to say that the term "refer" does or does not refer to anything, for example, except in the deflationary, non-theoretical sense.) Of course, from the object naturalist's perspective this looks like an investigation as to whether there are semantic properties, but the subject naturalist has no reason to construe it that way. Indeed, she has a very good reason *not* to construe it that way, if, as Boghossian has argued, that construal is simply incoherent.

The issue of the coherence of the object naturalist approach to the semantic terms is subtle and difficult, and I don't pretend to have made a case that the difficulty is conclusive. What I hope to have established is something weaker. A naturalist has neither need nor automatic entitlement to a substantial account of semantic relations between words or thoughts and the rest of the natural world – no automatic entitlement, because by naturalism's own lights, it is at best an empirical matter; and no need, because there are ways of being naturalist which don't depend on any such assumption. Nevertheless, the stronger thesis, the incoherency thesis, seems to me both fascinating and plausible, and I want briefly to mention another way of fleshing out the difficulty.

If there is a coherent object naturalist account of the semantic relations, then as we noted earlier, the object naturalist will want to say that the right account is not *a priori* – there is more than one coherent possibility, and the issue is in part an empirical matter. Let's consider just two of the coherent possibilities – two rival accounts of what reference is, for example. Account one says that reference is the natural relation R^*, account two that it is the natural relation R^{**}. Thus, apparently, we have two incompatible views as to what reference actually is.

But do we? Let's think a little more closely about what each of these views claims. The first account claims that the ordinary term "Reference" picks out, or refers to, the relation R^* – in other words, by its own lights, that

"Reference" stands in the relation R^* to the relation R^*.

The second account claims that the ordinary term "Reference" picks out, or refers to, the relation R^{**} – in other words, by its own lights, that

"Reference" stands in the relation R^{**} to the relation R^{**}.

Are these claims incompatible? Not at all. The term "Reference" might very well stand in these two different relations to two different things, even if we allow (as proponents of both views will want to insist), that in the case of each relation singly, no term could stand in that relation to both.

Again, the problem stems from the fact that the object naturalist is trying to ask a question which renders its own presuppositions fluid.

There is no fixed question, with a range of answers, but, so to speak, a different question for each answer. I leave as an exercise another puzzle of this kind. It is multiple choice:

> The option selected below is:
>
> A. Option A ☐
> B. Option B ☐
> C. Option C ☐
> D. None of the above ☐

The problem is not that there is no right answer, but that there are too many right answers[4]. Again, the upshot seems to be that in the light of the role of semantic notions in the object naturalist's conception of the task of philosophy, that task does not make sense with respect to the semantic terms themselves.

7 Does the Problem Lie with the Linguistic Conception of the *Explanandum?*

As I have emphasised, the above discussion has assumed a linguistic conception of the origins of the placement problem. Is this an optional assumption? Can a material conception get object naturalism off the hook? I close with two reasons for skepticism on this point.

A. The Cat Is Out of the Bag

It is clear that the linguistic conception of the placement issue is already in play. I noted earlier that to treat noncognitivism as an option in these debates is to commit oneself to a linguistic conception of the origin of the problem. The threat to object naturalism takes off from this point, noting that the representationalist assumption is non-compulsory – that there are other possible theoretical approaches to language, in which se-

---

[4] In a more detailed examination of these issues, it would be interesting to consider the connection between this kind of consideration (and indeed Boghossian's argument) and Putnam's "just more theory" concerns about the metaphysical use of a theory of reference (Putnam 1978, 1981).

mantic notions play no significant role. We have thus been offered the prospect of a (subject) naturalistic account of the relevant aspects of human talk and thought, from the perspective of which the material question ("What are Xs?") simply doesn't arise[5]. At this stage, the only way for object naturalists to regain control of the ball is to *defend* the representationalist assumption (a project fraught with difficulty, for the reasons noted above).

Couldn't an object naturalism challenge the current conception of the starting point? What is wrong with Stich's proposal, that we simply begin at the material level, and do metaphysics without semantic crutches? What is wrong with it, I think, is that it amounts to the proposal that we should simply *ignore* the possibility that philosophy might have something to learn from naturalistic – *subject* naturalistic – reflection on the things that we humans do with language. (If this seems controversial, note that it would be to ignore the possibility of noncognitivism.) So it is a radically anti-naturalistic move. For someone who takes science seriously, the only route to object naturalism is the hard one: to concede that the problem begins at the linguistic level, and to defend the representationalist view.

B. Semantic Notions Are Part of the Toolkit of Modern Metaphysics

The second consideration deserves a much more detailed discussion than I can give it here. Briefly, however, it seems that semantic notions such as reference and truth have become instruments in the investigative program of contemporary metaphysics. It has become common practice to identify one's objects of interest in semantic ways – as truth-makers or referents, say, or more generally as "realisers" of semantic roles.

However, the relevance of this observation about philosophical practice is far from straightforward. One of the difficulties is to decide which of the many uses of such semantic notions are "substantial" theoretical uses, and which can be regarded in a merely Quinean fashion – conven-

---

[5] That is to say, it doesn't arise as a question driven by naturalism. Such questions in many other contexts, of course – "What is justice?", "What is irony?", "What is choux pastry?", for example. If more or less commonplace questions of these kinds do give rise to puzzles of an object naturalist sort, the subject naturalist recommends a dose of linguistic therapy: Think carefully about what you are assuming about language, before you allow yourself to be convinced that there's a genuine ontological puzzle.

ient but theoretically uncommitted uses of deflationary semantic terms. For the reasons discussed earlier, the use of deflationary semantic notions in metaphysics is not incompatible with a material conception of the origins of the placement issue. But if more substantial notions are in play, then the linguistic domain seems to play a correspondingly more significant role. Claims about language come to play a role analogous to that of observational data in science, with the semantic relations supporting inferences to an unobserved reality. The enterprise thus becomes committed to a linguistic conception of its starting point.

There are many strands in this linguistic retooling of contemporary metaphysics – the Linguistic Return, as we might call it. One significant strand runs as follows, I think. In David Lewis's influential conception of theoretical identification in science (Lewis 1972, 1970), objects of interest are identified as occupiers of causal roles. If the theoretical term "X" is defined in this way, we know what to do to answer the question "What is X?" We experiment in the laboratory of the world, adjusting this, twiddling that, until we discover just what it is that does the causal job our theory assigns to X.

In the view of many, however, Lewis's program is fit not just for science but metaphysics as well[6]. Indeed, some who think this would reject the suggestion, implicit in my formulation, that metaphysics is something different from science. But there is one difference at least. In metaphysics, there is no guarantee that our objects of interest will be the kinds of things which have *causal* roles. We might be interested in numbers, or values, or indeed in causation itself, and for all of these things it is at least controversial whether they can be identified as the cause of this, the effect of that[7].

---

[6] See especially Jackson 1998.

[7] The claim that metaphysics extends beyond the causal realm is perhaps more controversial than I here allow. Someone who rejects it will be inclined to say that where causation stops, non-metaphysical modes of philosophy begin: formalism, perhaps, in the case of mathematics, noncognitivism in the case of value, and so on. For present purposes, it is enough to point out that such a view is thereby committed to a linguistic conception of the placement issue, for the latter views are linguistic in nature. However, it is worth noting that in a causally-grounded metaphysics of this kind, the notion of causation is likely to be problematic, in a way analogous to the semantic notions in a linguistically-grounded object naturalism. It will be a primitive notion, inaccessible to the program's own professed methods.

So in the global program, the place of causation must be taken by something else. What else could it be? It seems to me that there are two possibilities. One is that causal roles get replaced by semantic roles. In this case, the procedure for answering a question of the form "What is X?" is analogous to the one described above, except that the aim of our fiddling and twiddling – conceptual, now, rather than experimental – is to discover, say, to what the term "X" *refers,* or what *makes true* the claim that X is F.

That's the first possibility – that semantic relations play the same substantial role in the general program as causal relations played in the original program. If so, then the upshot is as we have seen. Language has become the starting point for metaphysics, and the resulting position is vulnerable in the ways described above.

The second possibility is that *nothing* specific replaces causation. It simply depends on the particular case, on what the Ramsey-Lewis method turns out to tell us about the X in question. Semantic terms may figure in the description of the task, but on this view they are no more than deflationary. We say, "X is the thing that makes this Ramsey-sentence true", but this is just a convenient way of doing what we could do by saying "X is the thing such that ..." and then going on to *use* the Ramsey-sentence in question.

I think that this second version does avoid essential use of nondeflationary semantic notions, and is hence compatible with a material conception of our starting point in metaphysics. The problem is that it thereby cuts itself off from any general argument for (object) naturalism, of a kind which would parallel Lewis's argument for physicalism about the mental (Lewis 1966). Lewis's argument relies on a premise to the effect that all causation is physical causation – the assumption of "the explanatory adequacy of physics", as Lewis puts it. Without such a premise, clearly, there is nothing to take us from the conclusion that a mental state M has a particular causal role to the conclusion that M is a physical state. The problem for the second of the two versions of the generalised Lewisean program is that without any single thing to play the role that causation plays in the restricted program, there can be no analogue of this crucial premise in support of a generalised argument for physicalism.

Thus it seems to me that object naturalists face a dilemma. If they appeal to substantial semantic relations, they have some prospect of an argument for naturalism, couched in terms of those relations – for example, an argument that all truths have natural truthmakers. In this case, however, they are implicitly committed to a linguistic conception of the "raw data" for these investigations, and face the problems identified earlier. If they don't appeal to substantial semantic relations, they avoid these difficulties, but lose the theoretical resources with which to formulate a general argument for naturalism, conceived on the object naturalist model.

Without the protection of such an argument, the difficult opponent is not someone who agrees to play the game in material mode but bats for non-naturalism, defending a primitive plurality of ontological realms. The difficult opponent is the naturalist who takes advantage of a non-representationalist theoretical perspective to avoid the material mode altogether. If such an opponent can explain why natural creatures in a natural environment come to *talk* in these plural ways – of "truth", "value", "meaning", "causation", and all the rest – what puzzle remains? What debt does philosophy now owe to science?

Summing up, it is doubtful whether an object naturalist can avoid a linguistic conception of the placement issue, and thereby escape the difficulties identified earlier. Some versions of object naturalism help themselves to the linguistic conception in any case, in order to put semantic relations to work in the service of metaphysics. In other cases, the inescapability of the linguistic conception turns on the fact that it is always available to the object naturalist's subject naturalist opponent, as the basis of an alternative view of the task of philosophy in these cases. The object naturalist's instinct is always to appeal to the representational character of language to bring the issue back to the material level; but this, as we have seen, is a recipe for grave discomfort.

8 Natural Plurality

Linguistically construed, the placement problem stems from a striking multiplicity in ordinary language, a puzzling plurality of topics of talk. Given a naturalistic conception of speakers, the addition of a representationalist conception of speech makes the object naturalist's ontological interpretation of the placement problem almost irresistible. Term by term, sentence by sentence, topic by topic, the representationalist's semantic ladder leads us from language to the world, from words to their worldly objects. Somehow, the resulting multiplicity of kinds of entities – values, modalities, meanings, and the rest – needs to be accommodated within the natural realm. To what else, after all, could natural speakers be related by natural semantic relations?

Without a representationalist conception of the talk, however, the puzzle takes a very different form. It remains in the linguistic realm, a puzzle about a plurality of *ways of talking,* of forms of human linguistic behaviour. The challenge is now simply to explain in naturalistic terms how creatures like us come to talk in these various ways. This is a matter of explaining what role the different language games play in our lives – what differences there are between the functions of talk of value and the functions of talk of electrons, for example[8]. This certainly requires plurality in the world, but of a familiar kind, in a familiar place. Nobody expects human behaviour to be anything other than highly complex. Without representationalism, the joints between topics remain joints between kinds of behaviour, and don't need to be mirrored in ontology of any other kind.

For present purposes, what matters is on the one hand, that this is a recognisably naturalistic project; and on the other, that it is a very different project from that of most contemporary philosophical naturalists. I have argued that the popular view (object naturalism) is in trouble by its own lights, in virtue of its semantic presuppositions. The availability of the subject naturalist alternative makes clear that the problems of object naturalism are not problems for naturalism *per se* – not a challenge to the view that in some areas, philosophy properly defers to science.

We began with the relevance of science to philosophy. Let's finish with the relevance of science to science itself. Object naturalism gives science not just centre-stage but the whole stage, taking scientific knowledge to be the only knowledge there is (at least in some sense). Subject naturalism suggests that science might properly take a more modest view of its own importance. It imagines a scientific discovery that science is

---

[8] This kind of linguistic pluralism is very Wittgensteinian in spirit, of course. One of Wittgenstein's main themes in the early sections of the *Investigations* is that philosophy misses important distinctions about the uses of language, distinctions which are hidden from us by 'the uniform appearances of words.' (§11) The view proposed here may be too naturalistic for some contemporary Wittgensteinians, but would Wittgenstein himself have objected to it? (He might have thought that it is science, not philosophy, but that's a different matter.)

not all there is – that science is just one thing among many[9] that we do with "representational" discourse. If so, then the semantic presuppositions of object naturalism are bad science, a legacy of an insufficiently naturalistic philosophy. The story then has the following satisfying moral. If we do science better in philosophy, we'll be less inclined to think that science is all there is to do.

References

Boghossian, Paul (1989). "The Rule-Following Considerations", *Mind* 98, pp. 507–549.

Boghossian, Paul (1990). "The Status of Content", *Philosophical Review* 99, pp. 157–184.

Jackson, Frank (1998). *From Metaphysics to Ethics,* Oxford: Clarendon Press.

Lewis, David (1972). "Psychophysical and Theoretical Identifications", *Australasian Journal of Philosophy* 50, pp. 249–58.

Lewis, David (1970). "How to Define Theoretical Terms", *Journal of Philosophy* 67, pp. 427–46.

Lewis, David (1966). "An Argument for the Identity Theory", *Journal of Philosophy* 63, pp. 17–25.

Price, Huw (1997). "Naturalism and the Fate of the M-worlds", *Proceedings of the Aristotelian Society, Supplementary Volume,* LXXI, pp. 247–267.

Price, Huw (1992). "Metaphysical Pluralism", *Journal of Philosophy* 89, pp. 387–409.

Putnam, Hilary (1978). *Meaning and the Moral Sciences*, Boston.

Putnam, Hilary (1981). *Reason, Truth and History*, New York, Cambridge University Press.

Quine, W.V. (1970). *Philosophy of Logic,* Prentice-Hall.

Stich, Steven (1996). *Deconstructing the Mind*, New York: Oxford University Press.

---

[9] Or more likely, I think, "several things among many", in the sense that scientific language itself is not monofunctional. I think that causal and modal talk has distinct functions in this sense, and, while essential to any interesting science, is not the whole of it. If so, this is enough to show that there is functional plurality within scientific language, as well as outside it. For more on this theme, and the program here envisaged, see Price 1997 and Price 1992.

10

Two Kinds of Nonscientific Naturalism

JONATHAN KNOWLES

Naturalism is a widespread position in contemporary analytical philosophy. It is not however a very specific one, embracing rather a range of different views each of which stress ideas and commitments that others calling themselves naturalists disavow. I take it that any naturalism worthy of the name must, at a minimum, subscribe to the idea that philosophy and science are not thoroughly disjoint enterprises, and that philosophy must defer to what we learn from science where there is, uncontroversially, overlap (such as in the question of the Euclidean versus non-Euclidean nature of space). (Cf. Price 2004: 71.) However whilst many naturalists would see in this track record grounds for a scientific metaphysics and epistemology, others are more chary. They urge us to ask what a reasonable understanding of the achievements of science actually commits us to by way of a general philosophy. Science has, it seems reasonable to say, placed us human beings firmly in the realm of space and time like all other organisms on earth. At the same time, we evince a range of properties and engage in a wealth of activities that seem very difficult to understand through science. We think, we act, we pass moral judgements, we appreciate music and visual art, we seek enlightenment through the study of other cultures and epochs, we carry out science (!). In relation to all of these things we discuss with each other using semantically structured language. There is nothing obviously unnatural about any of all this, seen as the activities of a particular, albeit rather remark-

Beyond Description: Naturalism and Normativity.
Marcin Miłkowski and Konrad Talmont-Kaminski (eds.).
Copyright © 2010 The Author.

able kind of biological entity; but nor is there obviously a way or even a need for understanding its significance and status in scientific terms – through a kind of experimental or theoretical enquiry. Relatedly, there is no obvious route to or need for understanding the objects of the everyday, common sense world in scientific terms – from hats and tables to unfinished symphonies. Common sense and/or broadly humanistic enquiry will suffice.

I dub views that stress this line of thought *nonscientific naturalism* (henceforth *NSN*), to be contrasted with the more usual *scientific* naturalism (henceforth *SN*). Both are naturalistic in that they disavow the existence of supernaturalistic, transcendent and/or immaterial entities and forces, thereby paying due respect to what science has taught us about the universe and our place within it. Both also accept the relevance of science and scientific understanding to at least some traditional philosophical problems. Where they differ is over acceptance of the following: that scientific knowledge is (or in some nontrivial sense could become) exhaustive of what there is to be known; that all facts are ultimately scientific ones; and/or that scientific knowledge and/or facts have a fundamental priority over other forms of knowledge/facts. Anything worthy of the name 'scientific naturalism' would at a minimum have to hold to the last of these disjuncts, whereas NSN would reject all of them. NSN as it exists in the contemporary literature is to a large extent the upshot of recent critical attention towards what can seem to be, and its supporters certainly present as, this highly committal idea of SN. For nonscientific naturalists (*NSNists,* who oppose *SNists*), it is implausible to hold that all or even the most fundamental facts are scientific. At the same time, rejecting this 'dogma' need in no way threaten the naturalistic credentials of one's view as far as a commitment to the wholly physical and biological constitution of human beings and their surroundings goes.

The critical attention towards SN such considerations have occasioned is very much to be welcomed. The idea that science can answer all our questions, or what this even means, has certainly been subject to too little scrutiny both in the popular press and in more standard naturalistic (often reductionistic) projects within philosophy and cognitive science. My view nevertheless is that NSN's resistance to the hegemony of science is ultimately unmotivated. The most fundamental reason for this is NSN's background allegiance to science, which, as I shall seek to show, renders it dialectically inferior to SN. This does not mean that I see SN as thereby vindicated. It may turn out, in the end, that there is no vindication of any overall metaphysical or philosophical position to be had (something I strongly suspect is the case). However, since this is a view I seem to share with many so-called nonscientific naturalists, it is interesting to see how their stand against science breaks down – from the inside, so to speak.

I have presented arguments against NSN previously (Knowles 2006), a paper which in turn presupposes arguments in Knowles (2002). In the sequel I partly build on but also seek to clarify and extend these arguments. Further, I distinguish between *two kinds* of nonscientific naturalism, the second of which requires a substantially different dialectical tack to defeat (there are of course subdivisions within these two broad categories but in the space available here I will have to paint with a broad brush). The first kind of nonscientific naturalism, which I dub *expansionist* NSN, is exemplified paradigmatically by John McDowell with his notions of *second nature* and *liberal naturalism* (cf. especially McDowell 1994, 1998, 2004). Similar ideas are defended by a number of McDowell's (originally) Oxford-based colleagues, such as Jennifer Hornsby with her notion of *naïve naturalism* (1997, 2009), David Wiggins (cf. e.g. 1987) and Greg McCulloch (cf. e.g. 2002). These views herald from the philosophy of mind and metaphysics, but the overarching idea is also evinced in recent epistemological work, such as that of the Susan Haack (1993) and Richard Feldman (2001 – a paper entitled 'We are all naturalists now'…), as well as informing the general tenor of many other contemporary critiques of SN (cf. e.g. the papers in de Caro & Macarthur 2004). Expansionist nonscientific naturalism seeks, as the name suggests, to *expand* or *liberalise* the notion of the natural to encompass *as such* realms of being – knowledge, rationality, morality and so on – that are often taken as problematic in unreduced form on a more standard construal of what is natural.

The second kind of nonscientific naturalism I dub *pragmatic* nonscientific naturalism, and can be seen as represented by thinkers such Richard Rorty (e.g. 1998), Huw Price (2004, 2007) and (perhaps) Hilary Putnam (1981, 2004). Pragmatic nonscientific naturalism seeks to deflate the significance of what is usually regarded as the bench-mark of the real, i.e. science, regarding this as just one amongst many competing vocabularies for coping in and with everyday life. At the same time, many of these thinkers also stress the naturalistic credentials of their position – Rorty, for example, in that he explicitly avows that we are biological beings, which explains why our needs in relation to the world are fundamentally pragmatic. In saying this Rorty echoes Quine's talk of the 'reciprocal containment' of science and epistemology (Quine 1969: 83). However, for Rorty, precisely this aspect of our nature – along with the many negative upshots of reductionist projects within the standard naturalistic camp – also renders the search for an absolute bench-mark of the true and the real forlorn. Rejecting this involves *a fortiori* rejecting the idea that science in particular 'is the measure of all things' (Sellars 1963: 1), that it 'limn[s] the true and ultimate structure of reality' (Quine 1960: 221).

In the following I seek to counter these two movements. Part 1 lays out my case against expansionist NSN (henceforth NSN *simpliciter*, since it is arguably the more standard and straightforward such position), part 2 against pragmatist NSN (henceforth NSN_P). In the latter I focus on Price's work, which to my knowledge presents the most honed version of NSN_P in the literature, as well as being pitched at a level of sufficient generality to be representative of a broad range of pragmatist positions[1].

Before getting under way, I should note that I do not exclude that there might be significantly different forms of NSN than those I consider in this paper. At the same time, the two I critique do it seems clear together constitute a large and significant faction within contemporary philosophy, evincing at root the same kind of general scepticism towards the hegemony of science.

1 Expansionist Nonscientific Naturalism

At the most general level, there are basically two kinds of argument that are deployed against SN by NSNists (i.e. expansionist NSNists). The first is most characteristically associated with McDowell and his followers. McDowell argues that it is mere prejudice to associate the natural with the 'realm of natural law', as he puts it, and that we should instead widen our conception of the natural to encompass phenomena associated with our peculiar kind of mindedness as such. McDowell builds on the well-known ideas of Sellars and Davidson that mental phenomena belong to 'the logical space of reasons' (Sellars 1963), and hence are in principle irreducible to physical events (Davidson 1980). But for McDowell this incommensurability is not just a matter of modes of understanding; we are in possession of a substantive, albeit 'second' nature which involves

---

[1] Or so it strikes me. Price relates his own brand of pragmatism to Rorty's in Price (2008). Rorty endorses Price's naturalism in Rorty (2007).

sensitivity to reasons or, to use the Kantian term, 'spontaneity' (rather than mere 'receptivity', as is the case in animals). To think saying this involves a lapse into some kind of supernatural dualism betrays a tendentious and nonobligatory conception of the natural.

The second argument is less metaphysically committing, though it can be seen as aiming at much the same conclusion[2]. In effect what it contends is that SN is, even from its own naturalistic perspective, either implausible (or at least unjustified) or vacuous. For example, a common variety of SN is physicalism: the view that all properties and objects are fundamentally physical in nature and that everything else we want to countenance as real has to in some way be discerned within the physicalistic universe (cf. Jackson 1998). However, it seems unlikely that science itself furnishes us with anything like sufficient reason to believe in anything beyond a very weak and unthreatening kind of supervenience physicalism, and certainly not the reductionist variety just outlined (see e.g. Dupré 1993; Kornblith 1994.) Physicalism (in this sense) does not seem to be acceptable by naturalists' own lights and hence should be discarded, whilst weaker varieties hardly enunciate a constraint on any explanatory undertaking or set of concepts.

A similar argument can be run with respect to method (or explanation, which I treat under the same heading for simplicity here). A methodological SNist is one who imposes the method of science on all genuinely cognitive enquiry[3]. The problem is, again, that no usefully precise such method, peculiar to all and only science, seems to exist (cf. Knowles 2003: ch. 4.5, Chalmers 1999: ch. 11 for overviews of the relevant arguments and literature). However, without either a metaphysical or meth-

---

[2] The following argument seems to be essentially that used by Haack (1993) and Feldman (2001). It is also at work in several papers from a recent volume largely sympathetic to NSN (of both varieties) edited by de Caro and Macarthur (2004); cf. e.g. Putnam (2004), Dupré (2004), Stroud (2004).

[3] Such a naturalist is not necessarily opposed to peculiarly philosophical or metaphysical enquiry, but will nevertheless insist that such enquiry employs basically the same methods as those of science (e.g. inference to the best explanation). Philosophers who espouse conceptual analysis as the method of philosophy (e.g. Jackson 1998) are of course not methodological SNists. Often these people are physicalists, but those who are not might it seems still consider themselves scientific naturalists (e.g. David Chalmers). My concern here is with naturalists who essentially balk at the idea of science as the mark of the natural, rather than those might who espouse the idea of a special philosophical method in addition to that of science.

odological basis of some relatively committing kind, it seems SN has very little bite and cannot require us to understand e.g. moral or mental talk in 'naturalistically kosher' terms.

The conclusion NSNists draw from these considerations is very close to McDowell's: that what generally goes under the name of (natural) science – physics, chemistry, biology, branches of psychology and social science – does not in fact have any necessarily privileged role to play in delimiting what exists and what can be known. History, literary criticism and other humanities and nonnatural social sciences, as well as everyday common sense explanatory practices, have just as much right to serious consideration as natural science – without their being anything 'supernatural' about their subject matter.

What are we to make of these two (admittedly abstract but nevertheless wide-spread) arguments? Note to begin with that they are in tension with one another. McDowell's argument presupposes a certain general conception of what science is, whereas the second presupposes that such a conception essentially does not exist. If we accept, as I think we should, the latter disjunct, then McDowell's argument is decisively weakened insofar as he cannot appeal to a neatly circumscribed 'realm of natural law' with which to contrast the 'logical space of reasons' (or 'the realm of spontaneity'). Of course, he can, and does, also appeal to what he thinks is distinctive about the latter realm – that it involves explanations of a special, normative sort. We shall return to this idea below.

What of the second argument? According to this, there is simply nothing within extant natural science that 'puts pressure', as it were, on traditionally nonscientific endeavours, such as (say) history and common sense psychology. However, though there may be no principled, *a priori* pressure, it doesn't of course follow that there is no *a posteriori* pressure. Below, I will seek to show that what we have learned within contemporary cognitive science suggests a way of understanding the above endeavours in a way that does render them in a significant way subordinate to natural scientific knowledge.

Before doing that however it is vitally important to be clear about the dialectical situation here. We must not forget that NSNists defer to science when it comes to physics, chemistry, biology and at least many parts of scientific psychology. At the same time, they want to draw a line somewhere between these disciplines/sub-disciplines and full blown scientism – a line which demarcates what, for simplicity's sake, can be broadly characterised as questions about 'the mind', properly so-called.

However, on the face of it such a demarcation can seem very arbitrary. Here is Hornsby, considering how we should rule out nonphysical, supernatural entities from our ontology:

> '[T]he easy answer is that, a hundred and fifty years on from Darwin, it is a reasonable view that nothing more than natural processes in a world of regular material stuff has ensured the presence here of beings with everyday psychological properties. The alternative can nowadays seem simply unmotivated. [...] I suggest that in the twenty-first century, rather little needs to be said in favour of a rather unexciting sort of physicalism.' (Hornsby 2008: 55)

There is something disingenuous about this statement viewed as a defence of a weak kind of physicalism amenable to NSN (how Hornsby intends it). Nothing very much needs to be said in favour of the general scientific world-view for us to be entitled to it, we are told. But one shouldn't need reminding that this is precisely an issue of hot controversy across the globe even today, and amongst inhabitants of our own 'secular' societies. Now it may be that there is no ultimately satisfying defence of science *vis à vis* alternative 'world-views' – that little here needs or indeed can in the final analysis 'be said'. Nevertheless, given we do pin our hopes to science when it comes to physics, chemistry and biology, why the chariness when it comes to psychology and cognitive science? Why are the latter, but not the former seen as up for grabs: as intellectual pursuits one might reasonably demur at (at least to some significant extent)? The rhetoric of NSN is replete with examples of this kind of strategy, whereby science and its basic ontological picture is presented as uncontroversial but also – and, it is often suggested, *in virtue of that very fact* – impotent in relation to answering questions of a more traditionally philosophical nature. But that misrepresents the dialectical situation: science in general is an achievement that we have to stand up for. Of course, more specific reasons for scepticism towards a full-blown cognitive science may exist. The present point is that the natural scientific world-view doesn't 'come for free', and that therefore all naturalists must start with a predisposition towards its general reliability and explanatory potential.

Another preliminary point needs to be registered before we continue. This is that being a SNist need not involve holding that everything can be explained scientifically or that everything there is to be known can be known scientifically. There may for reasons famously averred by Chomsky (e.g. 1988) and Fodor (1983) be limits on what we can understand scientifically (candidates include consciousness, language-use and scientific reasoning). However, these limits would not enunciate an alternative *nonscientific* kind of understanding that we are in possession of. NSNists need to establish more than that there are limits to what science can explain. Moreover, they need, as we have seen, to do this consonant with accepting and indeed promoting the achievements of science generally.

Let us now return to the relationship between scientific psychology, on the one hand, and humanistic understanding and common sense psychology on the other. The latter 'disciplines' are often seen as nonscientific insofar as they employ a certain mode of understanding or method allegedly peculiar to the human sciences: the method of *Verstehen* ('understanding'), as it is often termed (due to its prevalence in hermeneutically-inspired German philosophy). Exactly what *Verstehen* is has perhaps never been laid out wholly explicitly, but that something like it exists, in some form or other, is not something I want to question. It seems clear that we humans do deploy an intuitive form of understanding for predicting and explaining our fellows, revolving around the concepts of action, belief, meaning and (something like) desire that constrain one another holistically. In employing this understanding, we do not invoke, at least explicitly, laws or principles of explanation. It also seems reasonable to think that the study of history (etc.) extend this kind of everyday understanding to more *recherché* topics of study, such as temporally or spatially remote cultures, texts etc. However, the question for us is whether this intuitive 'hermeneutical' framework cannot be accommodated and accounted for within whatever uncontroversially natural scientific approaches to the mind are on offer today, or at least which it is reasonable to think will be on offer in the near future. If it can, though *Verstehen* could perhaps still be regarded as a special method for the human sciences, its viability as such would be dependent on facts revealed by natural science, and in that sense the latter will presumably have to be viewed as providing our most fundamental conception of human nature – from within which the activity of *Verstehen* is itself an object for scientific explanation.

To be a little bit more concrete, the idea within contemporary cognitive science is that we possess various intuitive, perhaps even in a sense innate 'modules' of understanding – naive (or *folk*) psychology, physics, biology and so on – whose use in unrefined form is a cognitively useful and significant activity for our organism[4]. We have a need to and therefore have evolved or developed a capacity for understanding other agents (*inter alia*) without engaging in science (a capacity that history and the rest simply extend to more recherché matters). Exactly what form such a module might take, what the capacity consists in (knowledge or off-line processing) and so on are issues of hot controversy within contemporary cognitive science. Nevertheless, the basic idea of folk psychological explanation and prediction being something we have a naturally explicable capacity for is not controversial.

The availability of this kind of explanation, coupled with NSN's general commitment to science, surely puts a deep dent in the idea of NSN insofar as this denies all fundamental knowledge is scientific. Even so, it does not challenge the autonomy of *Verstehen* per se. For some NSNists, *Verstehen* and science answer to fundamentally disparate explanatory projects. Here is a famous passage from McDowell:

> [P]ropositional attitudes have their proper home in explanations of a special sort: explanations in which things are made intelligible by being revealed to be, or to approximate to being, as they rationally ought to be. This is to be contrasted with a style of explanation in which one makes things intelligible by representing their coming into being as a particular instance of how things generally tend to happen. (McDowell 1985: 389)

According to this contrast, *Verstehen* is not (merely) an intuitive explanatory framework or a kind of proto-science; the insight it provides is of a fundamentally different kind from that of science.

However, this line faces many and I think decisive problems, as several authors have remarked (e.g. Henderson 1993, Knowles 2002). Unfortunately the issue is too large to go into in detail here, but two main points that can be registered. The first is that the position again involves a specific conception of scientific explanation that we saw above reason to be suspicious of. Science is not *a priori* restricted to causal-cum-law like explanations, *a fortiori* nor is cognitive science. Indeed some recent work aims precisely to take account of *Verstehen*'s explanatory features – often described as characterizing a so-called 'personal' level of explanation – within a nonreductive but fully scientific framework (see Hurley 1998). The second problem is that I think, in the final analysis, we can make nothing of the idea of primitively and irreducibly normative explanation,

---

[4] In relation to folk psychology, see e.g. Wellman (1990). For a more general overview of the area, see e.g. Carruthers (2006): ch. 3.

that is, of explanations that adumbrate what *ought* to be the case as explanatory – in and of itself – of things that *are* the case, such as someone's having done or thought something. This is plausibly the only idea that might really distinguish what people have called '*Verstehen*' from a more general notion of explanation employed in science or in relation to everyday events (like windows smashing); but it is not, unfortunately for this way of defending NSN, one that it seems we can give a coherent sense to (cf. Knowles 2002).

A possible response to this, discernible in the work of Hornsby (1997), is that what distinguishes folk psychology from science is something that distinguishes explanation at the level of ordinary, common sense objects and events *generally* – persons, actions, windows smashing, cricket balls etc. – from that of science. Put bluntly, science is concerned to show how very small events can generate ordinary sized ones, but there is no reason to think common sense, macro-level explanations, of either physical or psychological events, will be reducible to such microprocesses. But this line too faces insuperable problems. Firstly, there is a much greater acceptance that science acts as a corrective to common sense in the case of physics than in psychology. This undermines the parallel Hornsby builds on: whilst it is reasonable to think (as things stand) that at least one perfectly good explanation of why John threw the cricket ball was that he wanted to hit the stumps, it is not nearly so clear that the breaking of the window is as well explained by saying merely that the cricket ball hit it. Secondly, the argument, even if accepted, does not in any case undermine SN, at least as we have been developing it, since this eschews the kind of reductive programme for science the argument presupposes. Finally, much actual science (geology, zoology etc.) seems precisely concerned with macro-level objects and states of affairs as such. I conclude that the idea of a thoroughly autonomous level of common sense explanation for a thoroughly autonomous common sense world is without plausibility (cf. Knowles 2004)[5].

Many NSNists will of course still demur at the idea of a scientific intentional psychology – or for that matter at a scientific explanation of our

---

[5] A slightly different response, also prominent in Hornsby's work, would stress the idea of folk psychology as essentially involving talk of *persons* (though without any commitment to specifically normative explanation). This I think is not wholly implausible, but in light of a) the fact that animals would also seem to qualify as persons in the relevant sense b) the availability of nonreductive empirical work incorporating precisely the idea of personal-level explanations (Hurley 1998), this also strikes me as inadequate in holding SN at bay.

folk psychological practices. John Dupré (2001) sees such projects as a manifestation of *atavism*, bolstered by an ungrounded prejudice against the humanities. But, rhetoric aside, my plaint here has been to sketch an underlying dialectical situation that makes it hard to see how NSN can avoid the slide into SN. From the perspective of science generally, which NSNists endorse, I take it as uncontroversial that contemporary cognitive science both a) comprises a genuine research programme for explaining the cognitive basis of our folk psychological practices b) encourages a not wholly pessimistic attitude concerning the possibilities for scientifically understanding intentional psychology itself. Given a), NSN is already compromised insofar as scientific knowledge must then be viewed as fundamental relative to whatever disciplines our folk psychological capacities underlie (history, literary theory etc.). As for point b), this is formulated, deliberately, to allow pessimism to be something one might reasonably mount a case for. However, given that cognitive science itself opens for such pessimism (cf. the discussion of Chomsky and Fodor, above), NSN must be confessed to be on dialectically very thin ground. From within the general scientific world-view that NSNists themselves endorse, the derision often heaped on ambitious cognitive science can be explained without endorsing any alternative, nonscientific modes of explanation. NSNists cannot by contrast explain away what is surely a reasonable scepticism towards the idea of nonscientific modes of understanding, once McDowell's idea of a fundamentally different kind of insight and Hornsby's notion of an autonomous common sense world are rejected. Dividing through, what remains is the reasonable scepticism.

Needless to say, this doesn't end the debate between opponents and proponents of (ambitious) cognitive science, but then that would hardly be something a single paper could aim to do. What I do think I have shown is that, conceived at a certain level of abstraction, the ball is in the NSNists' court. The very general arguments that its supporters standardly employ against SN are inadequate to dislodging its place as our default form of naturalism.

2   Pragmatist Nonscientific Naturalism

I turn now from expansionist to pragmatic nonscientific naturalism (NSN_P), a position I see as most clearly articulated and defended in a couple of recent papers by Huw Price (2004, 2007, 2008). In Price (2004), reprinted in this volume, it is argued that a proper deference to science on the part of philosophers does not entail the position most commonly known as 'scientific naturalism' in contemporary analytical philosophy. According to this position, which Price himself terms *object naturalism* (henceforth *ON*), all there is is the world studied by science and all knowledge is scientific knowledge. The challenge for ON is to show how talk that on the face of it does not latch on to this world – talk about causation, modality, mathematics, intentionality, consciousness, morality and so on – nevertheless does so, or else can, with justification, be regarded as essentially meaningless, false, or at least 'second rate'. Price is highly suspicious of ON. However, he does embrace a position he calls *subject naturalism* (henceforth *SuN*), according to which 'philosophy needs to begin with what science tells us about ourselves' (ibid.: 73) – including our linguistic practices. According to Price, SuN is not, as one might initially surmise, a corollary of ON, but rather a view potentially, and perhaps even actually, in a position to undermine ON. In a word, science itself may or even will show us that there are limits to what can be understood scientifically.

Price argues as follows. On the standard ON-strategy, we begin with talk of something, call it 'X', and the question arises as to what place such talk can have in relation to the world described by science. What, in particular, are the occupiers of the *causal roles* identified by this talk? However, this strategy assumes that our talk of 'X' links us to something out there in the world, X itself. Of course, it is a platitude that 'X' refers to X (or Xes). However, as the possibility of minimalist or deflationist theories about reference should remind us, this is not necessarily a substantive truth, as opposed to a mere bi-product of the existence in our language of a device that allows us to say things about what people say, about words in general, and so on. To say "'snow is white' is true", for deflationists, is not to say anything more about the world than to say 'snow is white'. Something similar, it seems, might well apply to 'reference', and if so there is no automatic route from semantic platitudes to theories about how a certain kind of role is filled in reality.

Price thinks this kind of semantic deflationism is a live option when one takes a SuN-approach to language. Moreover, semantic deflationism avoids a problem for a more substantive naturalistic semantic theory which Paul Boghossian has pointed out, namely that, in being empirical, it leaves open the possibility that there may be no determinate semantic relations; in thus opening for the empirical possibility of semantic irrealism substantive semantics is incoherent, for it implies the same holds for the semantic terms themselves, which would disallow a formulation of the irrealistic thesis (cf. Boghossian 1990)[6]. Moreover, even if this objection fails and one could motivate a nondeflationary semantics, there is still what Price calls 'Stich's problem', to the effect that questions about what there is in the world aren't determinate given what we say about them (cf. Stich 1996). Stich used to worry whether or not there were beliefs, and gave a negative answer based on the falsity of folk psychology relative to a mature cognitive science. But does that really show there are no beliefs – or just that beliefs are very different from what we took them to be? We seem to be left with an indeterminacy in reference of a kind that again undermines the ON-approach to naturalization.

Now merely adopting a SuN approach to language is not to embrace semantic deflationism – though Price seems to suggest that it might well lead to this (2004:. 82). Moreover, as Price goes on to argue, if semantic deflationism is embraced, then the standard arguments for ON fail to go through, for then we cannot frame the kind of question object naturalists (such as Lewis and Jackson) standardly ask: *What are the truth-makers for such and such semantic roles?* [7] Ontological questions become instead internal to discourses, or perhaps lapse entirely. Science itself, then, as applied through the project of SuN, will show us that there are certain limits on what we can expect to explain scientifically. This suggests that, insofar as giving answers to questions about what exists and what is true are central to the project of ON, then ON is misconceived. Moreover, insofar as ON just is SN – *our* scientific naturalism – then so is the latter.

In my view, however, it would be a mistake to identify SN with ON. Moreover, I think SuN is unconvincing as a nonscientific naturalistic alternative to SN. To begin to see this, consider first what seems to be an

---

[6] Boghossian's paper also argues that deflationism is incoherent because it must take an irrealist stance with respect to nondeflationary truth and reference, which presupposes a robust notion of truth. Price (following a number of others) argues that deflationism can get around this objection by *not asserting* that there either exist or do not exist such substantive relations.

[7] Price also considers a nonsemantically-based version of ON that starts not with language but the world, so to speak (ibid.: § 7). The problem with this is that insofar as what we are seeking to motivate is a *metaphysical* picture ('the world is as described by science'), it fails to provide any overall motivation for this of the kind we had with the semantic picture, where truth-makers are seen as physical occupiers of causal roles. A possible response (made by the author in discussion with Price) would simply be to stress the role of causation as a criterion for the real, but as Price pointed out this merely begs the question of the ontological primacy of causal talk (cf. also Price 2007 on 'eleatic naturalism').

important ambiguity in the notion of SuN, as Price deploys it. As noted, SuN receives its central treatment in Price (2004), but he also discusses it in Price (2007), where the emphasis is rather different. In Price (2004), the main idea seems to be that SuN has a substantive philosophical role to play – that of undermining ON. The problem with this is that it doesn't seem to involve any kind naturalistic investigation at all. Price clearly wants SuN to involve recommendation of such investigation, such that it will be an open question whether an investigation of our linguistic practices will yield a substantive or nonsubstantive semantics: 'The subject naturalist's task is to account for the use of various terms – among them the semantic terms themselves – in the lives of natural creatures in a natural environment.' (ibid.: 82). She may in this task 'simply find no need for an explanatory category of semantic properties and relations' (ibid.). However, it turns out that this need not and had better not be construed as 'an investigation into *whether* there are semantic properties' (ibid., my emphasis), on pain of falling foul of Boghossian's argument (see above). But where does that leave us? It seems it leaves us in the position of having to say that SuN amounts to a more or less *a priori* insight that naturalistic representational semantics is bankrupt. Maybe that is right (as several other thinkers have argued). What I don't see is how it is something recognizably scientific, i.e. an empirical study, that is meant to be showing us this.

Now SuN is clearly intended by Price to be a position that involves naturalistic investigation into the different functions of different discourses play in our lives – moral, aesthetic, causal, mathematical and so on. He might thus say that it does indeed have an *a priori* element, as outlined above, but that rejecting substantive semantics still leaves a lot of work to be done in saying *how* our different discourses function. As he expounds upon it in Price (2007), SuN is the project 'of explaining our linguistic practices – for that way, if all goes well, lies a scientific foundation for the suggestion that different parts of language serve different functional ends' (ibid.: 24). Here Price also makes clear that he sees our linguistic practices as essentially ontologically committing, and hence plurality at the level of discourse amounts to a kind of ontological plurality, something which can sound very antiscientistic (i.e. contrary to the hegemony or priority of scientific knowledge).

However, if we bracket the ontology issue for the moment, what does the project of SuN as just described really amount to? I would seem to amount to a kind of naturalized epistemology of the kind cognitive science seeks to undertake, some of whose elements we outlined Part 1. In other words, it involves seeing language's conceptual functions in relation to our overall functioning as a biological organism. Moreover, if this is right, it surely thereby involves giving the discourse of scientific enquiry a priority over other discourses, something that any genuinely nonscientific naturalism would abjure.

This may sound too quick in neglecting the ontological commitments of the different discourses. Doesn't plurality here really sound the deathknell for a thoroughgoing scientific world-view? Well, I am prepared to admit that from, say, a moral or mathematical perspective our ontological commitments will look rather different than from a natural scientific one. I can also allow, for the sake of argument, that our talk in each case is equally cognitivist in its structure, allowing the construction of logical argument and reference to worldly properties that underscore the point of such argumentation. Nevertheless, if the *point* of all this in the different cases is something the scientific discourse is going to tell us and inform us more deeply *about*, then surely we are tacitly assuming the priority of that body of knowledge, i.e. what we call 'science'. Not just *what* we want to say exists within each discourse or language game, but also the fact *that* we make such commitments at all is in thrall to the scientific – in this case, psychological or anthropological – story about *why* we do all this. It is misleading, then, to sum up, as Price does, by saying that 'science is just one thing among many that we do with the linguistic tools of ontological commitment' (ibid.) – to say that science presents us with just *another* ontological view from just *another* perspective. For the very notion of what such views and interests are is, by Price's own reckoning, one that is beholden to scientific understanding. In a word: Given questions about ontology are posterior to, since responsible to questions about, explanation, then plurality with regard to the former does not impugn a scientific naturalism which is (in a certain important sense) monistic with respect to the latter.

On this second reading of SuN, then, it does emerge as a kind of naturalism, but it does not enunciate any deviation from SN – from which it clearly follows, insofar as SuN is not ON, that SN does not equal ON either. Now of course, whether there really can be a scientific representational semantics is big issue, and not one I can hope to say anything useful about here. I am in fact sympathetic to deflationism and something like Price's pragmatist line on ontological commitment, but that is not to the point in the present context. What is to the point is that SuN either is not distinct from SN or else isn't a way of being a naturalist at all, but merely a way of registering a certain scepticism to a certain kind of naturalistic project (perhaps in and of itself consistent with SN).

Since I take Price's views to provide an explication of the essentials of the view I have called NSN_P, I also conclude that the latter fails to represent any significant alternative to SN. Taken together with the conclusion of Part 1, nonscientific naturalism generally fails in a plausible way to distance itself from SN and must be considered undone.

Stepping back from the details, I think we can see a link between the two parts of the paper. Underlying Price's papers is a scepticism to the project of substantive naturalistic semantics and the associated idea of metaphysical realism. This is perhaps most clearly evinced in Price (2007), where he attempts to show that Quine's criterion for ontological commitment is either superscientific and nonnaturalistic or else lacks any kind of philosophical significance and is merely an internal affair: a matter of a science finding its own postulates reasonable. Ultimately, what one can countenance as existing must assume a certain practice, but practices are many and varied and not all of them scientific. Hence it can look as if SN is going to be in trouble, in lacking the wherewithal for vindicating the idea that all significant ontological commitment is to scientific objects and thereby all significant knowledge scientific. As we have just seen, however, this commitment is a not mandatory component of SN, as witnessed by the availability of Price's SuN which, though clearly not the same as ON, seems only nominally distinct from SN. But even without the idea of SuN (only fully developed in Price 2004), a reasonable question to ask Price would seem to be: *What positive programme is one left with on your conception of ontological commitment?* Should we stick at being idealists or ontological relativists of some stripe? Most philosophers, in any case, would want to be allowed to say that we humans are – really, *really* are – fully contained in the world of space-time and evolved organisms, even though they will also say we can make sense of it in various ways, perhaps some nonscientific. Thus are we returned to the dialectic played through in Part 1 above, the upshot of which was that nonscientific naturalism is not a dialectically stable position.

3 Conclusion

None of what I have said in this paper comprises an argument for SN that a sceptic of science or of naturalism generally would have to accept. However, the difficulty of maintaining a naturalism that does not fundamentally defer to science does strike me as a significant result.

As a final note, one should not get the impression that I place absolutely *no* weight on broadly epistemological arguments for naturalism, of the kind for example which says that natural science offers the hope of the most all-encompassing, coherent and consistent 'picture of the world' that we might ever hope to find. Having said that, there are almost certainly limits to this kind of argument, revolving centrally around the extent to which science can show itself to be precisely such a picture (cf. Knowles 2008). If scientific practice can show itself resourceful in the face of challenge, albeit only in a local, piecemeal fashion, that is perhaps some reason to stick with it. Ultimately, however, a thoroughgoing scientific naturalism will I think need to ally itself to a kind of *quietism*, according to which one is to a certain extent simply *beholden* to the practices of the dominating cognitive pictures and practices of one's epoch and culture (cf. Knowles 2003: ch. 1 for further discussion). This need not, however, be viewed as a concession, for such quietism is arguably a concomitant of any position worthy of the epithet 'naturalism'. Moreover, if, as seems reasonable to hold, science and scientific understanding do represent such a dominating practice in contemporary Western society, then the best option will arguably be to work within this framework – not in the reductive way some naturalists tend to do, but such that one doesn't neglect or renounce sources of insight which one's own practices in any case implicitly endorse[8].

References

Boghossian, Paul (1990). "The status of content". *The Philosophical Review* 99 (2): pp. 157–84.

Carruthers, Peter (2006). *The Architecture of the Mind: Massive Modularity and the Flexibility of Thought*. Oxford: Clarendon Press.

Chalmers, Alan (1999). *What is This Thing Called Science?* 3rd edition, Open University Press.

---

[8] Earlier versions of this paper were presented at KNEW'06 in September 2006 in Kazimierz, Poland, at Apeiron's 'Aporetisk aften' at NTNU in November 2006, and at the Fifth Conference of the Spanish Society of Logic, Methodology and Philosophy of Science in Granada, Spain, December 2006. I would like to thank Bjørn Ramberg and (especially) Huw Price for their comments on the first occasion, Kevin Cahill and Siv Dokmo for their comments on the second, and Jesús Vega Encabo for his comments (both oral and written) on the third. Thanks finally to David Macarthur for written comments on the version presented at KNEW'06.

Chomsky, Noam (1988). *Language and Problems of Knowledge: The Managua Lectures.* Cambridge, Mass.: MIT Press.

Davidson, Donald (1980). *Essays on Actions and Events.* Oxford: Oxford University Press.

de Caro, Mario, and Macarthur, David, eds. (2004). *Naturalism in Question.* Cambridge, Mass.: Harvard University Press.

Dupré, John (1993). *The Disorder of Things: Metaphysical Foundations of the Disunity of Science*, Cambridge, Mass.: Harvard University Press.

Dupré, John (2001). *Human Nature and the Limits of Science*, Oxford: Oxford University Press.

Dupré, John (2004). "The miracle of monism". In de Caro and Macarthur (2004), pp. 36–58.

Feldman, Richard (2001). "We are all naturalists now", ms., delivered at APA meeting 2001 (available at http:// www.ling.rochester.edu / feldman/ papers/naturalism.htm).

Fodor, Jerry (1983). *The Modularity of Mind.* Cambridge, Mass.: MIT Press.

Haack, Susan (1993). *Evidence and Inquiry.* Oxford: Blackwell.

Henderson, David K. (1993). *Interpretation and Explanation in the Human Sciences.* State University of New York Press.

Hornsby, Jennifer (1997). *Simple Mindedness.* Cambridge, Mass.: Harvard University Press.

Hornsby, Jennifer (2008) "Physicalism, conceptual analysis and acts of faith" In *Minds, Worlds & Conditionals: Essays in Honor of Frank Jackson*, ed. By I. Ravenscroft. Oxford: Oxford University Press, pp. 43–60.

Hurley, Susan (1998). *Consciousness in Action*, Cambridge, Mass.: Harvard University Press.

Jackson, Frank (1988). *From Metaphysics to Ethics.* Oxford: Oxford University Press.

Knowles, Jonathan (2002). "Is folk psychology different?". *Erkenntnis* 57, pp. 199–230.

Knowles, Jonathan (2003). *Norms, Naturalism and Epistemology: The Case for Science without Norms.* Palgrave Macmillan.

Knowles, Jonathan (2005). "Varieties of naturalism". In, *Synergies. Interdisciplinary Communications 2003/2004,* ed. by W. Østreng, Centre for Advanced Studies, Norwegian Academy for Science and Letters, Oslo.

Knowles, Jonathan (2006). "Non-scientific naturalism?". In *Science – A Challenge to Philosophy?*, ed. by S. Pihlström, R. Vilkko & H. Koskinen, Peter Lang.

Knowles, Jonathan (2008). "Is naturalism a threat to metaphysics?", *Norsk filosofisk tidsskrift* 43, pp. 23–32.

Kornblith, Hilary (1994). "Naturalism: both metaphysical and epistemological". In *Midwest Studies in Philosophy XIX: Philosophical Naturalism*, ed. by P. French, T. Uehling and H. Wettstein, University of Notre Dame Press.

McCulloch, Gregory (2002). *The Life of the Mind: An Essay on Phenomenological Externalism.* Routledge.

McDowell, John (1985). "Functionalism and anomalous monism". In *Actions and Events,* ed. by Brian McLaughlin and Ernie Lepore. Oxford: Blackwell.

McDowell, John (1994). *Mind and World.* Cambridge, Mass.: Harvard University Press 1994.

McDowell, John (1998). "Two kinds of naturalism". In *Mind, Value, and Reality*, John McDowell. Cambridge, Mass.: Harvard University Press.

McDowell, John (2004). "Naturalism in the philosophy of mind". In de Caro and Macarthur (2004), pp. 91–105.

Price, Huw (2004). "Naturalism without representationalism". In de Caro and Macarthur (2004), pp. 71–89. Reprinted in this volume.

Price, Huw (2007). "Quining Naturalism", *Journal of Philosophy* 104, 8, pp. 375–405. (page references to ms.).

Price, Huw (2008). "One cheer for representationalism". In *The Philosophy of Richard Rorty*, ed. by Randall E. Auxier. Open Court Library of Living Philosophers XXXII.

Putnam, Hilary (1979). *Reason, Truth and History.* Cambridge University Press.

Putnam, Hilary (2004). "The content and appeal of naturalism". In de Caro and Macarthur (2004), pp. 59–70.

Rorty, Richard (1998). *Truth and Progress.* Cambridge: Cambridge University Press.

Rorty, Richard (2007). "Naturalism and quietism", In *Philosophy as Cultural Politics: Philosophical Papers* (Vol. 4), Richard Rorty, Cambridge: Cambridge University Press, pp. 147–159.

Sellars, Wilfrid (1963). "Empiricism and the philosophy of mind". In Wilfrid Sellars, *Science, Perception and Reality*, London: Routledge & Kegan Paul, 1963.

Stich, Steven (1996). "Deconstructing the mind". In *Deconstructing the Mind*, Steven Stich, Oxford: Oxford University Press.

Stroud, Barry (2004). "The charm of naturalism". In de Caro and Macarthur (2004), pp. 21–35.

Wellman, Henry M. (1990). *The Child's Theory of Mind.* Cambridge Mass.: MIT Press.

Wiggins, David (1987). *Needs, Values, Truth.* Oxford: Blackwell.

11

Postscript: Reply to Knowles

HUW PRICE

In his essay 'Two Kinds of Non-scientific Naturalism' (this volume), Jonathan Knowles considers two kinds of opposition to what he terms 'scientific naturalism' (SN). These rival views—two different forms of 'non-scientific naturalism' (NSN), as Knowles calls them—are themselves naturalistic, in the following sense.

> [T]hey disavow the existence of supernaturalistic, transcendent and/or immaterial entities and forces, thereby paying due respect to what science has taught us about the universe and our place within it. Both also accept the relevance of science and scientific understanding to at least some traditional philosophical problems.

How then does non-scientific naturalism differ from scientific naturalism? Knowles characterises the difference as follows:

> Where they differ is over acceptance of the following: that scientific knowledge is (or in some non-trivial sense could become) exhaustive of what there is to be known; that all facts are ultimately scientific ones; and/or that scientific knowledge and/or facts have a fundamental priority over other forms of knowledge/facts. Anything worthy of the name 'scientific naturalism' would at a minimum have to hold to

Beyond Description: Naturalism and Normativity.
Marcin Miłkowski and Konrad Talmont-Kaminski (eds.).
Copyright © 2010 The Author.

the last of these disjuncts, whereas NSN would reject all of them. (2010: 158)

Knowles goes on to treat my 'subject naturalism' – and more particularly, the pluralism about ontologically-committing vocabularies that I see as its likely upshot – as a representative of the second of his two forms of NSN: *pragmatic* non-scientific naturalism, as he calls it. He then presents me with a dilemma: either the investigation I envisage of the likely role (or non-role) of semantic properties in a mature theory of human thought and language is too *a priori* to count as naturalistic at all; or, if it is intended to be an empirical investigation, then it accords a primacy to empirical science in virtue of which 'scientific knowledge and/or facts' do, after all, 'have a fundamental priority over other forms of knowledge/facts', so that my view is a form of SN, rather than NSN, after all.

The latter option would be one I could happily live with, I think. After all, the classification in question is Knowles's, not mine. If his SN is a broad enough church to accommodate my kind of pluralists, then so much the better – so long as we can still sit on the other side of the aisle from object naturalists and metaphysicians, at any rate!

Certainly, this horn of the dilemma is preferable to the other one, and I am grateful to Knowles for alerting me to the need for clarification on this matter. If there is anything *a priori* about my conclusion that mature science is unlikely to find a need for substantial semantic relations, it is only in the sense of a consideration of the likely shape of future theory, of a kind which is often, in practice, conducted from the armchair. (Think of thought experiments, after all.) In different ways, all three of the considerations I took to support the Invalidity Thesis lie at this level: at the broad-brush end of first-order theory, rather than at any distinctively philosophical level.

All the same, I think that Knowles's assimilation of my pluralistic subject naturalism to SN is a little too hasty. The crucial move occurs in this passage, where Knowles responds to the (self-posed) challenge that the plurality I envisage in the 'ontological commitments of the different discourses ... sound[s] the death-knell for a thoroughgoing scientific world-view':

> Well, I am prepared to admit that from, say, a moral or mathematical perspective our ontological commitments will look rather different

from a natural scientific one. I can also allow, for the sake of argument, that our talk in each case is equally cognitivist in its structure, allowing the construction of logical argument and reference to worldly properties that underscore the point of such argumentation. Nevertheless, if the *point* of all this in the different cases is something the scientific discourse is going to tell us and inform us more deeply *about*, then surely we are tacitly assuming the priority of that body of knowledge, i.e. what we call 'science'. Not just *what* we want to say exists within each discourse or language game, but also the fact *that* we make such commitments at all is in thrall to the scientific – in this case, psychological or anthropological – story about *why* we do all this. It is misleading, then, to sum up, as Price does, by saying that 'science is just one thing among many that we do with the linguistic tools of ontological commitment' (ibid.) – to say that science presents us with just *another* ontological view from just *another* perspective. For the very notion of what such views and interests are is, by Price's own reckoning, one that is beholden to scientific understanding. In a word: Given [that] questions about ontology are posterior to, since responsible to questions about, explanation, then plurality with regard to the former does not impugn a scientific naturalism which is (in a certain important sense) monistic with respect to the latter. (2010: 171)

I'd like to make three points in response to this passage. Firstly, I think it would be a mistake to think that there is some sense in which non-scientific discourses are 'in thrall' to the scientific facts, in a way in which the scientific discourse itself is not. On the contrary: *all* the discourses are human behaviours, and equally in thrall to the scientific facts, simply in the sense that we humans are natural creatures.

Secondly, I think it would be misleading to say that the *ontology* of the non-scientific discourses is in thrall to, or 'beholden to', that of science. I'm not sure whether Knowles has this kind of claim in mind, but on my view what science properly explains is *our use of vocabularies,* not the facts of which we speak from *within* those vocabularies. On the contrary, we can't even speak of those facts – that ontology – from the detached anthropological standpoint from which we seek to explain the use of the vocabularies themselves. (From that standpoint, we *mention* the vocabularies, but do not *use* them.) So once again, the dependence in question is of *vocabularies* on natural facts, not of *other facts* on natural facts.

Thirdly, and perhaps most importantly, I think that we shouldn't read too much into the fact that if we have our eyes on the explanatory project, then science will seem to be more than just 'science is just one thing among many that we do with the linguistic tools of ontological commitment', as I put it. It is true that *given that focus,* science is inevitably in the foreground. But other projects would put other vocabularies in the foreground. Explanatory projects accord priority to the explanatory vocabulary, evaluative projects to evaluative vocabulary, and so on. Only if the explanatory project were already privileged over others, would this amount to some kind of absolute privilege for science.

Thus it seems to me that Knowles perhaps overstates the case for the priority of science, in my kind of pragmatic pluralism. While I am certainly a naturalist - a subject naturalist - I think it remains unclear whether I should be counted a scientific naturalist, in Knowles's sense. There are various possible interpretations of the view 'that scientific knowledge and/or facts have a fundamental priority over other forms of knowledge/facts' (as Knowles states the basic commitment of SN), and my kind of naturalism seems to accord with some but not others.

References

Knowles, Jonathan (2010). "Two Kinds of Nonscientific Naturalism". This volume.

12

A Dilemma for Naturalism?[1,2]

SHANE OAKLEY

1 Introduction

The merits of a naturalized view of epistemology have been challenged on many fronts and for many different reasons. Here, I will be concerned with certain arguments against naturalized epistemology articulated by Harvey Siegel (1980, 1984) and Robert Almeder (1998). These arguments go right to the heart of the matter by questioning the feasibility of the entire program itself. They conclude that either naturalism is false because it is self-defeating or that naturalism is vacuous because it is circular. In order to respond to these critical arguments, I will here investigate in detail this apparently damning dilemma for naturalism[3].

Of course the conclusions of both horns of this dilemma do not bode well for naturalized epistemology, and so it is certainly a worthwhile project to see if the naturalists have sufficient resources to avoid it. My approach to this problem will be to argue that the dilemma presented by

---

[1] The following paper is a shortened version of a paper of the same title that is to appear as Oakley (forthcoming).
[2] I would like to thank Risto Hilpinen, AJ Kreider, Keith Lehrer, Peter Lewis, Jeremy Morris, Harvey Siegel, Mike Shaffer, and Mike Veber for very helpful and interesting conversations relating to the material in this paper.
[3] From this point on when I use the term "naturalism" I will have in mind only naturalism in epistemology as opposed to naturalism in other areas of philosophy.

Beyond Description: Naturalism and Normativity.
Marcin Miłkowski and Konrad Talmont-Kaminski (eds.).
Copyright © 2010 The Author.

Siegel and Almeder does not pose a special problem for naturalism, because the presuppositions that are required for the argument to go through are just the presuppositions behind the adequacy of *any* epistemological theory, naturalistic or otherwise. To show this I develop an analogous argument against *a priori* justification that has the same general structure as the argument leveled against naturalism. Given such an argument we can see that it is dialectically illegitimate to utilize such an argument to eliminate one theoretical standpoint in favor of another.

The reason that the problem presented by Siegel and Almeder is so interesting and in need of attention by naturalized epistemologists rests on a general failure on the part of many naturalists to appreciate the need to legitimize their position. In this respect, the dilemma that will be discussed here is akin to a skeptical challenge against a thesis. In the face of general epistemological skepticism it seems that most naturalists have simply waved their hands when confronted with the issue of justifying naturalism, and this seems to be intellectually unsatisfactory[4]. So, it is especially important to see what sort of response a naturalist might give to the challenge.

2 What is Naturalism?

One interesting observation that can be made with respect to the philosophical literature on Naturalism is that this position is often either inadequately defined or simply not defined at all. Also, some authors have offered such trivial accounts of naturalism that the justification of our beliefs includes rational insight or *a priori* judgment. Other authors seem to understand naturalism in a much more austere way taking it to be the thesis that what only counts as evidence is evidence of the sort characteristic of the empirical methods of the sciences. Between the two extremes there seem to be a variety of theses that form a continuum[5]. In order to facilitate discussion of the variants of naturalism in the context of an ar-

---

[4] I am not sure that this is really a fair statement as it appears that many naturalists do not necessarily neglect skeptical challenges to their view in so much as they concede something to the skeptic. In fact, I think that a concession of some sort to the skeptic puts the naturalists in a much better dialectical position than those who criticize the view, but that is an issue for another paper.

[5] E.g. reliabilism as developed by Goldman (1967) and (1979), just to take a couple of examples. One might also consider the view of Laudan (1996) as an in-between view as well.

gument against naturalism, it will prove fruitful to first give a schematic definition of naturalism that is broad enough to incorporate all of the naturalistic theses, from the most trivial to the most extreme. In so doing, we will be able to construct the alleged dilemma against "naturalism" in a more precise and comprehensive form.

Upon examination of both the extreme and trivial versions of naturalism, we find that the key idea they share is that principles of evidence and epistemic justification should be seen as those principles that are employed in or are discoverable by the methods of science. Hence, what one takes science to consist in will determine the form of the naturalized epistemology that one adopts. In order to capture the theses that constitute the total set of "naturalized" epistemologies let us first consider a set of propositions E having as members those propositions e that serve as evidence, and, hence justify one's beliefs. Assuming that it is possible for our beliefs to be justified and that the evidence for our beliefs is propositional evidence[6] we can presently understand the set E as a non-empty set with an undefined extension. The elements of E will be determined in accordance with the correct epistemological theory and will be those propositions that are implied by that theory to be evidential. Understanding E in this way we are now in a better position to understand why the trivial and extreme versions of naturalism are in fact trivial and extreme. According to the trivial version of naturalism the scope of E (were the trivial thesis true) would be quite large, as the set would consist of empirical propositions as well as *a priori* propositions. On the other hand, the extreme version of naturalism, were it true, would determine a set E with a very narrow scope and it would consist mainly of empirical propositions, although it would not necessarily include all empirical propositions. The triviality of the former view and the narrowness of the latter

---

[6] We could develop the notion of that which justifies a belief non-propositionally if we pleased, which is what I would be inclined to do in the end. However, utilizing the idea of a proposition and the concept of propositional justification will allow for a much less cumbersome presentation. I should note that my use of the notion of propositional justification is a bit idiosyncratic as what I mean for a proposition to justify a belief is for that proposition to express that something was observed, or something was intuited, or whatever the theory of justification says evidence for beliefs should be. Evidence in and of itself need not be propositional. If I believe p I will cite as my justification for that belief some proposition q expressing that which was my evidence for the belief in question, whether it is reason or experience or both. The proposition serves as my reason for the belief as that evidence is provided to a third party.

view will be even more apparent once we have developed a schematic version of naturalism.

Again, broadly speaking, naturalism in epistemology is the claim that the present principles of evidence and justification employed in the sciences, including those that will be discovered in accordance with presently employed principles, exhausts the set of epistemic principles. There are simply no more to be had. Given those principles of evidence and justification, we can determine the set of evidential propositions that follow from them, i.e. the set of propositions that provide probative support for our beliefs. Let the set S consist of those propositions e that are deemed to be justificatory in terms of both the presently employed and discoverable principles of evidence and justification employed in the sciences. So, it should be very clear that how broadly or narrowly one understands science will determine what one takes to be the elements of S. Assuming that a tenet of naturalism is that the principles of evidence and justification are those that are presently employed in science and the evidential propositions that follow from them, and only those that follow from them, determine the set S, we can see that the naturalists claim that the naturalistic thesis N entails the following general definitional scheme:

(1) $\forall(e)(e \in E^* \leftrightarrow e \in S)$

Here E^* is thought by the proponent of any particular theory to be coextensive with E.

Here we can see that (1), as a definition scheme, is rather trivial. However, the triviality of (1) is a virtue rather than a vice because it allows for a continuum of naturalistic theses to be defined dependent on how liberally or austerely each version of naturalism determines the extension of S. Although the definitions of the various theses might be rather thin, each thesis would nevertheless be uniquely identifiable. Given that the theses that are instances of (1) are provided by specifying identity conditions we can begin to construct a more refined set of definitions of "naturalism," thus allowing for more precise articulations of particular naturalized epistemologies. Of course, here (1) will remain in schematic form, as I have no intentions to defend any particular version of naturalism.

One thing to note about (1) is that using the general scheme one can schematically define a general continuum of epistemic theories. Again, this point makes (1) smack of triviality, but, as I will try to show below, this is a virtue, not a vice of (1) itself. Essentially this will allow us to underwrite the claim that the dilemma presented against naturalism is not a particular problem for naturalism, because it is a problem for any epistemological theory. In the next section I will give a non-formal exposition of the alleged dilemma against naturalism. Using (1), I will then prove that one of the premises of the dilemma is true and show that one of the premises is not obviously true. In doing this, I will formalize the tacit presuppositions that the proponents of the dilemma must accept in order to defend the premises of the argument. In any case, the response to the dilemma presented here is not meant to be a final refutation of the claim that this dilemma poses serious problems for naturalism, but it will at least undermine the initial *prima facie* force that the argument has.

3 An Informal Statement of the Dilemma

The dilemma to which I have been referring arises for a naturalistic thesis in the event that someone challenges that thesis. Hence, suppose that Jones confronts Quine and asks Quine why he, Jones, should accept a naturalized epistemology as the correct theory of knowledge and rationality. Should Quine respond that he is justified in accepting his naturalized epistemology on the basis of the Quine/Duhem thesis and his rejection of the analytic synthetic distinction, then it seems that Quine has presupposed that which he intends to deny by adopting an austere naturalized epistemology in the first place, viz. the utilization of reasons that are not sanctioned by or discoverable through the methods of the empirical sciences. For we are free to ask, as Siegel so poignantly does, "…is it the case that the Quine/Duhem thesis is justified by an appeal to empirical data or by reference to a scientific theory?"(Siegel 1984: 667) Moreover, is the rejection of the analytic/synthetic distinction based on empirical data or a scientific theory? The answer to both of these questions seems to be no. Both the Quine/Duhem thesis and the rejection of the analytic/synthetic distinction appear to be philosophical theses that were reached through philosophical argument and not through principles of justification sanctioned by or discoverable through the methods of empirical science. Hence, the Quine/Duhem thesis and the rejection of the analytic/synthetic distinction cannot be used in support of Quinean 'extreme' naturalism on pain of self-defeat. More generally, any independent reason that goes beyond those propositions that are declared to be evidence in terms of the naturalistic thesis will not serve to justify the thesis without also falsifying it. The only other response to Jones' request for a reason to accept Quinean naturalism that is then open for Quine is to offer some empirical, or otherwise scientifically sanctioned, proposition from within the epistemological theory itself. On the face of it, however, such a move seems to be viciously circular. It would, so the critic claims, be an illegitimate dialectical move on Quine's behalf to offer up such a proposition in defense of his own theory[7]. In a more schematic form then, the dilemma that is leveled by Siegel and Almeder is established as follows:

1. If there is an independent justification of naturalism, then it cannot be justification in the terms of the naturalistic thesis, i.e. naturalism is false.
2. If there is no independent justification for naturalism, then any defense of the thesis is viciously circular.
3. Either there is an independent justification for naturalism or there is not.

Therefore, either naturalism is false or any defense of naturalism is viciously circular.

The arguments that support premises 1 and 2 are obviously central to determining whether or not the argument is sound. Assuming that one of those arguments fails we would then have no reason to suspect that the dilemma presents a serious problem for naturalism. I will reconstruct a formal argument for premise 1 that shows the premise to be necessarily true given the definitional scheme of naturalism offered above. The focus of the attack on the purported dilemma will then be on premise 2. A formal examination of the tacit presuppositions that one must hold in order to maintain that the consequent of premise 2 follows from the antecedent will be made, and, given a variant of the definitional scheme offered above, it will be shown that it is in fact possible for there to be a justification of naturalism in terms of itself. Hence, the reasoning of the origi-

---

[7] For this sort of criticism see Siegel (1980). See Bealer (1992) and Shaffer and Warnick (2004) as well.

nal dilemma cannot be sustained in the form in which it has been presented.

4 A Formal Defense of the Self-Defeating Claim

The basic argument for premise one of the dilemma is elegantly stated by Siegel to be a deep problem for naturalized epistemology. This is because, in attempting to justify their own thesis, naturalists, "…must assume the legitimacy of, and strive to achieve, the very sort of justification [they] seek to show cannot be had"(Siegel 1984: 675). Hence, we seemingly must conclude that naturalism is in some way self-defeating, i.e. any justification that can be cited for the naturalistic thesis will need to be justified and such justification can only come by way of extra-scientific reasons. In terms of the definitional scheme provided above, we can thus provide a straightforward *reductio ad absurdum* against the possibility that there is such an extra-scientific reason, i.e. an independent reason, in support of any naturalistic thesis N. Recall that, according to a given thesis N, the set S is the set of propositions that are the evidential propositions capable of justifying the things that we believe. Again, the elements of S will be determined according to the way a particular thesis N specifies what science is like. Hence, for the set Ψ of every set S_i of evidential propositions there will be a one-to-one mapping of the elements from the set Φ of all naturalistic theses N_j to the elements of the set Ψ. Given this one-to-one mapping from Φ to Ψ we can prove by reductio that premise one is true for arbitrary N, S, and E* in terms of the definition scheme (1) above, and is thus true with respect to any naturalistic thesis.

In order to show this we must suppose that there is some proposition e that serves to justify some naturalistic thesis N, that e is an element of the set E* of evidential propositions, and that e is not an element of S. Under such a supposition we then have an independent proposition that is said to serve as a justification of some arbitrary naturalistic thesis N. Formally this would be represented as follows:

(2) $\exists(e)(eJN \ \& \ e \in E^* \ \& \ e \notin S)$.

Here 'xJy' is the two-place relation of justification and N is some arbitrary naturalistic thesis. Recall the definition scheme given above:

(1) $\forall(e)(e \in E^* \leftrightarrow e \in S)$.

187 / A DILEMMA FOR NATURALISM?

Here the domain of quantification is the set of all propositions. From (1) and the supposition of (2) one can easily deduce a straightforward contradiction[8]. Hence, it follows that:

(3) $\{(1) \& (2)\} \Rightarrow \bot$.

In other words, there is no model in which both (1) and (2) are true together. Also, given that (1) and (2) are mutually exclusive we can conclude that premise 1 of the purported dilemma for naturalism is necessarily true. There can be no independent justification of any thesis N such that the thesis comes out to be true. To put it another way, if there is an independent justification for some thesis N then that thesis is necessarily false.

That premise one of the argument above comes out true in accordance with our definitional scheme (1) seems to provide some support for considering (1) to be a comprehensive definition of the set of versions of naturalism with respect to the dialectical situation we have been considering. The proponents of anti-naturalism appear to accept that a general criterion that any epistemological theory must meet is that it cannot be justified by propositions or reasons that are not sanctioned as probative by the theory itself. As any epistemological theory that can be defined in terms of (1) meets this requirement, using (1) to combat the argument does not involve one in begging the question against the proponents of the dilemma. Moreover, as mentioned before, (1) must be formally correct in some way because in order to be non-self-defeating any epistemological theory must also conform to a formal scheme such as (1). This should come as no surprise because (1) is neither substantive nor controversial. Working within the constraints accepted by the proponents of the dilemma we must conclude then that not only is there no naturalistic thesis N such that N has an independent justification, but also that there is no epistemological theory of justification X such that X is true and there is an independent reason in favor of X. By extension then we see that premise 1 in the dilemma is true for any epistemological theory and so it cannot be a premise that is specifically problematic for naturalism.

From these reflections on (1) and its relation to premise 1 of the dilemma we can see that insofar as we accept as a criterion of adequacy for an epistemological theory that it not have a justification that is not sanc-

---

[8] For a proof of (3) please see the first appendix of Oakley (forthcoming).

tioned by the theory itself we can begin to appreciate the fact that premise 2 of the dilemma is doing all of the real work. In particular, given the generality of premise 1, viz. that it is true for any epistemological theory, it is apparent that the dilemma poses no special problem for naturalism unless premise 2 is true given the naturalistic thesis. Interestingly, there is no straightforward way to prove premise 2. In fact, once the underlying presuppositions that motivate the introduction of premise 2 into the argument against naturalism are uncovered we have a straightforward proof of the possibility of a self-justifying naturalistic thesis.

5 The Possibility of a Self-justifying Naturalism

Suppose that we accept as a negative criterion of adequacy for any epistemological theory of justification X that X cannot have as its meta-justification a proposition or set of propositions that are not entailed to be evidential by the theory itself. We have then committed ourselves at that point to a further positive criterion of adequacy if we accept the claim that it is possible for some theory to have a meta-justification at all. The positive criterion of adequacy that follows from our acceptance of the negative criterion states that an epistemological theory is justified just in case it is self-justifying. Hence, for any epistemological theory X and any evidential proposition e, e justifies X just in case e is an element of the set of propositions that are entailed to be evidential propositions by X. For clarity's sake, let us put this criterion of adequacy in symbolic form. This will make it easy to see if we can make use of it in justifying premise 2 of the argument:

(CA) $\forall(X)\forall(e) (eJX \leftrightarrow e \in E^*)$.

Here the extension of E is determined by an instance of X. Now, (CA) appears to be a condition of adequacy both on any actual and any possible X, at least insofar as we accept *tout court* the negative criterion of adequacy discussed above. Hence, it must be taken to be necessary if it is applicable and should be understood as follows:

(CA') $\Box\forall(X)\forall(e) (eJX \leftrightarrow e \in E^*)$

Taking (CA') to be the condition of adequacy imposed on epistemological theories, insofar as those theories are justified, we can now clearly see the underlying presuppositions behind the dilemma against naturalism. Moreover, if the conclusion of that argument is to follow, then what must be shown is that naturalism fails to meet (CA').

So, does naturalism fail to meet (CA')? Is it true that it is not possible for versions of naturalism to include internal mechanisms that allow the epistemological theory to justify itself? As I will show here this is not the case. It is in fact possible for a naturalistic thesis to justify itself. In fact, the proof goes through for arbitrary N, and so even if the extreme replacement version of naturalism is not justified, more must be said about why that is the case over and above the claim that replacement naturalism is circular. Despite these provisos, merely showing the bare possibility that naturalism is self-justifying is sufficient to cast doubt on the truth of the second premise of the argument. However, before giving the proof of this claim it is first necessary that we uncover a tacit presupposition of the debate to which the proponents of the dilemma are committed. The presupposition is quite simple, viz. if Siegel, Almeder, et al. want to avoid being epistemological skeptics, then they must believe that it is at least possible for there to be some epistemological theory X and some proposition e, such that e justifies X and $e \in E^*$, where E^* is determined by that particular instance of X. Moreover, the range of possible justified epistemological theories must be restricted to those theories that are possible to develop and verify in some way within the constraints of human cognitive limitations. Otherwise, there would be no reason to engage in this debate to begin with because we should simply be conceding that skepticism is true, i.e. *humans* can never be sure that we are ever justified in any of our beliefs[9]. Hence, formally, proponents of the Siegel/Almeder dilemma are committed to the following thesis:

(PE) $\Diamond \exists(X)\exists(e)(eJX \& e \in E^*)$.

---

[9] In formulating a proof for the possibility of a self-justifying naturalism I utilize the apparatus of possible worlds semantics for the sake of ease. The restriction of possibility and necessity with respect to epistemic theories should be understood to be a restriction on the possible worlds that are accessible from the actual world. Only those worlds where beings with relevantly similar cognitive structures to humans should be considered accessible, as other sorts of beings may have radically divergent epistemological features depending on the nature of their cognitive abilities. Some may say that this begs the question against the traditionalists. However, I think this to be a reasonable constraint insofar as the traditionalists are hoping to come up with some sort of necessary criteria of justification that is self-supporting. It begs the question to the skeptic to think that we, humans, would have the epistemological theory that is the best in all possible worlds given that we are cognitively constrained in many ways.

I take it that anyone who does not believe that skepticism about the justification of epistemic theories is true is committed to (PE) and that including the claim (PE) as a premise in an argument is unobjectionable.

Restricting the notion of possibility and necessity to worlds or situations in which humans are cognitively identical, or at least sufficiently similar, with respect to all essential properties of actual humans, we introduce a generalized version of (1) that serves as a definitional scheme for any epistemological theory. Here we are exploiting the broad generality of (1) that was noted above. When we speak of justification, evidence, and belief the general idea is that if a belief is justified then it is justified by the subjects possessing some evidence that supports the believed proposition. One role of a theory of justification then is to codify the types of propositions that are capable of serving as evidence for beliefs. In accord with the role that a theory of justification must play we can then say that any theory of justification, be it naturalistic or rationalistic, determines a unique set of evidential propositions constituted by a subset of the set of all propositions. Moreover, it seems reasonable to suppose that the set of evidential propositions that follows from an epistemic theory are, for the proponents of that theory, the exhaustive set of evidential propositions E. Hence, the following principle appears to be an extension of (1) as it applies to all epistemic theories of justification:

(1') $\Box \forall (Y) \forall (e)(e \in E^* \leftrightarrow e \in Y)$.

In this expression Y is a variable ranging over any set of evidential propositions corresponding to any possible epistemic theory. (1') should, however, be read carefully, especially under the supposition that there is some epistemological theory that is the correct epistemological theory. (1') explicates a commitment to the way in which we would go about providing a definition of an epistemological theory as determining the extension of E, whatever E may actually be. In any case, for any epistemological theory X there is a set Y of evidential propositions such that those propositions are claimed to be co-extensive with E. Presumably, this latter claim holds in any of our restricted possible worlds, and hence (1') is an acceptable definitional scheme. Necessarily, the quantified statement in (1') provides a definitional-scheme for any epistemological theory in any possible world.

To get a better handle on the content of (1') consider some set of evidential propositions Q that follow from the epistemic theory T. Proponents of T must then claim that the set Q of evidential propositions is coextensive with the set E, where E is the actual set of evidential propositions. We can then say that Q determines a set E* such that $\forall(e)(e \in E \rightarrow e \in E^*)$, which may actually be false. However, the proponents of a theory, insofar as they believe their theory to be correct, are committed to the truth of the co-extensiveness of E* and E. Hence, (1') should not be read as stating that it is necessarily the case that every epistemological theory determines the elements of E. Assuming that there is one correct epistemological theory, there will then be some Y and some E* such that Y, E*, and E are co-extensive. This is consistent with (1'). So (1') does not appear to be objectionable.

The reason for formalizing the scheme introduced earlier and for elucidating the underlying presuppositions of the proponents of the dilemma is, as stated earlier, to formally demonstrate that it is possible for some naturalistic thesis N to be self-justifying. For from (CE'), (PE), and (1') it follows that it is possible that there is some proposition e that justifies N where e is an element of S. Symbolically:

(4) $\{(CE'), (PE), (1')\} \Rightarrow \Diamond\exists(e)(eJN \ \& \ e \in S)^{10}$.

Given (CE'), (PE), and (1') it is possible that naturalism is self-justifying. In fact, accepting (CE'), (PE), and (1') commits one to the possibility that any epistemological theory X could be self-justifying[11]. As a result, we cannot maintain that the second premise of the above dilemma is obviously true. For, as this entailment demonstrates, if it is possible for any theory to be self-justifying, then it is possible for even extreme naturalism to be self-justifying. It simply does not follow that naturalism cannot be justified in this manner or, for that matter, that every self-justified epistemological theory is vacuous, at least insofar as we accept (PE). If this conclusion is denied then the proponents of the dilemma are simply skeptics about the justification of epistemic theories. To conclude I propose a dilemma for *a priori* theories of justification that is analogous to the argument stated above. Doing so will complete the project of showing that naturalism is not especially vulnerable to the dilemma.

---

[10] For a proof of (4) please see the second appendix of Oakley (forthcoming).
[11] I should note however that this result does not hold for relativism as there is no unique E* that is determined by the thesis. Relativism then does not fit the general schemata (1') and is non-self-justifiable. Thanks to Jeremy Morris for bringing the problem of relativism to my attention in a discussion of this paper.

6 A Dilemma for A Priori Justification

Constructing this dilemma is quite simple. In schematic form it can be stated as follows:
4. If there is an independent justification for rationalism, then rationalism is self-defeating, and hence false.
5. If there is no independent justification for rationalism, then any defense of the thesis will be viciously circular.
6. Either there is an independent justification for rationalism or there is not.

Therefore, either rationalism is false or is circular[12].

Formulating principle (R) as a schematic definition for any rationalistic thesis we get:

(R) $\forall(e)(e \in E^* \leftrightarrow e \in R)$, where R is the set of evidential propositions that follow from any particular rationalistic thesis and E^* is thought to meet the condition $\forall(e)(e \in E \rightarrow e \in E^*)$, where again this may well be false. Assuming R and that $\exists(e)(eJR \ \& \ e \in E^* \ \& \ e \notin R)$ is true, we can prove by *reductio ad absurdum* that premise 4 of this argument is true. Again, by reasoning similar to that used above, we can also show that it is possible that there is a self-justifying rationalistic thesis for arbitrary R, and hence for every R. Therefore, the dialectical situation from the standpoint of this sort of meta-epistemological dilemma is the same for both naturalism and rationalism. We cannot, therefore, legitimately use an argument of this form to favor one epistemic theory over another.

Reflecting on these results, I cannot claim to know how one might go about justifying naturalism in terms of itself. Moreover, I cannot claim to

---

[12] Casullo (2000) constructs a similar, if not identical argument, against the rationalists. He then proceeds to argue that what would be premise four of the above argument is false as the rationalists, insofar as they accept two sorts of justification, viz. rational and empirical, can feasibly offer a meta-justification for rationalism in terms of empirical evidence. I concede that certain rationalists may well have such a move open to them, but the target that I have in mind here is the theorists that either takes *a priori* justification to have more weight than empirical justification claiming that an empirical justification of rationalism somehow undermines *a priori* justification, e.g. BonJour (1998), or the rationalists that claims that *a priori* justification has the upper-hand in matters of meta-justification. With respect to the latter two sorts of theorists, premise four holds true of their theories.

know how one could go about justifying rationalism or *a priorism* in terms of itself. One might claim that those propositions that are *a priori* justified are so justified because they are self-evident. But the proposition that self-evident propositions are *a priori* justified is not itself self-evident[13]. Hence, it appears that the rationalist and the more empirically inclined naturalists are in the same dialectical position with respect to the sort of meta-epistemological argument offered by Siegel and Almeder. Therefore, the above metaepistemological dilemma is not a special problem for naturalists.

References

Achinstein, Peter (1962). "The Circularity of a Self-Supporting Inductive Argument". *Analysis* 22, pp. 138–141.
Almeder, Robert (1998). *Harmless Naturalism*. Peru, IL: Open Court Publishing.
Bealer, George (1992). "The Incoherence of Empiricism". *The Aristotelian Society Supplementary Volume* 66, pp. 99–138.
Bealer, George (1996). "A *Priori* Knowledge and the Scope of Philosophy". *Philosophical Studies* 91, pp. 121–142.
Bealer, George (1999). "The A Priori". In *The Blackwell Guide to Epistemology*, ed. by John Greco and Ernest Sosa. Oxford: Blackwell Publishing, pp. 243–270.
Black, Max (1958). "Self-Supporting Inductive Arguments". *Journal of Philosophy* 55, pp. 718–725.
BonJour, Laurence (1998). *In Defense of Pure Reason*. Cambridge: Cambridge University Press.
Casullo, Albert (2000). "The Coherence of Empiricism". *Pacific Philosophical Quarterly* 81, pp. 31–48.
Foley, Richard (1994). "Quine and Naturalized Epistemology". In *Midwest Studies in Philosophy* IX, ed. by Peter French, Theodore Uehling Jr., and Howard Wettstein. South Bend, IN: University of Notre Dame Press, pp. 243–260.

---

[13] See BonJour (1998, 142–6) where he repudiates the request for any sort of metajustification for rationalism. He proceeds to go back to the self-evidence criterion in order to support his repudiation. However, I think that he still falls prey to the objection here raised. We can still ask why the self-evidence of a proposition is conducive to its being the object of a justified belief. Other theories of *a priori* justification do not seem to have the available machinery to be self-justifying either. For example Bealer's account of the *a priori* probativity of intuition does not seem to be intuitively obvious. See, for example, Bealer (1996) and Bealer (1999).

Goldman, Alvin (1967). "A Causal Theory of Knowing". *Journal of Philosophy* 64, pp. 357–372.

Goldman, Alvin (1979). "What is Justified Belief?" In *Justification and Knowledge,* ed. by George Pappas. Dordrecht: Reidel Publishing, pp. 1–23.

Laudan, Larry (1996). *Beyond Positivism and Relativism: Theory, Method, and Evidence.* Boulder, CO: Westview Press.

Oakley, Shane (forthcoming). *A Dilemma for Naturalism?* In *New Perspectives on A Priori Knowledge and Naturalism* , ed. by Michael Shaffer and Michael Veber. La Salle, IL: Open Court.

Quine, W.V.O. (1951). "Two Dogmas of Empiricism". Reprinted in Quine (1953), pp. 20–46.

Quine, W.V.O. (1953). *From a Logical Point of View,* 2nd ed. Cambridge, MA: Harvard University Press.

Quine, W.V.O. (1969a.). *Ontological Relativity and Other Essays.* New York: Columbia University Press.

Quine, W.V.O. (1969b.). "Epistemology Naturalized". In Quine (1969a.), pp. 69–90.

Shaffer, Michael and Jason Warnick (2004). "Bursting Bealer's Bubble: How the Starting Points Argument Begs the Question of Foundationalism Against Quine". *Canadian Journal of Philosophy* 34, pp. 87–105.

Siegel, Harvey (1980). "Justification, Discovery and the Naturalizing of Epistemology". *Philosophy of Science* 47, pp. 297–321.

Siegel, Harvey (1984). "Empirical Psychology, Naturalized Epistemology, and First Philosophy". *Philosophy of Science* 51, pp. 667–676.

van Fraassen, Bas (2002). *The Empirical Stance.* New Haven, CT: Yale University Press.

13

Understanding Quine in Terms of the Aufbau: Another Look at Naturalized Epistemology

STEFANIE ROCKNAK

1 Introduction

True to at least Burton Dreben's word, lifelong friend and student of Quine, it is simply irresponsible to study Quine apart from Carnap (Dreben, 1990)[1]. It could even be said that Quine's dedication to Carnap as his "teacher and friend" (Quine 1960) was far more than a polite gesture; without Carnap, there might not have been a Quine. Or at least, Quine as we know him. In fact, as if to underline this very point, Quine writes in his short essay "Homage to Rudolph Carnap" (1970) that: "Carnap was my greatest teacher ... I was his disciple for six years. In later years his views went on evolving and so did mine in divergent ways." "But," he immediately continues: "Even where we disagreed he was still setting the theme; the line of my thought was largely determined by problems that I thought his position presented." (Quine 1976: 41) These problems, at their most general level, revolved around what Russell once gave the title

---

[1] Dreben also emphasized this point in the 1993 Carnap/Quine seminar that I attended at Boston University.

Beyond Description: Naturalism and Normativity.
Marcin Miłkowski and Konrad Talmont-Kaminski (eds.).
Copyright © 2010 The Author.

of a book: *Our Knowledge of the External World* (1914). For the fundamental questions that initially drove Russell, then Carnap, and eventually Quine, were simple, although perplexing: What does our knowledge of the external world consist of and how do we acquire it? In what sense is it certain, and/or justifiable, if at all?

But I certainly can't give an exhaustive account of how Carnap influenced Quine here—that would take a book. Instead, I focus on explicating just a small portion of what I think is the central tension between these two philosophers. In particular, I claim that Quine reacted to three epistemological circles he believed to be present in Carnap's work. Here, I focus on what we may identify as the first circle: The "rational reconstruction" (Carnap 1967: 158) of knowledge in the *Logische Aufbau der Welt*, where knowledge seems to paradoxically emerge from knowledge[2].

2   The Aufbau; a General Overview

The early Carnap was the champion of the great Russellian project in *Our Knowledge of the External World*[3], which was, according to Quine, the explication of the "construction" of the external world from bits of sense data. (Quine 1981: 83) In the *Aufbau*, this consisted of "attempt[ing] *to apply the theory of relations to the task of analyzing reality*." (Carnap 1967:7) That is, for his method of construction, Carnap em-

---

[2] To frame our discussion in terms of Quine's more comprehensive reaction to Carnap, realize that the other two circles are: [2] "The linguistic doctrine of logical truth" (Quine 1976: 108). This amounts to Carnap's conventional doctrine of logical truth, as spelled out in the *Logical Syntax of Language*. According to Quine, on this account, we seem to have to already know logic to acquire logic. In particular, in order to accept a logical inference as logically valid, one must *presuppose* the validity of that very inference (c.f. Stroud (1955: 38–39)) [3] Carnap's brand of analyticity, which is not be confused with the linguistic doctrine of logical truth. For as Quine points out in a number of papers and letters to Carnap, and most famously in "The Two Dogmas of Empiricism" (1950), to define analyticity, one must *already* have some definition of analyticity in mind. So, correspondingly, to know what 'analyticity' means in terms of grasping it by way of its definition, we must *already* know what 'analyticity' means (see "Truth by Convention" (1935) in Quine 1976 and letter #97 in Creath 1990.

[3] See Richard Creath's comments in his introduction to *Dear Carnap, Dear Van*, particularly: "Russell called for the rational reconstruction of our knowledge on the basis of sense experience and urged the narrowest and deepest selection of concepts [in Our Knowledge of the External World]. It seemed to speak directly to Carnap. In fact [Carnap] penciled in the margin of his copy 'This narrowing and deepening of the fundamental postulates is my task!'" (Creath 1990: 24).

ploys the theory of relations as it was laid out by Russell and Whitehead in the *Principia*. Broadly speaking, this means that Carnap attempted to show that *all* concepts/objects[4] may be understood as logically "reducible," or *translatable*[5] to the primary relation "remembering as similar" (what we may also refer to as R) and certain unanalyzable "elementary experiences" (what we may also refer to as E) (see Carnap 1967: Chapter C). In this respect, Carnap hoped to "rationally reconstruct" the concepts of *all* fields of knowledge (including science) by showing that they may be translated into the strictly formal world of a "constructional language." This constructed language served as a model for how all fields of knowledge may be redefined, or in other words, logically *reduced* to R and elementary experiences[6].

As far as reducing concepts/objects to other concepts/objects goes, and conversely, constructing concepts/objects out of other concepts/objects, Carnap explains that:

> if an object *a* is reducible to objects *b, c*, then all statements about *a* can be transformed into statements about *b, c*. To reduce *a* to *b*, or to *construct a* out of *b, c*, means to produce a general rule that indicates for each individual case how a statement about *a* must be transformed in order to yield a statement about *b, c*. This rule of *translation* we call a *constructional rule* or *constructional definition* (Carnap 1967: 6).

That is, "construction rules" are the rules that allow us to change any statement about **a** into given statements about **b** and **c**, provided that the concept/object **a** is "reducible to," namely, may be redefined as the concept/objects **b, c**. Keep in mind that an accurate "statement"—or as Car-

---

[4] According to Carnap, there is no logical difference between concepts and objects. Rather, this difference is, at best, a psychological difference, and so, for the purposes of the Aufbau's program, may be ignored (Carnap 1967:10).

[5] Note the following passage where Carnap makes it quite clear that at least in principle, all knowledge may be *translated* into E and R (where here, he is concerned with making it clear that by doing so, he may also account for the objectivity of knowledge): "Even though the subjective *origin of all knowledge lies in the contents of experiences and their connections*, it is still possible, as the constructional system will show, to advance to an intersubjective, objective world, which can be conceptually comprehended and which is identical for all observers" (Carnap, 1967: 7; emphasis added). That is, important for us to note, "all knowledge" is contained it, or in other words, "lies in" E and R.

[6] Carnap never intended to *complete* the constructional system in the Aufbau. Instead, he merely wanted to show in what respect it was possible (Carnap 1967: 176).

nap also puts it, a "definition"—concerning a concept/object should be understood as a knowledge claim (see Carnap 1967: Chapter A). Also note the following passage (which refers back to Chapter A): "[science] can restrict itself to statements about structures, since all objects of knowledge are not content, but form, and since they can be represented as structural entities (cf. §15 f)" (Carnap 1967: 107). In other words, the "object" of knowledge in this case is a "structure," where the knowledge claim is the "statement" about that structure.

Ultimately, as Carnap explains in Part III, Chapter C of the Aufbau, all basic concepts/objects may then, by a method he calls "quasi-analysis," be reduced to a network of "basic relations," (Carnap 1967: 98) where, as noted earlier, the relation that is logically primary is R, ("remembering as similar") and the components that these relations obtain of consist of E (unanalyzable "elementary experiences"). However, "analyzing" "unanalyzable wholes" (namely, "elementary experiences") appears to be somewhat problematic. As a result, Carnap explains that "quasi-analysis" is actually "a *synthesis* which wears the garb of an analysis." (Carnap 1967: 121; emphasis added). So, although the construction/reduction process of translating concepts/objects into other concepts/objects in the Aufbau is strictly *analytic*, the method of constructing-from/reducing-to concepts/objects by way of "quasi-analysis" is *synthetic*. As a result, a reduction to the objects created by quasi-analysis, is, *analogously*, a reduction *to* the elementary experiences and R, a point that is behind Carnap's remark that "the subjective origin of all knowledge claims *lies in* the contents of experiences and their connections" (Carnap 1967: 7; emphasis added). For our purposes, this means that according to Carnap, all knowledge claims are first reducible to the products of quasi analysis ("basic relations" (§§75–83) which obtain of elementary experiences), and then second, analogously, by way of quasi-analysis, to the elementary experiences themselves, and R.

3 Quine's Reaction to "Radical" Reductionism: A Sensitivity to Circularity

3.1 "Attenuated" v. "Radical" Reductionism

As is well-known, Quine rejects the idea that any claim can, both in principle and in practice, be confirmed or denied on the basis of just experience. This rejection is behind his attack on the "second" dogma of empiricism, i.e. "synthetic" claims. Quine's renouncement of the synthetic amounts to a repudiation of what he refers to as a "subtler and more tenuous form" (Quine 1980: 40) of reductionism, or what we can refer to, after Quine, as *"attenuated"* reductionism (Quine 1980: 41; emphasis added). Meanwhile, it is also well-known that Quine rejects what he construes as Carnap's *"radical"* (Quine 1980: 39; emphasis added) reductionism, where, as explained in §1 above, it is alleged that all statements may be reduced, or in other words, *translated* into sense data (E) and R. Or as Quine puts it:

"Radical reductionism, conceived now with statements as units, set itself the task of specifying a sense-datum language and showing how to *translate* the rest of significant discourse, statement by statement, into it. Carnap embarked on this project in the Aufbau" (Quine, 1980: 39; emphasis added)[7].

3.2 The Paradox of Radical Reductionism

On the face of it, it seems that Quine eschewed the notion of "synthetic" claims—and so, the theory of "attenuated" reductionism—because of his holism. According to the holist, no sentence stands or falls on its own, regardless of what the empirical evidence tells us. Instead, the Quinean story goes, whether or not we reject or accept a given sentence depends on its relationship to the rest of the theory at hand: "statements about the

---

[7] Quine says "sense-datum *language*" (emphasis added) here, not "sense-datum" *simpliciter*. So, contrary to what we just saw in §2, it seems that Quine thought that in the Aufbau, Carnap was attempting to reduce all knowledge to a primary language *about* sense data, rather than *to* the sense data (and R) itself. And in some respects, Quine is correct, "quasi-analysis," consists in constructing an analogous formal language *about* elementary experiences; particularly, the construction of the "basic relations" that obtain of elementary experiences. Nevertheless, Carnap clearly thought that "all knowledge *lies in* the contents of experiences and their connections" (Carnap 1967: 7), not just in sentences made *about* E and R. So we might take Quine's insistence on referring to a sense datum *language* as an artifact of Quine's behaviourism, where only sentences may be true or false, not mental entities (see for instance, Quine 1960: §30–31, 1992: 69,1995 90–92 and 1953). Meanwhile, so-called mental entities must be understood in physical terms (e.g. as nerves firing, etc. See at least Quine 1974: 34). However, regardless if in this respect Quine appears to be intermittently imposing his own epistemological predilections on the Aufbau, it may be argued that its "radical" reductionism *still* seemed paradoxical to Quine, or at the very least, struck him as an impossible task (see above for more detail).

external world face the tribunal of sense experience not individually, but only as a corporate body" (Quine 1980: 41)[8].

But I think that the reasons behind Quine's rejection of attenuated reductionism are more complex than this, although Quine never directly says as much. To see why this appears to have been the case, we must first understand how and why Quine rejected the paradoxical "radical" reductionism manifest in the Aufbau. To begin, note a particularly revealing line from Quine's 1993 paper "In Praise of Observation Sentences:" "The lively objection to [protocol sentences], as vehicles of evidence for our knowledge of the external world, is that they already assume such knowledge" However, he continues, "the answer is that they need not." (Quine 1993: 108; emphasis added). Here, Quine is defending the idea that his notion of an "observation sentence—" a term that he uses interchangeably in this paper with the term "protocol sentence—" is not, in the course of the human being's learning process, initially "theory-laden" (Quine 1993: 110). Rather, our initial use of language is purely *reflexive*; a product of our being habituated to say a given sentence S when we experience a given range of neural intake M (Quine 1993: 109). Only later (through a process that is not relevant for us to examine) do human beings acquire theory, and relatedly, knowledge. But why does Quine balk at the idea that our observation sentences somehow initially "assume" knowledge?

Two reasons, where the first, and most well-known is: According to Quine, science tells us that our initial input is remarkably "meager" (Quine 1995: 16), consisting of "the mere impacts of rays and particles on our surfaces and a few odds and ends such as the strain of walking uphill" (Quine 1995: 16). In this respect, our initial input consists of unrelated bits and pieces of sense data. So, we are not "aware" of such nerves firing (see at least Quine 1995: 17–18, and 1974: 2–4). Instead, this input must be understood as our body's initial and unconscious state of reacting to the world. This is the case not only when we are infants and first experience the world, but also as our "outermost" interface with the world assails us throughout our lives. Thus, "knowing"—where, ac-

---

[8] For more on Quine's notion of holism, see at least: "The Five Milestones of Empiricism" (1975) in Quine 1981, 1991 and 1992: 13–16. Keep in mind though, that in "The Two Dogmas of Empiricism," Quine credits Duhem (1906) and Lowinger (1941) for initially working out the fundamentals of holism. Quine's notion of "underdetermination" also comes into play here, but for our purposes, and given length restraints, we need not throw it into the mix. See Bergström (2004) for more detail.

cording to Quine, knowing consists of at least some kind of psychological ability to evaluate data such that we may say the right thing at the right time, and as a result, at the very least, be "aware" of what is being experienced and what to say[9]—is simply *not* an option at this stage of our data acquisition. Rather, according to Quine, our initial, most outermost interface with the world occurs at what he characterizes as the purely "*rec*eptual" (Quine 1995: 17) level of data acquisition. Accordingly, "awareness," and so, the possibility of knowledge occurs only at the "*per*ceptual" (Quine 1995:17) stage of data acquisition[10].

Second, although Quine never explicitly says so, it seems that assuming knowledge in our initial experience of the world incurs the second horn of Meno's Paradox, i.e., "[A man] would not seek what he knows, for since he knows it, there is no need of inquiry." (Cooper 1997: *Meno* 80 d-e). To see why, we must briefly re-examine what is going on behind the scenes in Carnap's Aufbau. In particular, realize that if any statements about a concept/object **a** are, in fact "translatable" (FLPV; TDE; 39) or in other words, are *logically equivalent* to some set of elementary experiences E and the relation of R, it seems that in virtue of just experiencing E and knowing R and the theory of relations, we must simultaneously know **a** and any statements about **a** as well—at least implicitly—much in the same way that if we know $A \supset B$ and we know our equivalence rules, then we know $\sim A \vee B$. For again, if it is the case that all concepts/objects may be *reduced* (namely, are logically equivalent to elementary experiences and R), then it seems that all our possible knowledge of the external world (including scientific theory) "lies in" (Carnap 1967: 7) our "elementary experiences" and R, if only in the respect that "lies in" means logically equivalent to[11]. For as noted above, the Aufbau's reduc-

---

[9] This is part and parcel of Quine's behaviorism; see at least Quine 1995 and 1992 where he gives a general outline of this position.

[10] For more on the distinction between "reception" and "perception," see at least Quine 1995: 17–18 and 1974: 2–4.

[11] With all the technical subtleties of the synthesis that occurs with quasi-analysis aside. For as noted earlier, the point we must grasp is Carnap's claim that all *knowledge* may, in principle, be reduced, or in other words, translated via logical equivalence (as manifest by theory of relations) to elementary experiences and R, regardless if the last step in this reduction (quasi-analysis) incurs a method of establishing "synthetic" equivalence. More importantly still, this is how Quine understood the Aufbau. Recall, for instance the following passage from "The Two Dogmas of Empiricism" where he writes: "Radical reductionism, conceived now with statements as units, set itself the task of specifying a sense-

tionist program was modeled after the logistic reduction carried out in the Principia (although the latter engaged in a fatally flawed reduction, as pointed out by Gödel (1931)). In fact, Quine writes in *From Stimulus to Science*:

> The conclusion [Whitehead and Russell] drew was that mathematics is *translatable* into pure logic (FSS 9) ... [The] *total translatability* [of mathematics and their basic laws and interrelations] into just elementary logic and a single familiar two-place predicate, membership, is of itself a philosophical sensation (FSS 9–10; emphases added) ... Russell adumbrated [the idea of this kind of construction] in *Our Knowledge of the External World*, and a dozen years later, Rudolf Carnap was undertaking to carry it out. Carnap's effort found expression in *Der Logische Aufbau der Welt* (1928) (Quine 1995: 10; first two emphases added).

However as far as I can tell, Quine did not *overtly* reject the Aufbau because all knowledge that is possibly derivative of a given elementary experience E, the relation R and the theory of relations, is it seems, "assumed" in these primary elements. Rather, he accuses Carnap of embracing a "mentalistic monism" in the Aufbau because, Quine asserts, "elementary experiences" were psychological "global units" (Quine 1995: 10) that consisted of "the individual's total experience at that moment" (Quine 1995: 10)[12]. As a result, Quine explains, these psychologically experienced wholes were, according to gestalt psychologists—as well as according to Carnap—units that one is necessarily "aware of" (Quine 1974:1–4) when they are being experienced. And in the respect that one would be "aware" of such units, one would, at least to some inchoate degree, *know* them. So, as Quine sees it, according to this psycho-epistemological account of the world, "awareness of" was roughly equiv-

---

datum language and showing how *to translate* the rest of significant discourse, statement by statement, *into it*. Carnap embarked on this project in the Aufbau" (Quine 1980: 39; emphasis added). See also the passages cited above from *From Stimulus to Science* and "Epistemology Naturalized," where Quine makes similar claims. However, as noted in footnote 7, it must be pointed out that at least at some level, Quine indicates that Carnap was not translating all knowledge into E and R, but instead, into certain *statements about* E and R. Either option however, as we see above, would have been problematic for Quine.

[12] Moreover, Quine thought that despite all the logically machinery that Carnap appealed to in the Aufbau, he could not adequately account for our ability to make spatial identifications. For more on this, see at least Quine 1980: 40 and 1969: 76–77.

alent to "knowledge of"—such "wholes" were alleged to be the psychological foundations of knowledge (Quine 1974: 1–4).

So, on the face of it, it does not appear that Quine calls the Aufbau a "sort of fiction" (Quine 1993: 116) and "make believe" (Quine 1969: 75) because it invokes the second horn of Meno's Paradox. However, this must be understood as his deeper objection; overt or not. Carnap's "mentalism," or what Quine also refers to as his "phenomenomalism" (Quine 1995: 15–16) is not just unconvincing because it incurs vague and suspicious mental entities ("elementary experiences"), but worse still, these entities allegedly admit of immediate awareness, and so, *knowledge of the world*. And not just rudimentary knowledge, but, it seems, knowledge that is logically equivalent to all the theories and knowledge claims possibly derivative of a given elementary experience or experiences. Note in fact, where Quine *does* somewhat obliquely admit as much in "Epistemology Naturalized" (1968), paying particular attention to the idea that it would be nice, Quine thinks, if we could show that all of science is *translatable* to "logic, observation terms and set theory" (Quine 1969: 76), and so, "[show] that everything done with the one apparatus could in principle be done with other" (Quine 1969: 76). But quite frankly, he tells us, this is *impossible*.

So, it's clear that Quine *did* think that the Aufbauian project was paradoxical, although not *quite* in Meno's respect that we would be *unmotivated* to learn what we already know. Rather, it is simply *not possible* that in virtue of just "elementary experiences" and R that we simultaneously know all of what we eventually come to learn, particularly, scientific theory. Or as Quine puts it: "certainly we *did not* grow up learning definitions of a physicalist language in terms of a prior language of set theory, logic and observation" (Quine 1969: 76; emphasis added). In fact, Quine had already put his finger on what seems to be the sheer impossibility of assuming such a cache of sophisticated logical ability some eighteen years earlier when he wrote in "The Two Dogmas of Empiricism:"

"The language which Carnap adopted as his starting point [in the Aufbau] was not a sense-datum language in the narrowest conceivable sense, for included also the notations of logic, up through higher set theory. In effect it included the whole of language of pure mathematics. The ontology implicit in it (that is, the range of values of its variables) embraced not only sensing events but classes, classes of classes, and so on. *Empi-*

ricists there are who would boggle at such prodigality." (Quine 1980: 39; emphasis added)

Who was "boggling?" We might, given what we have seen above, conclude that it was *Quine* who found himself gasping at such epistemological "prodigality." In fact, in so many words, Quine repeats this point in his last book, *From Stimulus to Science*, when he writes: "we are given a canon or procedure [in the Aufbau], and a brilliant one, but not one that makes the theory of the external world translatable into the language of sense experience. *That is too much to ask.*" (Quine 1995: 13; emphasis added)

4 The Naturalistic Circle

With Quine's rejection of "radical" reductionism in mind, where this rejection seems to turn on a somewhat implicit rejection of a form of Meno's Paradox, let's take two versions of what I characterize as the "naturalistic circle" into account. These two circles relentlessly plague naturalistic (empirical) philosophers, but, by rejecting the radical reductionism of the Aufbau (as it manifests itself in terms of Meno's Paradox) Quine appears to have escaped both.

4.1 The Naturalistic Circle: Hume's Version

According to Hume, the scientific method is a fallible method in the respect that its subject matter consists of "matters of facts" (Hume 1978: 1.3)[13]. This is the case because according to Hume, knowledge claims that are based on matters of fact are based on the relation of cause and effect. (Hume 1978: 1.3) However, no causal relation is, according to Hume, necessary, but instead, is a product of imagining certain constantly conjoined events as apprehended through any and/or all of our five senses. As a result, any causal relation can always be imagined otherwise without creating a contradiction. So, no matter of fact is necessarily true. Accordingly, because the scientific method is constructed from consideration of matters of fact, no result it yields is necessarily true (Hume 1978: 1.3). Consequently, by appealing to the scientific method to show that we must use the scientific method to philosophically examine the world, where a component of that world is the scientific method itself,

---

[13] Hume identified this as the method of "experience" (Hume 1978: xvi-xvii).

one makes a claim that is *not* necessarily true. No claim derivative of the scientific method is necessarily true, even if it's the claim: "We must use science to examine science." As a result, it is simply not *certain* that we should be doing naturalized philosophy at all. This is what we may identify as Hume's version of the "naturalistic circle," a circle that Hume intermittently torments himself with, particularly in the Treatise[14].

It's no surprise then, that Quine, latter-day Humean empiricist that he was, puts his finger on this circle approximately two hundred years later in *Roots of Reference*. However, here, Quine locates the circle in a historical venue that preceded Hume by thousands of years:

> Ancient skepticism, in its more primitive way, likewise challenged science from within. The skeptics cited familiar illusion to show the fallibility of the senses; but this concept of illusion rested on natural science, since the quality of illusion consisted simply in deviation from external scientific reality (Quine 1974: 2–3).

Ancient skepticism challenged science from a "scientific point of view" because the concept of an illusion is itself a scientific concept; an "illusion" is, by definition, a "deviation" from an empirically confirmable fact. As a result, the idea that the senses are fallible—and thus susceptible to illusion—is *itself* a claim that is derived from the senses. This means that the claim "The senses are fallible" seems to be fallible *itself*, and thus, is susceptible to illusion. So, just as Hume would complain thousands of years later, it seems that science may be "challenged ... from within" (Quine 1974: 2)[15].

4.2 The Naturalistic Circle; The Physicalist Version

With the general structure of the Humean version of the naturalistic circle in mind, let's now take a look at what I characterize as the physicalist version, which was brought squarely into focus by Quine. According to Quine, sense data, which he prefers to construe as "neural input," is fragmented, which—at least at the level that Quine identifies as *reception*—consists of experiences that we are in no way "aware" of. And so,

---

[14] See especially Hume 1978: 268–9.

[15] Also see "Epistemology Naturalized" (in Quine 1969), where Quine specifically mentions the "Humean predicament" (1969: 72) in regard to Hume's naturalistic method. Also see Pakaluk's (1989) citations from Quine's 1946 lecture notes on Hume, specifically 455, 457, 459.

these experiences, as explained above, could not possibly admit of knowledge, even knowledge in Quine's behavioristic sense of the word. Rather, as explained earlier, according to Quine, "awareness" and so, any possibility for knowledge, only emerges at the level of *per*ceptual similarity. In this respect, Quine's epistemology is fearlessly "physicalistic"—the primary source of all our knowledge consists of nerves firing, where "awareness" of such events is decisively absent. Recall that this way of looking at data acquisition is opposed to Carnap's "phenomenalism," where the source of all our knowledge consists of mentalistic entities that *are* related (at least by R). Moreover, we *are* aware of them.

However, adopting the physicalist stance seems to incur another version of the naturalistic circle: If one assumes physicalism *and* attempts to reduce, or in other words, claims to *translate* knowledge, particularly, knowledge of scientific theory, to nerve inputs, where such input does *not* admit of knowledge, then it seems that such knowledge is effectively equated to something that is *not* knowledge, namely, "smells, noises, feels, flashes, patches of color and the like" (Quine 1974: 1). As a result, it simply follows that if we *translate* science, say, the scientific claim X "All our scientific theory may be reduced to physical input" *to* physical input, then all of science, e.g. in this particular case, X, is equivalent to *nonsense*; that is, mere "impacts on our sensory surfaces" (Quine 1992: 1). This then, is the physicalist version of the naturalistic circle, which Quine discusses tirelessly throughout his work[16].

5 A Summary of What is at Stake

By now, it should be clear that Quine was faced with the following epistemological mess: If we "radically" reduce or translate knowledge to sense data it seems that:

a.) We must *assume* such knowledge in the sense data by way of the Gestalt psychologists' "wholes," or what Carnap preferred to call "elementary experiences." This constitutes what we might call, after Quine,

---

[16] See for instance, Quine 1974: 2–4, 1969: 71–72, 74–75, 83–84, 1981: 24, 1992: 1–20 and 1960: 2, 4. Note just one of these passages: "Science itself teaches that there is no clairvoyance; that the only information that can reach our sensory surfaces from external objects must be limited to two-dimensional optical projections and various impacts of airwaves on the eardrums and some gaseous reactions in the nasal passages and a few kindred odds and ends. How, the challenge proceeds, could one hope to find out about that external world from such meager traces? In short, *if our science were true, how could we know it?*" (Quine 1974: 2; emphasis added).

"phenomenalistic" radical reductionism. Yet as noted, according to Quine—with all suspect mentalistic overtures aside—this is simply impossible. The Aufbauian project smacks of the second horn of Meno's Paradox, i.e., the idea that we would not seek knowledge if we already *knew* such knowledge, where in this case, Quine translates the problem of a lack of motivation to seek what we already know into bleak impossibility: It's just *not* the case that in virtue of our "elementary experiences" and knowledge of R and all of set theory that we know all possible knowledge claims logically derivative of E and R. This would simply "be too much to ask" (Quine 1995: 13).

b.) If—unlike the Aufbau Carnap—we conclude that our sense input does *not* admit of knowledge, it seems that if we reduce, or in other words, translate scientific theory and/or knowledge into sense data conceived of from a physicalistic point of view (and so, engage in what we might call, after Quine, "physicalistic" radical reductionism), then knowledge, particularly knowledge of scientific theory, equates to nerves firing, and so, it seems, to *nonsense*. This is the physicalist version of the naturalistic circle.

c.) Regardless if we assume that knowledge is or is not present in the sense data (e.g. in terms of "elementary experiences"), empiricists widely accept the fact that empirical, and thus scientific claims, are *fallible*—as was made particularly clear by Hume. So, if the claim "We must use science to examine science" is a scientific claim, then it is a fallible claim; this is Hume's version of the naturalistic circle, and it, "challeng[es] science from within" (Quine 1974: 2).

6 The Solution: Naturalism Embraced; "Radical" and "Attenuated" Reductionism Rejected

Quine's three-fold solution to this mess is, as I see it, quite simple although many aspects of it have been much contested[17].

a.') We *cannot,* according to Quine, assume knowledge in our initial input. This means that Quine must flat-out reject Carnap's "phenomenalistic" radical reductionism. If we do *not*, we simply assume too much, causing us to "boggle at [the] prodigality" (Quine 1980: 39) inherent in such an endeavor. Meanwhile, as Quine sees it, contemporary scientific

---

[17] For some of these objections see *Perspectives on Quine* (1990), and *The Philosophy of W.V. Quine*, 1986 and 1998.

research shows that our initial input ("reception") does *not* admit of knowledge; science seems to favor the physicalistic approach. So, ironically[18], it seems that a simple Platonic Paradox appears to have justified Quine's endorsement of contemporary scientific research, but quite *independently* of Quine's pragmatic reasons for embracing naturalism. The paradox of "radical" reductionism may have made it quite clear to Quine that it is just *unreasonable* to assume knowledge in our initial interface with the world. As a result, problem a.) is avoided; our initial input is not only bereft of knowledge (even as adults), we are, according to contemporary scientific research, born knowing virtually nothing.

b.') However, if one *translates* knowledge claims into what science tells us constitutes our outermost interface with the world (i.e. fragmented sense data ("reception")) one effectively translates knowledge into nonsense. Recall that this is the physicalized version of the naturalistic circle. To specifically avoid this predicament, Quine *must* claim that at best, knowledge claims are "*evidence[d]*" by stimulus, where the notion "evidenced by" is not, equivalent to "equivalent to" (Quine 1981: 24). In other words, by "evidence," Quine is referring to the significant but *not* comprehensive influence that sense data has on a sentence. According to Quine, to grasp the given sentence's entire meaning, and likewise its truth value (and so to properly know it) it must be understood in terms of the theory it is embedded in. As a result, this means that a rejection of "radical" reductionism *entails* a rejection of "attenuated" reductionism. For if a knowledge claim is not reducible to, and thus, is not equivalent to sense data, but instead, its meaning, and *likewise*, its truth value can *only* be obtained upon considering it in terms of the theory it is embedded in, it simply follows that there are no knowledge claims whose truth values may be obtained solely in virtue of empirical confirmation or disconfirmation. So problem c.) is avoided; knowledge, knowledge of scientific theory in particular, is simply *not* equivalent to nonsense. And as an added bonus, the "synthetic" dogma ("attenuated" reductionism) is revealed for what it is—a dogma.

c.') With the rejection of "attenuated" reductionism, the expectation for "certainty" is also dropped because "the two dogmas are, indeed, at

---

[18] In the respect that Plato was, by no stretch of the imagination, a naturalistic philosopher. According to Plato, the way to the truth was by way of "pure" rationality, whereas empirical evidence only created confusion, if not knee-jerk relativism (see at least, the Theaetetus).

root identical" (Quine 1980: 41). For according to Quine, just as no claim may be proven true or false purely in virtue of sense data, no claim may be proven true or false purely in virtue of its meaning, where the latter ("analytic") claims, it is typically alleged, admit of "certainty" and the former ("synthetic") claims do not. But *no claim,* according to Quine, is "certain," or in other words, is "necessary" (see also Quine 1976). As a result, it simply doesn't *matter* if the scientific method, or our choice to employ it, is fallible. What *does* matter, according to Quine is that science *works*, "[the scientific, empirical method] is the best [method] we know" (Quine 1960: 4). Science allows us to make certain predictions about the world, which include predictions and hypotheses *about* scientific theory. And so, problem c.) is avoided; the Humean version of the naturalistic circle is simply *irrelevant*; it is a manifestation of misplaced expectations.

In conclusion, when faced with the question of: Where does our knowledge of the external world come from, Quine was forced to turn to science. In fact, it's no wonder that Quine's very last book, *From Stimulus to Science*, was devoted to "physicalizing" the Aufbau. For, the story goes, when we see that reducing knowledge *to knowledge* (e.g. "elementary experiences," R and all of set theory) is absurd (namely, when we see that phenomenalistic radical reductionism is absurd), we must turn to the more reasonable scientific account of knowledge acquisition, i.e. the idea that we are born knowing virtually nothing. But this does not mean that we should *equate* such an initial lack of knowledge (nerves firing, etc.) with what we *do* know. That is, we shouldn't engage in physicalistic radical reductionism either. And so, the physicalized version of the naturalistic circle is avoided. For although all our knowledge claims are *supported* by empirical evidence; they may not be translated into them, solving the problem of "if our science were true, how could we know it?" (Quine 1974: 2). Thus, the synthetic dogma is revealed *as* a dogma, and so, "attenuated" reductionism may be rejected. Simultaneously—because the two dogmas are, at root, identical—this means that no knowledge claim admits of absolute certainty, inspiring us to lower our somewhat childish philosophical expectations for science. As a result, we may simply sidestep Hume's torment and instead, exercise science for all that it's worth.

References

Carnap, Rudolf (1967). *The Logical Structure of the World; Pseudo problems in Philosophy,* Second Edition. Translated by R.A. George, Berkeley and Los Angeles: University of California Press (original publication date: 1928).
Cooper, J., ed. (1997). *Plato: Complete Works*. Hackett, 1997.
Dreben, Burton (1990). "Quine". *Perspectives on Quine,* eds. Robert Barrett and Roger Gibson. Oxford: Blackwell.
Dreben, Burton (1992). "Putnam, Quine—and the Facts". *Philosophical Topics* 20, pp. 293–315.
Dreben, Burton (1995) "In Medius Rebus". *Inquiry* 37, pp. 441–447.
Duhem, Pierre (1906). *La Théorie physique: son object et sa structure.* Paris: Chevalier et Rivière.
Gödel, Kurt (1986). *Collected Works: Publications 1929–1936*, New York: Oxford University Press.
Hume, David (1978). *A Treatise of Human Nature*, ed. by L.A. Selby-Bigge, 2nd ed. New York: Oxford (original publication date: 1739–40).
Lowinger, Armand (1941). *The Methodology of Pierre Duhem*. New York: Columbia.
Pakaluk, Michael (1989). "Quine's 1946 Lectures on Hume". *Journal of the History of Philosophy* 27, pp. 445–459.
Quine, W.V. (1953). "On Mental Entities". *Proceedings of the American Academy of Arts and Sciences* 80(3), pp. 198–203.
Quine, W.V. (1960). *Word and Object*. Cambridge, MA: MIT.
Quine, W.V. (1969). *Ontological Relativity and Other Essays*. New York: Columbia.
Quine, W.V. (1974). *The Roots of Reference*, La Salle: Illinois: Open Court.
Quine, W.V. (1976). *The Ways of Paradox and Other Essays*. Enlarged edition. Cambridge, MA: Harvard.
Quine, W.V. (1980). *From a Logical Point of View; 9 logico-philosophical essays*. Second edition, revised. Cambridge, MA: Harvard.
Quine, W.V. (1981). *Theories and Things*. Cambridge, MA: Harvard.
Quine, W.V. (1991). "Two Dogmas in Retrospect". *Canadian Journal of Philosophy* 21 (3), pp. 265–274.
Quine, W.V. (1992). *Pursuit of Truth*. Revised ed. Cambridge, MA: Harvard.
Quine, W.V. (1995). *From Stimulus to Science*, Cambridge, MA: Harvard.
Quine, W.V. (1993). "In Praise of Observation Sentences". *Journal of Philosophy* XC (3), pp. 107–116.
Russell, Bertrand (1961). *Our Knowledge of the External World*. London: George Allen and Unwin Ltd.

14

Descriptive Epistemology and Normativity: A Humean Approach[*]

TREASA CAMPBELL

1 Introduction

Emerging from Hume's account of belief formation is an understanding of causation in which the move made by the human mind from cause to effect is instinctual rather than rational. On this conception, the move from cause to effect is an unavoidable, indispensable and universal feature of how we as humans operate in the world. This specific description, 'unavoidable, indispensable and universal', sets out the unique character of the phenomena under investigation. My use of these terms may seem repetitive but I do this intentionally to emphasise the importance of the distinctive character which is being attributed to the causal move. It is as a consequence of being unavoidable, indispensable and universal that the causal instinct stands apart as a limit setting feature of the belief forming process. There is then a natural necessity which attaches to the causal instinct. The inescapable lived reality of the operation of the causal in-

---

[*] I would like to thank participants of the Kazimierz Naturalised Epistemology Workshop 2006 for extremely helpful comments and discussion. Dr. Stephen Thornton and Dr. Stephen Bond also provided many helpful suggestions in the preparation of this paper. Work on this research was generously supported by a Post-Graduate Scholarship from the Irish Research Council for the Humanities and Social Sciences.

Beyond Description: Naturalism and Normativity.
Marcin Miłkowski and Konrad Talmont-Kaminski (eds.).
Copyright © 2010 The Author.

stinct necessitates that its normative status be considered in very different terms.

As this conception of the causal move is based on Hume's descriptive account of how humans form beliefs, it has long been held to carry little normative value. It falls victim to the is/ought divide according to which descriptive theory can not generate evaluative prescriptions. Similar normative difficulties have been encountered by the various contemporary attempts to naturalise epistemology[1]. Traditionally, the central characteristic of epistemology is that it is a normative enterprise: it is concerned with how we *ought* to think, rather than with how we *happen* to think. However, the growing popularity of naturalistic approaches has seen the difficulty in generating normative prescriptions from descriptive theory become a central issue in contemporary epistemology. For this reason Hume's work has a strong contemporary resonance[2].

This paper is primarily concerned with the implications of the 'causal instinct' and the arguments relating to the normative status of this universal and unavoidable feature of our engagement with the world. Individual, content-specific beliefs inevitably emerge as our natural instincts are exposed to the stimuli provided by the senses. We have, for example, the individual, content-specific belief that the sun will rise tomorrow. Our causal instinct, combined with the stimuli of the senses, gives rise to this individual content-specific belief. Exposing the causal instinct as a fundamental component of how we form beliefs has implications not only for our understanding of the general process of belief formation but also for how we begin to address the process of evaluating the particular beliefs being formed. How does natural necessity, which concerns what *must* be the case, relate to normative necessity concerning what *ought* to be the case? If the key purpose of norms is for people to act on them, and if 'ought' implies 'can', do norms to which people cannot act lose their validity? Is it possible for natural necessity to serve as both explanation and justification? In identifying the causal move not as a belief (the outcome of a reasoning strategy) but as an unavoidable, universal feature of

---

[1] This need not be viewed as a problem which is faced solely by descriptive naturalist epistemologies. Bishop and Trout (2005) argue that standard analytic epistemologies (foundationalism, coherentism, reliabilism and contextualism) have at their core deceptive theory and as a result also share this normative difficulty.

[2] Resemblances between the paradigmatic naturalism of Quine and the earlier form of naturalism found in Hume have been acknowledged (Rea, 2002; Kitcher, 1992).

how we engage with the world, Hume's naturalism[3] can enrich our understanding, not only of the process of belief formation, but of the kinds of normative discourse which are appropriate within descriptive philosophy.

This paper sets out to give Hume's descriptive account a degree of normative worth, and in so doing, to draw the attention of contemporary eyes to the relevant normative insights contained in this earlier version of naturalism. I argue that the Humean account identifies the causal move as an unavoidable, instinctual feature of how we operate in the world, this feature determines how we pursue the epistemologist's tasks. It will be demonstrated that if we disregard such a universal and unavoidable aspect of how we engage with the world, the norms which we establish will have no legitimate force for human beings. Drawing upon Harold I. Brown's discussion of the interconnected relationship between epistemic norms and our cognitive abilities, I highlight the extent to which descriptive accounts form the framework within which normative accounts can arise, particularly when they reveal cognitive capacities, as is the case with Hume. With reference to Carnap's account of inductive intuition, I will argue for the removal of any viciousness associated with the circularity that arises from such an enterprise. The question of justification in relation to universal and unavoidable features which belongs to us by virtue of our nature will then be addressed, and the case will be made that justification in this context is neither possible nor necessary.

2 The Validity of Description

There has long been an uneasy relationship between norms and descriptions due in no small part to Hume himself. Indeed, in the context of ethical theory, Hume warns of the dangers involved in deducing "ought" from "is". In so doing, he makes the case for the illegitimacy of any

---

[3] Any survey of contemporary attempts to naturalise epistemology will quickly reveal that there is an array of theories, many contradictory, all claiming to be a form of naturalism. For an account of the various ways to disambiguate theses theories see Haack (1993), Kitcher (1992), Kornblith (1991), Maffie (1990). As with contemporary naturalism there is no single unitary account of what Humean naturalism entails. Norman Kemp Smith's seminal work on Hume led the way on naturalist interpretations of Hume and there now exists a wide array of competing naturalist readings of Hume, see for example Garrett (1997), Loeb (2002), Pears (1990), Stroud (1977), P.F. Strawson (1985).

move which attempts to arrive at an account of correct behaviour solely from a description of the way people do in fact behave. It would seem then that in both the ethical and the epistemological fields we must be able to establish norms separately and independently from any account of how people actually operate.

Fodor describes Hume's *Treatise* as "the foundational document of cognitive science" (Fodor 2003: 134). Hume's account of belief formation is primarily an investigation of the actual practice involved in belief formation; he does not study the logic of the structures of beliefs in abstraction from belief formation as it is actually carried out. Hence, Hume's ascription of a causal instinct to humans is a description of what we do, rather then a normative explanation of our action. Howson describes Hume's response as an attempt "to explain where he could not justify." (Howson 2000: 20) Passmore too held that in attempting to reconcile his sceptical conclusion with his positive description of how we do in fact form beliefs, Hume had provided at best a psychological resolution of the contradiction. Hume had simply described epistemic practices instead of evaluating them. Accordingly, Hume's answer to scepticism "is not a philosophical argument but a psychological fact" (Passmore 1952: 149). On such a reading, we must interpret Hume as being concerned more with action than knowledge, and attribute no prescriptive role to his account of belief formation. But the causal instinct which Hume's naturalism exposes cannot simply be ignored by philosophers and discarded as nothing more than "some psychological quirks of our constitution" (Popkin 1966: 64). When speaking of causal inferences, Hume famously said that "nothing leads us to this inference but custom or a certain instinct of our nature" (E190)[4]. Hume's descriptive account reveals that the operation of causation, which has traditionally been viewed in terms of a belief, must instead be considered in terms of a distinct form of instinct[5]. For Hume, the causal move is the result of a uni-

---

[4] I will use the following abbreviations in referencing works by David Hume:
T: *A Treatise of Human Nature*
E: *An Enquiry Concerning Human Understanding*
D: *Dialogues Concerning Natural Religion*

[5] Hume commentators such as Butler (1960), Gaskin (1974), McCormick (1993) and Kemp Smith (1905) regularly refer to the causal move as having an unavoidable and universal character, describing it as belonging to a unique class of belief which they term "natural belief". I have argued that Hume calls for more then a mere reclassification of this phenomenon as a unique form of belief. Rather, Hume's work necessitates that this phenomenon should no longer be viewed as any form of belief but as an instinct. See Campbell (2006) in which the case for this interpretation of Hume is set out.

versal, unavoidable instinct[6]. This instinct is a fundamental component of how we operate in the world, forming content specific beliefs. The causal move is to be understood in term of an unavoidable, indispensable and universal instinct, which, when exposed to external stimuli, produces content specific beliefs. In making this belief/instinct shift in relation to our understanding of the causal move, Hume enacts a dramatic transformation in the epistemological landscape.

The causal move is no longer viewed as the product of reasoning but as a cognitive resource. Thus, having provided a descriptive account of belief formation, Hume need not relinquish any attempt to address the critical normative aspect of epistemology. In an epistemological context, obedience to the dogmatic rigidity of the is/ought dichotomy blinds us to the interconnected relationship between epistemic norms and our cognitive abilities. There is a real sense in which a description of our cognitive abilities is essential to establishing any genuine epistemic norms. Harold I. Brown, in his article "Psychology, Naturalized Epistemology and Rationality", characterised the danger as follows:

> If we attempt to proceed a priori we may well end up with norms that have no legitimate force for human beings because they make demands on us that we cannot possibly fulfill. In other words, we need an account of the *appropriate epistemic norms* for human beings; an account of what is normatively rational, requires a prior account of what is rational in the descriptive sense—an account of what cognitive abilities human beings have available (Brown 1996: 20).

For Hume, the causal move is a universal, unavoidable feature of how we operate in the world; as such, any account of appropriate epistemic norms must incorporate it. As a specific feature of human beings the causal instinct determines how we pursue the epistemologist's tasks. If we attempt to construct norms in a vacuum, disregarding such permanent and irresistible aspects of how we engage in the world, then the norms we establish will have no legitimate force for human beings.

---

[6] It should be noted that not all instincts can be described as universal and unavoidable in fact this is a very stringent criteria.

The dominant objection to such an approach has always been that it is possible to provide a descriptive claim that is incorrect. This being the case, how can we escape the contradictions that arise when we attempt to choose between competing descriptions? It seems then that we must already have a set of epistemic norms in order to decide which competing descriptions are correct. Hence, normative epistemology, it seems, must proceed independently of any descriptive epistemology. Brown addresses this objection by demonstrating that descriptive epistemologies have been vital in providing the basis for specific norms and in determining what kinds of norms are appropriate for human knowers. Brown makes the case that "descriptive epistemology has played a much greater role in the development of normative epistemology than many contemporary epistemologists have acknowledged" (Brown 1996: 20). Brown argues that the manner in which traditional epistemological problems have been formulated rely on empirical claims about human cognition, giving as an example the problem of perception[7] in philosophy. He argues that the central role of this problem has only emerged because of changes that occurred in our understanding of the actual nature of human sense perception. He charts how the recognition of the existence of perpetual illusions necessitated a change in our understanding of sensory experience. In forgoing the belief that sensory experience provides an accurate image of the physical object that causes it, we have changed our understanding of sensory experience, with the consequential effect of initiating entirely new problems for the epistemology of perception. Such questions arise, however, only because of the particular understanding we have of the operation of our senses. Change the particular descriptive account of the operation of the senses and this particular problem of epistemology need not arise. Brown sums up the point as follows: "the very way in which traditional epistemological problems have been formulated depends on empirical claims about human cognition." (Brown 1996: 22) Goldman also makes clear that cognitive science is relevant to certain epistemological questions, stating that "to the extent that human epistemic attainments critically depend on human cognitive endowments, those endowments are relevant to epistemology." (Goldman 2002: 146) In the introduction to the *Treatise* Hume goes further emphasising the importance of providing a "science of Man", for there is no question of any importance which "can be decided with any certainty, before we become acquainted with that science" (T43).

---

[7] For Brown this problem is not one concern, but a problem-cluster made up of a variety of questions concerning the reliability of our senses and use of the data of sense perception.

Even in the light of this interconnectedness between norms and descriptions, there still remains a very enticing argument to continue to strive to locate a means by which epistemic norms can be established *a priori*. We can and do appeal to explanatory theories, but if we believe these are themselves supported and must be supported by observation, the problem is simply pushed back a stage; it is not solved. The causal instinct on which Hume must draw in order to arrive at his account of human cognition is established empirically. But this requires that we already have a set of methodological rules that will allow us to evaluate empirical claims. It would seem then that we are trapped in a vicious circle: "We need a body of psychology in order to choose an appropriate methodology, but we need a methodology in order to evaluate psychological hypotheses." (Brown 1996: 22) Having encountered such circularity, the need for *a priori* norms seems pressing, for without such norms how are we to provide an anchor outside of the process of empirical investigation that would provided a noncircular foundation for empirical inquiry? Hume's empirical study can only provide a description of how we come to particular beliefs, but, as has been claimed by Siegel, "an account of the mechanisms of knowledge-acquisition cannot, in principle, serve as well as an account of the justification of knowledge-claims."(Siegel 1980: 309) It is the instinctual rather than the propositional nature of the causal instinct that enables us to move beyond the vicious circle.

3 Beyond the Vicious Circle

Even the most analytic of thinkers accept that there are genuine features of how we engage with the world that are not in need of any prior justification, because they are simply constitutive of the kind of beings we are. Carnap, for example, held that a certain amount of circularity is not only necessary but also legitimate in certain investigations. In his paper "Inductive Logic and Inductive Intuition", which he delivered to The International Colloquium in the Philosophy of Science in 1965[8], Carnap says:

---

[8] Though presented to The International Colloquium in the philosophy of science in 1965, it was not published until 1968.

> I think that it is not only legitimate to appeal to inductive reasoning in defending inductive reasoning, but that it is indispensable. This is a rather audacious statement to make, because it looks like defending a vicious circle. But I believe all procedures of self-clarification, of making clear to ourselves what it is we have in mind, are in a way circular. We clarify B through A, and then we turn around and explain A with the help of B. I think we cannot do without it (Carnap 1968: 265).

Carnap goes on to argue that human beings are not "inductively blind", and that a crucial part of our ability to engage in inductive reasoning stems from the fact that we have what he calls "the ability of inductive intuition." (Carnap 1968: 265) Carnap adds the important caveat that he does not mean by "intuition" a source of knowledge that is infallible. Though Hume never makes reference to intuition in his account of inductive reasoning, he grounds induction in an instinct without which we would be, as it were, inductively blind. Hume argued that humanity has an inborn expectation that factors observed to be constantly conjoined in the past will continue to be conjoined in the future and that this expectation arises instinctually from our very nature. This propensity to extrapolate such conjunctions is always with us. No more than Carnap, Hume cannot step outside his humanity to give an account of the inseparable features of how we, as functioning human beings, operate in the world.

Indeed, for Carnap, the same mysterious intuitive foundations are also to be found in the operation of deductive logic. He gives the example of someone who is "deductively blind", viz., an individual who is unable to distinguish between valid and invalid arguments. He sets out the following scenario involving the deductively blind individual:

> You tell him, 'You just told me that it is raining now.' 'Yes,' he says. 'You told me before that if it is raining then the lawn is wet.' 'Yes.' 'So then you believe now that the lawn is wet.' 'Why should I?' he replies. Then you go through the whole procedure again in a different order, and with different words. If all efforts were in vain, you would have to conclude that he is deductively blind, and you would give up (Carnap 1968: 266).

Carnap concludes that no normal person is deductively blind in this sense, though differences in the speed of learning do occur. The vital point for Carnap is that you must appeal to an individual's deductive intuition in order to teach him deduction, and the same, he holds, is true of induction. Carnap does not, nor should he, conclude that all deductive reasoning must be disregarded as unfounded or unjustified because one component in the emergence of this reasoning is a deductive intuition innate to the human species. Nor should Hume be compelled to regard induction as unjustified or unfounded because its operation engages an innate indispensable instinct of the human species. The causal move should not be considered unjustified because of its instinctual grounding, but it does not seems to follow that the causal move can be justified on the basis of its instinctual grounding. I will deal more with what kind of justification we can speak of when dealing with a universal unavoidable instinct in the following section.

In 'Theories and Things' Quine rejected the transcendental question stating that:
> What evaporates is the transcendental question of the reality of the external world - the question whether or in how far our science measures up to the *Ding an sich* (Quine 1981: 22).

In expanding the knowledge of our limitations, Hume makes no attempt to answer the transcendental question. From Hume's naturalist viewpoint, the question disappears. We can never take up a vantage point outside our very nature from which we can answer such questions. Hume's descriptive philosophy, which begins by investigating how it is we do go about moving from our data to the formation of belief, is then a necessary step in providing epistemological norms. Without such an understanding, we run the danger of creating norms which are irrelevant to the kind of species that we are. Hume's descriptive account makes claims about the content of human cognition and in so doing provides a radically different view of how we acquire beliefs. Those characteristics which Hume classed as arising from our nature are to be regarded as features of human cognition, and we cannot proceed as if we were organisms of a very different kind. The causal instinct is a fundamental element of enquiry, or the substrata of thought; as such it can only be described, because there is nothing in terms of which it could be explained. If normative epistemology is to be relevant to human beings, it must itself be built on a descriptive account of human cognitive abilities. Hence a descriptive account is vital and forms the framework within which normative accounts can arise. Any account of norms depends on the cognitive abilities to which we have access.

4 The Requirements of Justification

When we ask for the impression behind a supposed idea, we are seeking the sources of knowledge. Establishing the source is crucial, for in establishing the source we not only determine the conditions under which a particular claim is made, but we come to see the type of justification appropriate to it. For Hume, our causal instinct is an unavoidable operation of our being. When we have sensory experience this universal, inescapable instinct will always be in operation, giving rise to a variety of content specific beliefs. The kind of justification, if any, demanded of an instinct characterised as unavoidable and universal is not the same as that required of a proposition. When we speak of causation in Humean epistemology what is at stake is not a belief or set of propositions but an instinct. Causal inference arises from an instinct which we bring to our experience in the world; the body of belief that it gives rise to are not founded on self-evident, self-justifying or indubitable propositions, but rather on a permanent, universal, unavoidable instinct. The body of belief which rests on self-evident, self-justifying and indubitable propositions are deemed to have some form of rational justification; but what of the status of justification of the body of belief that rests on a permanent, universal, unavoidable instinct?

As a feature of cognition the causal instinct can not be grounded by philosophers, but for Hume this is no reason to attempt to dispense with the products of this central aspect of cognition. Individual content specific beliefs are formed when our causal instinct is exposed to external stimuli, and despite the fact that these input data can be flawed or incomplete, there is little indication that Hume was committed to the idea that beliefs arising from our causal instinct are to be regarded as unjustified or irrationally held. Swinburne points out in his book "Epistemic Justification", that:

> My beliefs are true if (and only if) things are as I believe them to be. My belief that the earth revolves annually round the sun is true if (and only if) the earth does revolve annually around the sun. But my beliefs are ones that I am justified in holding if in some sense they are well grounded; if in some sense I have reason for believing that they are true (Swinburne 2001: 1).

For Hume individual content specific beliefs which arise from the unavoidable universal causal instinct are in some sense well grounded. Their regress stopper is an inescapable cognitive capacity.

The case for justification then seems to pivot on whether we are justified in acting on our causal instinct, but as it is a universal and unavoidable feature of how humans engage in the world this is clearly a pseudo-proposition. Asking for justification here is to lapse back into treating it as propositions. Broughton refers to Hume's naturalism as a form of "deflationary naturalism" because "it sets aside the philosophical assumption that cognitive worth is possible only when philosophical reflection can supply a general rationale for the kind of cognition in question." (Broughton 2003: 2) A demand for a grounding of the causal move, as Hume describes it, is not possible. As Strawson points out, such features are "outside our critical and rational competence, in the sense that they define, or help to define, the area in which that competence is exercised" (Strawson 1985: 19).

To attempt to provide a rational justification for the causal instinct is to show a profound misunderstanding of the role it plays in belief formation. For Hume, then, we must clearly distinguish between "what it is vain" to make a matter of inquiry (that which "we must take for granted in all our reasoning"), and that which is a genuine matter for inquiry. Hume is not concerned "to refute the cavils of total scepticism" because there is no need to:

> Whoever has taken the pains to refute the cavils of this total scepticism, has really disputed without an antagonist, and endeavour'd by arguments to establish a faculty, which nature has antecedently implanted in the mind, and rendered unavoidable (T234).

A principle can be taken to be original, Hume says, when we "despair of explaining its causes" (T672) or when they "cannot be accounted for." (T640). In this respect, we can see how Hume's naturalism differs substantially from the contemporary forms of scientific naturalism, in accordance with which the whole of reality, in principle at least, may be revealed by scientific inquiry. In his book *Hume's Naturalism*, H.O. Mounce points out that, in believing that the whole of the universe or experience may be accounted for by methods like that of the physical sciences, these naturalists must opt for the position that nothing is mysterious but only problematic, and that any difficulty may be removed given sufficient persistence by human reason. In contrast, a central element of Hume's naturalism is that there is a point beyond which rational justification cannot go; beyond which, indeed, the demand for rational justification ceases to make sense. Recognition of the limits and boundaries set out by our cognitive capacities is a requirement of sound philosophy[9]. The limitations of the human mind and the structure within which the mind operates delineate key limits within which rationality operates. I would argue that Hume belongs to a variety of naturalist thinkers described by Knowles (2005) as having argued for a form of "cognitive boundedness" but who "have not seen it as implying the availability of an alternative mode of understanding of the things we will never understand scientifically" (Knowles 2005: 26).

5 Conclusion

In Hume there is a sense of a positive relation between the natural and the justified; indeed there are places where he seems to be upholding the view that only reasonable doubt precludes justification. Not all doubt that is possible is thereby reasonable, and only reasonable doubt precludes justification[10]. In the case of the causal instinct and the beliefs that flow from it, Hume considers himself to be acting in a just and reasonable manner when operating in accordance with them. Hume has demonstrated, as Penelhum puts it, that "most topics of human enquiry belong in a sphere where the certainties of the rationalist and the chronic doubts of the sceptic are equally beyond us" (Penelhum 1975: 19). Hume's descriptive epistemology provides us with a universal unavoidable instinct beyond which we cannot go. In foregoing the search for ultimate explanations, in the rationalist sense, Hume is content to found epistemology on what happens in human life and on how we as human beings function in the world. As Brown states, "epistemic norms that are based on a particular account of our cognitive abilities become suspect if that account is rejected, and norms that require us to do what is beyond our capabilities are surely unacceptable" (Brown 31: 1996). The request for justification

---

[9] I am not saying that science will not arrive at a point where it becomes possible to evaluate critically the causal instinct but simply that such evaluations may have little effect on the process it is evaluating.

[10] See Ferreira 1985.

of the causal instinct is ultimately incoherent. It is a feature of the kind of beings that we are. A philosopher, Hume says, "must act ... and live, and converse like other men; and for this conduct he is not obliged to give any other reason than the absolute necessity he lies under of doing so" (D134). Hume has done away with the notion of perceiving a split in man's nature between rational man and natural man. What emerges is a human philosophy which takes account of the cognitive capacities of our species.

The fundamental insight of Hume's naturalism is that it alerts us to the fact that some of our key operating principles[11] are not to be classed as beliefs; rather they are vital components of our belief forming structure. They exist not as a *product* of the belief forming structures of the mind, but as an indispensable, instinctual part of those very belief forming structures. That I operate in the world as if the reliability of inductive belief formation is a reality is not the consequence of any belief which I affirm. Rather, it is a result of universal, unavoidable instincts. Before contemporary naturalists begin the task of addressing the standard normative objection against naturalist approaches to epistemology they should take on board Hume's belief/instinct shift, for it gives us a much richer understanding of the cognitive resource at play in belief formation. It is on this broadened account of cognitive resources that activities such as providing an epistemic justification of belief or developing normative reasoning strategies should begin. In this way the norms which may arise will be tailored to the demands made by the real world on creatures embodied in the way we are embodied.

References

Bishop, Michael A. and J.D. Trout (2005). *Epistemology and the Psychology of Human Judgment*. Oxford: Oxford University Press.
Broughton, Janet (2003). "Hume's Naturalism about Cognitive Norms". *Philosophical Topics* 31(2), pp. 1–19.

---

[11] It is not only the causal move which Hume identifies as being universal and unavoidable. A similar case can be made for a belief instinct/shift in relation to our affirmation of the existence of the external world as well as our affirmation of the existence of the self.

Brown, Harold I. (1987). "Normative Epistemology and Naturalized Epistemology". *Inquiry* 31, pp. 53–78.
Brown, Harold I. (1996). "Psychology, Naturalized Epistemology, and Rationality". In *The Philosophy of Psychology,* ed. by William T. O'Donohue and Richard F. Kitchener. London: Sage Publications, pp. 19–32.
Butler, R. J. (1960). "Natural Belief and the Enigma of Hume". *Archiv Für Geschichte Der Philosophie* 40, pp. 71–100.
Campbell, Treasa (2006). "Human Philosophy: Hume on Natural Instincts and Belief formation". In *Content, Consciousness, and Perception: Essays in Contemporary Philosophy of Mind*, ed. by Ezio Di Nucci and Conor McHugh. Newcastle: Cambridge Scholars Press, pp. 62–72.
Carnap, Rudolf (1968). "Inductive Logic and Inductive Intuition". In *The Problem of Inductive Logic*, ed. by Imre Lakatos, pp. 258–315.
Ferreira, M. J. (1985). "Hume's Naturalism-'Proof' and Practice". *The Philosophical Quarterly*, Vol. 35, No. 138, pp. 45–57.
Fodor, Jerry (2003). *Hume Variations*. Oxford: Clarendon Press.
Garrett, Don (1997). *Cognition and Commitment in Hume's Philosophy*. New York: Oxford University Press.
Gaskin, J.C.A. (1974). "God Hume and Natural Belief". *Philosophy* 49, pp. 281–294.
Gochet, Paul (1986). *Ascent to Truth: A Critical Examination of Quine's Philosophy*. München: Philosophia Verlag.
Goldman, Alvin (2002). "The Sciences and Epistemology". In *The Oxford Handbook of Epistemology*, ed. by Paul K. Moser. Oxford: Oxford University Press, pp. 144–176.
Haack, Susan (1993). *Evidence and Inquiry: Towards Reconstruction in Epistemology*. Oxford: Blackwell.
Howson, Colin. (2000). *Hume's Problem*. Oxford: Clarendon Press.
Hume, David (1988). *An Enquiry Concerning Human Understanding*. Ed. by Antony Flew. Chicago: Open Court.
Hume, David (1985). *A Treatise of Human Nature*. Ed. by Ernest C. Mossner. England: Penguin Books.
Hume, David (1947). *Dialogues Concerning Natural Religion*. Ed. by N. Kemp Smith. Edinburgh: Thomas Nelson and Sons.
Kemp Smith, Norman (1941). *The Philosophy of David Hume*. London: Macmillan.
Kitcher, Philip. (1992). "The Naturalists Return". *Philosophical Review* 101, pp. 53–114.
Knowles, Jonathan (2005). "Varieties of Naturalism". In *Synergies: Interdisciplinary Communications 2003–4*, ed. by W. Østreng. Norway: Centre for Advanced Studies, Norwegian Academy of Science and Letters, pp. 26–29.

Kornblith, Hillary (1985). "What is Naturalistic Epistemology?" In *Naturalizing Epistemology,* ed. H. Kornblith. Massachusetts: MIT Press, pp. 1–13.
Loeb, Louis (2002). *Stability and justification in Hume's treatise*. Oxford: Oxford University Press.
Maffie, James (1990). "Recent Work on Naturalized Epistemology". *American Philosophical Quarterly* 27, pp. 281–294.
McCormick, M. (1993). "Hume on Natural Belief and Original Principles". *Hume Studies* 19, pp. 103–116.
Mounce, H.O. (1999). *Hume's Naturalism.* London: Routledge.
Passmore, John A. (1952). *Hume's Intentions*. Cambridge: Cambridge University Press. 3rd edition 1980 London: Duckworth.
Pears, David (1990). *Hume's System: An Examination of the First Book of his Treatise.* Oxford: Oxford University Press.
Penelhum, Terence (1975). *Hume*. London: Macmillan.
Popkin, Richard H. (1966). "David Hume: His Pyrrhonism and His Critique of Pyrrhonism". In *Hume*, ed. V.C. Chappell. New York: Doubleday, pp. 53–98.
Quine, W.V. (1981). *Theories and Things.* Cambridge, MA: Harvard University Press.
Rea, Michael (2002). *World Without Design: The Ontological Consequences of Naturalism*. Oxford: Clarendon Press.
Siegel, Harvey (1980). "Justification, Discovery, and the Naturalizing of Epistemology". *Philosophy of Science* 47, pp. 297–320.
Simon, Herbert A. (1982). *Models of bounded rationality*. Cambridge, Massachusetts: MIT Press.
Strawson, Peter F. (1985). *Skepticism and Naturalism: Some varieties.* New York: Columbia University Press.
Stroud, Barry (1977). *Hume*. London: Routledge and Kegan Paul.
Swinburne, Richard (2001). *Epistemic Justification*. Oxford: Clarendon Press.

15

Naturalising Logic. The inference-marker view[1]

MARÍA J. FRÁPOLLI

The project of naturalism

The project of naturalisation is an essential aspect of the general project of analysis. Naturalising a theoretical domain amounts to redefining its essential notions and relations in terms of a different domain, that is considered acceptable by the standards of natural science. Thus stated, the project is compatible with several different proposals with varying degrees of radicalism.

Mathematics and logic challenge the general project of naturalisation precisely because of their formal character. Being formal implies that, from an epistemological perspective, mathematics and logic are also a priori. It is hard to accommodate a priori knowledge within a naturalistic framework. The reason is that, most of the time, the endorsement of a non-empirical way of acquiring knowledge goes along with the acceptation of methods, procedures and skills — introspection and intuition, among others — that are not sanctioned by the current state of natural

---

[1] This paper has been written as a part of a general research project, financially supported by the Spanish Ministry of Education (Project HUM2004–00118).

Beyond Description: Naturalism and Normativity.
Marcin Miłkowski and Konrad Talmont-Kaminski (eds.).
Copyright © 2010 The Author.

science. The kind of formality proper of logic is nevertheless different from the kind of formality proper of mathematics, and the same happens with the way in which they can be said to be a priori. Consequently, the enquiries on the status of mathematics and logic in the general context of the naturalisation project have distinctive aspects and are logically independent.

In this paper I am only concerned with the project of naturalising logic. In order to assess the project's viability it is not necessary to change the view we all have of logic as a science, although a better understanding of some well-established ideas about the nature of logic is required. Logic is the science of valid inferences, inferences are sets of propositions, and propositions are the outputs of speech acts that have the force of claims. This characterization of logic is not in dispute, as it is not the claim that validity is a property of arguments, a property that is independent of the empirical features of the external world. Nevertheless, although logic can be argued to possess the mentioned independence, the inferences that are its subject-matter are not independent of our linguistic practices. For this reason, the project of naturalising logic is relative to the more basic project of naturalising some relevant components of human linguistic activity such as the meaning of terms and expressions and the content of speech acts. Naturalising logic comes, so to speak, on a second step. The foundational level of a completed process of naturalising logic is the naturalisation of content and meaning, i.e. the naturalisation of our linguistic practices and their results, on which it is reliant. In turn, the project of naturalizing meaning and content is an aspect of the general project of naturalizing normativity. M. Bickhard (2010) proposes to change from substance and object metaphysics to a process metaphysics. His proposal places normativity at the core of the natural world offering thus a scientifically sound way out from the Cartesian dichotomy.

I will not directly argue for the possibility of naturalising logic, instead, I propose a conditional argument: *If* meaning and content can be naturalised at all, so can logic. In spite of being conditional, the argument offered here is very strong, since the whole project of naturalism rests on the possibility of the truth of its antecedent. If meaning and content turned out to be nonnaturalisable, naturalism would not be possible. The naturalisation of meaning and content is thus the possibility condition of the naturalisation of logic and, in general, of the whole naturalisation project.

Let's assume then that a naturalistic account of meaning and content can be given. In the following pages, I will present an explanation of how the meanings of logical constants arise from the aims of some of our linguistic acts. Part of our linguistic activity imbues logical terms with their significance, which appears in scenes as a product of our use of language. To show how logical terms emerge, the relation between material inferences and formal inferences must be made clear.

There is however a previous concern, which is the already mentioned characterization of logic as a formal science. This will be the topic of the next section. In Section 3, I will work out the process by which formal inferences supervene from material ones, explaining thus in which sense logic results from the ordinary use of language and how logical terms acquire their meanings from what we, agents, do with words. In Section 4, I will display the main features of the two contemporary competing paradigms in the philosophy of language, i.e. truth-conditional semantics and inferential semantics, and contrast my view on logical words against them. Finally, in Section 5, I will offer my definition of what a logical constant is.

1 What does it mean that logic is a formal science?

My examination of the way in which logic is formal will proceed by focusing first on the traditional claim that logical constants are syncategorematic terms, and in relation to this, on the claim that logic is topic-neutral.

Logic-as-a-science is concerned with the inferential relations among propositions irrespective of their subject matter, and this fact has motivated the idea that logical constants are *syncategorematic* and that logic is *topic-neutral*. Both terms, correctly understood, pick up an essential aspect of logic. According to the classical definition, *syncategoremata* are terms that can be neither subject nor predicates in a sentence. Medieval logicians that defined logical constants this way considered, following Aristotle, that being either the entity named by the subject or the property expressed by the predicate were the only two possible elements of a proposition. Therefore, according to this view, syncategorematic terms didn't contribute a component to the proposition at the same level as subject and predicate do. A modern variation of this view on logical constants is found in Wittgenstein's *Tractatus*². It picks up an essential facet of logical terms, i.e. that they are not names of anything; their meaning is expressive as opposed to representational. Representational meaning is the aspect of the significance of words that is connected either with entities in the world or with their characteristics. Besides depicting the world, speakers may use language with many other purposes. Some of these purposes have to do with the different ways in which an agent can affect their natural or social surroundings. The pragmatist tradition in the Philosophy of Language, the speech act theory for instance, has offered detailed explanations of these alternative kinds of meaning. Coming back to logic, the meaning of logical constants is of this pragmatic kind. By using them, speakers convey information other than the merely descriptive. In particular, logical constants serve to display the structure of an inference. In the current Philosophy of Logic, this view is known as "logical expressivism". Robert Brandom (Brandom 1994) is presently a renowned defender of it, as was Wittgenstein in his time, and it is congenial with relevant parts of the medieval treatments. Kneale and Kneale (Kneale and Kneale 1962: 233) explained syncategoremata in the following terms: "*Syncategoremata* are words such as 'and', 'or', 'not', 'if', 'every', 'some', 'only', and 'except' which cannot function as terms but are of special importance in logic because they show the forms of statements." William of Ockham and his followers provide an example of this view on logical words. They defended a kind of "ontological liberalism", as Klima (Klima 2006: 8) calls it, that attached to syncategoremata reduced degrees of reality. Syncategoremata did not refer, in this view, to the external reality but rather to some mental acts that modify the way in which categoremata signified.

According to tradition, logic is *topic-neutral*. The insight that this characterisation attempts to capture is that logically valid arguments are logically valid independently of their subject matter. Topic-neutrality is

---

² "My fundamental idea", Wittgenstein said in 4.0312, "is that the 'logical constants' are not representatives." In Wittgenstein's view there are atomic facts and their components. Logical words are not components of facts. It would be possible to completely describe the world, any world, without using logical constants. Listing the true atomic propositions would be enough. I am not particularly fond of Wittgenstein's metaphysical style, but I consider his insight about logical constants correct. And it defines the theoretical position known as "logical expressivism".

another essential aspect of logic, although it has not always been correctly understood, and has often been confused with the (false) claim that logical constants have no meaning. Logical terms do not name, it is true, but there are other kinds of meaning besides naming. Logic's topic-neutrality is not relative to the expressions that function as logical terms but to the *meanings of the propositions* that function as their arguments. It is claimed that these propositions can be part of valid arguments no matter what their particular meanings are.

That logic is topic-neutral does not suggest either that logical relations hold between uninterpreted strings of signs, but that any proposition whatsoever independently of its meaning may work as an argument of a logical constant. The confusion of these two ways of understanding topic-neutrality is in part responsible for the widespread belief that logic deals with syntactic items.

That logic is a formal science is thus a short way of making a cluster of claims; among them, (i) that logical constants are not names of anything — the old syncategorematic characterization and the most recent expressivist view — and (ii) that their arguments are propositions of any kind — the old topic-neutrality of logic. Putting all these insights together, the shortest claim that correctly embodies the thesis of the formality of logic is that logical constants are *higher order functions used to mark the structure of inferences*.

Mathematics is another formal science. Nonetheless, the ways in which mathematics and logic are formal are entirely different. Logic doesn't deal with uninterpreted strings of signs. Logic is a relational enterprise concerned with the inferential relations among truth-bearers. The items related by logical relations —the relations of consequence, equivalence, incompatibility — are *begriffliche Inhalten*, i.e. judgeable contents, to use Frege's terms, and not uninterpreted structures. In *Begriffsschrift*, Frege, the father of modern logic, attempted to offer a "formula language of pure thought modelled upon the formula language of arithmetic". This is the subtitle of the booklet. The resemblances of *Begriffsschrift* to arithmetic are limited, however, to the use of a symbolic language and to the use of the categories of argument and function instead of the older subject and predicate. Frege was aware of the superficiality of the resemblances: "The most immediate point of contact between my formula language and that of arithmetic is in the way letters are used." (Frege 1879: 104). I doubt then that Frege would share the equation introduced by Sher (Sher 1991: 133): "The difference between the new conception [her view of logic] and the 'old' logicism regarding mathematical constants is a matter of perspective. Both approaches are based on the equation that being mathematical = being formal = being logical." And the rejection of the equation does not imply an automatic rejection of Frege's logicism. The basic mathematical notions might have been defined in logical terms, and mathematical truths defined in terms of logical truths, without being the task of logic identical to that of mathematics. Logicism is false, we know now, but if it were true, it still wouldn't guarantee that logic and mathematics are formal in the same sense.

Mathematics works on syntactic structures, whereas logic does not. What is often called "logical syntax" is not grammar, but conceptual structure. Logical syntax is independent of the grammatical rules of particular languages. Logical syntax as opposed to grammatical syntax is what logic is about, and logical forms represent the logical category of the ingredients of the conceptual contents expressed by sentences and the way in which they are put together[3]. Mathematics is formal because it is concerned with structures, whereas logic is formal because its operators are used to *mark* the structure of inferences among items that possess content. Since structures are relevant in both cases, the word "formal" is justified in both cases.

2 Formal inferences

In the last few decades, there has been intermittent debate about whether material inferences are logical inferences at all (Sellars, Brandom, Harman). The standard opinion among logicians and philosophers of logic is that material inferences fall short of being logical inferences for they are incomplete arguments, "enthymemes" in the traditional terminology. An enthymeme is a truncated argument with at least one hidden premise. They are valid or not in a derivate sense, depending on whether they can

---

[3] I shall not pursue this point further. For an already classical explanation of this line of thought, see Etchemendy (1983).

be restored to become instances of formally valid structures. This is the classical view that I will confront.

If the semantic definition of validity, i.e. that an argument is valid if, and only if, it is not possible that its premises are true and its conclusion false, is taken seriously, then material inferences have to be accepted as genuine inferences. On this definition, the following arguments are incontestable:

(A)$_{material}$ Today is Friday,
tomorrow is Saturday

(B)$_{material}$ Victoria is a girl,
Victoria is a human being.

The question now is to decide whether (A)$_{material}$ and (B)$_{material}$ are logical inferences or not. Obviously the answer depends on what one means by "logical inference". The standard explanation of why (A)$_{material}$ and (B)$_{material}$ are not logical inferences is that they do not instantiate a valid form.

What are ultimately the differences between (A)$_{material}$ and (B)$_{material}$ and their corresponding formal counterparts, (A)$_{formal}$ and (B)$_{formal}$?

(A)$_{formal}$ *If* today is Friday, *then* tomorrow is Saturday
Today is Friday
Therefore, tomorrow is Saturday.

(B)$_{formal}$ *All* girls are human beings
Victoria is a girl,
Therefore, Victoria is a human being.

At first sight, there are logical constants in the surface of (A)$_{formal}$ and (B)$_{formal}$. Material inferences do not include expressions that signal their status as inferences. Their premises and conclusions are inferentially connected because of the meanings of the concepts involved and the information we possess about the reality they purport to represent. Possessing the concept Friday implies familiarity with the sequence of the days of the week, possessing the concept girl implies the knowledge that it designates a stage of a female human being's development. This information is part of the inferential meaning of Friday and girl.

Although material inferences don't essentially use logical constants, they can be presented as formal inferences simply by placing the relevant logical words in the relevant places. (A)$_{formal}$ and (B)$_{formal}$ are qualified as logical inferences because they instantiate logically valid structures, i.e. structures that are valid by virtue of the meanings of its logical words. This, although correct, is hardly informative. (A)$_{material}$ and (B)$_{material}$ are as truth-preserving as (A)$_{formal}$ and (B)$_{formal}$. The only difference between them is that in the formal cases the principle of inference at work is explicitly displayed. Neither the conditional sentence in (A)$_{formal}$ nor the generalization in (B)$_{formal}$ should be seen as further premises. They are principles of inference, rules; neglecting this distinction would lead us to the infinite regress of the paradox of Achilles and the Tortoise[4]. Formal inferences, in conclusion, are inferences the inferential status of which has been made explicit by the use of logical constants. The propositions expressed by the sentences in (A)$_{material}$ and (B)$_{material}$ are inferentially related. By asserting the first one, one is committed to assert the second, for because of the meanings of the terms in them the second follows from the first. Even if this is so, a hearer might overlook this relation, or the speaker might have reasons to stress it. In these cases, logical constants enter the scene: logical terms are used for the purpose of bringing into the open the inferential relations among propositional contents. Claiming that only formal inferences are logical inferences might be correct in some sense, but the sense that makes it a true claim also makes it a trivial one. Material and formal inferences can both be truth preserving; the difference is only that the latter, unlike the former, are explicitly presented as inferences. And they are material inferences the ones that lend support to formal inferences, and not the other way around. Valid material inferences are not logically valid insofar as they can be seen as instances of formal structures, but the other way around. Valid formal inferences display the implicit inferential structure of already valid material inferences[5].

3 Truth-conditional semantics vs. inferential semantics

The notion of inferential meaning has been mentioned in connection with valid material inferences. All concepts, logical or not, have their dose of

---

[4] The statement of the paradox is due to Lewis Carroll (Carroll 1895); but the underlying distinction between premises and principles of inference is found in the thought of the best philosophers of logic, Frege (1879) and (1884), Peirce (1932) and Prior (1976) among them.

[5] Overlooking the relationship between material and formal inferences leads to the disconnection between logic and human reasoning, a view that I consider completely unjustified, but that has been argued for by philosophers such as Harman: "My conclusion is that there is no clearly significant way in which logic is specially relevant to reasoning" (Harman 1986: 20).

inferential meaning. But, in spite of some similarities, there is a contrast between the way in which run-of-mill concepts signify and how logical words do. I am not going to argue for the contrast, which has been neglected by the realist accounts of logic and, generally, by the naïve views of language that assume that the basic word-world relation is that of naming. The contrast is, nevertheless, widely recognised and it lies behind the medieval distinction between categorematic and syncategorematic terms.

How run-of-the-mill concepts acquire their meaning and express a content[6]? There are currently two paradigms that account for the process of meaning acquisition: one of them is truth-conditional semantics and the other is inferential semantics. In truth-conditional semantics, and in its contextualist follow-up, truth-conditional pragmatics, the core explanatory notions are those of *reference, representation* and *truth*. Terms acquire their meanings because they are connected one way or another to extralinguistic entities; sentences represent states-of-affairs, they are models of possible situations. When the modelled situations are actual, the sentences in question are said to be true. Philosophers such as Wittgenstein, Tarski, Quine, and Davidson belong to the tradition of truth-conditional semantics, as do the followers of possible world semantics, such as Stalnaker and Lewis. This has been the dominant view in the twentieth century Philosophy of Language. Recanati and Carston endorse its pragmatist version; the difference between the two, which will be neglected for our present purposes, lies on the role of context in the determination of the content of utterances.

Inferential semantics, on the other hand, places the notion of *inference*, together with the normative pragmatic notions of *commitment* and *entitlement* at the basic level. The content of an utterance is defined by the propositions from which it follows and the propositions that follow from it. In other words, propositional content is determined by the circumstances that entitle a speaker to assert it and the commitments the speaker acquires by its assertion. The contents of a concept are the cir-

---

[6] The meaning of a word is the linguistic information that the speakers systematically relate to it; the content is the contribution of the word to the proposition expressed by the sentences in which it occurs. In general, meaning is related to expressions and content to their utterances. A more technical account of the distinction is given by the Kaplanian pair of *character* and *content*, or by the more traditional distinction, used by Austin and Strawson, between a sentence's *linguistic meaning* and the *statement made* by its utterances.

cumstances and consequences of its application. Inferential semantics is argued for in (Brandom 1994 and 2000).

It is now time to return to the discussion of naturalism. Both paradigms of meaning acquisition and content expression have naturalistic versions. As a general claim, externalism, the view on meaning that stems from the works of Putnam and Kripke in the 70s, is an attempt to offer a naturalistic interpretation of truth-conditional semantics, as they are the more specific theories on concepts defended by Fodor, Dretske, Millikan, Prinz, the Churchlands, etc. Brandom's normative pragmatics, on the other hand, is an attempt to naturalise inferential semantics, making meaning and content rest on the activities that connect speakers with other speakers and with their natural milieu. The acts of the speakers gain content by means of the commitments undertaken by the linguistic agents to act in a certain way as a result of their linguistic actions.

My view on logical constants is that their meaning emerges from the speaker's intentions of showing as a formal inference a previous material inference whose validity or invalidity rests on the non-logical concepts involved in it. The inferential behaviour of speakers makes possible the use of logical constants, which become completely defined by the kind of inferential commitments and entitlements assumed by the speaker when she explicitly presents an inferential transition between propositions. The presence of logical words does not add anything to the content of the propositions expressed, they signal conceptual movements either endorsed or permitted by the speaker. Here lies the interest of this view of logic for the general project of naturalism. The principles of inference in $(A)_{formal}$ and $(B)_{formal}$ just show the propensity of the agent to connect the concepts involved in the way indicated by the argument, and by displaying these principles overtly she is both showing her inferential dispositions and giving permissions to others to borrow them. Therefore, if propositions can be naturalised, formal inferences can be too. And from the naturalisation of formal inferences, logic also becomes naturalised. Formal logic is only an artefact, a human creation that purports to model real linguistic practices.

The other disturbing feature of logic for the naturalist project is the assumed fact that logical relations are known and assessed a priori[7].

---

[7] The sense in which *a priori assessment* or *a priori knowledge* is needed in this context is not new. It is exactly the sense that Lisa Warenski (this volume) takes from Burge and attributes to Kant: "A priori justification is justification that does not rely upon the particulars of sensory experience for its justificational force. The locution 'justificational force' is due to Tyler Burge. (Burge 1993; 1998), and it makes explicit Kant's original

Logic is an a priori science, but the sense in which it is so is quite harmless and, in any case, it does not present any challenge for naturalism. Again, the argument here is conditional: if our knowledge of language does not suppose a problem for naturalism, our knowledge of logical relations is not a problem either.

The point of departure is linguistic competence. Every proficient speaker of English knows that she cannot assent to $(A.1)_{material}$

$(A.1)_{material}$ Today is Friday,

and dissent to $(A.2)_{material}$

$(A.2)_{material}$ Tomorrow is Saturday,

in the same context, if she wants to be consistent. The crucial point here is that "consistency" is not an a priori formal relation, but the basic notion of rationality. Rational behaviour consists of being aware of the consequences of one's actions and undertaking them. Otherwise, communication would not be possible. By understanding the content of other agent's linguistic actions, one can infer her subsequent acts, and some of her previous assumptions. And both speaker and hearer are placed in the position of taking part in the game of giving and asking for reasons. Being consistent in this way is not a formal luxury, demanded by sophisticated logicians, but the condition of possibility of rational behaviour[8].

Once it is assumed that the transition from $(A.1)_{material}$ to $(A.2)_{material}$ is obliged by the meaning of concepts concerned and by the background requirements of rational behaviour, it should be obvious that the correctness of $(A.1)_{formal}$

$(A.1)_{formal}$ *If* today is Friday, *then* tomorrow is Saturday,

is also obliged by the same reasons.

There are several different senses in which a piece of knowledge can be said to be a priori. The most radical sense in which a priori means "independent of all experience" is hardly applicable. Most of time, the concept is relative to some kind of experience or other. Then, if there is a sense, acceptable to naturalism, in which linguistic knowledge can said to be a priori, the same sense also covers logical knowledge.

So far, I have outlined a way out of the difficulties of naturalising logic. My purpose has not been to defend naturalism, but to offer a conditional argument: logical terms are parasitic to ordinary concepts, and

---

understanding of a priori justification as justification that is independent of the particulars of experience, but allowing that experience may be needed to acquire the relevant concepts involved in an a priori claim."

[8] This connexion between rationality and behaviour has been stressed from different philosophical perspectives. Ramsey and Brandom defended it.

logical behaviour is parasitic to rational linguistic behaviour. Thus, if meaning and content can be naturalized, logic does not present an added difficulty. If, on the other hand, meaning and content were not naturalisable, the whole project of naturalism would collapse (and logic would not present an added difficulty either).

The argument defended here depends on a view of logic that is independent of the problems derived from naturalism. In the next section, I will offer a brief outline of what is, in my opinion, the syntactic status, the semantic meaning and the pragmatic role of logical constants. I will leave many topics untouched, many discussions open and many difficulties unanswered, for presenting a completed view on logical terms is not the aim of this paper. Nevertheless, the following outline will serve as the theoretical background of the topics addressed here.

4 Logical words as inference-markers

The meaning and role of logical terms emerge from the practice of drawing material inferences. As mentioned in Section 2, the logical expressivist view that I take from Wittgenstein and Brandom amounts to the following claims: that logical words do not name entities and that they don't contribute a component to the proposition expressed by the use of sentences in which they appear. From a pragmatic point of view, logical words are inference markers, their role is stressing that an inference is in progress.

My proposal is to return logic to language, its natural home, and to place the philosophy of logic within the philosophy of language. What logic is cannot be decided by backing out of the inferential linguistic practices of human beings, and the same can be said of the task of identifying the features that make a term a logical constant.

The users of natural languages bring logical words into play for a purpose, and their formal features have to adapt to it. The main purpose is making explicit inferential connections among concepts and propositional concepts; this is the pragmatic role of logical constants. Making explicit inferential connections is not only possessing inferential meaning. All concepts have inferential meaning to some extent, and the inferential meaning justifies the material inferences in which they are involved. In this sense my proposal goes further than Gentzen's and Prawitz's, for it is not that the meanings of logical constants can be given as sets of rules, introduction and elimination rules, but rather that the pragmatic significance of logical constants is being used as inference-markers.

[DEF] Logical constants are higher-order predicables that have 0–adic predicables as arguments. They don't name any kind of entity but rather are natural language devices for making explicit the inferential relations among concepts and propositional contents.

DEF involves a syntactic claim, that logical constants are higher-order; a semantic claim, that they do not name; and a pragmatic claim, that by using them a speaker signals the presence of an inference. The semantic claim is sometimes called "logical expressivism" and has been defended by Wittgenstein and Brandom. The pragmatic claim can be dubbed "the inference-marker view".

Being higher-order is only a necessary condition for being a logical constant. The same thing occurs with the semantic aspect. In language, there are many different expressions that don't name anything, and shouldn't be catalogued as logical constants for this reason alone. But as logic is the science of inferences, logical constants are essentially inference-markers; particular logical constants mean the specific inferential movements they allow.

A 0–adic predicable is a predicable with 0 argument places, i.e. a proposition. That logical words are higher order predicables that have propositions as arguments should be obvious if one recalls, as has been stressed in Section I, that the basic notion of logic is validity, that validity is a property of inferences, and that inferences are sets of propositions.

An immediate objection to my definition is that, although it fits sentential connectives well, it leaves out identity and first order quantifiers. Let's see if this is so. But before answering the objection, let me state the terms of my commitment with DEF.

DEF is not intended to be *ad hoc*. It has not been developed to fit a rigidly determined set of expressions, or abstracted to cover the more general aspects of a selected group of terms, although it has been guided by some pre-theoretical intuitions that include reference to some expressions. A philosophical account of logical constants that aims for any depth has to begin by asking what the task of logic is, and by comparing it with the pragmatic significance of the terms that belong in the intersection of most available accounts of them: quantifiers, truth-functional connectives, and also modal and epistemic operators. Its concern should be to understand why these terms have enjoyed logicians' favour. The direction of an enlightening inquiry has to run contrary to Quine's "list view". For what is at stake is not a formal characterization that may have extensional success, which in any case is impossible, since there is no generalized agreement about what the set of logical constants is, but rather a general philosophical understanding capable of illuminating their status as such. And what I submit is not an explanation of what makes them logically *interesting*, but the cluster of features that makes them *logical* terms. If I am right, we should count as logical constants any terms that fit the definition, and only these, with the only proviso that I am not concerned with the project of understanding non-standard expressions of Twin-English as used by silicon-based rational creatures, but with the project of finding a philosophical account that sheds light on the meaning and use of some ingredients of our everyday language.

Besides, DEF can have two readings, one weaker that the other. They are the following,

[DEF]$_{weak}$ Logical constants are higher-order predicables that can admit 0–adic predicables among their arguments. They don't name any kind of entity but rather are natural language devices for making explicit the inferential relations among concepts and propositional contents.

[DEF]$_{strong}$ Logical constants are higher-order predicables whose arguments are 0–adic predicables. They don't name any kind of entity but rather are natural language devices for making explicit the inferential relations among concepts and propositional contents.

[DEF]$_{weak}$ predicates logical constanthood of types, while [DEF]$_{strong}$ predicates it of tokens. Under the former, a type, say a quantifier, is a logical constant if, among other characteristic, it has tokens that are functions of 0–adic predicables. Propositional quantification would be an obvious case that would provide quantifiers with the required feature. Under the stronger definition, what is classified as a logical constant is a token, i.e. a particular instance of a type together with its particular aspects. If one selects exclusively [DEF]$_{strong}$, it makes no sense asking whether quantifiers or any other kind of expression are or are not logical constants.

Fortunately, it is not necessary to choose one of the two options and reject the other. We can assume the charitable position of classifying types as logical constants in a weak sense if, and only if, they have tokens that are so in a strong sense.

DEF assembles three aspects that are individually necessary and jointly sufficient for being a logical constant. Removing some aspect while leaving others, we get broader sets of expressions still related to the class of logical constants. Table 1 shows different expressions with different sets of properties.

My definition rules out:

(i) First-order predicables, and hence it rejects first-order identity and membership as logical constants

(ii) Predicate-formers such as some cases of negation, conjunction and disjunction, higher-order identity and the reflexivity operator

(iii) Monadic sentential operators that act as circumstance-shifting operators, such as modal, epistemic and temporal operators

(iv) Monadic sentence-formers, such as monadic quantifiers

Nevertheless,

(v) DEF doesn't imply that first-order identity, conjunction and disjunction should be removed from standard calculi. They shouldn't. They all have jobs to perform there.

(vi) It doesn't imply that modal, epistemic and tensed logics shouldn't be considered as logics. They are, although they all include at least two sets of constants, genuine logical constants, which earn them the title "logic", and specific constants that make them modal, or epistemic or tensed logics, in each case.

(vii) DEF doesn't imply that quantifiers are not logical constants. Rather, it distinguishes different kinds of quantifiers. Monadic quantifiers don't act as inference-markers, but binary quantifiers standardly do. This does not mean any rejection of Frege's (1884) account. Frege rightly understood the nature of numerical expressions as higher-order concepts, and rightly defined existence as an expression of quantity. Neither does my point signify any criticism of Mostowski's insights that monadic quantifiers help us to construe propositions out of propositional functions, or that logical quantifiers cannot be used to single out individuals. Both theses are correct. But none of them define logical constants.

All these apparent difficulties of my view on logical constants can be answered, and it can be argued that the inference-marker view, with its syntactic, semantic and pragmatic aspects, fits surprisingly well into our intuitive understanding of logic. It is compatible with the Fregean account of logical constants and quantifiers, with the Wittgensteinian view of logic and with our ordinary practice as linguistic agents and as working logicians. It, nevertheless, is at odds with some theoretical positions on logic that place it in the realm of syntax. In any case, it is more difficult for syntacticists to explain how their view is compatible even with the basic definition of validity and in which sense their syntactic proposal is useful for our inferential practices, than for me to demonstrate why syntacticism in logic should be abandoned.

To conclude, I would insist that logic is an essential part of our rational behaviour, and that its significance and the meanings of its concepts cannot be understood by ignoring the kind of actions the speakers use logical terms for. There is no isolated problem that logic poses to the project of naturalism. Inferential practices are just a kind of linguistic actions. If the latter are naturalistically explainable, so are the former.

References

Bickhard, Mark (2010). "Is Normativity Natural?". In this volume.

Brandom, Robert (1994). *Making it Explicit. Reasoning, Representing, and Discursive Commitment*. Cambridge, Mass.: Harvard University Press.

Carroll, Lewis (1895). "What Achilles said to the Tortoise". *Mind* 15, pp. 279–80.

Dretske, Fred (1995). *Naturalizing the Mind*. Cambridge, Mass.: The MIT Press.

Etchemendy, John (1983). "The doctrine of logic as form". *Linguistic and Philosophy* 6, pp. 319–334.

Frege, Gottlob (1879). "Conceptual Notation. A formula language of pure thought modelled upon the formula language of arithmetic". In Frege (1972), pp. 101–203.

Frege, Gottlob (1972). *Conceptual Notation and Related Articles*, transl. and ed. by Terrell Ward Bynum. Oxford, Clarendon Press.

Frege, Gottlob (1884). *The Foundations of Arithmetic*. Oxford, Basil Blackwell, 1980.

Frege, Gottlob (1892). "On Concept and Object". In *Translations from the Philosophical Writings of Gottlob Frege*, ed. by Peter Geach and Max Black. Oxford: Basil Blackwell, 1952.

Gentzen, Gerhard. (1969). *Collected Papers*. Amsterdam, North-Holland

Harman, Gilbert (1986). *Change in View. Principles of Reasoning*. Cambridge, Mass.: The MIT Press.

Klima, Gyula (2004). "Syncategoremata". In *Encyclopedia of Language and Linguistics,* vol. 12. 2nd edition, ed. by Keith Brown. Oxford: Elsevier, pp. 353–356.

Kneale, William and Kneale, Martha (1962). *The Development of Logic*. Oxford: University Press.

Kornblith, Hilary, ed. (1985). *Naturalizing Epistemology*. Cambridge, Mass.: The MIT Press.

Koslow, Arnold (1992). *A Structuralist Theory of Logic.* Cambridge, Cambridge University Press.

Mostowski, Andrzej (1957). "On a Generalization of Quantifiers". *Fundamenta Mathematicae* 44, pp. 12–36.

Peirce, Charles S. (1932). *Collected Papers of Charles Sanders Peirce*, ed. by Charles Hartshorne and Paul Weiss. Volume II. *Elements of Logic*. Cambridge, Harvard University Press.

Prawitz, Dag (1978). "Proofs and the Meaning and Completeness of the Logical Constants". In *Essays in Mathematical and Philosophical Logic*, ed. by Jaakko Hintikka. Boston: Reidel, pp. 25–39.

Prawitz, Dag (2006). *Natural Deduction. A proof-theoretical study*. Dover Publications.

Prior, Arthur N. (1976). "What is logic?". In *Papers in Logic and Ethics*. Amherst: University of Massachusetts Press.

Quine, W. V. O. (1986). *Philosophy of Logic.* 2nd edition. Cambridge: Harvard University Press.

Sellars, Wilfrid S. (1963). "Empiricism and the Philosophy of Mind". Reprinted in *Science, Perception, and Reality.* London: Routledge and Kegan Paul.

Sher, Gila (1991). *The Bounds of Logic. A Generalized Viewpoint*. Cambridge, Mass: The MIT Press.

Warmbrod, Ken (1999)."Logical Constants". *Mind* 8, pp. 503–538.

Williams, C. J. F. (1992). "Towards a Unified Theory of Higher-Level Predication". *Philosophical Quarterly* 42 (169), pp. 449–464.

Wittgenstein, Ludwig (1922). *Tractatus Logico-Philosophicus*. London: Routledge and Kegan Paul.

Wittgenstein, Ludwig (1978). *Remarks on the Foundations of Mathematics*, ed. by Georg Henrik von Wright, Rush Rhees, G. E. M. Anscombe. Revised edition. Cambridge, Massachusetts. The MIT Press.

16

Naturalising Illocutionary Rules[*]

MACIEJ WITEK

In this paper I consider the concept of an *illocutionary rule* – i.e., the rule of the form "*X* counts as *Y* in context *C*" – and examine the role it plays in explaining the nature of verbal communication and the conventionality of natural languages. My aim is to find a middle ground between John R. Searle's view, according to which every conventional speech act has to be explained in terms of illocutionary rules that underlie its performance, and the view held by Ruth G. Millikan, who seems to suggest that the formula "*X* counts as *Y* in context *C*" has no application in our theorising about human linguistic practice. I claim, namely, that the concept of an illocutionary rule is theoretically useful, though not explanatorily basic. I argue that using the formula "*X* counts as *Y* in context *C*" we can classify illocutionary acts by what Millikan calls their *conventional outcomes*, and thereby make them susceptible to naturalistic explanation.

My paper consists of three parts. In the first section I discuss Searle's account of illocutionary acts, assessing its strengths and weaknesses. In the second section I analyse Millikan's conception of illocutionary com-

---

[*] Work on this paper was supported by the research grant No. N101 012 31/1708 of the Polish Ministry of Science and Higher Education. I want to thank to Edoardo Fittipaldi, Maciej Makarewicz, Jakub Martewicz, Jurġis Šķilters and two anonymous reviewers for their helpful critical comments on an earlier version of this paper.

Beyond Description: Naturalism and Normativity.
Marcin Miłkowski and Konrad Talmont-Kaminski (eds.).
Copyright © 2010 The Author.

munication. In the third section I develop a naturalistic account of speech acts, the central idea of which is that conventional illocutionary acts are complete linguistic signs conceived as structured states of affairs that embrace both lexical and environmental elements.

It is worth stressing that in what follows I focus on communicative illocutionary acts whose performance requires no extra-linguistic institutions. It is not my aim to examine such formal acts as pronouncing a couple husband and wife, returning a verdict, adjourning a parliamentary session, and so on.

1 Searle on Illocutionary Rules

In his essay *Speech Acts* (1969) Searle adopts the Austinian view on human linguistic practice, the central idea of which is that "speaking a language is engaging in a (...) rule-governed form of behavior" (Searle 1969: 12). In particular, he assumes that to perform an illocutionary act of a certain type – such as stating, requesting, warning, advising, promising, and so on – is to utter certain words in certain circumstances in accordance with a certain set of rules that he calls *constitutive*. Roughly speaking, a rule is constitutive if its collective acceptance by the community creates the possibility of a new form of behaviour.

In order to define the central concept of his theory, Searle draws a distinction between constitutive and regulative rules, which differ in their form and function. Constitutive rules have the form "X counts as Y in context C". Their function is not only to regulate, but to create the possibility of a new form of behaviour. The rules of chess, for example, define what counts as playing the game or, more accurately, what counts as making particular moves in the game, such as castling or checkmating. Regulative rules, by contrast, have the form "Do X" or "While G-ing, do X". Their function is to regulate the conduct of antecedently existing form of behaviour G. For example, the rule of etiquette "While talking to others, do not yawn" does not create the possibility of a conversation, but determines how to make it in a polite manner.

Searle's crucial point is that in some respects speaking a language resembles playing a game. To wit, types of illocutionary acts – e.g., stating, promising, requesting, and so on – can be likened to types of moves in the game of chess, such as castling or checkmating. A particular arrangement of the pieces on the chessboard, for instance, is not checkmating in virtue of its physical properties alone. What makes it checkmating is the fact that it instantiates the relevant move type. The type, in turn, is defined by the system of rules that jointly determine that such and such a position in chess counts as checkmating. By analogy, the utterance of a sentence in a context is not itself the performance of a certain speech act unless it instantiates the relevant illocutionary act type. The type, in turn, is defined by the set of illocutionary rules according to which the use of certain linguistic devices – words, syntactic structures, moods, and so on – in such and such a context counts as the performance of such and such an act.

The idea of rules that create the possibility of certain forms of behaviour, though popularised by Searle, has been independently put forth by other philosophers. Amedeo G. Conte (1997), an Italian legal philosopher, offers his own conception of eidetic-constitutive rules. He remarks that it was Wittgenstein who used the "verb 'to constitute' when talking of the rules of chess" (Conte 1997: 135). According to Conte, the idea that the types of moves in the game of chess are constituted by its rules can be found in the work of Czesław Znamierowski, "the Polish philosopher who put forward the concept of *norma konstrukcyjna* [a constructive norm]" (Conte 1997: 135). Another interesting conception of constitutive rules comes from William P. Alston, who in his *Illocutionary Acts and Sentence Meaning* (2000) accounts for illocutionary acts in terms of the speaker's taking a normative stance with respect to his utterance (for a critical discussion of this topic see Harnish 2005). Timothy Williamson, in turn, in his paper "Knowing and Asserting" (1996) claims that what is constitutive of assertions is the so-called knowledge rule (for a discussion of this topic see García-Carpintero 2004).

Constructing his theory, Searle focuses on a few closely related topics concerning (*i*) the nature of speech acts and linguistic conventions, (*ii*) the nature of illocutionary competence and (*iii*) the explanatory standards that every adequate account of language has to meet. In short, his aim is to construct a comprehensive theory that solves ontological, epistemological and methodological puzzles connected with speech acts. Let me, therefore, reconstruct it as a conjunction of the following four theses:
(1) Illocutionary acts are performed within language in virtue of the system of constitutive rules.

(2) Illocutionary conventions of different languages are different realisations of the same underlying constitutive rules; the rules, in turn, are conventional because they are collectively accepted by the language community.
(3) An agent knows how to perform and interpret certain illocutionary acts if and only if he has internalised the appropriate system of constitutive rules.
(4) In order to explain a linguistic characterisation of the form "In uttering sentence T in context C speaker S performs illocutionary act $F(p)$" – where "F" stands for the type of which the act is a token and "p" stands for the propositional content – one has to formulate the set of constitutive rules in accordance to which speaker S utters sentence T.

Thesis (1) defines the nature of illocutionary acts that are conceived as real components of our social environment. We describe them by means of sentences of the form "S performs illocutionary act $F(p)$" – e.g. "John states that Peter is a secret agent", "Sue asks whether Peter is a secret agent" and "Paul requests Peter to become a secret agent" – that can be true or false in virtue of facts. According to Searle, statements about illocutionary acts are *epistemically objective*, since they "can be established as true or false independently of the feelings and attitudes of the makers and the interpreters of the statement" (Searle 2005: 4). Facts that these statements register, in turn, have *subjective ontology*, because "their mode of existence requires that they be experienced by a human or animal subject" (ibid). Notice, then, that the necessary conditions for the successful performance of an illocutionary act token made in uttering sentence T are, *inter alia*, that (*a*) the speaker intends the hearer to recognise that the state of affairs specified by the rules of the relevant components of T obtains and (*b*) this intention is fulfilled (see Searle 1969: 49–50). In short, what constitutes the particular illocutionary act token are, *inter alia*, certain intentional states – feelings and attitudes – of the speaker and the hearer. These intentional states, nevertheless, can only function against the presupposition of the system of illocutionary constitutive rules, whose existence requires the collective acceptance by the community to which the speaker and the hearer belong. Illocutionary acts, then, have subjective ontology because, first, every act *token* requires for its successful performance that the speaker and the hearer have certain intentional states and, second, every illocutionary act *type* exists in virtue of the collective acceptance of the relevant set of constitutive rules by the linguistic community.

As Robert M. Harnish points out, "the utterance of a sentence in a context is not sufficient for the performance of a speech act" (Harnish 2005: 11). To determine the nature of speech acts, therefore, is to specify what must be added. According to Searle, we must add both the speaker's individual intentionality and the set of constitutive rules that are collectively accepted by the linguistic community. The rules jointly constitute the possibility of performing acts of certain types or, in other words, the possibility of the speaker's expressing and the hearer's recognising certain illocutionary intentions (see Searle 2002: 150–151 and Searle 2005: 5–10). It turns out, therefore, that Searle attempts to reconcile two competing views on the nature of speech acts: the Gricean view, the central idea of which is that the performance of a speech act is best understood as the speaker's successful expression of a complex intentional state, and the Austinian view, according to which performing speech acts is engaging in a rule-governed form of behaviour.

Thesis (2), in turn, concerns the nature of linguistic conventions. Notice, however, that it involves two different criteria of conventionality which, it seems, fail to delimit a coherent class of conventional items. First, in different natural languages there are different conventional devices – illocutionary verbs, moods, syntactic structures, and so on – by means of which the speaker can indicate the illocutionary force of the act he performs. To call them conventional is to state that their forms are arbitrary in relation to their function. Second, there are underlying constitutive rules of language. To call them conventional is to state that they are products of collective intentionality.

Consider, first, the criterion of conventionality defined in terms of the arbitrariness of an item's form in relation to its function (call it the *arbitrariness-criterion*). Indeed, it is a matter of convention that the function of the French expression "Je promets" – as well as the German expression "Ich verspreche" and the English expression "I promise" – is to make a promise. In other words, these expressions are three different conventional devices for performing acts of the same type. In other words, they are arbitrary in relation to their illocutionary function, i.e., the function to bring about the institutional fact that Searle describes as *the undertaking of an obligation*. Generally speaking, to issue an utterance with a certain illocutionary force is to express the intention to get the hearer to recognise that such and such an institutional fact obtains. Provided this intention is recognised by the hearer – i.e., the *illocutionary uptake* or *effect* is secured – the act is successfully performed. In short, Searle classifies illocutionary acts, *inter alia*, in terms of their illocutionary effects that are determined by what he calls *essential rules*. The essential rule of promising, for example, is "The utterance of *Pr* counts as the undertaking of an obligation to do *A*", where "*Pr*" stands for a linguistic device indicating the illocutionary force of promise (see Searle 1969: 63). It is a matter of convention that in French *Pr* is "Je promets" and in German it is "Ich verspreche".

The second criterion of conventionality – that I call the *agreement-criterion* – is met by the set of underlying illocutionary rules that are realised in one way or another by different natural languages. The rules exist – or, more accurately, are in force – in virtue of their collective acceptance by the community of speakers (see Searle 2005). In other words, they have subjective ontology, since they exist as correlates of acts of collective intentionality.

It turns out, therefore, that we are faced with two distinct criteria of conventionality – the arbitrariness-criterion and the agreement-criterion – that delimit two different domains of conventional items. According to Searle, the latter is explanatorily prior to the former, i.e., one cannot understand the conventional nature of illocutionary verbs – as well as other illocutionary force indicating devices – without a prior understanding of their function. The function, in turn, is conventional because it results from the collective agreement or acceptance. In other words, a considerable portion of linguistic conventions remain unintelligible unless they are conceived as particular realisations of the constitutive rules of language.

Thesis (3) is epistemological. It defines the kind of competence that underlies illocutionary communication. According to Searle, every agent who knows how to issue and understand illocutionary acts of certain types must have internalised the appropriate system of illocutionary rules. The individual knowledge of such a system constitutes the agent's illocutionary competence. According to Searle's modified definition of non-natural meaning, the speaker intends the hearer to recognise the intention to produce the illocutionary effect in virtue of the hearer's knowledge of the relevant set of constitutive rules. Moreover, due to this kind of competence the agent is able to issue and understand novel speech acts, i.e., acts they have never encountered before. Such an ability – that can be, following Chomsky, called the *creative aspect of normal language use* – is, according to Searle, an important mark "of rule-governed *as* opposed to merely regular behavior" (Searle 1969: 42). In this respect – though, of course, not in others – Searle's individualistic account of illocutionary competence can be likened to Chomsky's conception of I-languages. "In addition to what is internalised in the minds/brains of the speakers – Searle declares – there isn't some social practice that is, so to speak, out there independent of them. Social capacities are realised entirely in the individual brains of the members of any given society." (Searle 2002: 154)

Theses (1), (2) and (3) support methodological principle (4). According to Searle, to perform an illocutionary act is to utter words in accordance with the relevant system of illocutionary rules. Moreover, the agent's knowledge how to perform and interpret illocutionary acts amounts to his mastery of the rules he has internalised. In order to explain illocutionary act tokens, therefore, one has to formulate the relevant rules that underlie their performance. What is more, every speaker who is able to participate in illocutionary communication is also able, after careful and systematic reflection, to provide such an explanation. Why? Because they can speak the language they investigate and, in this connection, can come to know explicitly the rules that shape *their* linguistic behaviour.

Searle's account of speech acts in terms of constitutive rules offers a unified explanation of various linguistic phenomena, such as indirect speech acts and performative utterances. It also provides the basis for an interesting taxonomy of speech acts. Moreover, it accommodates the Gricean idea – that meaning is a matter of expressing a complex intentional state – within the broader Austinian framework. Despite these and similar advantages, however, Searle's account faces at least two serious problems.

First, there seems to be something wrong with Searle's two-step account of the conventionality of natural languages. To wit, it fails to delimit a coherent region of conventional items. First, Searle explains conventions of particular languages in terms of their arbitrariness-conventionality and the underlying constitutive rules. Next, he claims that the underlying rules have subjective ontology, which means that they exist in virtue of the collective acceptance by the linguistic community and, in this connection, are agreement-conventional. It seems to me, however, that for an item to be conventional it has to meet both the arbitrariness-criterion and (a version of) the agreement-criterion: a pattern of behaviour is conventional only if its form is arbitrary in relation to its function and its performance presupposes a kind of collective attitude. I return to this topic in the second section of this paper, where I consider Millikan's account of natural conventionality.

Second, there are reasons for doubting whether illocutionary competence does require the internalisation of the system of illocutionary rules. Notice that claim (3), though epistemological, carries one disputable metaphysical assumption. It presupposes, namely, that the speaker's illocutionary competence comes down to his knowledge of the system of illocutionary rules and, as such, is a natural property of his brain. The point is that, according to Searle, (*i*) the system of illocutionary rules is a product of the collective intentionality and (*ii*) intentionality is a biological phenomenon (Searle 1992). It turns out, therefore, that Searle attempts to provide a naturalistic account of constitutive rules. In the third section I offer an alternative view on skills that underlie illocutionary communication. I claim that our ability to issue and interpret illocutionary acts rides piggyback on our ability to read natural signs, an ability that is further extended by our capacity to imitate what others do. Illocutionary rules are not in the head.

2   Millikan on Illocutionary Conventions

In her "Proper Function and Convention in Speech Acts" (2005) Ruth G. Millikan offers a uniform account of illocutionary acts. She claims, namely, that they all can be grouped and defined by their purposes. Allowing for the fact that speech acts do not form a homogeneous class, however, she mentions three different kinds of purposes one may attribute to them: (*i*) the purpose of the speaker in speaking, (*ii*) the purpose of the linguistic form used and (*iii*) the purpose of the extra-linguistic conventional move (if any) the speaker makes. Purpose (*i*) is the intention that underlies the speaker's utterance, whereas purpose (*ii*) can be identified with the conventional outcome of the utterance, i.e., the effect it has under the relevant convention (constraints it puts on what can count as the hearer's conventional response). Millikan claims that purposes (*i*) and (*ii*) normally coincide in content. But they can diverge: the speaker can be insincere or uncooperative; they can also perform an illocutionary act in a non-conventional way, thereby generating the Gricean implicature.

In this section I examine Millikan's idea of illocutionary acts as conventional moves. I start, however, with a brief presentation of her conception of *locally recurrent natural signs* (henceforth "LRNSs"), a conception that explains how it is possible for an organism inhabiting a certain domain to learn about one of its elements from the other. Millikan's point is that conventional signs in general and linguistic signs in particular are nothing but natural components of the human environment and as such "are read in exactly the same way that natural signs are read" (Millikan 2004: 109).

Consider a fox who perceives certain tracks left on the snow – call them, following Dretske and Millikan, "ε-tracks" (Millikan 2004: 38) – and recognises that there was a quail in its vicinity a short time ago. How is it possible? First – Millikan claims – in the wood the fox inhabits there has to be a nonaccidental recurrent correlation between ε-tracks and the presence of quails. Second, the fox's cognitive system has to be adapted to this correlation, i.e., it has to be able to keep track of it. The correlation in question does not have to be global: the fact that in a different wood ε-tracks are correlated with something else – or even with nothing at all – has no bearing on the fox's ability to read ε-tracks left in its local environment as signs of quails. By analogy, consider a beaver who splashes the water with its tail to signal the presence of a predator (Millikan 1989: 288). Other beavers who hear the splash looks for a place to hide. We can say, therefore, that in the beavers' local domain there is a recurrent correlation between certain splashes and the presence of predators. A beaver who is not able to keep track of this correlation has little chance to survive. In sum, as part of their adaptation to their environments, organisms have become sensitive – by means of learning or natural selection – to recurrent correlations characteristic to *local* domains they inhabit.

Notice that a LRNS of a thing is not a simple quality – such as a track of a certain shape or a characteristic splashing sound – but a structured state of affairs. The same holds for what it signifies. In the fox's wood, for example, states of affairs of the form "ε-track-of-size-*s*-at-*p*-and-*t*" signifies states of affairs of the form "a-quail-of-size-z-at-p-and-the-moment-preceding-t" (where "p" and "t" are locational and temporal variables, respectively). Notice that there are systematic correlations between the time, place and size of a particular ε-track and the time, place and size of the quail it signifies. By the same token, in the beaver splash semiotic system the time and place of a splash vary systematically with the place and time of a predator. In other words, there is an isomorphism – which Millikan calls a *semantic mapping function* – between the class of signifying states of the form "a-splash-at-p-and-t" and the class of signified states of the form "a-predator-at-p-and-t" (Millikan 2004: 49). The former class is a sign type, which can, following Charles S. Peirce, be called *legisign*. Its every token, in turn, is a *sinsign*, within which one can distinguish (*i*) a characteristic splashing sound and (*ii*) the particular time and place of its production. Component (*i*) is qualitative and as such can be called *qualisign*. Components (*ii*) are *reflexive*: the time and place of a splash stand for the time and place of danger. Both (*i*) and (*ii*) are singled out by abstraction, since the real semiotic unit is a sign token that represents a respective type. Only in the context of the beaver semiotic system does a splash signify something. "It is a serious mistake" – Millikan points out – "to suppose that the architectural or compositional meaning of a complex sign is derived by combining the prior independent meanings of its parts or aspects. Rather, the meanings of the various significant parts or aspects of signs are abstracted from the prior meanings of complete signs occurring within complete sign systems." (ibid.: 50).

Consider now the concept of natural conventions. According to Millikan (1998), natural conventions consist of reproduced patterns of activities that proliferate due to weight of precedent rather than due to their capacity to perform certain functions. In other words, a reproduced item is conventional if its form has been reproduced from other items and is arbitrary relative to its function. For example, what explains the proliferation of chopsticks in the East and forks in the West – two different though equally effective devices for placing food in the mouth – is weight of their respective precedents.

In some cases, to reproduce an activity – for example, wearing green clothes on St. Patrick's Day – is to copy directly its relevant aspects or form. Another possibility is to follow explicit instructions. Consider, for example, a radio presenter who advises her listeners how to decorate a Christmas tree. The predominant form of reproduction, however, is what

Millikan calls *counterpart reproduction*. Within every counterpart-reproduced pattern one can single out two complementary portions. Their production does not consist in direct coping, but is guided by the need to fit in with one another. For example, "the traditional positions assumed by men and women for ballroom dancing were commonly reproduced in part by [counterpart reproduction], each woman settling into the traditional woman's posture in response to the postures of the men with whom she danced, and vice versa" (Millikan 1998: 164). The custom to greet each other by shaking right hands and the driving-on-the-left convention are other examples of counterpart-reproduced patterns.

According to Millikan, most language conventions consist of counterpart-reproduced patterns. It is a matter of convention – she claims – that we use the indicative mood to make assertions and the imperative mood to issue directives. Moods and syntactic forms, however, are not handed down by direct coping. They are abstract components of complex speaker-hearer patterns whose reproduction involves two complementary acts that are supposed to fit in with one another. Normally – Millikan claims – a speaker who utters an indicative sentence initiates the reproduction of the relevant pattern; the reproduction is completed if the hearer believes what the speaker says. Normally, the conventional pattern whose speaker's portion involves the utterance of an imperative sentence is completed when the hearer complies with what he is told. In short, we acquire our illocutionary competence by fitting in with what others say and do.

Two tokens – such as phrases and structures – are of the same type in virtue of their history rather than their shape. Roughly speaking, language conventions are sequences of pattern tokens that have the same evolutionary history. To recognise the type to which a given token belongs is to identify the family from which it comes.

I assume that Millikan's reproduction-requirement is an analogue of Searle's agreement-criterion. To reproduce a pattern of activity is to do what *others* have done before. When I do something in a conventional manner, *my* doing it this way presupposes *our* doing it the same way. It should be stressed, however, that this presupposition is not normally consciously represented by the agents who are engaged in the reproduction of conventional patterns. Note, next, that not all reproduced patterns are conventional. Technologies and skills, for example, are handed down as well. That is why Millikan adds the second requirement, which is an analogue of Searle's arbitrariness-criterion: reproduced patterns are conventional if their form is arbitrary relative to their function. What, then, is the function relatively to which linguistic conventional patterns are arbitrary? According to Millikan, language conventions proliferate, in part, due to the fact that they perform *coordinating functions*.

Let me say a word on the relationship between three concepts: *cooperation*, *coordination*, and *convention*. It is worth stressing that (*a*) not all cases of cooperation involve coordination and (*b*) not all cases of coordination involve conventions.

To illustrate thesis (*a*), let me consider a cognitive system made up of two cooperating input-output subsystems: the perceptual system and the executive system. Assume, for simplicity, that the former consists of the retina, the optic nerve and the primary visual cortex. When triggered by a distal stimulus (e.g., a predator), it produces a topographically organised neural pattern in the primary visual cortex. The function of the executive system, in turn, is to translate such a perceptual pattern into a corresponding behavioural reaction (e.g., to fly away). Following Millikan, we can call the perceptual system a *sign producer* and the executive system a *sign consumer*. Provided the former operates *normally* the pattern it produces is a LRNS of the relevant distal stimulus. (Note that "normally" is a historical rather than statistical term; for an item to operate normally is to operate in a way that explains the item's continuous reproduction; for a discussion of this topic see Millikan 1989: 284.) The sign, next, is consumed by the executive system. The crucial point here is that these two systems in question cooperate with each other. They have a purpose in common – or, borrowing the term from Searle, a *collective purpose* – which is to adapt the organism's behaviour to variations in its environment. Moreover, it is their collective purpose – or, more accurately, their *collective proper function* – that explains their continuous reproduction within the relevant species. The producer's part of the collective purpose is to engender whatever the consumer needs for doing its part in a normal way. The consumer's function, in turn, is to adapt the organism's behaviour to variations in perceptual patterns. The consumer performs its function normally only if its triggering pattern is a true representation. Therefore, the producer function is to produce representations that are true as the consumer reads them. Provided the producer performs its function in a normal way, the sign it engenders is not only true, but is also a LRNS.

In short, the representation that stands midway between the producer and the consumer is a *cooperative intentional sign* (see Millikan 2004: chapter 6), which, unlike a LRNS, can be false.

It is not my aim in this section to reconstruct Millikan's concept of intentional signs and her original theory of proper functions. What I want to stress now is the fact that the cognitive system under discussion contains two subsystems that have been designed to cooperate with each other. In other words, they have been selected for performing their collective proper function. We cannot characterise proper functions of the perceptual system and the executive system without reference to their collective purpose. In short, the purposes we attribute to both the producer and the consumer are *cooperative* purposes. These two subsystems cooperate despite the fact that their interactions involve no coordination. Generally speaking, what underlies the most primitive forms of cooperation is evolutionary design rather than coordination.

Now consider thesis (*b*). Notice, first, that what Millikan calls the producer and the consumer can be two distinct organisms. Consider, then, two or more partners that have a collective purpose. Assume, next, that "achieving this purpose requires actions by each of the partners", and that "more than one combination of actions will achieve the purpose" (Millikan 1998: 168). In order to achieve their collective purpose, then, the cooperating participants have to be able to predict each others' moves and, as a result, adapt their individual actions to what others are predicted to do. In short, their collective behaviour has to involve a form of coordination.

Millikan maintains three types of coordination: *open, blind* and *half-blind*. Open coordination is completely unproblematic and as such requires no conventions. Consider, for example, two people whose collective purpose is to sit at the same table in the restaurant. One of them – the leader – sits at an arbitrary table, whereas her partner follows after. In other words, the follower does not have to predict the leader's move in order to achieve coordination; he just sees what he is supposed to do. Blind coordination, by contrast, necessarily involves conventions. Consider, for example, the driving-on-the-left convention, whose function is to achieve coordination between drivers that otherwise – i.e., in the absence of such a convention – would not be able to predict each other's behaviour. Their collective purpose is to avoid the oncoming traffic. An interesting type of coordination is half-blind coordination. Like open coordination, it involves interaction between a leader and a follower. Like blind coordination, however, it involves conventions. In short, half-blind coordination is conventional leader-follower coordination. Examples of this kind of coordination "began when a leader reproduces a certain portion of a pattern, which portion is observable to a follower. The follower is familiar with the pattern, recognises it, and reproduces the complementary part, resulting in a coordination of a sort that is partly responsible for the proliferation (due to precedent) of the pattern." (Millikan 1998: 172) Consider, for example, two mechanics whose collective purpose is to repair a car engine. One of them (the leader) wants to remove a broken carburettor, but cannot do this until his partner (the follower) undoes certain nuts. The leader's intention to get the hearer to undo the nuts is an unobservable part of the collective activity under discussion. In other words, the follower cannot directly recognise it. This intention, however, is an unobservable part of the relevant speaker-hearer pattern that involves (*i*) the use of the imperative mood on the part of the speaker and (*ii*) complying with what the speaker says on the part of the hearer. Reproducing his portion of the pattern, the leader makes his intention overt, thereby facilitating the achievement of coordination.

To sum, only blind and half-blind coordination necessarily involves conventions. Most language conventions, in particular, have coordinating purposes. Speaker-hearer conventional patterns proliferate because they help to achieve half-blind coordination between cooperating partners.

Recall that "the utterance of a sentence in a context is not sufficient for the performance of a speech act" (Harnish 2005: 11). According to Millikan, what must be added are conventional patterns that are reproduced by cooperating speakers and hearers. In other words, to perform an act of a certain type is to initiate or complete the reproduction of a corresponding speaker-hearer conventional pattern. For example, to perform an assertive act is to utter an indicative sentence in such and such a context and thereby initiate the reproduction of a corresponding conventional pattern. Normally – Millikan claims – the speaker's portion of the pattern involves two components: the speaker's belief and his publicly observable utterance. In other words, the speaker who performs an assertive act translates his belief into an *outer cooperative intentional sign*. The hearer's portion of the pattern, in turn, is to believe what the speaker says. In other words, the hearer's cooperative response is to translate the sign produced by the speaker into a corresponding belief. In short, assertive communication, when it proceeds in a normal way, can be best understood as a transfer of knowledge, the purpose of which is to achieve coordination between the leader (i.e., the speaker who is a sign producer) and the follower (i.e., the hearer who is a sign consumer). To perform a directive act, in turn, is to utter an imperative sentence and thereby initiate the reproduction of a corresponding conventional pattern. What completes the reproduction is the hearer's cooperative response, i.e., his complying with what the speaker says.

The speaker who initiates the counterpart reproduction of a conventional pattern makes a *conventional move* that can be characterised by its *conventional outcome*, i.e., in terms of constraints put on what counts as the hearer's cooperative response (Millikan 1998: 178). To perform an illocutionary act, then, is to make a conventional move. Every illocutionary act type can be defined as a set or family of conventional move tokens that have the same conventional outcome or, in other words, have the same cooperative purpose. It should be kept in mind, however, that an utterance token can be a determinate conventional move even though the hearer to whom it is addressed behaves uncooperatively. What matters is the fact that the speaker who makes the utterance initiates the reproduction of the relevant pattern. Whether the reproduction is completed or not has no bearing on the identity of the illocutionary act the speaker makes. (Of course if hearers were systematically uncooperative, speakers would not be motivated to initiate the reproduction of the pattern in question.)

3 Natural Sign and Convention in Speech Acts

Following Millikan, I assume that the central class of illocutionary acts is conventional in nature. Normally, to perform an illocutionary act is to make a conventional move that can be defined by its conventional outcome. Unlike Millikan, however, I am far from claiming that the conventional outcome of an act is usually identical to the purpose of the linguistic form used. My point is, rather, that the latter should be analysed in terms of what it contributes to the former. I claim, moreover, that in order to characterise an illocutionary act type Y – i.e., a class of act tokens that have the same conventional outcome – we can invoke the formula "X_n counts as Y in context C_n" and represent the tokens of Y as ordered pairs of the form "$\langle X_n, C_n \rangle$", where "X_n" stands for the utterance made by a speaker and "C_n" stands for its environmental context, i.e., the context that is built of LRNSs that are readable to the speaker and the hearer..

Let me reconstruct my view as a conjunction of the following four theses:

(1) Illocutionary acts are performed within a given domain in virtue of (*a*) the system of LRNSs that are specific to that domain and (*b*) the relevant system of speaker-hearer conventional patterns, where the latter is built on the former.

(2) Illocutionary conventions consist of speaker-hearer patterns whose form is arbitrary relative to their coordinative function; to perform a conventional illocutionary act is to initiate the reproduction of the corresponding pattern by supplementing LRNSs that are available to the speaker and the hearer with an appropriate utterance.

(3) An agent knows how to perform/interpret certain illocutionary acts if and only if he is able to (*a*) read the relevant LRNSs and (*b*) initiate/complete the reproduction of the relevant speaker-hearer patterns.

(4) In order to explain a linguistic characterisation of the form "In making utterance X_n in context C_n speaker S performs illocutionary act Y" – where "Y" stands for the type of which the act is a token – one has to identify family Y of tokens of the form "$\langle X, C \rangle$" to which the token $\langle X_n, C_n \rangle$ can be assimilated.

Let me justify my view by testing it against the following three examples. The first one comes from Grice (1989: 32):

Scenario 1.
A is standing by an obviously immobilised car and is approached by *B*. The following exchange takes place:
A: I am out of petrol.
B: There is a garage around the corner.

According to Grice and his followers, *B*'s utterance carries a conversational implicature: by saying that there is a garage around the corner, *B* non-conventionally means that the garage is open and selling petrol. Notice, however, that *A*'s opening remark can be also analysed along the Gricean lines: by saying that he is out of petrol, *A* non-conventionally asks *B* for help in finding petrol for his car (see Korta and Perry 2006: 169).

I claim that there is nothing unconventional in *A*'s and *B*'s behaviour. I assume that *A* and *B* reproduce a speaker-hearer conventional pattern, whose speaker's portion is to produce a *complete cooperative linguistic sign* (henceforth "CCLS") that is a conventional request for help in finding petrol for the speaker's car. The hearer's portion of the pattern, in turn, is to respond cooperatively. The main idea behind my account comes from Millikan, who claims that "there are many conventional ways of using context as a proper part of a linguistic sign" (Millikan 2004: 139). Hence thesis (2): to produce a CCLS by uttering certain words is to add something to the domain of LRNSs that are available to the hearer. The resulting sign is a structured state of affairs one aspect of which is the speaker's utterance. Its other aspects are LRNSs that constitute the *external* or *environmental context* of the utterance as opposed to its *internal* or *cognitive context* (see Carston 2002: 81). External context is a complex world affair, whereas internal context can be represented as the set of propositions that are mutually believed by the hearer and the speaker.

Assume – in agreement with thesis (1) – that in the traffic domain there is a trackable and non-accidental correlation between structured states of the form "x-stands-by-immobilised-*car*-at-*p*-and-*t*" and states of the form "x-needs-help-with-*car*-at-*p*-and-*t*". (Note that the way the signified states are characterised presupposes the existence of a cooperative society: only members of a cooperative society can be described as being in need of help.) "*Car*", "*p*" and "*t*" are variables representing reflexive elements of sign tokens, i.e., elements that stand for themselves (see Millikan 2004: 49). We can say, therefore, that there is a semantic mapping function that defines an isomorphism between the class of signifying states and the class of signified states. States of the form "x-stands-by-immobilised-*car*-at-*p*-and-*t*" naturally signify (i.e., carry natural information of) corresponding states of the form "x-needs-help-with-*car*-at-*p*-and-*t*".

According to thesis (2), *A*'s utterance supplements the LRNS token whose structure can be described as *A*-stands-by-*CAR*-at-*P*-in-*T* (where "*CAR*" stands for the immobilised car under discussion and "*P*" and "*T*" stands for the location and time of the utterance respectively); to wit, words uttered by *A* specify the kind of problem that *A* is currently facing and, in the process, the kind of help he needs. The CCLS produced by *A* is the state A-stands-by-CAR-at-P-and-T-and-utters-[I am out of petrol] and can be represented as an ordered pair $\langle X_1, C_1 \rangle$, where X_1 is A's utterance of the sentence "I am out of petrol" and C_1 is the state A-stands-by-CAR-at-P-and-T. Notice that what determines the illocutionary force of $\langle X_1, C_1 \rangle$ is its contextual component, i.e., the LRNS token A-stands-by-CAR-at-P-and-T. In the traffic domain, it naturally signifies the state A-needs-help-with-CAR-at-P-and-T. Although the sentence uttered by A is indicative in form, the communicative act he performs is best understood as a conventional request. The point is that what A reproduces is not merely the sentence "I am out of petrol", but a complex state of affairs to which the sentence contributes; the resulting state is a conventional move whose conventional outcome can be described in terms of what can be counted as B's cooperative response.

Observe – in agreement with thesis (3) – that what underlies B's understanding of A's opening remark – the understanding that is manifested in B's cooperative response – is nothing but B's ability to keep track of locally recurrent correlations that is essentially enriched by his capacity to reproduce speaker-hearer patterns.

By analogy, consider scenario 2:

Scenario 2.:
A four year old boy runs into the kitchen and cries: "I'm thirsty, mum!"
His mother gives him a glass of juice.

Note that according to the Gricean view, the boy directly states that he is thirsty and indirectly (*via* non-conventional implicature) asks his mother for something to drink. I claim, by contrast, that the act the boy performs is a conventional request. More precisely, it is a complex conventional sign within which we can single out its linguistic and contextual component. The former – element X_2 – is the utterance of the sentence "I'm thirsty, mum", whereas the latter – element C_2 – is the state boy-runs-into-the-kitchen-at-T. From the mother's point of view the occurrence of her son in the kitchen at t is a LRNS of his being in need of something at t. What she interprets, however, is a CCLS, i.e., a state whose structure can be described as boy-runs-into-the-kitchen-at-T-and-cries-[I'm thirsty, mum]. By giving him a glass of juice, she completes the reproduction of the relevant conventional pattern.

Consider the third example, which is borrowed from Carston (2002: 17):

Scenario 3.:
D and *E* live together. *D*, who notoriously eats marmalade on toast for breakfast, holds a slice of toast in his hand and visibly looks around for something. *E*, who is sitting at the kitchen table, says: "On the top shelf!"

Note that *E* behaves cooperatively. To wit, she recognises that her partner needs help – more precisely, that he is looking for the marmalade – and provides him with the relevant piece of information. How is it possible for *E* to come to know what *D* wants? My hypothesis is that in their kitchen domain there is a trackable and recurrent correlation between states of the form "*D*-holds-a-slice-of-toast-at-*t*" and states of the form "*D*-wants-the-marmalade-at-*t*" (or "*D*-looks-for-the-marmalade-at-*t*"). State tokens that exemplify the first type naturally signify corresponding state tokens that exemplify the second type. Note, that some elements of every signifying state contribute as such to the state it signifies. Agent *D*, for example, who is an element of the signifying state, stands for himself. The same holds for the moment *t* which is an abstract component of both the signifying and the signified state. It can be said, therefore, that there is a semantic mapping function that defines an isomorphism between the class of states of the form "*D*-holds-a-slice-of-toast-at-*t*" and the class that comprises states of the form "*D*-wants-the-marmalade-at-*t*". Being adapted to it, *E* is able to interpret *D*'s behaviour as the LRNS of his want of the marmalade.

Do *D* and *E* reproduce a speaker-hearer conventional pattern? Strictly speaking, they do not. Only cooperating agents can be in need of coordination and, a fortiori, in need of coordination achieved by means of language conventions. There is no reason to suppose that *D*'s behaviour is a cooperative intentional sign. Rather, it is a natural sign that has no cooperative function.

Notice, however, that *E* behaves cooperatively. She recognises that her partner is looking for the marmalade and, as a result, she provides him with the relevant piece of information. We can say, therefore, that what scenario 3 illustrates is a borderline case. It involves, namely, a natural non-cooperative sign produced by *D* and *E*'s cooperative response to it. That is why I am inclined to regard the former as a quasi-illocutionary act that evokes a proto-conventional, though entirely cooperative response.

Consider now the following three states of affairs:

1. A-stands-by-CAR-at-P-and-T-and-utters-[I am out of petrol]
2. boy-runs-into-the-kitchen-at-T-and-cries-[I'm thirsty, mum]
3. D-holds-a-slice-of-toast-at-T

States 1 and 2 are conventional CCSLs: they initiate the reproduction of relevant speaker-hearer patterns, i.e., patterns involving two complementary acts that are supposed to fit in with one another. State 1 – and the same holds for state 2 – can be represented as an ordered pair $\langle X_1, C_1\rangle$, where "X_1" stands for A's utterance of the sentence "I am out of petrol" and "C_1" stands for the state A-stands-by-CAR-at-P-and-T. In other words, state 1 exemplifies a type of illocutionary act that can be represented – in agreement with thesis (4) – as a sequence of ordered pairs of the form "$\langle X_n, C_n\rangle$" that share the same evolutionary history and, as a result, can be counted as having the same conventional outcome Y. It is not required, however, that all tokens of a given act type have exactly the same shape. Consider, for example, speaker F who enters a small shop, looks at the assistant, and says: "My car is on the shoulder. I am out of petrol". Like sign 1, the sign produced by F can be represented as an ordered pair of the form "$\langle X_n, C_n\rangle$". These two signs under consideration differ in their linguistic and contextual components. Nevertheless, they can be counted as instantiating *the same* illocutionary act type Y (two different cases of asking for help with finding petrol for the speaker's car). As John L. Austin put it, "'The same' does not always mean the same. (…) it is a (the typical) device for establishing and distinguishing the meanings of ordinary words. Like 'real', it is part of our apparatus *in* words for fixing and adjusting the semantics *of* words." (Austin 1961: 88, footnote 2) We can add that it is also part of our apparatus for fixing and adjusting the typology of illocutionary acts.

It turns out, therefore, that illocutionary rules of the form "X_n counts as Y in context C_n" do not *constitute* but *describe* types of illocutionary acts. The latter are nothing but sequences of ordered pairs of the form "$\langle X_n, C_n\rangle$" that are taken by members of the linguistic community to be of *the same* type. Illocutionary rules do not constitute our linguistic practice; rather, it is our linguistic practice that constitutes what they describe.

Observe, next, that what underlies the interpretation of signs 1, 2 and 3 is our ability to keep track of natural semiotic domains that is essentially enriched by our capacity to imitate certain aspects of what others do. In other words, there is a continuity between our ability to read

LRNSs – an example of which is state 3 – and our capacity to interpret CCLSs such as 1 and 2. Both *B* and *E* are trying to be helpful. *E* reacts cooperatively to the LRNS produced by her partner (i.e., to state 3), whereas *B* reacts cooperatively to the CCLS produced by *A*. The latter (i.e., state 1) is also a LRNS, provided *A* is truthful, sincere and cooperative. The correlation between states of the form "*x*-stands-by-immobilised-*car*-at-*p*-and-*t*-and-utters-[I am out of petrol]" and states of the form "*x*-needs-help-in-finding-petrol-for-*car*-at-*p*-and-*t*" spreads over a local time and place "through the medium of competent, reliable, and sincere speakers of the language who have learned from one another" (Millikan 2004: 109).

Let me end my paper with four remarks.

First, the view I develop here is a bit more radical than the one offered by Millikan in her "Proper Function and Convention in Speech Acts" (2005). She assumes, namely, that the conventional outcome of the speaker's move can be identified with the cooperative purpose of the linguistic form used. The problem is, however, that this assumption can hardly be reconciled with the observation that the primary bearers of linguistic meaning are CCLSs – complex states of affairs that essentially involve contextual elements carrying local natural information. That is why I claim that the cooperative function of a linguistic form should be analysed in terms of its systematic contribution to the meaning of CCLSs.

Second, Millikan's conception seems to be an attractive alternative to Searle's two-step account of language conventions. Unlike Searle's two criteria of conventionality, the reproduction-constraint enables us – together with the weight-of-precedent-constraint – to delimit a coherent region of conventional activities.

Third, the ability to issue and understand illocutionary acts does not require the internalisation of the set of illocutionary rules. Rather, it involves a more primitive and evolutionary older capacity to read LRNSs – signs that make up the environmental context of an utterance – that is enriched by the ability to reproduce what others have done before, i.e., the ability that underlies the proliferation of linguistic conventions.

Fourth, it turns out that formulas of the form "*X* counts as *Y* in context *C*" are theoretically useful. To wit, they are convenient devices for classifying illocutionary act tokens.

References

Alston, William P. (2000). *Illocutionary Acts and Sentence Meaning*. Ithaca and London: Cornell University Press.
Austin, John L. (1961). *Philosophical Papers*. Oxford: The Clarendon Press.
Carston, Robyn (2002). *Thoughts and Utterances. The Pragmatics of Explicit Communication*. Oxford: Blackwell Publishing.
Conte, Amedeo G. (1997). "Eidetic-Constitutive Rules". In *Law and Language: The Italian Analytical School*, ed. By Anna Pintore and Mario Jori. Liverpool: Deborah Charles Publications, pp. 133–146.
García-Carpintero, Manuel (2004). "Assertion and the Semantics of Force-Markers". In *The Semantics/Pragmatics Distinction*, ed. By Claudia Bianchi, Stanford: CSLI Publications, pp. 133–166.
Harnish, Robert M. (2005). "Commitments and Speech Acts". *Philosophica* 75, pp. 11–41.
Korta, Kepa and Perry, John (2006). "Three Demonstrations and a Funeral". *Mind & Language* 21, pp.166–186.
Millikan, Ruth G. (1998). "Biosemantics". *The Journal of Philosophy* LXXXVI, pp. 161–180.
Millikan, Ruth G. (1998). "Language Conventions Made Simple". *The Journal of Philosophy* XCV, pp. 161–180.
Millikan, Ruth G. (2004). *Varieties of Meaning. The 2002 Jean Nicod Lectures*. Cambridge Mass.: MIT Press.
Millikan, Ruth G. (2005). "Proper Function and Convention in Speech Acts". In Ruth G. Millikan. *Language: A Biological Model*. Oxford: Oxford University Press.
Searle, John R. (1969). *Speech Acts: An Essay in the Philosophy of Language*. Cambridge Mass.: Cambridge University Press.
Searle, John R. (1992). *The Rediscovery of the Mind*. Cambridge Mass.: MIT Press.
Searle, John R. (2002). "Individual Intentionality and Social Phenomena in the Theory of Speech Acts". In John R. Searle. *Consciousness and Language*, Cambridge: Cambridge University Press, pp. 142–155.
Searle, John R. (2005). "What is an institution?" *Journal of Institutional Economics* 1, pp. 1–22.
Williamson, Timothy (1996). "Knowing and Asserting". *Philosophical Review* 105, pp. 489–523.

17

Naturalising the Design Process: Autonomy and Interaction as Core Features

ARGYRIS ARNELLOS, THOMAS SPYROU, JOHN DARZENTAS

Abstract/Introduction

This paper attempts to provide a naturalized description of the complex design process. The design process may be abstractly conceived as a future-creating activity that goes beyond 'facticity' and creates visions of a desirable future among groups of agents. It requires the engagement of individual or groups of cognitive systems in purposeful and intentional (meaning-based) interactions with their environment and consequently with each other. It is argued in this paper that a design process should be interactive, future-anticipatory and open-ended. Furthermore, a framework to explain and support the design process should have in turn its basis in a framework of cognition. It is suggested that the design process should primarily be examined within an interactive framework of agency based on 2nd order cybernetic epistemology. Future-oriented anticipation requires functionality which can be thought of as future-directed activity; indeed all but the simplest functionalities require anticipation in order to be effective. Based on the fundamental notions of closure, self-reference and self-organisation, a cybernetically-inspired systems-theoretic notion of autonomy is proposed. This conception of autonomy is immediately

Beyond Description: Naturalism and Normativity.
Marcin Miłkowski and Konrad Talmont-Kaminski (eds.).
Copyright © 2010 The Authors.

related to the anticipative functionality of the cognitive system, which constructs emergent representations while it interactively participates in a design process.

Consequently, the design process is seen as an interaction between two or more self-organising autonomous systems thereby constructing ever more adaptive representations directed towards ill-defined outcomes. It is argued that this kind of autonomy is fundamental for the interactive establishment and definition of the design process as an essentially open-ended process.

1 Defining the Design Process

In the contemporary literature, there have been many efforts to define the design process and furthermore attempts to identify its most essential features. The nature and the purpose of the design process been much disputed and these issues have taxed various researchers over the last decades.

Defining the design process is certainly not an easy task and so, as one might expect, views are pretty diverse. As a matter of fact, Banathy (1996, pp. 11–13) lists up to twenty-four (24) definitions of design. Jones (1970) argues that design provides a means by which change is initiated in man-made things and in a somewhat parallel way Simon (1999, p. 111) states that, "…everyone designs who devises courses of action aimed at changing existing situations into preferred ones." Friedman (2003) argues that most definitions of design describe it as a goal-oriented process, where the goal is a solution to a problem, the improvement of a situation or the creation of something new and useful. Glanville (2007, p. 1178) states that, "…design is an activity that is often carried out in the face of very complex (and conflicting) requirements…" In Glanville (2006) he furthermore agrees with Jonas (2007) in arguing that design can be considered the primary human activity.

All these definitions may differ from each other, but they appear to share a common opinion, namely, that the design process should be considered a cognitive activity. Furthermore, design should primarily be attributed to a cognitive agent and hence, it should have as its basis the cognitive process[1] (Arnellos, Spyrou, Darzentas, 2007a, 2007b).

---

[1] This is of course not limited only to humans.

But why attempt to give a definition of the design process? The main reason is that a proper definition will probably indicate the most suitable theoretical framework in which the design process can be thoroughly analyzed and explained. Thus far design activities have usually been considered a discourse situated between problem-framing and problem-solving (Simon, 1995). From this perspective, certain related activities include: the construction, elaboration and modification of the representations of the problem. In the problem-framing phase, designers refine their mental representations related to the problem, while during the problem-solving stage they elaborate their representations and then evaluate them (Bonnardel, 2000). Most often, the explanation of the activity of design is given by showing the ways an agent engaging in a design activity uses his representations (Simon, 1999) and the ways these representations are generated during the design activity. Regarding the latter, the main focus is on interaction with the environment and other design systems that play an important role in the generation of these representations (see e.g. Schön & Wiggins 1992, Gero & Kannengiesser 2004).

Is an explanation like this - based on the functionality of the problem-framing and problem-solving related representations - enough? That depends on what the main aims of such a framework are. At this point it should be noted that the rationale for an analytical framework to explain the design process is not to find a formalism to reduce the complexity of the design process, nor to produce models of structured representations to guide potential computer simulations. Such models would necessarily be much impoverished versions of reality, while any such framework would run into problems regarding contextuality and evolvability issues (Macmillan et. al., 2001) - it would be like trying to compute the transcomputable (Glanville, 2007).

However, as has been shown in (Arnellos, Spyrou, Darzentas, 2007a), an in-depth understanding of the complex and dynamic nature of a design process requires a framework to support the modelling of said processes so as to provide further understanding to provide better explanations and facilitate the emergence of creativity in the design process. Overall, it might be said that explaining the design process means trying to describe what the participating cognitive systems are doing and also, how they are doing whatever is that they do. In other words, a naturalized explanation of the design process should be provided.

2 What does it mean to naturalize the design process?

There are many different kinds of naturalism, but almost all of its adherents - especially those in favour of epistemological naturalism (see e.g. Feldman, 2006) – share the view that they provide different answers from those of traditional epistemologists to key epistemological questions such as the ways a cognitive system acts and the reasons for its actions.

Naturalization requires the justification of an explanation based on facts, i.e. based on natural relations or interactions. It is primarily an attempt to look inside the system under consideration and try to understand and explain how it works. This seems to be the most valid strategy for naturalism, as in this case the respective explanations can be objectively verified. Science is inherently progressive and so 'scientific' explanatory principles and rules should also be progressive; naturalization should have no end or a specific and discrete final state - it is an ongoing and open-ended process of scientific inquiry. Naturalization should be viewed as a constant process of reformulation of questions concerning a given phenomenon, making use of both quantitative and qualitative advances in the relevant field, thus aiming towards a better understanding, explanation, and description and modelling of this phenomenon.

We have argued elsewhere (Arnellos, Spyrou, Darzentas, 2007a, 2007b) that the design process has an interactive nature, realised at the social level by acts of communication, which in turn are mediated by acts of cognition by individual cognitive agents.[2] Hence, providing a naturalised description of the notion of agency (Arnellos, Spyrou, Darzentas, in press) could not be enough to amount to a naturalisation of the design process. Actually, a properly naturalised explanation of the design process should include the main characteristics of that process, characteristics which also have their source in the relevant communicative and social (cooperative) dimensions. These fundamental characteristics are briefly presented in the next section.

---

[2] Another approach to the design process is the one which primarily considers the designer as a system which is able to engage in a circular and conversational process of creating innovative concepts and artefacts (e.g. Glanville, 2002, 2007). The approach adopted in this paper accounts for this case, as well as for the case where two or more cognitive agents are engaging in the design process. These two approaches are almost coinciding given that, during the design process, the respective agents are informed and reformed, irrespectively if one is designing on its own (i.e. by interacting with himself) or he is just in the phase of using (interacting with) the artefact of a design process.

2.1 Ill-definedness and the Open-Ended Nature of the Design Process

Most design problems are defined in terms of the features and needs of the people who will use the outcome of the design process (an artefact, which can be material or immaterial), the purpose it has for them and the form the artefact should posses in order to be deemed successful. Such design problems are ill-defined and the possible solutions are not clear from the beginning. Particularly, finding a solution also requires us to find out what the 'real' problem is, which in respect to human-centred problems is impossible. In such a complex process where solutions and problems co-evolve, one may well think that it is the solution that defines the problem. As such, the goal-oriented nature of the design process is usually related to a problem, or to a set of problems, the nature of which is constitutive of the design process itself.

On the other hand, there may be no 'problem' at all. Banathy (1996, p. 29) states that design confronts "...a system of problems rather than a collection of problems..." and he strongly argues in favour of viewing design as the attempt to find out what should become real, in terms of discerning what would be a desirable addition to the real word. From this perspective, the design process seems to be a form of inquiry driven by intentional action. Accordingly, the meanings of each cognitive system participating in the design process are continuously evolving and they are always incomplete and imprecise, however much problem-solving advances. So, design problems are also open-ended. There are different logical paths leading to a design solution - different cognitive systems construct different meanings of the design problem and consequently provide different meaning-based outcomes as solutions. This makes designing into a process that is difficult to model and even more difficult to prescribe.

2.2 The Design Process Needs an Interactive Network

The ill-defined and open-ended nature of a design problem makes both the goal and the respective constraints highly ambiguous. An internal evaluation of a possible solution is not enough – it would be subjective and disregard real-world needs. Internal evaluations of a closed system's actions are bounded to its initial organizational complexity. The result will always be satisfactory for the system itself but rarely for its environment and hence for other systems. The lack of valuable information from the system at all stages of the design process is confronted by the opening of its boundaries to interact with the environment.

Banathy stresses the interactive and participatory nature of the design process arguing that a design system cannot design for others, but it can only design *with* others. Otherwise, as Laszlo (2001) also suggests, the design system cannot be said to engage in authentic design, it is merely trying to impose its visions and values, a situation represented by the conception of a design system operating solely in a cognitivist mode. As it is mentioned by Jonas (2001), there is a need to increase the internal complexity of a design system to deal with the increasing external complexity. Banathy (1996), Glanville (2001, 2007) and Arnellos, Spyrou, Darzentas (2007a, 2007b), all argue that the design process has a systemic nature implemented in an interactive and iterated mode. These two modes are both deemed necessary for they allow the testing of alternative solutions, the integration of insights, the formulation of viable strategies and attention to shifting parameters - factors that are all crucial to complex design processes.

2.3 The Content of the Design Process Is Not the Artefact Itself

As is thoroughly analysed in (Arnellos, Spyrou, Darzentas, 2007a), the assignment of the design process to an interactive framework raises the question of the importance of the user of the design process outcome (the artefact). Users and stakeholders evaluate the artefact on the basis of their own individual experience. Considering that each user's experience and hence representational structures are different, the content of the design process should not be understood to be merely the artefact itself.

Indeed, the content should not be attributed to the aesthetic and practical properties of a fixed object (Kazmierczak, 2003). The content of the design process is subjectively interpreted and is changed by the user's cognitive processes while (s)he, in turn, is purposefully engaging in future design processes. The design system should now provide a form for dynamic and ill-defined content in such a way that will facilitate its creative interpretation by the user/receiver and, ultimately, other design systems.

From this perspective, validating the design outcome is an extremely difficult task, as there can be quite unexpected benefits for the other design systems issuing from the use of that outcome. So the next difficult question might be where the design process ends. Of course, as mentioned before, design is an open-ended and iterated process, and as such it never comes to an end. But the designer should be able to take an open-ended decision in this process and since the content under discussion is in fact a meaning understood by the participants; it would seem that their anticipation must have a key role in the design process.

2.4 The Design Process Is Future-Anticipative

The varied interpretation of content from multiple receivers implies that the design process should have the potential to be directed towards many different possible outcomes and their consequences. In other words, the design process has an anticipatory nature by which it will be placed in a pragmatic context and simultaneously be projected towards the future, using different directions and time scales (Banathy, 1996; Nadin, 2000; Jonas, 2001). It is this orientation towards the future that makes design different from mere problem-solving. Its interactive nature implies a new kind of anticipation for each cognitive system engaging in the design process, a cognitive system which learns from the past and appraises what is presently useful and desirable by simultaneously projecting content into the future.

According to the fundamental characteristics of the design process presented above, its naturalized explanation should incorporate in its description the engagement of individual cognitive systems (agents) in intentional and purposeful interactions with their environment and consequently with each other – actions undertaken in order to be able to fulfil their ill-defined goals. As argued in (Arnellos, Spyrou, Darzentas, 2007b) cognitive systems like these should have an autonomy that will guide them through this kind of interaction, based on their open-ended anticipative functionality. As expected, a complete analysis and description of the design process in a naturalised framework is not an easy task. We therefore begin this endeavour with a naturalised account of agency presented in detail in (Arnellos, Spyrou, Darzentas, in press) and we will try to show how the main characteristics of the design process are constructively supported within the resulting framework. Autonomy and interactivity will turn out to be core features in this naturalised framework.

3 A Naturalized Description of Agency

3.1 Autonomy drives agency via the intentional creation of functional meaning

There are many frameworks explaining agency in contemporary scientific literature and thus many diverse definitions of a cognitive agent. On the other hand, and as we have repeatedly suggested in (Arnellos, Spyrou, Darzentas, 2007b, 2008, in press) a strong notion of agency calls for: *interactivity* – the ability of an agent/cognitive system to perceive and act upon its environment by taking the initiative; *intentionality* – the ability of an agent to effect a goal-oriented interaction by attributing purposes, beliefs and desires to its actions; and *autonomy*, which can be characterized as the ability of an agent to function/operate intentionally and interactively based on its own resources.

This definition mentions three fundamental capacities that an agent should exhibit in a somewhat integrated way regarding their existence and their evolutionary development. According to this definition, agency requires interactivity – which in turn implies action on the environment. This action is not accidental but intentional; it is purposeful action directed towards a goal and it is driven by content such as beliefs and desires. In addition, an agent like this exhibits the property of autonomy as it interacts with the environment in an intentional manner based on its *own* resources, including its own internal content. These three properties seem quite interdependent, what becomes clear when one attempts to consider if it is possible for one of them to increase qualitatively while the others remain at the same level.

This interdependency is emphasized by Collier (1999) when he suggests that there is no *function* without *autonomy*, no *intentionality* without *function* and no *meaning* without *intentionality*. The interdependence is completed by considering *meaning* as a prerequisite for the maintenance of system's *autonomy* during its purposeful *interaction* with the environment.

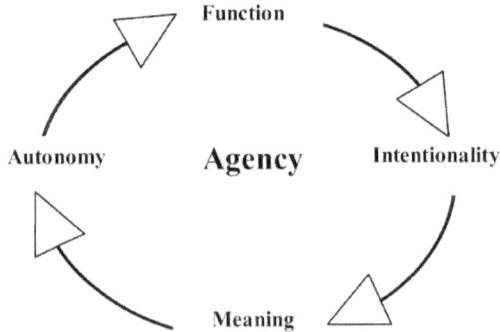

Figure 1. Interdependence of autonomy, functionality, intentionality and meaning in an autonomous agent.

These properties and their interdependence are characteristic of the strong notion of agency (i.e. they are features of living systems) – that which is emergent in the functional organisation of a living/cognitive system. The term 'functional' is used here to denote the processes of the network of components that contribute to the autonomy of the cognitive system and particularly, to the maintenance of the system as a whole (see e.g. Ruiz-Mirazo and Moreno, 2004). In this sense, meaning should be linked with the functional structures of the system. So meaning should guide the constructive and interactive processes of the functional components of the system in such a way that these processes maintain and enhance its autonomy. As such, the enhancement of autonomy means setting certain goals by the system itself. So the intentionality of the system is guiding its behaviour through meaning.

It should be noted that in such a theoretical set-up, meaning and its functional substratum are the defining properties of an autonomous agent that can act intentionally. In other words, an autonomous system may act intentionally if its actions are mediated by meaning. The foundations of functional emergence of this sort have been established in the systems-theoretic framework of second-order cybernetics.

3.2 Closure and Self-Reference for Self-Organisation

In second-order cybernetic epistemology, a cognitive system is able to carry out the fundamental actions of distinction and observation. It observes its boundaries and it is thus itself differentiated from its environment. As the cognitive system is able to observe the distinctions it makes, it is able to refer the result of its actions back to itself. This makes it a *self-referential* system, with the ability to create new distinctions (actions) based on previous ones, to judge distinctions, and to increase its complexity by producing new meanings in order to interact. The self-referential loop can only exist in relation to an environment, but it nevertheless goes beyond classical system-environment models, which hold that the external control of a cognitive system's adaptation to its environment is replaced by a model of *systemic* and *operational/organisational closure* (von Foerster, 1960, 1981).

Due to this closure, the self-reference of an observation produces meaning inside the cognitive system, which is used as a model for further observations in order to compensate for external complexity. Indeed, this closure is functional in so far as the effects produced by the cognitive system produce the maintenance of its systemic equilibrium through the emergence of more complex organizations. With system closure, environmental complexity is based solely on system observations, so system reality is observation-based. As von Foerster (1976) argued, the results of an observation do not refer directly to the objects of the real world; they are instead the results of recurrent cognitive functions in the structural coupling between the cognitive system and the environment. So each emergent function based on observations is a construction; it is an increase of the organisation and cognitive complexity of the agent. This process of emergent increment of order through the internal construction of functional organisations and simultaneous classification of the environment is a process of *self-organization* (von Foerster, 1960, 1981).

The nature of this systemic closure means that all the interactive alternatives of the cognitive system are internally generated and their selection is an entirely internal process. So, autonomous cognitive systems like this must construct their reality by using internally available structures. We should note that the respective self-organised structures (eigenvalues) are specific to the particular functionality of the cognitive system. Specifically, the functionality of the cognitive system is entirely dependent on its structural components and their interrelationships – interrelationships that establish the respective dynamics. So the functionality of the cognitive system is immediately related to the maintenance of its systemic cohesion (Collier, 1999), and consequently its self-organising dynamics. This inclination of a self-organising cognitive system to maintain its own self-organisation constitutes the core of its intentional and purposeful (goal-oriented) interaction with the environment. This pattern of self-organising dynamics requires a certain type of cohesion.

3.3 Cohesion via Process Closure for Self-Organisation

Cohesion is an inclusive capacity of an autonomous system and it indicates the existence of causal interactions among the components of the system in which certain capacities emerge - the respective components are constituents for the system itself. As such, cohesion can only be explained with respect to the causal roles that the constituent components and the relations among them, that is, their functional processes, acquire in the dynamic organization of the system.

Cohesive systems exhibit different kinds of correlations between different processes with respect to the degree (or the type) of cohesion that they exhibit. Systems with very strong and highly local bonds exhibit powerful cohesion which does not necessarily provide them with genuine autonomy and agency. The essential type of cohesion emerges in systems that are thermodynamically open and function in conditions that are far from equilibrium (Collier and Hooker, 1999). As Collier (2007) has stressed, since there is an internal need in these systems for the coordination of the processes to be able to achieve viability (self-maintenance), one should expect to find holistic organization in which organizationally/operationally open aspects of lower level are closed at higher organizational levels. This is a highly constructive type of autonomy (see Arnellos, Spyrou, Darzentas, 2008) and it requires what Collier (1999) suggests we call *process closure* (in the convention of 'organizational/operational closure'), to stress the fact that in such autonomous systems there are some internal constraints controlling the internal flow of matter and energy, and by doing so, the whole system acquires the capacity to carry out the respective processes, since these processes will contribute to its self-maintenance.

The preceding analysis of agency is a useful basis for understanding and explaining the design process. However, the description given is not adequately naturalized. Agency comes in degrees and at various levels in nature (Arnellos, Spyrou, Darzentas, in press). Genuine autonomous systems, such as living systems, are distinguished by a high degree of disentanglement from the environment, not in terms of their interactive processes, but on the contrary, in terms of their ability to adapt in various environmental disturbances. The systems described so far seem to exhibit a functional organization that is too tightly connected with their environments, but with minimal interactive characteristics, and as such, they cannot evolve beyond a certain threshold. Such systems are at the threshold of achieving autonomy, but at most this is a reactive kind of agency, insufficient to be able to engage in genuine design processes, where interaction is a vital asset.

Agency and the design process cannot be solely a matter of internal constructive processes and process closure. The need for open-endedness calls for interaction of the autonomous agent with the environment, while, the functional aspects of such an embodiment and its anticipatory content calls for advanced and efficient mechanisms of controlling and purposefully managing these interactions.

3.4 Interaction Closure and the Emergence of Normative Functionality

In section 4.2 it was mentioned that any system (defined and considered under the more general framework of second-order cybernetics) makes a distinction between the components that constitute itself and the rest of the elements that form its environment. The respective qualitative and quantitative imbalance indicates an asymmetry between a system and its environment. In the self-organizing systems described so far, this asymmetry is created and maintained by the functionality of the system through the establishment of internal constructive relations that organizationally differentiate the system from its environment and specify its autonomy and its identity.

This is an interpretive asymmetry (Hoffmeyer, 1998; Arnellos, Spyrou, Darzentas, in press) with some very interesting implications. Bickhard (1993, 2000) exemplifies the implications of this asymmetry by postulating a recursive self-maintenant system: a self-organizing system that has more than one means at its disposal to maintain its ability to be self-maintenant in various environmental conditions. This is a self-organizing system which functions far from thermodynamic equilibrium by continuously interacting with the environment, from where it finds the *appropriate conditions* for the success of its functional processes. Processes which are far from equilibrium cannot be kept in isolation, as they will lose their dynamic-functional stability.

So, the interactive opening of the system to the environment is considered the most important point in its evolution towards genuine autonomy and agency, as it first of all enhances the stability of the system and its ability to maintain its maintenance. Specifically, the interactions in which an autonomous agent engages will be *functional* and *dysfunctional* (Moreno and Barandiaran, 2004). The former corresponds to those interactions which are integrated in the functional organization of the agent and in this way they contribute to its self-maintenance. The latter corresponds to interactions that cannot be properly integrated in the functional organization and hence do not contribute or/nor disturb the self-maintenance of the system.

So the primary goal of such a self-organizing system is to maintain its autonomy in the course of its interactions. Since it is a self-organizing system, its embodiment is of a kind that its functionality is immediately related to its autonomy, through the fact that its apparent inclination to maintain its autonomy - in terms of its self-maintenance (its *purpose*) - constitutes the intentionality of its actions and hence its interaction with the environment. As such, autonomous systems do not only exhibit process closure, but also *interaction closure* (Collier, 1999, 2000, 2007), a situation where the internal outcomes of the interactions of the autonomous system with its environment contributes to the maintenance of the functional (constructive/interactive) processes of the system that are responsible for these specific interactions. It is cohesion via process and interaction closure that truly distinguishes autonomous systems from other kinds of cohesive systems. An autonomous system is not only able to maintain itself, but it can also meaningfully alter its internal functionality in order to adapt to complex and changing conditions around the environment.

This capacity for meaningful critique regarding the functional (the 'good') and the dysfunctional (the 'bad') with respect to the maintenance of the system is a normative one. Self-maintenant systems that exhibit *normative functionality* are truly autonomous systems and they present genuine agency. In this way, the overall functional closure (process and interaction closure) of an agent is guided by its autonomy - in the sense that the former contributes to the maintenance of the latter - while its intentionality derives from this specific normative functionality, as the latter is being directed towards the primary purpose of maintaining self-maintenance. This cohesive combination of process and interaction closure is responsible for the emergence of functional norms within the autonomous system and for the autonomous system itself.

These functional norms, in a way, attribute values of truth or falsity, and they are emergent in the system's interactions with the environment. Particularly, they are internal constructions that attribute binary values of to processes and/or the interactions of an autonomous system. The binary nature does not imply explicitness, but on the contrary, it can be said that the higher the autonomy and agency of the cognitive system, the higher the degree of abstraction of the concepts to which some of its norms can be related. This means that even though norms are constructed by the autonomous system itself, there are too many cases where their interactive satisfaction is not immediately recognizable by the autonomous system.

It would appear, according to the strong notion of agency introduced in 4.1, we are still lacking *meaning* - on the basis of which the cognitive system decides which of the available functional processes to make use of in order to successfully interact with a specific environment, i.e. to fulfil its goal or to satisfy its functional norms. An autonomous system anticipates via the respective representational content (meaning). But where exactly is this content to be found? The naturalistic requirement for an explanation of the constructive and interactive aspects of normative functionality - i.e. of the efficient control and management of the constructive/interactive capabilities of an autonomous agent - calls for the introduction of interactive, emergent representations.

3.5 Anticipations and the Emergence of Representational Content

Bickhard argues that an autonomous system of the aforementioned kind should have a way of differentiating the environments with which it interacts, and should possess a switching mechanism to choose among the appropriate internal functional processes that it will use in the interaction in question. The differentiations are implicitly and interactively defined, as the internal outcomes of the interaction - which in turn depend on the functional organization of the participating subsystems and on that of the environment. These differentiations create an epistemic contact with the environment, but they do not carry any representational content at all. However, they are indications of the interactive potentiality of the functional processes of the autonomous system itself. As such, these differentiations functionally indicate that some type of interaction is available in the specific environment and hence implicitly anticipate that the environment exhibits *appropriate conditions* for the success of the indicated interaction.

In this model (Bickhard, 1993; 2000), differentiated indications like the aforementioned constitute *emergent representations*. The conditions of the environment that are functionally and implicitly responded to by the differentiation, as well as the internal conditions of the autonomous cognitive system (i.e. other functional processes or conditions), that are supposed to be supporting the selected type of interaction, constitute the *dynamic presuppositions* of the functional processes that will guide the interaction. These presuppositions constitute the *representational content* of the autonomous cognitive system regarding the differentiated environment. This content emerges in the interaction of the system with the environment. What remains to be shown is how this representational content is related to the anticipations of an autonomous system.

Anticipation relates the present action of an agent with its future state. An anticipatory system has the ability to organise its functional state, in such a way that its current behaviour will provide the ability to successfully interact with its environment in the future. Such a system needs to be able to take into consideration the possible results of its actions in advance, hence, anticipation is immediately related to the meaning of the representations of the autonomous cognitive system (Collier, 1999). In this way, anticipation is one of the most characteristic aspects of autonomous systems due to their need to shape their dynamic interaction with the environment so as to achieve future outcomes (goals of the system) that will enhance their autonomy. In the context of the autonomous systems discussed so far, these future outcomes should satisfy the demand for process and interaction closure of the system and in general, for system's normative functionality.

Normative functionality is evaluated on the basis of the functional outcomes of the autonomous system; therefore, anticipation is immediately related to functionality (Collier, 2007). Even the simplest function requires anticipation in order to be effective. As mentioned before, anticipation is goal-directed. As a matter of fact, anticipation almost always requires functionality, which is, by default, a goal-oriented process. From this perspective, anticipation guides the functionality of the system through its representational content. In the model of the emergence of representations in the special case of an autonomous agent presented above, *the representational content emerges in a system's anticipation of interactive capabilities* (Bickhard, 2001). In other words, the interactive capabilities of a system are the subject of anticipation by the self-same system. This anticipation may be erroneous, potential errors being detectable by the system. Anticipation is an integral part of the functional context of a goal-directed system (a system which exhibits what we call 'emergent normativity').

These anticipations guide the interpretive interactions of an autonomous agent. In case these interactions contribute to the agent's self-maintenance, its capability for interactive anticipation progressively increases and as such its intentional capacity increases too (Christensen and Hooker, 2002; Arnellos, Spyrou, Darzentas, in press).

4 The Design Process as Interaction between Autonomous Systems

Following on from the analysis made above, each autonomous cognitive system participating in the design process is considered a self-organising system with the ability to maintain its autonomy in terms of its self-maintenance in different and dynamic environments. Hence, an autonomous cognitive system acquires the identity of a UD system[3] the very moment that it intentionally decides to engage in a design process. Con-

---

[3] In a serial description (applicable only for demonstrative purposes) of the design process, each one of the participating autonomous systems could be defined as design-systems or user-systems at different time instances. However, the systemic and interactive approach adopted in this paper calls for a more participative and cooperative term, such as 'user-designer' (called as UD, hereinafter), used by Banathy to denote the 'designing-within-the-system' approach to design (Banathy, 1996, p. 226)

sequently, in the framework described so far, *the design process is viewed as an interaction between two or more autonomous UD systems, in order to maintain their capacity for self-maintenance, or in other words, in order to maintain the type of autonomy that permits them to internally create representational content.*

In the analysis sketched before, autonomy guides functionality; so *the functional aspect of the design process in which each UD system interactively participates becomes the purposeful and ongoing transformation and expansion of their already existing representations.* For each UD system, a different representational content is internally emerging from their mutual attempts to incorporate the results of each other actions (the artefact in each instance of the design process), as a perturbation and not as a static informational structure nor as a content in itself, into their functional organisation. In addition, *a group of autonomous UD systems such as these, engaging in the design process constitutes a design **system**, which (as expected from the interactive nature of the design process) it is defined on the communicative/co-operative level.*

A logical sequence of the interaction cannot be implied, but for the benefit of this analysis let's just assume that a UD system attempts to communicate its representations, regarding a possible solution towards an ill-defined goal, to the other UD systems participating in the design process, via the creation of an artefact. Considering the participative and co-operative aspects of the design process, the aim of this communication is to induce, in the other UD systems, the emergence of the necessary representational content that will guide their functional organisation towards the ill-defined goal.

From the perspective of autonomy, the aim of this communication, *from the point of view of the UD system that decides to communicate an artefact*, is to indirectly enhance the degree of variety found in the environment, so that the interaction of the UD system with this environment will facilitate the emergence of richer representational content that will further enhance its autonomy. Since, as discussed in 4.5, the representational content of each autonomous cognitive system partly depends on the dynamic presuppositions provided by the environment with which it chooses to interact, and partly on the functional dynamics of the system itself, the only way for an autonomous cognitive system to enhance its content is to provide for the enhancement of the representational content of all the other participants in the design process. Furthermore, this mutual enhancement should take place in a way that furthers the achievement of the specific but ill-defined goal standing before the system, since, according to the framework we have adopted; its attainment will implicitly enhance the autonomy of the cognitive system.

4.1 The Role of Ill-Definedness

Initially, in the early stages of an autonomous cognitive system this mutual dependence upon an ill-defined goal can be easily overcome. The achievement of goals becomes harder as those ill-defined goals become more complicated. This happens when different cognitive systems construct different meanings of the design problem and provide different outcomes as possible solutions. This means that the ill-defined goal of the design process will never have a genuine and mutual recognition between its participants. Indeed, the degree of mutuality will decrease as far as the ill-defined goal becomes more complicated. On this basis, it can be concluded that *the design process is purposeful communication between two or more autonomous UD systems, in order to shape their dynamical interaction with the environment, so as to achieve a kind of functionality that contributes to the enhancement of their autonomy, by attempting to direct their functional organisations (i.e. themselves) towards an allegedly common, ill-defined goal.*

At this point, it has been argued that two or more self-organising systems engage in an intentional and purposeful interaction with each other, in order to maintain and enhance their autonomy. In other words, self-organising systems engage in a design process out of necessity. From an observer's point of view, the design process could be considered as the attempt of two or more cognitive agents to provide each other a specific solution regarding a specific problem. In the interactive framework of second-order cybernetics, *the design process should be seen as an attempt of two or more autonomous systems to communicate their representational content regarding a possible solution to an ill defined goal – which is internally and differently formulated by each autonomous system –in order to maintain and enhance their autonomy.*

The ways this enhancement takes place in the face of complicated ill-defined goals and the ways the design process might acquire a greater directionality towards these goals are discussed in the following section.

4.2 The Design Process Is Directed By Dynamic Anticipation of the Participating Autonomous Systems

As mentioned above, the design process is open-ended and emerges out of the ill-defined goals and purposes of its participants (autonomous systems), while it also results in ill-defined outcomes with ill-defined consequences. The anticipatory content of each autonomous system engaging in the design process should be open to revision and evolution. Considering the dynamic and future-oriented type of anticipation described in 4.5, it can be said that *each UD system participating in a design process should have the capability for anticipative interaction with the environment, in order to achieve the closure conditions that will contribute to its autonomy.*

As already said, the only way for an autonomous system to enhance its autonomy is by constructing even more adaptive representations towards its ill-defined goal. But this can only be achieved through the enhancement of its environment, that is, the emergence of new and more complex representations in the other UD systems which belong in the same overall design system. If this is to move in the direction of the otherwise subjectively formulated ill-defined goal, then the ability of each one UD system to anticipate the variety of the functional structures of all the other UD systems is crucial for the enhancement of autonomy. Actually, the higher the degree of anticipation in each UD system, the higher its capacity to evaluate its interaction and the greater its ability to incorporate multiple possibilities in its performance, and also, the higher its capacity to consider the ill-defined consequences of the outcome of the design process, that is, the multiple ways in which each one of the other UD systems may choose to interact with the artefact.

In general, it can be said that the more the representational content of an autonomous system is evolved, the more dynamic its anticipative structures become (Collier, 1999; Bickhard, 2001). This has a positive effect in the anticipatory capacity of the autonomous system and in its capacity to evaluate its future interactions. The increase of the system's capacity for dynamic anticipation expands that what Christensen and Hooker (2000) call the *anticipatory time window*, which provides a certain degree of directionality (Christensen and Hooker, 2002) in the goal-directed interaction of the autonomous system. Overall, these capacities result in the emergence of new cognitive abilities for the autonomous system, thus, implicitly increasing its interactive autonomy.

4.3 The Design Process as Learning

Nevertheless, no matter how large the window of anticipatory interaction may be, not all possibilities and selections regarding the outcomes and the ill-defined consequences of the design process can be inherent in the organisation of each UD system. A possible solution to this predicament is for the UD system to evolve learning capabilities. This would provide a way to expand its dynamical anticipation capacity and its ability to evaluate a possible interaction. The UD system becomes less dependent and more sensitive regarding its contextual interactive capabilities. It increases its ability to better recognize its environment, evaluate conditions and better formulate its goal regarding the problem. This provides an infrastructure better suited for the UD system to be able to define the design problem and anticipate the possibility of success in the emergent interactions between the other UD systems and the communicated artefact. Structural coupling is strengthened and the new and more adaptive representational content acquires a more prosperous field of emergence. Consequently, autonomy is increased.

However, in the proposed framework closure is achieved at the level of differentiations and of the respective emergent representational content, so autonomy cannot be statically identified. Instead, as Collier (2000, 2002) suggests, it has a gradual nature. So *autonomy should be considered an anticipative and future-directed property and it is a vital asset directly related to the variety with which the UD systems participating in the design process will internally create adaptive emergent representations towards their ill-defined goals*. The artefacts are not objects any more, but interfaces functioning as triggers that drive the formation of new representational content. Therefore, each UD system should exploit each artefact, as both a means of maintenance and a source of enhancement of its own autonomy. A consequence of this point of view is a paradigm shift: from focusing on designing static things to focusing on designing the emergence of thoughts and of novel representational content. Interaction with an artefact results in a differentiated indication of the interactive capabilities of each UD system engaging in the design process. From this perspective, *autonomy depends on the degree to which the communicated representational content of each UD system, through the artefact, gives the other UD systems the proper indications of the potentialities of their interactive capabilities*. Ultimately, the increase of autonomy is the result of a creative design process (Arnellos, Spyrou and Darzentas, 2007a).

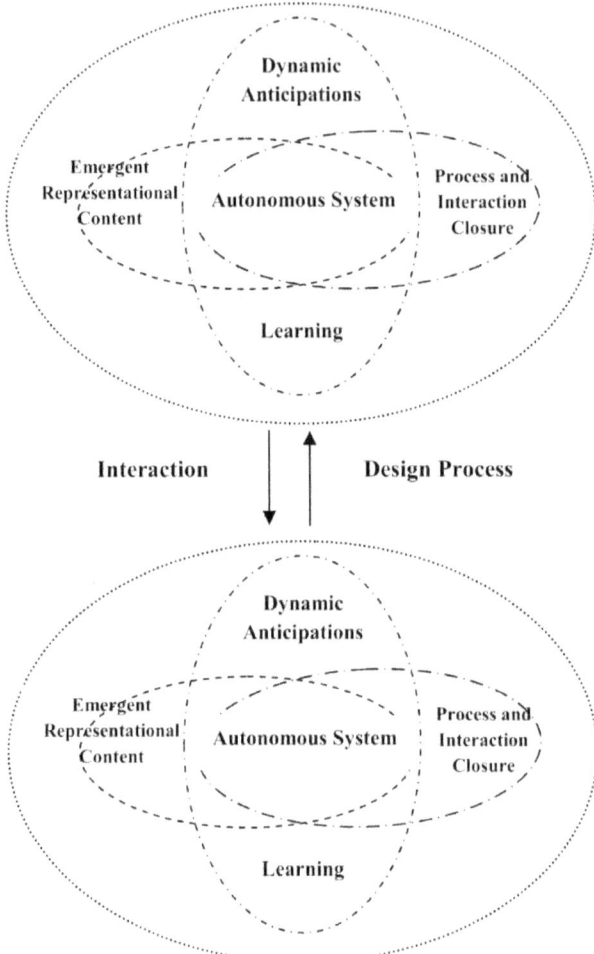

Figure 2. The design process as the interaction between two autonomous systems that guide their learning through the use of dynamic anticipations with emergent representational content.

The design process together with its key aspects, supported by its participating autonomous systems, is abstractly depicted in Fig. 2. What should be noted at this point is that from this perspective, the content of the design process is not the artefact itself. It is not static, since it is the attempt to communicate the UD system's representational content to the other UD systems actively participating in the design process. Moreover, due to the capacity for directed interaction, all UD systems engage in a mutual dependence with each other, while they are trying to increase their anticipatory capacity, no matter the degree of mutual recognition of their ill-defined goals. In their attempt to create richer representational structures towards their ill-defined goals, they are continuously interacting with the artefacts and hence, they learn to anticipate, or as it is suggested by Bickhard (2001) they anticipate the necessity to acquire new anticipations. Furthermore, the progressively increasing capability of the UD system's anticipation also creates an intentional capacity. This is not the same as the traditional notion of intentionality considered as the sum of all system's representations. Intentionality derives from the UD system's functional capability of anticipative and purposeful interaction, and aims to enhance each UD system's autonomy.

5 Conclusions

Naturalization is quite controversial: one has to proceed with a continuous formulation of questions about the phenomenon in question, taking into consideration both the quantitative and the qualitative progress of science with respect to relevant notions and beliefs. Design should have a cognitive foundation. Agency appears to be one of the most complicated capacities that nature presents and the quest for its naturalized explanation is not easy (Arnellos, Spyrou, Darzentas, in press).

An attempt has been made to provide a naturalized analysis of the design process by considering the latter as the purposeful interaction between two or more autonomous agents. The interaction of each cognitive system is guided by its self-organising functionality, which arises from its autonomy and it is directed towards the maintenance and/or the enhancement of this autonomy. The respective analysis departs from the systemic framework of second-order cybernetics, where an agent is viewed as a self-organising system exhibiting self-reference and organisation closure. The respective functional circularity is the result of interaction closure, which combined with process closure provides the means for the emergence of functional norms in each autonomous system.

This normative nature is grounded in values produced within the system and used in order to guide its interactions. As an agent evolves, some of its norms cannot be immediately identified and hence satisfied in its functional organization – so some mediation of their uncertain interactive potentialities is required. This mediation takes place through the formation of relevant anticipations with the respective representational content. These dynamic anticipations guide the autonomous system in the design process and provide the system with the ability to bring itself closer to its ill-defined goals. In this way, autonomy drives the interactive design process and at the same time profits from it.

References

Arnellos, Argyris, Spyrou, Thomas, Darzentas, John (2007a). "Exploring creativity in the design process: A systems-semiotic perspective". *Cybernetics and Human Knowing* 14 (1), pp. 37–64.
Arnellos, Argyris, Spyrou, Thomas, Darzentas, John (2007b). "Cybernetic embodiment and the role of autonomy in the design process". *Kybernetes* 36 (9/10), pp. 1207–1224.
Arnellos, Argyris, Spyrou, Thomas, Darzentas, John (in press) "Towards the Naturalization of Agency based on an Interactivist Account of Autonomy". *New Ideas in Psychology* (*doi:10.1016/j.newideapsych.2009.09.005*).
Arnellos, Argyris Spyrou, Thomas, Darzentas, John (2008). "Emergence and Downward Causation in Contemporary Artificial Agents: Implications for their Autonomy and Some Design Guidelines". *Cybernetics and Human Knowing* 15 (3–4), pp. 15–41.
Banathy, Bela H. (1996). *Designing Social Systems in a Changing World*, Plenum, New York.
Bickhard, Mark H. (1993). "Representational Content in Humans and Machines". *Journal of Experimental and Theoretical Artificial Intelligence* 5, pp. 285–333.
Bickhard, Mark H. (2000). "Autonomy, Function, and Representation". *Communication and Cognition – Artificial Intelligence* 17 (3–4), pp. 111–131.
Bickhard, Mark H. (2001). "Function, Anticipation, Representation". In *Computing Anticipatory Systems, CASYS 2000 - Fourth International Conference* ed. by D. M. Dubois, NY American Institute of Physics, Melville, pp. 459–469.
Bonnardel, Nathalie (2000). "Towards understanding and supporting creativity in design: analogies in a constrained cognitive environment". *Knowledge-Based Systems* 13, pp. 505–513.
Christensen, Wayne D. and Hooker, C. A. (2002). "Self-directed agents". *Canadian Journal of Philosophy*, Special Supplementary 27, pp. 19–52.
Collier, John (1999). "Autonomy in anticipatory systems: significance for functionality, intentionality and meaning". In *Computing Anticipatory Systems, CASYS'98 - Second International Conference, American Institute of Physics* ed. by D. M. Dubois, New York: Woodbury, pp. 75–81.
Collier, John (2000). "Autonomy and Process Closure as the Basis for Functionality". *Annals of the New York Academy of Science* 901, pp. 280–291.

Collier, John (2002). "What is Autonomy?". *International Journal of Computing Anticipatory Systems* 12, pp. 212–221.
Collier, John (2008). "Simulating autonomous anticipation: The importance of Dubois' conjecture". *BioSystems* 91, 2, pp. 346–354.
Collier, John and Hooker C.A. (1999). "Complexly Organised Dynamical Systems". *Open Systems and Information Dynamics* 6, pp. 241–302.
Feldman, Richard (2006). "Naturalized Epistemology". In *The Stanford Encyclopaedia of Philosophy (Fall 2006 Edition)*, ed. by Edward N. Zalta, URL = http://plato.stanford.edu/archives/fall2006/entries/epistemology-naturalized/.
Friedman, Ken (2003). "Theory construction in design research: criteria: approaches, and methods". *Design Studies* 24 (6), pp. 507–522.
Gero, John S. & Kannengiesser, Udo (2004). "The situated function–behaviour–structure framework". *Design Studies*, 25 (4), pp. 373–391.
Glanville, Ranulph (2001). "A (Cybernetic) Musing: Constructing my Cybernetic World". *Cybernetics and Human Knowing* 8 (1–2), pp. 141–150.
Glanville, Ranulph (2006b). "Design and mentation: Piaget's constant objects". *The Radical Designist*, zero issue, available at: www.iade.pt/designist/jornal/jornal.html (accessed 14 April 2007).
Glanville, Ranulph (2007). "Try again. Fail again. Fail better: the cybernetics in design and the design in cybernetics". *Kybernetes* 36 (9/10), pp. 1173–1206.
Hoffmeyer, Jesper (1998). "Surfaces inside surfaces. On the origin of agency and life". *Cybernetics and Human Knowing* 5 (1), pp. 33–42.
Jonas, Wolfgang (2001). "A Scenario for Design". *Design Issues* 17 (2), pp. 64–80.
Jonas, Wolfgang (2007). "Research through DESIGN through research. A cybernetic model of designing design foundations". *Kybernetes* 36 (9/10), pp. 1362–1380.
Jones, John C. (1970). *Design methods: seeds of human futures*. London, New York: Wiley-Interscience.
Kazmierczak, Elżbieta T. (2003). "Design as Meaning Making: From Making Things to the Design of Thinking". *Design Issues* 19 (2), pp. 45–59.
Laszlo, Alexander (2001). "The epistemological foundations of evolutionary systems design". *Systems Research and Behavioral Science* 18, pp. 307–321.
Macmillan, Sebastian, Steele, John, Austin, Simon, Kirby, Paul & Spence, Robin (2001). "Development and verification of a generic framework for conceptual design". *Design Studies* 22 (2), pp. 169–191.
Moreno, Alvaro and Barandiaran, Xabier (2004). "A naturalized account of the inside-outside dichotomy". *Philosophica* 73, pp. 11–26.
Nadin, Mihai (2000). "Anticipation: A Spooky Computation". *International Journal of Computing Anticipatory Systems* 6, pp. 3–47.
Ruiz-Mirazo, Kepa & Moreno, Alvaro (2004). "Basic Autonomy as a fundamental step in the synthesis of life". *Artificial Life* 10 (3), pp. 235–259.
Schön, Donald A. & Wiggins, Glenn (1992). "Kinds of seeing and their functions in designing". *Design Studies* 13 (2), pp. 135–156.

Simon, Herbert A. (1995). "Problem forming, problem finding and problem solving in design". In *Design & Systems*, ed. by Arne Collen & Wojciech Gasparski. New Brunswick: Transaction Publishers, pp. 245–257.

Simon, Herbert A. (1999). *The sciences of the artificial*, The MIT Press, Cambridge, MA.

von Foerster, Heinz (1960). "On self-organizing systems and their environments". Reprinted in von Foerster, Heinz (2003), pp. 1–19.

von Foerster, Heinz (1976). "Objects: tokens for (eigen-) behaviors", *ASC Cybernetics Forum* 8, pp. 91–6. Reprinted in: von Foerster, Heinz (2003), pp. 261–71.

von Foerster, Heinz (1981). *Observing Systems*. CA: USA, Intersystems Publications.

von Foerster, Heinz (2003). *Understanding Understanding. Essays on Cybernetics and Cognition*. New York: Springer-Verlag.

18

Causality Naturalised?

PIOTR LEŚNIAK

In his well known argument, Putnam (1983) discourages us from any attempt to define causal relations in terms of physics. His argument turns on the irrevocably epistemic character of causal concepts. If we accept Putnam's conclusion, we have to redefine scientific naturalism or alternatively exclude the concept of causation from scientific discourse. Although the latter option has had eminent defenders in the empiricist tradition such as Russell, when we note that causal explanation constitutes an essential feature of the whole scientific stance, the first option is initially much more attractive for a naturalist. A good example of the first option, redefining scientific naturalism, is Price's 'subject naturalism' (2004).

I take it for granted that to be able to embrace the idea of causality, naturalism requires modifications similar to those suggested by Price. But I am not going to refer to his 'perspectival' account of causation (Price 2007), instead I am going to concentrate on the sensory aspect of causal experience and its objectivity. We should not extrapolate the 'view-from-nowhere' model of objectivity taken from physics to the whole area of human experience. In the epistemology of causation, as well as in cognitive psychology, especially in work on human and nonhuman forms of causal cognition, it is useful to distinguish between two different concepts of the objectivity of experience. The dual view of the objectivity of experience, presented below, has Kantian roots. Kant found two pillars of the objectivity of experience in its conceptual structure and in the forms of sensory intuition. While the all-pervading character of the conceptual

Beyond Description: Naturalism and Normativity.
Marcin Miłkowski and Konrad Talmont-Kaminski (eds.).
Copyright © 2010 The Author.

structure, the first 'pillar', is today accepted as a kind of contemporary philosophical truism, the non-conceptual character and significance of the forms of sensory intuition, is not so often recognized.

1 Two Concepts of the Objectivity of Experience

What is the object of our common experience when we see a stone? Is it a certain mixture of chemical compounds, or is it a heavy, browny-grey looking thing which we identify as stone? The possibility of an unlimited number of answers to that question reflects a feature of our experience which may be called 'Quinian' – there are a number of possible ontologies, according to which we may interpret our sensory input in the situation in question.

But let's assume that 'we' in the above question refers to all primates. Then, it is not a mixture of chemical compounds that is the object of our common experiences (we should doubt that even the brightest chimps could see anything *as* a certain chemical compound). But still, there is quite a large scope of 'agreement' between us and apes in the matter of stones. They are visible, tactile, movable and even throwable for us – probably in a very similar way. It even seems reasonable to claim that a stone, as an object of sensory experience, must look similar to all primates. By saying this, we do not mean that we all share a given ontological or conceptual framework. We would have to postulate a single ontological framework if there were only one 'Quinian' concept of the objectivity of experience.

When approaching the problem of causal cognition I am going to use the distinction between the *sensory* (or 'ecological') and the *conceptual* (or intersubjective) model of the objectivity of experience. In the conceptual model of experience, the ontological status of its objects is determined on the ground of the conceptual system to which experiential judgment belongs and it is relatively independent of the phenomenal content of perception. The ontology of *ecological* experience, conversely, depends on the phenomenal content of perception and is not deducible from assumptions of the conceptual system in which it could be verbalized.

2 Two levels of causal cognition

Contemporary approaches to causality may be roughly divided into Humean and non-Humean (Psillos 2003). Humeans exclude any direct cognitive access to causation and regard it as reducible to non-causal facts (like spatiotemporal contiguity, succession and regular conjunction). According to them there is no necessary connection between the cause and the effect that goes beyond their regular association. Contrary to the *prima facie* impression we might get, this account actually appears to be at odds with scientific naturalism. It can hardly draw a line between non-causal (accidental) and causal relations and between mere regularities and the laws of nature without appealing to some 'epistemic' or 'pragmatic' mark. In the conception of R. Braithwaite, A. Ayer, N. Goodman and others: it is **our attitude** towards certain sentences which imposes a law-like or necessary character on them. Other Humeans like J.S. Mill, F. Ramsey or D. Lewis recognize certain regularities as nomic by appealing to the idea of the best (the simplest and the strongest) deductive system. This idea, although expressed in a more objective manner, is also hardly expressible without reference to our **cognitive interests or values**. As mentioned above, this excludes only traditional scientific naturalism and is reconcilable with its modified forms. But the 'subjectivist' picture of causal explanations which emerges from these Humean accounts seems to be problematic, especially when we want to view scientific methods as paradigms of *objectivity*.

In the non-Humean account, causation is an autonomous, irreducible element of the world. There is an intrinsic feature of **nomic neccesitation** between elements of causal relation which distinguishes causation from mere succession. Armstrong and Dretske define this feature as an objective relation between properties (universals). An undeniable virtue of Armstrong's (1997) conception is that it does not ignore the question of scientific objectivity. It is a bold attempt to understand why empirical science is so successful in causally explaining the world of our experience. Doubts appear, however, when we look at the details of his theory. According to Armstrong, there are two levels of causal cognition. We have direct knowledge of singular causes (like feeling pressure on one's body), which may be the starting point for causal explanations we offer. First, we infer the existence of universals (first order) from the sameness of the instances of the patterns in which singular 'causings' appear. Then we posit the existence of a necessitating relation between these universals. This (second order) relation is a causal relation. I list some of the premises of Armstrong's account, from which two (3 and 4) I reject as false, and two (1 and 2) I accept and elaborate in the following part of this essay.

(1) It is possible to distinguish two levels in our causal cognition of the world: sensory (singular) and conceptual (universal).

(2) There is direct sensory causal cognition.

(3) There are singular causal statements expressing our sensory causal knowledge from which we may infer universal causal statements.

(4) The relation between universals and the relation between singular instantiations of these universals is the same causal relation.

Premise (3) is 'inductionist'. It is at odds with the contemporary holistic post-Quinian picture of empirical knowledge. The idea of a set of observational statements expressing our immediate sensory cognition, which may constitute 'a basis' for theoretical propositions is no longer acceptable. Simple, singular empirical statements contain some universal, theory-laden element – and this implies circularity for the Armstrong view.

The gap between the two levels of our causal cognition is deeper than Armstrong wants to admit. It may be expressed in terms of the distinction of section 1: his singular causal statements are objective in the ecological sense, while universal statements are objective in the conceptual sense. Armstrong ignores that difference in interpreting the former in terms of the ontology of the latter. That allows him to posit the existence of logical inferences between two levels but at the same time it diminishes the justifying power of singular statements.

(4) is obviously false. The relations between universals, according to Armstrong, constitute laws of nature, which by definition must embrace cases which are not actually instantiated. The identity conjectured by Armstrong would require the unacceptable redefinition of the concept of law. Armstrong wants to reconcile non-singularism with causal realism which is not an easy task. His failure on this point illustrates problems which any seriously ontological theory of causation must probably face. The advantage of his view is again its attempt to do justice to the objectivity of scientific experience.

3   Are causal relations directly observable?

The conclusion of Hume's analysis of experience is that, since causal relations are not directly perceived, causal judgments are inferred from the regular conjunction of perceptions. Some contemporary philosophers have attacked this conclusion presenting a variety of couterexamples which purportedly represent directly experienced causation. D. Armstrong and E. Fales appeal to the impression of pressure upon one's body as a paradigmatic example of directly perceived causation. E. Anscombe from her 'singularist' position, claims that we don't need any regularity or law to perceive certain events as causally related. She gives the example of knives cutting butter and stones breaking windows as typical examples of immediately observed causation. She also appeals to quantum mechanics, where relations between observables do not fall under universal deterministic laws although we think of them as parts of causal processes. P. F. Strawson writes about experiences of certain natural relations which "...supply wholly satisfactory explanations of their outcomes..." (Strawson 1992: 118) like "...seeing the man pick up the suitcase and lift it..." or seeing "...the boulder flatten the hut."

What do all these examples have in common? They all describe simple natural situations when we spontaneously ascribe causal powers to objects. They all present themselves as if causal relations appeared before our eyes: no prior assumptions nor conditioning is necessary to perceive observed events as causally related. Hume would say that there is an 'unavoidable instinct' which makes us believe in causal powers acting there, but it is only **spatiotemporal relations** that we actually observe. To answer Humean causal scepticism is not easy. I am going to concentrate here on the question of the perceptual accessibility of causal powers and to attack the Humean idea of causality at the point supposed to be its weakest – his atomistic theory of sensual cognition. My claim is that there do exist dynamic dispositions which are directly cognizable.

Obviously, we cannot see directly the power which produces the light when we turn on the switch. In general, it is difficult to distinguish the following situations: cases where we 'perceive' causality, but in reality only as the result of 'conditioning'; cases in which we really do perceive causal powers directly; and cases in which we understand causal relation thanks to the theories that we have mustered. Take the case of an 18 month child who learned how to switch on the light in his room. It could be an example of simple causal understanding based on mere association of stimuli, but he had some primitive ideas of the mechanism of electricity. Is there some primitive dynamics, primitive psychology, etc. that enables nonlinguistic subjects to posit the existence of causal powers or is their knowledge of causation always the result of earlier experiences? There is also the third option of causal powers being directly given. At this point it is worth confronting philosophical ideas with those of cognitive psychology.

4 Piaget on Causality

Piaget places the origin of our concept of causality in the first two years of our life, in the sensorimotor period. He conjectures that there are two roots of the concept: our feeling of efficacy (children are vaguely aware that it is their own volition that produces certain effects) and the regularity of events that are contiguous in time (e. g. mother's undressing and the availability of milk). He suggests that the infantile concept of causality is quite different from an adult's until the child reaches the age of 6–10. The peculiar feature of the child's conception is that anything can cause anything even if the cause and effect are not physically connected in space and time. This 'pancausalism' is connected with a magical view of objects which are believed to be endowed with hidden powers. The development of the concept of causality is connected with progress in the understanding of space and time. There is no idea of an all-pervading space and universal time in children under 5. In one of Piaget's experiments, children were asked about the parameters of motion of two objects moving with different speed and stopping at the same time. Children generally gave correct answers to questions of the type: Did the objects start at the same time? Did they move at the same speed? Have they moved the same distance? But when asked if the objects had stopped at the same time children generally replied incorrectly – that the faster object stopped later. Piaget concludes from this and similar experiments that **speed** is our **primary** intuitive category in this period. It is not the case that we infer kinetic categories from judging distances covered in certain time; it is the other way round: we derive temporal relations like simultaneity from the assessment of speed.

The ontology of experiences in the sensorimotor period is not 'Quinian' or language-bound – it is rather the sensory model of the objectivity of experience which should be applied here. Our perception viewed 'from outside' may consist in transforming singular neural input into a complex picture, but the primitive world of preconceptual sensory data **does not** consist of spatially and temporally ordered elementary units like sensations or color dots, from which we infer dynamic categories. The powerless colored surfaces or sensations should be treated as **abstracts** inferred from the dynamic world of our experience.

5 Michotte's Experiments

Michotte explored the visual experience of causality in adults. Scenes of 'launching' and 'entraining' were presented to people who were asked to describe precisely what they were observing. In the launching situation, object A moves towards stationary object B, makes contact with it and then B starts to move without delay. Entraining looks the same except that A after 'touching' moves along with B. Michotte tried to discover the exact parameters of motion which evoked causal descriptions in these cases. In some of the experiments the moving objects were not ordinary heavy objects but light or shadows projected on the screen. All these scenes were described by adults in causal terms ('moved', 'pushed', etc.) independently of any knowledge they had about the situations (that shadows or light cannot 'push' anything, for example). Michotte conjectured that it is something other than our beliefs about was happening that is responsible for the causal descriptions we offer. He called this sensory source of our causal beliefs the *causal impression*.

What are the features of that experience? First of all, the 'causal impression' is the source of the meaning of causal statements – not the other way round. It is not the causal concepts used to express the 'causal impression' verbally that impose causal meaning on the impression. Conversely, we understand primitive causal concepts because we associate them with the causal impression in question. So it is clear that we should interpret these experiences in terms of sensory and not conceptual objectivity. That is why the 'causal impression' is not just a 'subjective' feeling. It refers to the primitive kinetic sensory dispositions of objects, which are real although they are not objective in the conceptual sense – they are objective in exactly the same way as sounds and colors are.

6 What does it mean to be 'immediately' or 'directly' perceived?

(1) Directness as qualitative indistinguishability

M. Tooley (2003) presents the following argument against the possibility of causal relations being immediately given in experience. According to him, a property or relation is immediately given in experience only if "…for any two qualitatively indistinguishable experiences, the property must either be given in both or given in neither." A causal relation cannot be given in this sense because it is logically possible that appropriate, direct stimulation of the brain might produce two qualitatively indistinguishable experiences, one of which did not involve any causally related elements. That sense of immediateness is too strong. It is logically possible in the case of any pair of perceptually indistinguishable experiences that they are the effects of the same direct stimulation of the brain. That excludes the directness of cognition in general – and not only in the case of causal cognition.

(2) No mediator in the perception of objects

This is the sense of directness exploited in the classic debate between direct realism and representationism. According to direct realists it is the object itself and not its representation which is given to us in perception. Cognitive states like perceptions, sensations or ideas do not mediate in the process of sensory cognition. They are at the most *transparent mediators*[1] for us. This classical debate was revitalized on the occasion of cognitive psychology – by Gibson and his followers (reviving traditional questions of the ontological status of subject and object, of 'normal' and illusionary perceptions). The difficulties involved in the precise formulation of that sense of directness lies in the ambiguity of the concept of an object of perception, namely the equivocation between its intentional (conceptual) and sensory (ecological) sense.

(3) Sensual directness

Sensory modes of knowing which we share with non-human animals are phenomenally direct. Contrary to the cognitivist model of knowing, there is no mental representation mediating in the process of sensory cognition. There are other features of sensory direct knowledge. It is not *inferential* (it doesn't imply any kind of inference or reasoning). *It is temporally homogeneous* (there are no distinctive or separate stages in it). *It is structurally homogeneous* (does not engage different levels of our cognitive structure). *It is self-sufficient* (no prior belief is necessary for it).

7 Between associative learning and conceptual causal reasoning

In work on animal cognition (Hurley 2003: 6), the attempt has sometimes been made to escape the crude dichotomy between context-bound stimulus response learning and fully-fledged conceptual reasoning. Hurley tries to do this, claiming that in the middle between classical conditioning and language-bound rationality there lies the rationality of instrumental behaviour. Having practical reasons, according to her, does not entail conceptual abilities. Although intentional agency of nonhuman animals is not based on a system of verbalized beliefs, it involves a certain kind of 'hol-

---

[1] The idea of forms of sensory intuition as transparent mediators was developed by Thomas Aquinas, where their counterpart is called *species impressa*. The parallels between this account and Gibson are examined in my (Leśniak 2006).

ism and normativity'. The actions of an intentional agent are normatively constrained by relations between her intentions and perceptions (an intentional animal may err and try to achieve a certain end by different means). Hurley rejects the view (Dennett 1996) that unconceptualized reasons for an action cannot be the agent's own reasons. Perceptions and intentions make certain actions reasonable from the animal's own perspective.

Premack (1995) distinguishes between *arbitrary causal knowledge* (ACK) resulting from associative learning and *natural causal knowledge* (NCK). The first results from repetition and contiguity and is not domain specific. NCK is not dependent on repetition, it has a "deductive" and "*a priori*" character and is not domain specific. According to Premack, it is difficult if not impossible to attribute NCK to nonhuman animals. If he were correct in this, it would follow that all causal knowledge of nonhuman animals would consist in ACK. That would explain the differences but not the common ground between human and nonhuman forms of causal cognition. There are accounts according to which there is no gap at all between the species on this point (Wasserman 1990) because their structures are similarly Humean. That is at odds not only with Premack's conjecture but also with the empirical conclusions of such researchers as Tomasello (1998), Povinelli (2000), Vonk (2006) and others.

To explain the similarities as well as discrepancies between human and nonhuman causal cognition, it is useful to introduce a third type of causal knowledge: *immediate causal knowledge* (ICK) which is the result of neither inductive nor deductive reasoning and refers to situations where causal powers are directly perceived. ICK would consist of the perception of so-called *manifest powers* (Pettit 2003).

It is commonly held among researchers on primate cognition (Tomasello, Povinelli, Vonk, Bering) that only humans are capable of reasoning about abstract, unobservable theoretical entities. But if all causal powers were entities of this sort, they could not be, *ex definitione*, cognizable for apes. This conclusion, however, is not widely accepted. Tomasello (1998) defends it by appealing to examples of 'irrational' behavior of chimps where they seem blind to certain obvious simple forces of objects (for instance, they retrieve food through an empty space in a 'trap table, which they should avoid doing if they understood the effect of gravity.) But there are also experiments (Call 2004) where chimps directly observe the presence of food as the cause of the sound produced by shaking the cup.

This debate turns on the applied concept of causal force. It is his 'abstract" definition of causal force (as a mediating variable between cause and effect) that makes Tomasello reject the possibility of direct causal cognition in chimps. Two different meanings of the concept of 'causal force' should be distinguished. There are *abstract powers* which get their ontological status from their conceptual framework and those which are directly perceived. In the group of manifest powers are included sensual dispositions (taste, smell, sound, color, different modalities of sense of touch) and *affordances*. There are both passive affordances (being graspable, movable, stand-on-able, eatable etc.) and active ones (being-able-to-move, being-able-to-crush, being-able-to-burn). Passing over the controversies connected with the very concept of affordances they may be treated in general as accessible for apes. They may appear closely connected with the anatomic peculiarities of an organism and its ecological niche, but they constitute a kind of 'perceptual basis' for our fully-fledged conceptual causal understanding, 'mediating' between sensory dispositions and abstract powers. It should be clear now that their being immediately given situates them in the sphere of the perceptual and that their ontological status cannot be established in a Quinian way i.e. on the basis of the conceptual model of objectivity.

8 Conclusion

There is a sense in which causal powers are immediately perceived. The concept of immediateness presented here is hardly explicable in terms of so-called 'conceptual objectivity'. The alternative to this account of objectivity, given above, may seem archaic and, in fact, it is pre-Cartesian. But for the naturalist it opens the perspective of getting rid of the remnants of Cartesian dualism without falling into the traps of reductionism.

Attributing to perceived causal powers a similar status to colors and sounds may seem discouraging, especially for those who accept ontological physicalism. But naturalism may do without physicalism. In return he gets an ontological tool to deal with both Hume's and Putnam's causal skepticism. And though there is no straight road from direct causal perception to causal laws (as in Armstrong 1997), the perceptual objectivity of some causal powers gives us an argument for the nonarbitrariness of the very idea of causation.

References

Anscombe, Elizabeth (1975). "Causality and Extensionality". In *Causation and Conditionals*, ed. by Ernest Sosa. Oxford: Oxford University Press, pp. 63–81.

Armstrong, David (1997). *The World of States of Affairs*. Cambridge: Cambridge University Press.
Call, Josep (2004). "Inferences about the location of food in the great apes". *Journal of Comparative Psychology* 118, pp. 232–241.
Hurley, Susan (2003), "Animal Action in the Space of Reason". *Mind and Language* 18(3), pp. 231–257.
Leśniak, Piotr (2006). "Spostrzeganie barw w świetle epistemologii ewolucyjnej". *Ruch Filozoficzny* 1, pp. 81–91.
Premack, David (1995) "Cause/induced motion: Intention/spontaneous motion. Origins of the human brain". In *Origins of the human brain. Symposia of the Fyssen Foundation*, ed. by Jean-Pierre Changeux and Jean Chavaillon. New York: Clarendon Press/Oxford University Press, pp. 286–309.
Price, Huw (2004). "Naturalism without representationalism". In *Naturalism in Question*, ed. by David Macarthur and Mario de Caro. Harvard: Harvard University Press, pp. 71–88.
Price, Huw (2007). "Causal Perspectivalism". In *Causation, Physics and the Constitution of Reality: Russell's Republic Revisited,* ed. by Huw Price and Richard Corry. Oxford: Oxford University Press, pp. 250–292.
Pettit, Philip (2003). "Looks red", *Philosophical Issues* 13(1), pp. 221–252.
Putnam, Hilary (1983). "Realism and Reason". In *Philosophical Papers*, vol. 3, Cambridge: Cambridge University Press, pp. 213–220.
Povinelli, Daniel J. (2000). *Folk physics for apes: The chimpanzee's theory of how the world works*. Oxford: Oxford University Press [Reprinted with revisions, 2003].
Psillos, Stathis (2002). *Causation and Explanation*. Durham: Acumen Publishing.
Strawson, Peter F. (1992). *Analysis and Metaphysics: An Introduction to Philosophy*. Oxford: Oxford University Press.
Tomasello, Michael (1998). "Uniquely primate, uniquely human". *Developmental Science* 1, pp. 1–16.
Tooley, Michael (2003). "Causation and supervenience". In *The Oxford Handbook of Metaphysics*, ed. by Michael J. Loux and Dean W. Zimmerman, Oxford: Oxford University Press.
Vonk, Jennifer & Povinelli, Daniel J. (2006). "Similarity and difference in the conceptual systems of primates: The Unobservability Hypothesis". In *Comparative Cognition: Experimental Explorations of Animal Intelligence,* ed. by Edward A. Wasserman and Thomas A. Zentall. Oxford: Oxford University Press.
Wasserman, Edward A. (1990). "Attribution of Causality to Common and Distinctive Elements of Compound Stimuli". *Psychological Science* 1 (5), pp. 298–302.

19

Can Mental Illness Be Naturalised?

ANDRZEJ KAPUSTA

1 Introduction

The aim of research into and consideration of mental disorders is to understand the character of these disorders and to present the actual status of present-day psychopathology. Attempts to discover the biological foundations of mental diseases have accompanied psychiatry ever since its evolution into an independent medical discipline. The various attitudes to the biological analysis of the essence of these disorders have been strongly influenced by disputes on the very definition of mental illness. The issue of alleviating psychological problems involves both the question of the prospects for an objective, descriptive discussion of psychopathology and the question of the role of valuation and assessment in the diagnostic process. Christopher Boorse (Boorse 1975) provides an example of the approach that distinguishes between the normative and descriptive elements. He recognises the difference between *disease* and *illness*. *Disease* is a condition perceived by scientific medical theory and *illness* is the actual, experienced condition of being sick – the feeling of illness. Fulford (Fulford et al. 2006) points to the hidden assumption behind this dispute and distinction which is significant not only for the status of the mental disorder but also for assumptions made regarding the notion of disease as such.

In this paper, I would like to take a biologically and evolutionarily based stance in the discussion of the notion of mental disease. At the same time, by referring to contemporary systems of classification and diagnostic practice, I shall point to a number of limitations and obstacles for a radical naturalist programme within psychopathology. I would like to avoid becoming entangled in complex conceptual analyses – I merely wish to cast light on the notion of mental disease as it emerges from present-day psychiatric practice and point to a number of criteria indispensible for developing a good-quality definition of psychic disorders. In proposing a definition like this we are hindered by the 'abundance' of existing mental conditions and the tension that exists between folk and strictly scientific approaches to those cases. Are we more interested in the common perception of such disorders, involving our linguistic intuitions, or should we only base our classifications on purely scientific, clear and reliable criteria? Ultimately, it appears today that we cannot opt for a purely scientific classification of mental disorders, since we do not in fact possess good theoretical models of most psychiatric disorders and if we did, their application would entail a radical redefinition of basic concepts in modern psychiatry and would reveal the heterogeneous nature of officially recognized classifications. Naturalisation is not only about discarding commonsense concepts of mental illness but also about removing social constructivist approaches where the reality of mental illness is rejected. Nevertheless, besides its social costs, the naturalisation of some aspects of disorders seems workable and necessary if we expect to see any realistic progress in therapy requiring, as this would, the search for causes of illness and the ability to forecast and control psychiatric phenomena.

2 Naturalisation in Cognitive Sciences

The naturalisation of psychiatric phenomena seems feasible only if we are in a position to naturalise the mind, intentionality and our common-sense beliefs. The philosophy of mind and cognitive science has seen attempts of this kind in relation to the issue of mental content. A naturalist approach to content seeks to reduce intentionality (so-called 'aboutness') to something else. Fodor (Fodor 1987) assumed that it is possible to prove that "R represents x" without referring to intention notions – instead invoking internal states typical of material processes within the brain. Were it not for this possibility, Fodor claims, intentionality would not be something real but something distant and magic - operating only in a common but pre-scientific perspective. This approach is present in modern cognitive psychology where the human cognitive capacity is defined through the concept of a flow of information between different subpersonal systems. The semantic properties of mental states can be expressed by the data processing of lower-order levels. This approach has been criticized because it is not capable of expressing the normative aspect of human convictions - the fact that they can be right or wrong – nor is it capable of establishing relationships to the outer world.

As T. Thornton points out:

> The problem is that the subject described by a cognitivist account appears to be out of touch with or alienated from the world. Even the mental state that corresponds to opening ones eyes to and experiencing the world is construed as a free-standing state in inner space connected to the outer world only by causal relations. But how can such a state be *about* anything? How can such inner states be anything but blind? The general explanatory picture at work here seems not to contain the right sort of materials to explain how thought and experience is able to bear on the world at all. (Thornton 2002: 245).

The problem of the normativity of our beliefs, as well as the problem of when beliefs can be attributed at all have both been addressed by the evolutionary biological account. According to this view, represented, inter alia, by R.G. Millikan (Millikan 1984), mental content is rooted in natural, biological functions.

In psychiatry, there is already a developed discussion of biological approaches and criticisms have been levelled against the bio*medical* approach which seeks explanations in the physiological and genetic factors responsible for mental disorder. The biological and evolutionary approach, on the other hand, aims to discover the source of the disorders by appealing to the notions of function and dysfunction. Internal states code the content whose adequacy is supposed to be explained by its biological usefulness.

Besides the evolutionary account of dysfunction we may also distinguish between:

1. the clinical understanding of dysfunction in the biomedical model (which in turn invokes the physiological or genetic level) and classification systems (e.g. DSM-IV)

2. the common-sense or 'folk' understanding of the notion of dysfunction (described in social, rational or emotional terms).

3 Mental Diseases in Contemporary Classifications

Modern psychiatric classifications do not offer definitions of diseases *explicite*. They are rather referred to by pointing to standardized or paradigmatic definitions (stereotypical). The notions of 'clinically recognizable', 'symptom' or 'dysfunction' are not exhaustively defined. The World Health organization gives the following definition of 'disorder':

> The term 'disorder' is used throughout the classification, so as to avoid even the greater problems inherent in the use of terms such as 'disease' and 'illness'. 'Disorder' is not an exact term, but it is used here to imply the existence of a clinically recognizable set of symptoms or behaviour associated in most cases with distress and with interference with personal functions. Social deviance or conflict alone, without personal dysfunction, should not be included in mental disorder as defined here (World Health Organization (1992, 5).

DSM-IV offers a similar definition of 'norm' and 'pathology' to that of ICD-10:

> In *DSM*4, each mental disorder is conceptualized as a clinically significant behavioural or psychological syndrome or pattern that occurs in an individual and that is associated with present distress (e.g. a painful symptom) or disability (i.e. impairment in one or more important areas of functioning) or with a significantly increased risk of suffering death, pain, disability or a significant loss of freedom. In addition, this syndrome or pattern must not be merely an understandable and culturally sanctioned response to a particular event, for example, the death of a loved one. Whatever its original cause, it must currently be considered a manifestation of a behavioural, psychological or biological dysfunction in the individual (DSM-IV 1994: XXI-XXII).

As in the case of ICD-10, there are a number of terms whose meaning has not been elucidated. Some additional clues as to how to define individual symptoms are to be found elsewhere in DSM-IV. However, there is the recurring reference to the *implicite* established norm/standard. The classification criteria often mask a qualitative element; they refer to clinically significant changes or a change in relation to standard functions. The external and behavioural criteria do not make mention of the biological markers or specific cognitive or brain mechanisms. The reader is left with the strong suspicion that despite the relatively well-defined and reliable criteria of the recognized diseases, there could be different causes and mechanisms involved in what is putatively the same disease. However, in any case the probability of symptoms does not necessarily translate into the consistency of aetiology or pathophysiology and the descriptive criteria of contemporary classification systems are far from being a matter of free interpretation. Nevertheless, human action and behaviour cannot be isolated altogether from interpretation, understanding and social background. And this background in turn may represent a considerable limitation to the naturalisation of psychiatric disorders.

4 Mental Disorder as a Dysfunction

A central notion to the naturalisation of disorders is biological function. Dysfunction implies a defect of a natural body mechanism which has been acquired through evolution to respond to the external environment. The notion of *disease* refers to a 'dysfunction' interpreted as a biological disadvantage. On the other hand, *illness* is a consequence of a biological defect and has a normative character: it is something wrong and unwanted. The 'naturalisation cascade' described by Fulford (Fulford 2000: 78) shows passage from the descriptive to the prescriptive in relation to psychopathology. As is well known, a disease is something undesirable and painful for the patient and their surroundings. Medicine endeavours to unveil the true causes of diseases and through naturalisation make their essence visible. Disputes largely revolve around the notion of dysfunction which, according to Wakefield (Wakefield, 2000), is of a normative character - whereas for Boorse and Kendell (Kendell 1975) it is a more descriptive concept. Conversely, Fulford (Fulford et al. 2006) assumes that the descriptive definition of a disorder can be given whereas its *practical* application cannot do without evaluation – without normativity. While it is possible to define murder as a conscious and unjustified taking of somebody's life, we cannot name such a deed without expressing equal contempt towards it.

Let us try to define the concept of mental disease beginning with a classic, biomedical model and then go on to compare this with a functional conception. Of crucial importance is the factual element understood as an external factor. The disorder is caused by an injury, i.e. structural or anatomic damage (to cells, tissue, organs). As pointed out by Szasz: "Literally, the concept of a disease refers to the substantiated damage to cells, tissue or organs." (Szasz 2000: 4). At the same time, Szasz does not challenge the occurrence of functional disorders. However, this radical approach does not present suitable tools to grasp the character of functions or dysfunctions involved in disease, i.e. it cannot deal with the specific character of living organisms as revealed in the cases under consideration.

Disorders conceived of as a partial dysfunction (or harmful dysfunction) concern a physiological or biochemical process not necessarily being the result of an underlying anatomic damage. Pathology has a functional character which we cannot explain by a purely causal approach free from the language of teleology and function (this approach only considers self-organizing systems). We can speak of disease only where there is defective internal functioning of the body and if these internal dysfunctions explain the symptoms observable across the whole organism (e.g. at the behavioural level). This is definitely still a reductive approach which takes no account of the quality of the sick person's life but stresses the fact that certain mechanisms within the body are no longer as efficient as they used to be.

Dysfunction can be viewed from two angles: biologically and statistically. A biological defect is understood in evolutionary terms as a decrease in the chance of survival and as a reduction in reproductive capacity. Statistical anomaly, on the other hand, means departure from a statistical norm. The biological and evolutionary approach points to the failure of some internal mechanisms with respect to their natural functions. 'Natural' means compliance with nature's - i.e. evolution's - design. The failure is believed to cause damage and a depletion of certain bodily advantages and results from the inability of the internal mechanisms to initiate and sustain the natural functions in question. However, attempts to define psychotic disorders in this way face a number of obstacles.

A mental disorder is often described as a breakdown in the connections between our beliefs and other mental states and actions. We first attempt to explain someone's behaviour in rational and intentional terms – with reference to an object which is the main focal point of the mental states in questions – however we might judge the true significance of that object. Once we have exhausted our attempts to find an explanation of this kind, the natural step is to turn to 'lower-order' explanations, which assume that some irrational behaviour is in play. Furthermore, it is not the case that every intentional disorder results in a disease at all. We certainly encounter minor mistakes or errors in the form of habits, minor mood swings or incoherence between beliefs and action. According to current clinical practice - and sometimes folk-psychology as well – we are faced with a real disorder when improper intentionality is accompanied by suffering or impairment of everyday functions. In the case of erroneous or irrational convictions, it is necessary to provide for cultural context when some false convictions are enhanced by commonly accepted educational patterns which mean that false beliefs are widely held even despite adverse evidence or other widely recognized beliefs. The explanation of irrational beliefs may be sought at the biological and physical level, but we may also be able to explain certain disorders at the intentional level. Human goals are so complex that the various sets of rules and factors that come into play in a specific situation may be in conflict. Another instance is the sacrifice of one of the functions (goal, desire) in order to realize another. The intentional approach is supported by Daniel Dennett (Dennett 1987) who defines it in rational terms. It serves to provide a satisfactory explanation of the actions in question and helps forecast their effects. However, intentional explanations may also concern actions which, in specific conditions, do not seem rational for an ideally rational observer. For this reason Derek Bolton allows for the possibility that we accept an attitude intentional towards goals whose achievement may require us to be more flexible in relation to variable environmental factors and thus we should take into consideration the specific prejudices or fears of the acting subject. So the notion of understanding is revealed to be broader than that of rationality. We are able to understand actions which do not seem entirely rational. (This can also be said of a computer which is so programmed as to refrain from implementing certain otherwise optimum solutions (e.g. while playing chess).)

Certainly some defects of intentional explanations prompt us to 'reject' the intentional stance altogether – however flexible we are in its application. In cases like these, to forecast the action of the system, we need the functional attitude (or the 'design stance') rather than, for example, the physical attitude. For, as we have noted elsewhere, a purely physical attitude is too irregular to comprehend the specificity of living organisms. There have been a number of attempts to elucidate psychiatric disorders by reference to evolutionary adaptation. That is why Kendell sees a mental disease in a subgroup of diseases and speaks of biological disadvantage defined as the increase in mortality and decrease in fertility of the sick individual. The issue is that in the case of psychiatric disorders it is hardly possible to tell the difference between the biological defect and the social defect as, for example, with homosexuality - which adversely impacts fertility but whose status as a pathology seems at the very least controversial.

5 Naturalisation of Mental Diseases and its Limitations

The natural functions of mind according to contemporary psychiatry and commonsense – perception, thinking, emotion, convictions or desires –

do not necessarily correspond to natural functions acquired through evolution. Moreover, some groups of specific mental symptoms, perceived as the effect of a given biological dysfunction, do not have to display *neurological* similarity. The functional group does not have to share the same biological conditions with respect to source, course and treatment of the disease. Besides this limitation, it also happens that there is no biological dysfunction lying behind a mental disorder. Someone may be mentally suffering even if there is no 'evolutionary error' involved. For many natural functions are not direct outcomes of evolutionary adaptation but are rather neutral by-products of that adaptation (e.g. the ability to read):

1) Disease may result from damage to mechanisms which lack adaptive capacity. They are a type of exaptation or the remnants of adaptation mechanisms (e.g. the spandrel, an ornamental part of an arch).

2) Mental disorders may also be caused by mechanisms which are fulfilling their naturally acquired functions, they are in accordance with the design of evolution (the disorder may be prompted by atypical content which, when processed by the body, results in pathology).

When we adopt an evolutionary and theoretical perspective, we search for the elements of the adaptation of biological mechanisms to the environment - even if we cannot find such elements at first. This approach belongs to the level of 'design' (and not the 'intentional' level), to use Dennett's terminology, and concerns the adaptive capacity of systems in diverse internal and external environments. Evolutionary epidemiology points to the high rates of major and minor mental disorders that survive in the population despite their discernible biological defects. So if their genotypic and phenotypic features have been preserved, the disorders must have somehow benefited human beings (Baptista 2008). According to Bolton, the high level of pathological features exceeding the standard indicator of mutations and phenotype reactions forces us to take a fresh look at psychopathology: "what we are inclined to call a disorder may turn out not to be a disorder at all, from the evolutionary perspective, but indeed perhaps something more in order, more adapted, than normal." (Bolton 2001: 193). A number of hypotheses have emerged dealing with the adaptive capacity of disorders such as sociopathy, anxiety, neurosis, depression or schizophrenia. T. Crow (Crow 1995) underlines the fact that the loss of certain functions in schizophrenia is strictly connected, in terms of genotype and phenotype, with the biological achievement of speaking languages.

There is also another explanation of these discrepancies, namely that our environment is very different to that of our ancestors. This explains why something adaptive for a previous age today appears to be a dysfunction, not fitting with nature-developed functions. From the evolutionary and theoretical viewpoint, a mental disease consists in damage to basic psychological abilities and has a modular character. To justify this approach, Baron-Cohen proposes a theory of the failure of the function of the theory of mind in autistic patients or the impairment of concentration processes in schizophrenia. However, the evolutionary approach is much richer that the physical or functional view might lead one to suggest. Any damage to the function, even if the underlying factor is a neurological defect, is accompanied by mechanisms facilitating the survival of the organism such as recreation, plasticity and compensation which allow a crisis situation to be positively handled. After Dennett, we can observe cases where the intentional strategy becomes incorporated into the organism's design which allows the body to overcome physical and functional obstacles. So schizophrenic or autistic patients tend to avoid conditions in which it is particularly important to use the impaired functions such as social cooperation and simulation, or stimulation. With psychiatric disorders, Wakefield (Wakefield 2000a) discusses 'harmful dysfunctions'. On the one hand, he describes dysfunction as damage to what has been designed through natural selection, on the other hand he looks at the 'failure' from the perspective of today's patient's interests and values. So he appreciates the role of the environment which may at times *favour* some biological dysfunctions. Finally, Wakefield rejects the requirement of providing a dysfunctional mechanism when defining a disease – though he does not admit this straightforwardly (see Bolton 2000: 144). The problem of telling the difference between an evolutionary drawback and an everyday case of non-standard behaviour pushes us to accept less restrictive definitions of dysfunction. A function is every mechanism or structure which contributes to the general operation of the systems containing that function. This definition is supported by Cummins, where function is just a causal role in a system (see Cummins 1975); he says that spandrels, exaptations or the adaptation of mind also constitute functions. In my opinion (and to some extent against Cummins' intentions), this makes a disorder (as a dysfunction) an evaluative notion - pathological functions are ultimately harmful and against the patient's interest; we can't strictly differentiate between the descriptive and normative aspects of dysfunctions.

When Megone (Megone 2000) analyzes the notion of mental disease in terms of dysfunctions, he holds out hope that it will be possible to separate the descriptive element from the evaluative, normative element. Dysfunction adds to the limitation of the individual's capacity to fulfil their life goals, yet it does this instrumentally. Dysfunction technically blocks the realization of somebody's rational being in the world. In order to distinguish pathological dysfunctions from simple human problems, e.g. social, ethical or legal, we look for the internal cause, state or process that results in feeling 'ill' - i.e. unfit or incapable. This definition raises doubts as it will count many conditions and states as diseases including ones which do not seem to be diseases at all. These are, for example, ignorance, sadness or a fanatic belief. A similar definition was proposed by Culver and Gert (1982) who defined the phrase 'internally caused' as 'the absence of a distinct sustaining cause'. They further point out:

> We could say that to be a malady, the evil-producing condition must be part of the person. However, for reasons of conceptual rigor, a more formal negative statement is preferable: the person has a malady if and only if the evil he is suffering does *not* have a sustaining cause which is clearly distinct from the person (Culver and Gert 1982: 72).

Handcuffs on one's hands impose a limitation but they are an external factor. The internal cause might be a deadly virus or a clamp left accidentally in the patient's body after an operation. In the case of mental disorders, the cause may be mental or biological and the impairment itself may concern free will or cognitive functions. The definition still seems problematic as, for example, fundamental religious beliefs may count as maladies since they can be taken as an integral part of an individual. Moreover, sorrow caused by the loss of a close relative may seem an independent factor in the world whose change would bring the mourning person back to their normal condition. However, one can always conclude that the sorrow has emerged due to the internal conviction of the mourner concerning the loss. Still more dubious are the conditions of sensory deprivation or phobias which are strictly connected with the external environment and yet are invariably treated as types of psychiatric disorders. Boorse's classic definition took disease to be somehow interconnected with failure in regular biological processes. Nevertheless, the reference here to the biological and evolutionary dysfunctions runs into a number of difficulties. As Dominic Murphy emphasizes:

> In the biomedical and cognitive sciences, function concepts get their sense from the role they play in mechanistic, rather than evolutionary,

explanation. Ever since Harvey showed that the heart is a pump, medicine has ascribed functions to organs without worrying about (or, in Harvey's case, even knowing about) the possibility of showing that the function is a naturally selected one. The tasks performed by the organism are broken down into subtasks and these are localized in subcomponents. So the function of a mechanism is the activity that it performs so as to contribute to the overall system (Murphy 2005: 124).

Exclusive reference to functional break-down would fundamentally alter our perception of mental diseases and psychiatric classification. For many psychiatric diagnoses rely upon a hard-to-define notion of irrationality. After all, the idea of mental disease encounters problems not encountered in the case of somatic diseases. It is not easy to pin down the concept of mental breakdown precisely.

6 Development Prospects for Naturalised Psychopathology

The disputes and difficulties we find in defining mental disorders partly stems from misconception in our linguistic intuitions and in the perspective of scientific objectivism. When juxtaposing our linguistic intuitions with the scientific endeavours to define diseases, it appears that some of them are unjustified, e.g. make no mention of biological dysfunction but only of the culture-dependent notion of irrationality. If the starting point is the commonsense interpretation of a mental disease, scientific research should only determine the conditioning mechanism. It can happen, however, that out common intuitions are totally undermined by scientific discoveries. The current dispute over the status of psychopathology vacillates between objectivism and constructivism. The followers of constructivism assume that mental disorders are basically a social phenomenon. They base their explanations on social norms and rules, claiming that the biomedical approach will not contribute much to the problem as it moves in a conceptual area which is not adequate to account for mental diseases. Mentally ill patients often break or bend social rules. Even if constructivists agree that we may search for the biological and psychological mechanisms underlying such disorders, the fundamental decision consists in the classification of given behaviour as pathological (negatively evaluated). On the other hand, objectivism concentrates solely on biological change as determining the status and desirability of a disorder. Conversely, Dominic Murphy (Murphy 2005) proposes a distinction between a *conservative* and *revisionist* approach. The former invokes our everyday intuitions which determine whether a given case is an actual disease or merely a reaction to some external, disadvantageous situation/surroundings. The revisionist approach subscribes to the idea that our scientific discoveries alter our cognition and classification of diseases even if it contradicts common intuitions. Interestingly enough, even constructivists sometimes adopt the revisionist approach by criticizing socially pejorative classifications of 'madness'. These criticisms question the concepts of mental diseases being used.

The attempts to naturalise mental diseases will surely not enjoy full success. On the other hand, we cannot ignore the biological foundations of disorders. Contemporary psychiatric classification tends to be descriptive and neutral towards possible causes of most mental disorders. In fact, it is neurocognitive theories that have played a major part in the breakthrough in schizophrenia research or depression analysis. After all, the field of psychiatric disorders is so extensive that some conditions will have to be reclassified as a result of our growing understanding and some apparently unified phenomena will likely turn out to be collections of diverse afflictions. The current discussion on schizophrenia testifies to this trend as it aims to replace the notion of schizophrenia with a number of particular conditions (for more on this point, see Bloom 2004 and Boyle 2002).

References

American Psychiatric Association (1994). *Diagnostic and Statistical Manual Of Mental Disorders* (4th ed., DSM-IV). Washington, DC: American Psychiatric Association. (DSM-IV)

Baptista, Trino et al. (2008). "Evolution theory: An Overview of its Application in Psychiatry". *Psychopathology* 41 (1), pp. 17–27.

Bloom, Jan Dirk (2004). *Deconstructing Schizophrenia*. Amsterdam: Boom Publishers.

Bolton, Derek (2000). "Continuing Commentary: Alternatives to Disorder". *Philosophy, Psychiatry, & Psychology*, 7(2), pp. 141–54.

Bolton, Derek (2001). "Problems in the Definition of 'Mental Disorder'". *The Philosophical Quarterly*, 203, pp. 182–99.

Boorse, C. (1975). "On the distinction between disease and illness". *Philosophy and Public Affairs*, 5, pp. 49–68.

Boyle, Mary (2002). *Schizophrenia. A Scientific Delusion?*, London: Routledge.

Crow, Timothy J. (1995). "A continuum of psychosis, one human gene, and not much else - the case for homogeneity". *Schizophrenia Research 17*, pp. 135–45.

Culver, Charles M. & Gert, Bernard (1982). *Philosophy in medicine*. New York: Oxford University Press.
Cummins, Robert (1975). "Functional analysis". *Journal of Philosophy*, 72, pp. 741–64.
Dennett, Daniel (1987). "True believers: the Intentional Strategy and why it works". In Daniel Dennett, *The Intentional Stance*. Cambridge, MA: MIT Press, pp. 13–35.
Fodor, Jerry A. (1987). *Psychosemantics*. Cambridge, MA: MIT Press.
Fulford, Bill (2000). "Teleology without Tears: Naturalism, Neo-Naturalism and Evaluationism in the Analysis of Function Statements in Biology (and a Bet on the Twenty-first Century)". *Philosophy, Psychiatry, & Psychology* 7(1): 77–94.
Fulford, Bill, Thornton, Tim and Graham, George (2006). *Oxford Textbook of Philosophy and Psychiatry*, Oxford: Oxford University Press
Gillett, Grant (1999). *The Mind and its Discontents*. Oxford: Oxford University Press.
Kendell, R.E. (1975). "The concept of disease and its implications for psychiatry". *British Journal of Psychiatry*, 127, pp. 305–315
Millikan, Ruth G. (1984). *Language, thought and other biological categories*. Cambridge, MA: MIT Press.
Megone, Christopher (2000). "Mental Illness, Human Function, and Values Philosophy". *Psychiatry, & Psychology* – 7 (1), pp. 45–65.
Murphy, Dominic (2005). "The Concept of Mental Illness – Where the Debate Has Reached and Where It Needs to Go". *Journal of Theoretical and Philosophical Psychology*. 25, pp. 116–131.
Szasz, Thomas Steven (2000). "Second Commentary on Aristotle's function argument". "Philosophy, Psychiatry, & Psychology", 7(1), pp. 3–16.
Thornton, Tim (2002). "Thought insertion, Cognitivism and inner space". *Cognitive Neuropsychiatry*, 7, pp. 237–249
Wakefield, Jerome C. (2000). "Aristotle as sociobiologist: the "function of a human being" argument, black box essentialism, and the concept of mental disorder". *Philosophy, Psychiatry, & Psychology*, 7(1), pp. 17–44.
Wakefield, Jerome C. (2000a). "Spandrels, vestigal organs, and such: reply to Murphy and Woolfolk. The harmful dysfunction analysis of mental disorder". *Philosophy, Psychiatry, & Psychology*, 7(4), pp. 253–270
World Health Organization (1992). *ICD-10. International Classification of Diseases and Related Health Problems* (10th ed.). Geneva: World Health Organization.

20

Technologised Epistemology

MAREK HETMAŃSKI

1 Introduction

Technologised epistemology is a type of naturalised epistemology that is interested in the process of knowledge acquisition and transmission, and looks upon cognition as well as its results as psycho-social phenomena; changeable and dependent on manifold circumstances particularly technological ones. It considers cognition and knowledge as mediated by tools, instruments and communication media, as well as putting important epistemological questions in that context: Does technological mediation really change the nature of knowledge (from individual and subjective to dispersed and impersonal)? Does it subsequently make the knower, sender, or receiver (who become anonymous and depersonalised agents) more effective but less rational, responsible, and reliable? Does knowledge in such cases cease to be true and justified? Who is the agent – the individual person who introspectively experiences their own subjective mental states, or the networked group of individuals who participate in commonly shared (but impersonal) knowledge?

At the same time, technologised epistemology is confronted with the same – unavoidable as well as troublesome – traditional problems of uncertainty, unreliability, and falsehood. It shares the same characteristics (i.e. meta-theoretical, normative analysis of cognition and knowledge) by which traditional epistemology is still identified. Its interest in cognition's instrumentation nevertheless reveals new tendencies to which cognitive and communicative phenomena are increasingly subjected. It is also obliged to answer the old epistemological question of how reliable knowledge (data-bases, the news, public opinion, or any type of information and knowledge exchange) might be gained if the means of its gathering, processing, and conveying are technologically mediated to such an extent? New tendencies oblige epistemologists to think over anew the problem of normativity, understood in the paper in two ways: (1) as values, norms such as truth, evidence, certainty, reliability etc. (properties of beliefs used in the agent's evaluation acts); and (2) prescriptions and rules telling how to obtain true (as well as how to avoid false) cognitive results (taking the form of imperative, normative sentences). The problem how values such as truth or evidence undergo changes, not only in their linguistic meaning but in their factual content, is worth discussing.

2 Increasing knowledge naturalisation

"Naturalising" does not assume only one particular form – several versions of it can indeed be found in the history of philosophy. It concerns both objective and theoretical levels of knowledge (I shall analyse them in sec. 6); in other words, the term "naturalisation" applies to processes and tendencies constituting knowledge as well as to the theories which describe and postulate new epistemology. Naturalisation occurs in many areas of human cognitive and communicative endeavour. It is, generally speaking, the intellectual consequence of the many changes that took place within philosophy as well as in Western culture and modern European societies at the turn of the eighteenth century.

Naturalisation in a broad sense, as I want to define it, concerns, to a varying degree, several things: (1) the *real processes of cognition* (natural human faculties and abilities, perceptive or intellectual) improved and facilitated by different instruments and media of communication; (2) the psycho-social *position of an agent* (involved in technological endeavours and communication with other human beings or machines) as well as the *epistemologist* who provides analyses of naturalisation; (3) a *subject of knowledge* (real and objective things, events, and processes as well as virtual and fictional phenomena); and (4) the *knowledge justification* procedures (scientific and commonsensical) negotiated and constructed by agents who obtain as well as evaluate knowledge. These characteristics may be treated as a general model describing how naturalisation takes place in commonsensical knowledge, public opinion, and science. Naturalised epistemology is then, firstly, a theoretical view-point that reduces epistemological analyses to science, especially to psychological studies. But one can also treat knowledge naturalisation as, secondly, an objective process which human cognition and knowledge (not reduced exclusively to science) have undergone in the last centuries and decades, and which have been taking place in science and public affairs. Taking this into account, I suggest that the above characteristics fit very well with the tendencies that are analysed by technologised epistemology.

With the beginning of the so called computer revolution human cognitive processes and knowledge have changed their nature, as its theorists maintain (See Bolter 1984; Sloman 1978), becoming more dispersed and impersonal, but at the same time less reliable and comprehensible. These socio-cultural tendencies are now a challenge for epistemology. Technologised epistemology, unlike traditional epistemology, ought to provide a theoretical description of cognitive phenomena (especially mediated cognitive phenomena) and an evaluation of the cultural changes which human cognition and knowledge are increasingly subject to. It may, on the basis of case studies and historical investigations, provide forecasts and long-term predictions concerning knowledge development, particularly the tendencies observed in science, public opinion, or mass communications. These predictions, being neutral, objective, and self-correcting (science-based) evaluations, may be treated as normative. Not in the traditional meaning – as following arbitrary epistemic rules that are presented as objective – but in a more realistic and critical way, as value-related epistemological analysis.

3 Normativity in the broader context

Epistemic norms, to put the problem generally, are the result of the manifold human endeavours, properties of individual agent beliefs used in their evaluation acts. Such norms as truth, evidence, certainty, reliability lead human achievements. But they function in a context much broader than just the cognitive (individual or subjective). All norms and values originate from human processes or acts of evaluation, and function not only in internally but externally, as well. They are the results of effective human efforts undertaken in order to achieve some cognitive goals. These goals look for their manifold completion or fulfilment. The agent's satisfaction called certainty is mainly ascribed to the gained knowledge, while unsatisfactory beliefs are deemed mistaken. Most of the goals are in fact collective, not individual, and many social influences are reflected in them. It cannot be denied that evaluating (i.e. ascribing significance to things or events) is a more substantial human activity than any cognitive process. This is the case because perception (visual evidence) as well as thinking (conceptual evidence) or conveying what is conceived as a true justified belief (its truth *per se*) are usually undertaken in the course of deciding or estimating what is good or wrong. Truth as obviousness, perceptual or intellectual, is then a value or norm that emerges through perpetual human evaluative and normative endeavours that, I wish to argue, are prior to the generalised norms themselves. The norms are, therefore, the cultural embodiment of individual and social understanding that people acquired through trying to experience a variety of things. This can be observed not only in science, where truth plays the crucial role, but also in areas of commonsense knowledge or public opinion, as well as in communicational behaviours.

Because of its introspective and subjective concept of 'the knower', traditional epistemology usually did not take the above perspective into account. As most of epistemology's concerns (i.e. agent's identity, scope and limits of knowledge, concept of truth and evidence, etc.) were traditionally considered within the internalistic (introspective) framework (in the first-person perspective) any solution to the problem of norms usually took the form of an absolute. Epistemic norms and values were conceived as the final goals of personal cognitive acts; they preceded, not followed them. But since Cartesian-Husserlian epistemology has been critically reconsidered many times, a new perspective has been developed. Externalism (See BonJour 1994; Goldman 1995; Zieminska 1998) re-evaluates all epistemic concepts and issues, including the problem of normativity. But there is a number of noteworthy ways in which this change is realised.

Socio-historical epistemological studies are one of the currents of externalism, and Alvin Goldman's veritistic epistemology (situated in the analytical tradition) plays the crucial role therein. Goldman says that veritistic epistemology, "a specialised subject, analogous to environmental studies and nutritional studies", deals with special social values, a circumscribed kind of things that people and institutions take into account.

"Veritistic epistemology is such a special field, where the selected good is knowledge and the selected bads are error and ignorance. [...] It has the distinctive *normative* purpose of evaluating or appraising such practices on the veritistic dimension, that is, in terms of their respective knowledge consequences. Practices currently in place will be veritistically good or bad in varying degrees; they will rarely be ideal. To investigate prospects for improvement, social epistemology must be prepared to transcend previously realised practices. It must be ready to consider the probable veritistic properties of practices that have not yet been, but might be, adopted." (Goldman 1999: 6–7) Social practices which play a role in evaluating some achieved cognitive results as true beliefs, constitute certain goods as true or false. They are then the subject of epistemology's meta-theoretical analyses (veritistic in their nature). This obliges, if not compels, the epistemologist to take the role of "the disinterested participant of analytical social epistemology, which aims to acquire knowledge first-hand above all else" (See Fuller 2007: 110).

Steve Fuller goes much further in his critical analyses of the problem of normativity. His externalist approach takes into account social circumstances as important conditions for knowledge making and evaluation. What matters is not only the scientific methods and results but also the social and public strategies and policies ("knowledge regimes"). Epistemic norms emerge in the course of knowledge production and distribution; they do not function independently of the social situations which generate them. Fuller holds that "Social epistemology's normative concerns largely reflect the bureaucratic context of modern resource-intensive 'big science'. It situates the points of critical intervention not in the laboratory, but in the policy forums were research is initially simulated and ultimately evaluated. Part of this shift is due to the gradual demystification of scientific work that has attended the rise of science and technology studies.[...] Another part of the story is the increasing realization that bodies of the knowledge can be evaluated, not merely in terms of their conception, but also in terms of their consequences. Given the increasing access to resources that science commands, research has become – if it was not already – both in investment opportunity and a public trust." (Fuller 2007: 110) In other words, epistemic norms and values originate and function in the context of social structure and public opinion, not only in individual activity. Their status and importance are due to the constant change and re-evaluation that takes place outside philosophy.

One consequence of this is the change that occurs at the meta-theoretical level. It concerns the position of the philosopher providing epistemological analyses (See part 2, point (3) above). The epistemologist becomes "the interested non-participant in the knowledge system", as Fuller puts it (this position is opposed to that which was ascribed to Goldman). This happens that because "interest in knowledge policy is grounded in the idea that, generally speaking, the *prescribers* and *evaluators* (or, respectively, *legislators* and *judges*) of knowledge production are not the same – in terms of identities or interests – as the first-order knowledge producers. Knowledge serves as a means to other human ends (which themselves may be epistemic) but one's participation in the knowledge process is usually confined to the meta-level of inquiry, that is, the design and evaluation of knowledge production regimes that *others* carry out. [...] Thus, the social epistemologist's position is, generally speaking, *rule-utilitarian*: if the people subjected to an epistemic regime can live well with its consequences, then that is success enough. [...] A progressive knowledge regime institutionalizes both the exploration and the criticism of alternative research trajectories." (Fuller 2007: 110–111) Finally, one can say that the problem of normativity which epistemology deals with lies in the fact that knowledge (as any other epistemic concept and value) is indispensably intervolved with social phenomena that influence it. Technology and social or political practices and infrastructures (i.e. information and computer technologies) that enable wide and pervasive knowledge functioning in a social structure, have to be then the subject of epistemology's interest.

4 What do knowledge and technology have in common

The traditional perspective on knowledge considers it as the idealised result of an agent's individual cognitive efforts which ought to be realised in one particular way. The agent has privileged, introspective to this knowledge and there is no demand for any external means of mediation or improvement; indeed, such options are excluded. The issue of the circumstances that accompany the cognitive acts or influence their results is either omitted or treated as a serious and troublesome epistemic obstacle.

Nobody will deny that knowing means doing and making, at the same time. Most of our ordinary cognitive acts are involved in various practical activities. Only certain, very simple and evident cognitive acts, such as perceiving objects around us, may be actually realised without any assistance or help from instruments or tools. In order to be acquainted with more distant objects that are more distant or which are somehow obscure, we must use a variety of instruments for observation, differentiation, calibration, preparation, modelling, simulation etc. Most scientific or common cognitive activities executed by people looking for knowledge are based on the tools and instruments they use deliberately. In other words, cognition and knowledge in their substance are tool-related human activities.

Does an instrument- and tool-related cognitive activity really mean a new epistemic situation which requires a new (technologised, as well as social or cultural) epistemology, however? In what sense and to what extent is the instrumental involvement of human knowledge really the subject for epistemological meta-theoretical level of analysis? Considering that complex, reciprocal relations between knowing and doing are obvious in our everyday life (in pre-theoretical experience), why is this such a controversial and troublesome issue for traditional epistemology? Why should a new theoretical perspective arise from studying these connections? There are, in my opinion, a few important reasons why we can believe that and, respectively to these facts, try to sketch the concept of technologised epistemology. One needs only to state precisely what is the area of interest and study; in short, how, where, and why is knowledge (beliefs, opinions, information, databases, the news, etc.) constituted by the technological means of processing, conveying, gathering, and improving it.

But what do we mean by 'technology'? Which of its epistemic aspects could require a new epistemological perspective? Human activity is simultaneously practical and cognitive. Both sides of human life involve the tools, signs, symbols, and language that serve as its instruments. Only in very specific situations are people not compelled directly or urgently to use some instruments, and then we may rely on what we perceive, imagine, memorise, or think immediately. Subjective, intensive and seemingly evident experience is traditionally treated as pure, unmediated cognition that possesses the special epistemic value of being "uncontaminated" by the use of instruments and tools. As such, it is still the ideal for traditional epistemology. But even though this cognition model describes mathematical knowledge very well (yet, there are branches in mathematics where computers are used to obtain proofs of theorems), it does not function in other areas of human knowledge (i.e. natural sciences) where facts and events are brought into the light of scientific interest thanks to instruments and communication media.

Technology is the use of various tools for achieving various practical goals, including cognitive ones. But knowledge is entangled in practical human activity in two ways: as (1) a result of using instruments and tools when new information is gathered or processed thanks to the technological support; and which couldn't be achieved by other means (such as pure intellectual reasoning); (2) a starting point when new technological instruments or inventions that constitute so called information infrastructure emerge thanks to intellectual scientific discoveries (i.e. computers and information technology as a result of mathematical discussions on algorithmic computability). In other words, technology is the application of knowledge (commonsensical, scientific, or other) that brings about and controls human activities, as well as the production of knowledge that is otherwise unobtainable. It is for this reason that any type of technology is characterised by its intellectual ingredient.

The essence of modern technology is its collective functioning within society. It is the production, engineering, and management of material things, where information processing and conveying is substantial and constitutive. Knowledge (information) and its technological involvement function within the social structure, at the same time being an important aspect of its change and development, as many theorists hold (See Laver 1989; Hughes 2005; Baird 2004; Lash 2002). There are still many human collective endeavours and types of experience in which sophisticated and complex technology systems constitute new kinds of knowledge unachievable without them. These new phenomena, considered on the epistemological level (by description and by normative evaluation) open new intellectual horizons, but at the same time imply novel and paradoxical theoretical problems.

5 Telepistemology – new facts and new theory

The consequences of technology – the good or bad results it may bring about as well as the optimistic or pessimistic opinions (both overestimated, as is usually the case) it may lead to – are neither unknowable nor evident. They require our ability to recognize what is hidden under technology's spectacular achievements and apparent successes. Sophisticated and complex information technologies that pervade our lives must be constantly subject to investigation and critical evaluation, and this is the task for technologised epistemology.

Some of these issues may be dealt with by a *telepistemology* that emerges from recent technology and art performances[1] described in Ken Goldberg's monograph (See Goldberg 2000). "Access, agency, authority, and authenticity are central issues for the new subject of telepistemology: the study of knowledge acquired at distance. [...] Although epistemology has lost primacy within philosophy, each new invention for communication and measurement forces us to recalibrate our definition of knowledge. [...] Telepistemology asks: To what extent can epistemology inform our understanding of telerobotics and to what extent can telerobotics furnish new insights into classical questions about the nature and possibilities of knowledge?" (Goldberg 2000: 3–4) It approaches both the technical and the moral questions that arise from these new phenomena: Do telerobotics and the Internet really provide us with knowledge? Is it reliable knowledge? How should we act in the technologically mediated environment? How does our sense of agency change? Hubert L. Dreyfus, following Descartes' line of sceptical argumentation toward perceptual knowledge, admits that the rise of technologically mediated communication and knowledge confronts us with the same old epistemic situation: why and how to believe mediated experience, and how to cope with sceptical arguments? "And if telepresence became ubiquitous and we became dependent on electronic prostheses to mediate *all* our relations to the world, the epistemological questions that troubled Descartes and three centuries of epistemologists could again come to seem, not just intelligible, but disturbing." (Dreyfus 2000: 55) This situation compels us to answer anew the old pragmatists' question of whether our relation to the world should be that of a detached spectator or an involved actor? If there are serious reasons to doubt the authenticity and reliability of Internet communication or highly mediated mental representation that are so easily experienced, how are we to dismiss scepticism? If our background trust is missing, Dreyfus continues, we might be suspicious of the trustworthiness of every type of technologically mediated cognition and, what would be the worst, all mediated social interactions; our life would then become unbearable.

---

[1] http://goldberg.berkeley.edu/garden/Ars/

A similar perspective is considered by Catherine Wilson who investigates the consequences of the 'telefictive experience', 'proximal experience', and 'mediated agency' for the newest scientific, cultural, and ordinary endeavours. For her, these phenomena show that the old, constant bifurcation (traceable back to Greek theories of tragedy) that one can find in human experience between 'here' and 'away' is still operating and takes the form of dramatic self-awareness. "My central claim is that human ability to distinguish simulacra from real things and simulations from real events, has been made to carry too much psychological weight. [...] The real world and fictional worlds are not emotionally, psychologically, or morally insulated from each other [...] our everyday experience is permeated by the fictive. If we see fictive modes – including imagination and fantasy – as weakened forms of what I will characterize as *telefictive experience*, we obtain quite different results from the standard theories." (Wilson 2000:76) People using internet mediated instruments and performing actions at a distance are confronted with very specific and unique situations. Their subjective experience, being technologically mediated to such an extent, changes itself as do their remote actions. Nobody is the same subject after being involved in internet communication, where they realise an increasing number of their activities. "We can nevertheless venture the claim that, to the extent that an agent is screened off from the proximal experiences that would otherwise accompany his agency, his agency appears to us to be remote. Conversely, to the extent that experience is screened off from the possibility of agency, it is regarded as remote." (Wilson 2000:78) In other words, the nature of agency becomes more and more complex and not evident even to the agent; as such it is a challenge for the new type of epistemology as well as aesthetics.

In what sense, if at all, are technologically mediated cognition or communication trustworthy, and their results reliable? If they are fictional and misleading to such a degree, might it be impossible to ascribe to them such traditional epistemic values as truth, rationality, or reliability? However, the question seems to be still open, and there are approaches that try to solve it in the realist and critical way. Alvin Goldman's theory of causal factors in knowledge (his *no relevant alternatives* (NRA) approach) holds that whether a true belief is knowledge depends on the real reasons the belief is held, on the psychological as well as sociological processes that cause the belief and sustain it in the knower's mind as knowledge. If the causes actually bring about particular beliefs, and if they are experienced by the subject, then the cause of such beliefs is only sustainable for reliable knowledge on the condition that "there is no relevant alternative on which the belief would be false" [REFERENCE]. The above circumstance of reliability may be extended to all cases of technologically mediated cognition and communication, especially those provided by the Internet. Even though they produce many apparent and obscure effects, they are of central interest to the theory of knowledge. As Goldman holds: "Telerobotically acquired beliefs raise interesting difficulties for the theory of knowledge. Unlike papier-mâché barns and boxes of thermometers, deception on the Internet is common. This implies that telerobotic knowledge may be deeply difficult to come by. Given that the threat of Internet deception is always present, can beliefs that are produced by telerobotic installations on the Internet satisfy the requirements for knowledge? The answer is not clear." (Goldman 2000:141–142) But what are the most important questions that arise from such new epistemic situations? Do they really concern only counterfactual cases (irrelevant alternatives) one can construct giving the technologically mediated communication? Do they concern their general reliability? What are other epistemological problems that one can put forward and consider?

6 Conclusions

The technologically mediation of human endeavours and cognitive processes is the cultural fact that characterises the last few decades of the computer revolution since information technology has penetrated deeply and broadly into our lives. But mediation of human experience took place long before that and was introduced to facilitate many social and cultural exchanges, to mention only such examples as writing, print, the press, radio, or television systems of mass communication. In all of these cases of 'technologising' and 'making of the typographic man', human collective and individual experiences were mediated by the tools, instruments, and means of communication (See McLuhan 1962; Ong 1982). Thanks to these technological mediations new types of mentalities and minds, especially scientific thought, have emerged in European civilization, along with new kinds of social relations and structures. As McLuhan holds, "The use of any kind of medium or extension of man alters the patterns of interdependence among people, as it alters the ratios among our senses."

(McLuhan 1965:90) The linear, mono-causal, predictable, commonsensical and scientific ways of thinking, created concurrently with the rise of modern science by such inventions as the printing press, microscope, telescope, and mathematical calculus, gave rise to epistemology.

The Cartesian-Lockean model of the theory of knowledge ("considerations concerning human understanding") as well as its other versions (e.g. Kantian, Husserlian) were in fact the theoretical implications of the instrumentally mediated knowledge gained in astronomy, physics, or geometry. But paradoxically, this knowledge has been misleadingly presented by philosophers as a domain of 'pure reason', as a result of an ideal subject who is free of any mediations which would only 'contaminate' his process of cognition. In this context - on the one hand, the real and successful instrumentally-achieved scientific knowledge and, on the other, the meta-theoretical analyses – traditional epistemology has emerged. Its ambiguous nature is evident as far as one discerns the two levels on which it realises itself: the *epistemic* (objective) – where real instrumental mediation has been appropriately recognised, and the *epistemological* (meta-theoretical) – where this phenomenon has unfortunately been obscured and refined specifically into the shape of a normative philosophical theory of knowledge. Both comprise epistemology as such, but the dominance of the later, making epistemology normative and taking it far from the social context of cognition, must be at present counter-balanced by more realistic analyses of what really happens when technology is involved in human cognition. In conclusion I wish to formulate several theses, some seemingly obvious and naive but which nevertheless have important consequences, by answering what technologised epistemology is or ought to be.

6.1. Organic vs. Artificial mediation

Only these technologically mediated human cognitive processes have meaningful epistemological consequences that produce really new epistemic situations. Mediation in human activity, both practical and cognitive, can be observed in the two ways it can function: (1) *organic* – when a human being uses parts of their body as well as very simple tools to perform ordinary cognitive tasks, and (2) *artificial* – when more complex, intentionally constructed, instruments and tools are used to circumvent natural limitations. Mediation is an indispensable precondition for almost all human endeavours aimed at gaining knowledge. But only when mediation brings about effects that could not appear in natural (organic or very simple artificial) situations does it becomes an epistemological problem. In other words, the domain where epistemologically interesting new cognitive situations occur is much narrower than the areas of human activity where habitual mediation takes place; the former, being a subdomain of the later, is of theoretical interest only in so far as it is set free from traditional epistemology's restrictive assumptions.

6.2. Technologically mediated communication

Instrumentally mediated knowledge emerges in information technology systems where signals and signs characterising the objects and processes are encoded and transmitted between different material objects and processes. Information technology allows mutual and repeated coding (encoding and decoding) of any possible state of matter or energy, which people deal with in the physical world (excluding black holes or absolute zero temperature). It enables transition between analogue and digital information. Dematerialised strings of zeros and ones may be conveyed between different senders and receivers (human beings as well as machines) regardless of speed and place, making communication the form and matter of modern civilization. Technologised (i.e. computerised) communication has absorbed not only all previous means of communication such as the telegraph, radio, or television but also means of transport and ways of doing everyday things. Thanks to its effectiveness, almost everything becomes 'networked communication', including most human cognitive undertakings. Cognitive processes and their results are realised more and more on the Internet, which is the proper environment for them, giving them the opportunity for reciprocal exchange of information, signals, signs, and respectively symbols, intensions, thoughts, emotions, knowledge etc.

6.3. Simulations and Simulacra

Digital coding, implemented in computer systems, allows precise presentations of manifold aspects of reality. It makes scientific, as well as common, cognition and practice more effective. Models and simulations built on the digital platform are mainly presentations of non-existing and imaginary worlds that come into existence through them. They are results of the pervasive penetration into the different levels of both micro- and macroscopic areas of the world. Thus, the question of their adequacy arises. If they are instruments of successfully conducted scientific or business endeavours that enhance natural cognition, are we really obliged, as traditional epistemology would have it, to evaluate them by asking the question of their truth or falsity? Simulation or modelling seem not to fulfil strict epistemic standards because they are tools for practical rather than simply cognitive tasks. If they work, help to solve important questions or open new cognitive horizons (while producing uncertainty), they are sufficiently adequate representations of investigated objects and events. Therefore, the epistemological question seems to be less important or urgent than the practical one. Still, this does not imply epistemic carelessness or assent to relativism. In the realm of simulations and simulacra traditional epistemological values and perspectives do not maintain their validity.

6.4. Dispersed and Mythologized Agency

As a result of technologically mediated cognition and communication, a new type of human experience emerges, especially in areas of intellectual endeavour where people are confronted with challenging situations such as described above. It would be naive and excessive to claim that a person utilising information technology becomes an entirely new cognitive subject, radically different from one relying only on speech, writing, print media or television. As we become increasingly involved in complex information technology systems, becoming dependent on them in more and more areas of our lives – possibly even addicted to them – we remain the agents of simple, natural cognitive actions within the factual (physical, natural, and social) worlds. It is not our senses and simple intellectual functions (inference, argumentation, etc.) that have been improved or altered by the use of computerised tools, but rather our memory, imagination and self-identification. The greatest impact of these tools can be observed in higher functions and mental processes, particularly in the concepts and speculations used by cognitive sciences and artificial intelligence studies. These fields of knowledge have created myths of an artificial human being (looking back to the legends of the golem), which reflect the understandable desire to not only construct fully functional robots, but also to uncover and conclusively understand the secret of human thought. As pointed out by many researchers studying the phenomenon (See Turkle 1996; Hetmański 2005), visions and theories of artificial intellect have led, in a broad cultural perspective, to a significant change in the human experience of one's own agency and subsequently in personal as well as self-cultural identity. They involve, for instance, identifying the mind with the Turing Machine, reducing cognition to algorithmic calculations and information processing. Eventually, this results (due to the impact of those concepts on common thought, particularly via computer games and multimedia education) in the specific self-identification of the users of computerised cognitive and communicational tools as cyborgs, avatars or zombies. I believe that this phenomenon is not only of interest to developmental psychology, pedagogy or mass communication studies, but also to epistemology, in particular the type herein referred to as technologised epistemology.

References

Baird, Davis (2004). *Thing Knowledge. A Philosophy of Scientific Instruments*. Berkeley: University of California Press.

Bolter, David (1985). *Turing's Man. Western Culture in the Computer Age*. The University of North Carolina Press.

BonJour, Laurence (1992). *Internalism/externalism*, In *A Companion to Epistemology*, ed. by Jonathan Dancy and Ernest Sosa. Oxford: Oxford University Press, pp. 132–137.

Dreyfus, Hubert L. (2000). "Telepistemology: Descartes's Last Stand". In *The Robot in the Garden. Telerobotics and Telepistemology in the Age of the Internet,* ed. by Ken Goldberg. Cambridge, Mass., London: The MIT Press, pp. 48–63.

Fuller, Steven (2007). *The Knowledge Book. Key Concepts in Philosophy, Science and Culture*, Stocksfield, Acumen.

Goldberg, Ken, ed. (2000). *The Robot in the Garden. Telerobotics and Telepistemology in the Age of the Internet*. Cambridge, Mass., London: The MIT Press.

Goldman, Alvin (1995). "Internalism exposed", *The Journal of Philosophy* 96, pp. 271–293.

Goldman, Alvin (1999). *Knowledge in a Social World*, Oxford: Clarendon Press.

Goldman, Alvin (2000). "Telerobotic Knowledge: A Reliabilist Approach". In *The Robot in the Garden. Telerobotics and Telepistemology in the Age of the*

Internet, ed. by Ken Goldberg. Cambridge, Mass., London: The MIT Press, pp. 126–142.

Hetmański, Marek (2005). "Artificial Intelligence: The Myth of Information Science" In *Ethical Problems in the Rapid Advancement of Science* , ed. by Mariusz M. Żydowo. Warsaw: Polish Academy of Sciences, pp. 46–58.

Hughes, Thomas (2005). *Human-Built World. How to Think About Technology and Culture.* Chicago: The University of Chicago Press.

Lash, Scott (2002). *Critique of Information.* London: SAGE Publications.

Laver, Murray (1989). *Information Technology: Agent of Change.* Cambridge, Cambridge University Press.

McLuhan, Marshall (1965). *Understanding Media: The Extentions of Man,* New York-London-Sydney-Toronto: McGraw Hill Book Company.

Ong, J. Walter (1982). *Orality and Literacy. The Technologizing of Word*. London-New York:

Sloman, Aaron (1978). *The Computer Revolution in Philosophy: Philosophy, Science, and Models of Mind.* New Jersey: Humanities Press.

Turkle, Sherry (1996). *Life on the Screen. Identity in the Age of the Internet.* London: Phoenix.

Wilson, Catherina (2000). "Vicariousness and Authenticity". In *The Robot in the Garden. Telerobotics and Telepistemology in the Age of the Internet,* ed. by Ken Goldberg. Cambridge, Mass., London: The MIT Press, pp. 64–88.

Ziemińska, Renata (1998). "What is Epistemic Externalism". *Reports on Philosophy* 18, pp. 53–70.

Index

Achinstein, Peter, 193
Ahlstrom, Kristoffer, 119, 120
Alexander, Joshua, 113, 122
Almeder, Robert, 180, 181, 185, 189, 193
Alston, William, 33, 57, 245, 263
Anscombe, Elizabeth 292, 299
Antony, Louise, 36, 57, 93, 98
Aristotle, 15, 29, 228, 312
Armstrong, David, 291, 292, 298, 299
Arnellos, Argyris, 12, 13
Austin, John, 234, 244, 247, 249, 262, 263
Austin, Simon, 287
Auxier, Randall, 175
Ayer, Alfred, 291

Bénard, Henri, 21
Baird, Davis, 320, 327
Banathy, Bela, 266, 269–271, 280, 286
Baptista, Trino, 307, 311
Barandiaran, Xabier, 276, 287
Baron-Cohen, Simon, 308
Barrett, Robert, 210
Bealer, George, 102, 109, 120, 185, 192–194
Bering, Jesse, 297
Bianchi, Claudia, 264
Bickhard, Mark H., 4, 5, 7, 9, 11–13, 80, 83, 97, 98, 128, 134, 227, 241, 276–279, 282, 285, 286
Bishop, Michael, 8, 9, 51, 56, 57, 85, 212, 224
Black, Max, 193
Bloom, Jan Dirk, 311
Boghossian, Paul, 29, 145–150, 168, 170, 173
Bolter, David, 315, 327
Bolton, Derek, 306–308, 311

Bond, Stephen, 211
BonJour, Laurence, 103, 109, 121, 316, 327
Bonnardel, Nathalie, 267, 286
Boorse, Christopher, 300, 304, 309, 311
Boyle, Mary, 311
Bradley, Francis, 15
Braithwaite, Richard, 291
Brandom, Robert, 8, 124–126, 132–134, 229, 231, 234–238, 241
Brooks, Rodney, 28
Broughton, Janet, 221, 224
Brown, Harold, 213–217, 223, 224, 241
Burge, Tyler, 86, 98
Butler, R. J., 214, 224
Bynum, Terry, 241

Call, Josep, 297, 299
Campbell, Donald, 21, 24, 28, 29
Campbell, Treasa, 11
Cao, Tian Yu, 19, 29
Carnap, Rudolf, 11, 143, 195–203, 206, 207, 210, 213, 217–219, 224
Carroll, Lewis, 233, 234, 241
Carruthers, Peter, 79, 83, 164, 173
Carston, Robyn, 234, 259, 260, 264
Casullo, Albert, 192, 193
Chalmers, Alan, 39, 46, 57, 161, 173
Chalmers, David, 161
Chang, C. C., 29
Cherniak, Christopher, 44, 57
Choi, Incheol, 111, 122
Chomsky, Noam, 36, 163, 167, 173, 248, 249
Chrisman, Matthew, 97, 98
Christensen, Wayne D., 22, 26, 29, 279, 282, 286
Christiansen, P. V., 28

Churchland, Patricia, 235
Churchland, Paul, 235
Ciecierski, Tadeusz, 13
Claxton, Guy, 103, 121
Clifton, Rob, 19, 29
Cohen, Jonathan, 36, 57, 103, 121, 308
Collen, Arne, 288
Collier, John, 13, 272, 274–279, 282, 283, 287
Conte, Amedeo, 245, 264
Cooper, J., 201, 210
Couvalis, George, 39, 46, 47, 57
Craver, Carl, 75, 76, 83
Crow, Timothy, 307, 311
Culver, Charles, 309, 311
Cummins, Robert, 79, 83, 308, 311

Darwin, Charles, 83, 124, 125, 163
Darzentas, John, 12
Davidson, Donald, 160, 173, 234
Democritus, 14
Dennett, Daniel, 7, 75, 78, 79, 83, 84, 297, 306–308, 312
DePaul, Michael, 109, 121
Descartes, Rene, 15, 60–62, 90, 125–128, 227, 298, 316, 321, 324, 327
Devitt, Michael, 85, 98, 103, 121
Dewey, John, 2
Dostoyevsky, Fyodor, 124
Doyle, Jon, 29
Dreben, Burton, 195, 210
Dretske, Fred, 234, 241, 251, 291
Dreyfus, Hubert, 321, 322, 327
Duhem, Pierre, 184, 200, 210
Dupré, John, 161, 166, 173

Empedocles, 14
Etchemendy, 231, 241
Ewald, William, 89, 98

Feldman, Richard, 159, 161, 173, 267, 287
Feltz, Adam, 8, 9
Ferreira, M. J., 222, 224
Feyerabend, Paul, 39, 58
Field, Hartry, 97, 98
Flew, Antony, 224
Fodor, Jerry, 99, 163, 167, 173, 214, 224, 234, 301, 312
Foley, Richard, 51, 95, 98, 193
Ford, Kenneth, 81, 83
Frápolli, María, 11, 12
Freedman, Karyn, 51, 58
Frege, Gottlob, 230, 231, 233, 240, 241
French, Peter, 98, 174, 193
Friedman, Ken, 266, 287
Fulford, Bill, 300, 304, 312
Fuller, Steven, 317, 318, 327

Gödel, Kurt, 82, 202, 210
Galilei, Galileo, 39
García-Carpintero, Manuel, 245, 264
Garrett, Don, 213, 224
Gaskin J. C. A., 214, 224
Gauss, Carl Frederich, 89
Geach, Peter, 241
Gentzen, Gerhard, 94, 237, 241
Gero, John, 267, 287
Gert, Bertrand, 309, 311
Gettier, Edmund, 75, 110, 116
Gibbard, Alan, 97, 99
Gibson, James, 12
Gibson, Roger, 95, 99, 210, 296
Giere, Ronald, 51, 58, 95, 99
Gill, Mary-Louise, 29
Gillett, Grant, 312
Glanville, Ranulph, 266–270, 287
Glymour, Clark, 81, 83
Gochet, Paul, 224
Godfrey-Smith, Peter, 25, 29

Goldberg, Ken, 321, 327
Goldman, Alvin, 44, 51, 58, 61, 63, 65–70, 93, 99, 102, 121, 181, 193, 216, 224, 316–318, 323, 327
Goodman, Nelson, 37, 38, 49, 58, 291
Graham, Daniel, 15, 29
Graham, George, 312
Green, Thomas, 15
Grice, Paul, 247, 249, 250, 258, 260

Haack, Susan, 87, 95, 99, 133, 134, 159, 161, 173, 213, 224
Hahn, Lewis, 59, 71, 99
Hale, Bob, 29
Hale, Steven, 103, 121
Halvorson, Hans, 19, 29
Harman, Gilbert, 11, 231, 233, 241
Harnish, Robert, 245, 247, 256, 264
Hartshorne, Charles, 241
Hayes, Patrick, 81, 83
Heidegger, Martin, 82, 135
Heinz, Christoph, 288
Henderson, David, 38, 51, 55, 58, 165, 174
Hendricks, Vincent, 13
Heraclitus, 20
Hetmański, Marek, 13
Hilbert, David, 17, 29, 98
Hintikka, Jaakko, 241
Hobbes, Thomas, 15
Hoffmeyer, Jesper, 276, 287
Hooker, Cliff, 274, 279, 282, 286, 287
Hookway, Christopher, 74, 83
Hornsby, Jennifer, 159, 162, 163, 166, 167, 174
Horsten, Leon, 83
Howson, Colin, 214, 224
Huggett, Nick, 19, 29
Hughes, Thomas, 320, 328
Hume, David, 2, 5, 11, 12, 15–18, 29, 61, 64, 70, 82, 126, 129, 130, 134, 136, 139, 204–225, 290–293, 297, 298
Hurley, Susan, 165, 166, 174, 296–299
Husserl, Edmund, 127, 316, 324

Jackson, Frank, 9, 113, 121, 152, 156, 161, 169, 174
Jonas, Wolfgang, 266, 270, 271, 287
Jones, John, 266

Kannengiesser, Udo, 267, 287
Kant, Immanuel, 7, 12, 15, 74, 76, 77, 83, 86, 98, 125–130, 160, 289, 324
Kaplan, Mark, 109, 121, 234
Kapusta, Andrzej, 12, 13
Kazmierczak, Elżbieta, 270, 287
Keisler, Howard, 17, 29
Kemp Smith, Norman, 129, 134, 213, 214, 224
Kendell, R. E., 304, 306, 312
Keynes, John Maynard, 57
Kim, Jaegwon, 16–19, 29, 62, 68, 70, 72, 83
Kirby, Paul, 287
Kitcher, Patricia, 77, 83
Kitcher, Philip, 51, 58, 212, 213, 225
Klima, Gyula, 229, 241
Kneale, Martha, 229, 241
Kneale, William, 229, 241
Knowles, Jonathan, 5–7, 9–11, 62, 66, 70, 72, 74, 78, 83, 91, 92, 99, 126, 128, 134, 176, 179, 222, 225
Kolaitis, Phokion, 29
Kornblith, Hilary, 51, 58, 68–71, 95, 99, 103, 121, 161, 174, 213, 225, 241
Korta, Kepa, 258, 264
Koslow, Arnold, 241
Kosso, Peter, 39, 58
Kripke, Saul, 116, 121, 234

Krohs, Ulrich, 80, 83
Kuhlmann, Meinard, 19, 29
Kuhn, Thomas, 3, 46, 58

Lakatos, Imre, 39, 58, 224
Lash, Scott, 320, 328
Laszlo, Alexander, 269, 287
Laudan, Larry, 39, 40, 46, 51, 52, 58, 95, 99, 181, 193
Laver, Murray, 320, 328
Lavoisier, Antoine, 39
Leśniak, Piotr, 12
Lehrer, Keith, 132, 134, 180
Leiter, Brian, 125, 134
Lepore, Ernest, 99, 174
Lewis, David, 71, 102, 121, 151–153, 156, 169, 180, 291
Locke, John, 127, 129, 324
Loeb, Louis, 213, 225
Lowinger, Armand, 200, 210
Lynch, Michael, 97, 99
Lyre, Holger, 29

Macarthur, David, 175
Macmillan, Sebastian, 267, 287
Maffie, James, 51, 59, 213, 225
Masuda, Takahiko, 111, 121
McCormick, M., 214, 225
McCulloch, Gregory, 159, 174
McDowell, John, 9, 10, 124, 126, 132, 134, 159–162, 165, 167, 174
McHugh, Conor, 224
McLuhan, Marshall, 324, 328
Megone, Christopher, 308, 312
Meno, 201, 203, 204, 207
Miłkowski, Marcin, 6, 7, 12, 62
Michotte, Albert, 294, 295
Mill, John Stuart, 8, 12, 23, 24, 29, 30, 41, 46–50, 59, 80, 83, 235, 243, 250–259, 263, 264, 291, 302, 312

Millikan, Ruth, 8, 12, 23, 24, 29, 30, 80, 83, 235, 243, 250–259, 263, 264, 302, 312
Moore, George Edward, 2, 61, 71
Moreno, Alvaro, 273, 276, 287
Mostowski, Andrzej, 240, 241
Mounce, H. O., 222, 225
Murphy, Dominic, 121, 122, 309, 310, 312

Nadin, Mihai, 271, 288
Nagel, Ernest, 96, 99
Nagel, Thomas, 96, 99
Neurath, Otto, 35
Newton, Isaac, 39, 108, 125, 129, 130
Nichols, Shaun, 110, 122
Nietzsche, Friedrich, 73
Nisbett, Richard, 111, 112, 121, 122
Norenzayan, Ara, 111, 122

Oakley, Shane, 10, 180, 186, 191, 193
Ockham, William of, 229
Ong, J. Walter, 324, 328
Osbeck, Lisa, 102, 122
Otero, Mario, 17, 30

Pakaluk, Michael, 205, 210
Papineau, David, 46, 59
Passmore, John, 214, 225
Pears, David, 213, 225
Peirce, Charles, 2, 233, 241, 252
Penelhum, Terence, 222, 225
Peng, Kaiping, 111, 122, 135, 224
Perry, John, 258, 264
Pettit, Philip, 297, 299
Piaget, Jean, 287, 293, 294
Plato, 89, 90, 125, 208, 210
Pollock, John, 36, 59, 97, 99
Popkin, Richard, 214, 225

Popper, Karl, 29
Povinelli, Daniel, 297, 299
Prawitz, Dag, 237, 241
Premack, David, 297, 299
Price, Huw, 8–10, 12, 13, 124, 125, 128, 135, 157, 159, 160, 167–175, 289, 299
Prinz, Jesse, 235
Prior, Arthur, 29, 85, 86, 88–90, 98–100, 121, 144, 191, 193, 233, 242
Psillos, Stathis, 290, 299
Pust, Joel, 121
Putnam, Hilary, 72, 84, 116, 122, 150, 156, 159, 161, 175, 210, 234, 289, 298–299

Quine, Willard V. O., 1, 6, 11, 12, 15, 16, 33–36, 38–40, 51, 59, 61, 63–66, 71–74, 83, 84, 91, 93, 95, 99, 121, 124, 125, 128–131, 135, 142, 143, 151, 156, 159, 160, 171, 184, 185, 193–196, 198–210, 212, 219, 224, 225, 234, 238, 242

Ramberg, Bjørn, 125, 126, 135, 173
Ramsey, Frank P., 121, 153, 236, 291
Rawls, John, 37, 38, 59
Rea, Michael, 212, 225
Recanati, François, 234
Rescher, Nicholas, 29
Rey, George, 93, 94, 99
Rocknak, Stephanie, 11
Rorty, Richard, 8, 124–135, 159, 160, 175
Rosenberg, Alex, 52, 59
Ruiz-Mirazo, Kepa, 273
Russell, Bertrand, 195, 196, 202, 210, 289, 299

Schön, Donald, 267, 288
Schilpp, Paul A., 29, 59, 71, 99

Searle, John, 12, 243–250, 253, 254, 263, 264
Seibt, Johanna, 28
Sellars, Wilfrid, 8, 124, 126, 131–135, 160, 175, 231, 242
Shaffer, Michael, 180, 185, 193, 194
Shakespeare, William, 124
Sher, Gila, 230, 242, 328
Siegel, Harvey, 56, 57, 59, 91, 99, 109, 122, 180, 181, 184–186, 189, 193, 194, 217, 225
Siemek, Marek, 83
Simon, Herbert, 78, 83, 84, 225, 266, 267, 287, 288
Skorupski, John, 46, 59
Sloman, Aaron, 315, 328
Sosa, Ernest, 102, 108, 122, 193, 299, 327
Spence, Paul, 287
Spurr, Jane, 13
Spyrou, Thomas, 12
Stalnaker, Robert, 234
Stanley, Jason, 114, 115, 122
Steele, John, 287
Stein, Edward, 38, 43, 45, 59
Stich, Steven, 43, 45, 51, 59, 95, 100, 104, 110, 121, 122, 146, 151, 156, 168, 175
Strawson, Peter F., 213, 221, 225, 234, 293, 299
Stroud, Barry, 161, 175, 196, 213, 225
Swain, Stacey, 113, 122
Swinburne, Richard, 220, 221, 225
Szasz, Thomas Steven, 304, 312

Tarski, Alfred, 82, 234
Thornton, Stephen, 211
Thornton, Tim, 302, 312
Tomasello, Michael, 297–299
Tooley, Michael, 295, 299
Trompiz, Patrick, 13

Trout, J. D., 51, 56, 57, 119–121, 212, 224
Trybulec, Barbara, 6
Turkle, Sherry, 327, 328

Van Cleve, James, 132, 134, 135
Van Fraassen, Bas, 194
Van Gelder, Tim, 30
Veber, Michael, 180, 193
Von Foerster, Heinz, 273, 274, 288
Vonk, Jennifer, 297, 299
Vuorio, Timo, 8, 9

Wakefield, Jerome, 304, 308, 312
Warenski, Lisa, 7–9, 11
Warmbrod, Ken, 242
Warnick, Jason, 185, 194
Wasserman, Edward, 297, 299
Wayne, Andrew, 29
Weatherson, Brian, 107, 122
Weinberg, Steven, 19, 30, 110, 113, 122
Wellman, Henry, 164, 175
Wheeler, Michael, 82, 84
White, Morton, 59, 65, 71, 95, 99
Whitehead, Alfred North, 196, 202
Wiggins, David, 159, 175
Wiggins, Glenn, 267, 288
Williams, C. J. F., 242
Williamson, Timothy, 245, 264
Wilson, Catherina, 322, 328
Witek, Maciej, 12
Wittgenstein, Ludwig, 125, 131, 154, 155, 229, 234, 237, 238, 240, 242, 245
Wright, Crispin, 29, 96, 100
Wright, Larry, 80, 84

Zarpentine, Chris, 114, 115, 121
Zee, Anthony, 19, 30
Ziemińska, Renata, 316, 328

www.ingramcontent.com/pod-product-compliance
Lightning Source LLC
Chambersburg PA
CBHW050333230426
43663CB00010B/1848